IN THE COMPANY OF KILLERS

norman parker

BLAKE

Published by Blake Publishing Ltd,
3 Bramber Court, 2 Bramber Road,
London W14 9PB, England

First published in 1999

ISBN 1 85782 3036

British Library Cataloguing-in-Publication Data:
A catalogue record for this book is available
from the British Library.

Typeset by BCP

Printed and bound in Great Britain by
Creative Print and Design (Wales), Ebbw Vale

3 5 7 9 10 8 6 4 2

For Janice

Dear Reader

Welcome to the third title in Blake's True Crime Library, the series that brings you the most high-profile true crime stories for you to read in the comfort of your own armchair.

If you've read his bestselling books *Parkhurst Tales* and *Parkhurst Tales 2*, you will know that Norman Parker is the country's foremost commentator on the bizarre truths of prison life. His amazing anecdotes are sometimes funny, sometimes disturbing — but always intriguing. What is more, they present us with an important psychological insight into the criminals that populate Britain's jails.

Between the pages of this book, Norman Parker will take you on a journey to a special kind of prison — a prison for men who have committed the most serious crimes. The identities of the jail have been changed so that Parker can reveal its darkest secrets.

Read on — and if the book makes you uncomfortable, then remember, every word is true …

Adam Parfitt
Editor
Blake's True Crime Library

glossary

AG Assistant Governor.

agg Aggravation, trouble.

Albany Top-security jail on the Isle of Wight.

bang-up Lock up.

berk Idiot, fool.

bird Time, sentence; also girl, woman.

blank Ignore, refuse.

block Punishment block, chokey (*see below*). 'To be blocked': to be sent to the punishment block.

bottle Nerve, courage.

brief Solicitor, barrister, QC.

Category B Second highest security category.

Category C Third highest security category.

Category D Lowest security category.

Chief Most senior uniformed officer in a jail.

chin, to To punch (someone) on the chin.

chokey Punishment block.

coating Volley of verbal abuse.

come on top To be found out.

con Convict, prisoner.

CRO'ed Checked out (CRO=Criminal Records Office).

Dep Deputy Governor.

dispersal system System whereby top-security prisoners are mixed in with lower-security prisoners.

face Well-known prisoner, one with criminal status.

firm Gang.

frit Frightened.

Gartree Top-security jail in Leicestershire.

GBH Grevious bodily harm.

go into one Explode in rage; throw a tantrum.

Gloucester Local prison in Gloucester.

Good Order and Discipline Rule used to segregate a prisoner suspected of being disruptive.

grass Informer. 'To grass': to inform on someone.

half-sheet Disciplinary form given to prison officers.

khazi Toilet.

Lincoln Local prison in Lincoln.

lollied Grassed (*see above*).

Long Lartin Top-security jail in the Midlands.

LRC Local Review Committee.

made one Took part in, joined in.

manor Local area, neighbourhood.

moody False.

nonce Sex offender.

PO Principal Officer – below Chief but above SO.

PTI Physical Training Instructor.

screw Prison officer.

shanghaied Immediately and involuntarily transferred from one prison to another.

smack-head Heroin junkie.

SO Senior Officer – below PO but above Basic Grade.

SP Form, low-down (SP=starting price).

straightened Corrupted.

stretch Length of sentence – e.g. 'two-stretch'=two-year sentence.

sussed Figured out, exposed.

tie-up Robbery in which victims are tied up, usually in a domestic setting.

volley Insult loudly and/or publicly.

Wakefield Top-security jail in Yorkshire.

Winchester Top-security and local jail in Hampshire.

wrecked 'Stoned'; confused/stimulated state brought on by the use of drugs, usually cannabis.

1

As the first signs for Dartville appeared, I began to think more deeply about the jail to which I was headed. Knightsford was supposed to be a good jail, an easy jail.

In all my years in the dispersal system, I had never met anyone who had been there. This supported the rumour that, although Knightsford was 'home' to men who had committed very serious crimes indeed, it was for model prisoners only, the cream. The sort who never returned to the dispersals.

I hoped that all the good things I had heard were true. I had had a hard time of it over the past thirteen months. It had started when I was shanghaied from Long Lartin after being blocked for an attack on a big black fella. I wasn't exactly delighted to arrive at Albany. I had been shanghaied from there five years earlier following my leading role in an escape and the subsequent riot.

Sure enough, after only three weeks I was shanghaied on a pretext and ended up in the chokey at Winchester for twenty-eight days' 'good order and discipline'. Other than the chokey screws, I didn't see another human being for a whole month.

After the solitary, I thought I would be pleased to go to any long-term jail. Wakefield, though, was the worst possible option. Apart from the fact that it was hundreds of miles north of London, it had a bad regime and very few fellow Londoners. An added negative was that it was the jail where a close pal of mine had been stabbed to death fifteen years earlier. I had been only nineteen at the time and Terry had died in my arms. As far as traumatic experiences went, I couldn't remember a worse one.

Whether by ill luck or design, when I arrived I was lodged on the wing where it had happened. That night, I awoke to the agony of conjunctivitis in both eyes. Then, within days, the summons arrived charging me with GBH with intent on the big black fella. I took little consolation from the fact that I had four co-defendants.

A GBH conviction on top of my life sentence would have ensured that it would be many, many years before I could hope to be released. The preparation of a defence took up all my attention at a time when I was on the verge of a crucial Open University exam. A couple of months passed and I was taken down to Gloucester jail for the committals at Evesham magistrates. The armed police ringing the court and the helicopter circling overhead did nothing to ease the pressure. Following committal, it was back up to Wakefield for another couple of months. All too soon I was returned to Gloucester and the trial at Worcester Crown Court. The acquittal was a relief, but it came as no surprise. There had been no evidence, just the usual prison innuendo. Within days, I was back at Long Lartin.

If I had thought that that was the end of a painful and unpleasant interlude, then I was soon to be disabused of that notion. The senior screws hadn't been at all impressed by the acquittal. Before three months were out, I had been shanghaied on a pretext again.

Gartree, not long after the latest riot, wasn't the best of places to arrive at. But I was punchy from all the travelling around, and I resolved to keep a low profile. When a sit-down took place, I didn't take part, the first time in many years that I hadn't. Little good it did me though: I was one of the first to be shanghaied. Barely three months had passed.

Lincoln chokey on indefinite Rule 43 would have been hard even if I had done something to deserve it. Sitting there for having done absolutely nothing, with the added irony that I had actually avoided the sit-down, brought me to the lowest point of my sentence to date.

Perhaps that cosmic scriptwriter who had been directing my life for so many years at last showed some mercy. Perhaps he was just looking the other way for a while. Anyway, Gartree informed the Home Office that a mistake had been made and that I had been moved for nothing.

An AG came to my cell and asked me where I would like to go. For a moment, I thought he was taking the piss. In similar spirit, I said, 'Knightsford,' never dreaming I would get it.

Now I was sitting in a Lincolnshire taxi with three screws, nearing the outskirts of Dartville. Short of an act of God, it looked like I was going to Knightsford.

'Whatever it's like, put up with it for a while and regain some strength,' I said to myself. But I knew that the most important thing was for my spirit to be strong. If Knightsford had a regime that tried to humiliate me, I was sure to react against it. My pride wouldn't allow me to back down to the screws. That would be the start of a long, slippery slope to spiritual oblivion.

But I had been significantly weakened by the cumulative effect of the past years, and especially the last thirteen months. I desperately needed a rest. And my mother did, too. She was over seventy now, and as she dragged around from jail to jail to visit me, the strain was telling on her. She had asked me recently to give her a couple of years' peace. I could envisage my continued rebelliousness actually killing the one person I loved and who loved me in return. I would try to stay out of trouble.

The problem was that I now had such a reputation that it preceded me. I didn't actually have to do anything; it was enough for me to just be in the vicinity of trouble. It didn't help either that many of the staff I was meeting on my travels had been working in jails with me when I had been in my particularly disruptive phase. Men who had been ordinary screws were now SOs and POs; AGs and deps were now governors. With their new-found power, they were even more dangerous adversaries. The negative possibilities were infinite. All I could do was hope for the best.

Suddenly, as we rounded a bend, there was the front of the jail. Knightsford looked no different from the scores of other Victorian jails across the country. The twin turrets either side of the gate-lodge, the Gothic arch and the massive wooden doors gave me no clues as to the interior.

The PO got out from beside the cab driver as we pulled up before the doors. He pressed a bell on one of the turrets and a small, picket-gate opened almost immediately. There was a hurried conversation, the PO climbed back in the car and the massive doors swung open.

We drove into the gate-lodge and stopped before a similarly massive pair of barred gates. Thus far Knightsford was still no different from other jails.

Although I was sitting passively back in my seat, I was surreptitiously examining these outer defences. Knightsford was the first Category B jail I would do some time in on my present sentence. I could expect the security to be something less than the dispersal jails I had been in.

Although I was looking for a period of relative peace, my overriding priority was still to escape. I knew I had too long left to do to settle down and accept it. I didn't kid myself about the GBH acquittal either. That would be fully written up in my record with only slightly less detriment than if I had been convicted of the crime.

The PO handed over some paperwork, the gates swung open and we were directed to reception. We immediately found ourselves in a 'sterile area', just inside the gates. A sixteen-foot-high wire fence topped with barbed wire curled in a semi-circle around the back of the gate-lodge.

Such sterile areas were commonplace in security jails, and no inmate was ever allowed in the area unescorted. Any hope I had had that Knightsford was going to be a soft touch security-wise began to recede.

A gate-screw unlocked a massive pair of gates set in the fence, close to the gate-lodge. I noticed a similar pair on the opposite side.

We drove through, along a narrow roadway between the wings and the wall. I was reassured to see that there was no wire fence in front of the wall, as was the custom in most security jails, but any pleasure I took from that was quickly dissipated when I noticed the plastic canopy set atop the wall. It was like a massive, inverted guttering that ran all along the wall as far as the eye could see. Its rounded smoothness made it impossible for a rope-and-hook to find any purchase. Only a ladder would reach the top of that wall, and the prison staff were unlikely to leave ladders lying about.

We pulled up alongside some stairs that led down to a basement. A board fixed to the wall of the wing read 'RECEPTION' in large red letters. Beneath it stood a bulky figure in screw's uniform. The corpulent face looked vaguely familiar. The small, piggy eyes stared back at me as the head shook slowly backwards and forwards, causing the fleshy jowls to dance beneath the chin like pink jelly.

The screws on either side of me opened the back doors of the car and I got out. Sweet fresh air washed over me. Other than for a short stop at a motorway café to use the toilet, the three of us had been jammed in the back seat for nearly three hours.

I stepped out into the bright sunlight, still cuffed to the screw on my left. The escort PO hurried over and unlocked the cuffs.

I stood there massaging my wrist in a reflex action that every prisoner throughout history must have repeated. My wrist was stiff and sore from the restrictive steel bracelet, but the gesture was something more than that. It was an act of reassurance, to confirm that I was no longer chained to my guard.

'Hello, Parker,' said a deep voice with the lilt of the Welsh valleys to it. 'Fancy meeting you again.'

I looked up and saw that the speaker was the screw standing beneath the reception sign. I had developed a habit over the years of rarely looking screws in the face, except when challenged. It had happened subconsciously. They were faceless people, so I tended to look at the whole person, never making eye contact. But now as I stared into the fleshy face, recognition dawned. It had been six years earlier but it seemed like aeons ago. Time had etched age in him far beyond the true number of years that had passed. Cons often carried their years well, but screws seemed to age much more quickly.

Suddenly I was back at Parkhurst. A brief memory of the youthful rage that had consumed me there now washed through my consciousness as I realised who the screw was: the bulky figure standing in the middle of the parade ground as we went to work, the large face emotionless and impassive, the porcine eyes observing our passing contemptuously.

The hatred had been mutual. We had passed like water washing around a rock. Not close, but keeping a careful distance. In his arrogance, he had never turned his head once we were past. He had looked at us, but had never seen us.

Occasionally he would bark: 'No newspapers in the workshops' or 'Don't wear trainers to work.' It hadn't been communication. He hadn't expected a reply. And if ever there was any argument, he would turn to the nearest screw and shout, 'Put this man on report!' –

then forget about the individual as he was led off to the chokey.

We had known him as 'God'. Not that we had looked up to him or revered him in any way. It had just been that his breathtaking arrogance and studied remoteness had set him far above normal men. And no doubt he had viewed himself in this way. To us lowly cons, he had had the power of a god.

As all this flooded back, a sinking sensation gripped my stomach. What a start. One of the worst dogs ever to walk the landings of Parkhurst, and here he was waiting to welcome me to Knightsford.

But there was a smile on his face. And his tone, while not being actually friendly, lacked the harshness that had characterised the 'God of Parkhurst'.

I walked over to him. I nearly flinched in surprise as he suddenly stuck out his hand.

'You remember me, Parker,' he said. 'PO Hughes from Parkhurst. I'm the Chief here, though.'

It was a weakness to shake his hand. A couple of years earlier, I would have just stared impassively into his face and ignored the outstretched hand. But I was stronger then. I just hoped that no con was watching as I shook it. It wasn't much of a price to pay if it brought me a bit of peace. After all, he was the Chief, the most powerful uniformed screw in the jail.

'You know, me and the wife were only talking the other night about old Fred at Parkhurst. You know, Fred who died later up at Hull,' he chuntered on. 'Me and the wife often talk about old times.'

'You mean Freddy Sandon, guv.'

'That's him!' he cried animatedly. 'The wife and I were trying to think of his name for hours.'

Prison is all about the bizarre. I had learned to size up a situation, to work out what all the underlying meanings were, and never to change the expression on my face while doing it. I realised I was in the presence of a strange and unbalanced man. The whole performance was wrong for a chief welcoming a new prisoner to his jail. And a very troublesome prisoner at that.

These weren't old friends he was talking about. Back at Parkhurst, we had hated him with a passion and he had fully re-ciprocated our feelings. Now here he was, six years later, talking about the 'old times'. And he regularly discussed these things with his wife. It wasn't only cons who went mad in prison.

I quickly assessed my situation. He genuinely seemed pleased to see me. All I could do was humour him. Perhaps the situation wouldn't turn out too bad after all.

The Chief had been so engrossed in talking to me that he only now noticed my escort screws. They had been shifting uneasily from foot to foot, obviously wanting to get me into reception so that they could leave. But they were in the presence of a chief and were reluctant to interrupt.

'Well, Parker, we mustn't keep you hanging about. I'll talk to you again later. The wife will be so pleased.' With that, the Chief spun around and walked towards the gate, chuckling to himself and shaking his head.

If the escort screws had been surprised by his behaviour, they didn't say. No doubt they saw enough bizarre behaviour on their travels. Anyway, they would be leaving shortly and would probably never see either of us again.

The PO led the way down the basement steps with me close behind him. The two screws followed, carrying the two large boxes containing my property that they had taken from the boot of the taxi.

We passed through an open gate and into a dimly lit passage, coming to a brightly lit office where a screw in shirt-sleeves sat at a desk. He looked up as we all filed in. The PO handed him some papers and my property sheet. Behind me the two screws put my boxes on the floor. In less than a minute, the papers had been signed and my escort had left.

'I won't be a minute,' said the shirt-sleeved screw. 'I've just got to finish this.' He carried on writing on a sheet in front of him.

I looked around the office. The vaulted ceilings and Gothic archways showed that it had once been two cells. In these old jails, they made the best use of available space that they could.

The screw finished writing and looked up. He was pleasant enough in an absent-minded sort of way. He unpacked my boxes and went through the contents with me. Surprisingly, I was allowed to keep the vast majority of the stuff. You can often judge a jail by the reception. Good jails let you have all sorts of things from civilian sweatshirts to record players. Bad jails only allowed you to have a radio. I was pleased with the way things were going. I had all my sweatshirts, my record player, a couple of pairs of trainers and several pairs of white gym socks. All my books and my OU materials were handed to me, together with several posters. I jollied the screw along before he could change his mind.

'We'd better get you some new prison kit,' he said as he finished with the boxes. He turned towards the door through which I had entered and suddenly yelled, 'Harold!'

It was a loud noise in such a confined space and it startled me. I guessed that whoever he was shouting to must be several rooms away along the corridor. I heard a door slam, then the sound of footsteps approaching.

I suppose I should have known. This jail was already a bit like an enchanted castle. For every pleasant person you encountered, the next one could be an ogre. The creature that entered the office was certainly one of those. I had been around dangerous mental patients for many years now, and was no stranger to abominations in human form. Harold, though, was a revelation.

The short, wiry figure shuffled sideways through the door. It was dressed from head to toe in prison clothes, the crumpled grey jumper and grubby blue jeans adding to the impression of a creature from a dungeon. Its back was fearsomely hunched, the curvature bending it nearly double from just above the waist. Unruly black hair covered its head; separate clumps stuck out in all directions, clear evidence that it never saw a comb.

As Harold neared the desk, I got a sideways view of his face. Beetling brows underscored a bony, lined forehead. Deep-set, dead-fish eyes peered out of dark sockets. A corner of his mouth was pulled sideways into a permanent rictus, one half of a devilish grin. A malign scowl was fixed on his face.

I had seen too many terrible things to betray any physical reaction. But inwardly, I did gasp. Harold was a frightening, horrible demi-human. In a busy street, on a bright summer's day, he would still scare the life out of anyone. Scuttling about the subterranean corridors of Knightsford, he was a creature straight out of a Hammer horror.

For a brief second, I marvelled at the ugliness of the world I inhabited. Ogres and demons, personified in the flesh, wandered briefly through the footlights of the stage. As long as I was strong and fit, they would not drag me down. But if I weakened and strayed into the shadows, then an awful fate awaited me.

As Harold drew close I bristled involuntarily. A protective reflex caused me to radiate hostility and I growled without uttering a sound. He got it immediately. Like myself, he was delicately tuned into bodily vibes. The outcomes of too many dangerous situations had depended on the ability to read subliminal warning signs.

He turned his face slightly to glance at me. I stared into his eyes and I saw his gaze flicker as a bolt of psychic hostility struck him. He turned away.

Yes, you fucker, I told him speechlessly. *Look and know that if you so much as make one hostile move towards me, my fists will break the bones of your ugly face and my booted feet will kick that twisted spine straight again. Understand from the very beginning that I read the evil in your soul. I don't know it for a fact, but I can feel it in every fibre of my being that you are a fucking nonce. Some poor woman or child has been at your mercy and died horribly. Go your evil way, for I won't bother you. But fuck with me just once and I will show you a viciousness to marvel at.*

A thousand words passed in a glance. The screw missed it all. Harold and I, though, knew exactly where we stood. Our relationship had been irrevocably formed.

Another five minutes saw me finished with reception. My personal stuff was crammed into one of the boxes, the new prison gear piled on the top. The screw directed me up some narrow stairs and told me how to find my way to C wing office.

I staggered up the stairs with the heavy box. No doubt Harold helped some new arrivals, but I would make do on my own. I surfaced in another narrow corridor then emerged, blinking, into the dazzling brightness of Knightsford's 'centre'.

All Victorian jails have a 'centre' – the open place, the hub, where all the wings meet. Knightsford had four of them. Each had a ground floor, called the 'ones', and a raised catwalk landing: the 'twos'. Along both sides, cell doorways receded into the distance. The centre must have been thirty feet in diameter, its floor covered with thousands of small, narrow tiles laid in an intricate pattern. Right in the middle stood a full-sized snooker table, the green baize hidden by a stained-oak cover.

Coming from the cramped darkness, the first impression was one of space and brightness. It was like a dazzling arena awaiting a show. As I stepped out on to it with my piled-up box, I saw that all the wings were just as brightly lit.

I made my way across the centre towards the wing that lay opposite, which the screw had told me was C wing. I circumnavigated the snooker table, noticing as I passed a massive barred gateway that blocked off the entrance to a wide, well-lit corridor that lay between A and C wings. Curtains hung at windows along its length, and here and there were dotted pieces of civilian furniture. It looked thoroughly incongruous, as if part of a domestic house had been grafted on to the prison. This could only be an office area for civilian staff and governors.

'Well, fuck me, Norm. What are you doing here?' The deep, gruff voice came out of nowhere. I heard a London accent, but an exaggerated one. I could also discern a West Country lilt beneath the Cockney tones.

I was just entering C wing. Directly in front of me a massive steel staircase led up to the twos. It threw its shadow across a doorway on the left where I had been told the wing office would be. In the gloom, I could see someone sitting in a chair against the wall, and as the figure hauled itself to its feet and ambled towards me, I saw that it was Hall, a screw I had seen at Parkhurst many years before.

Parkhurst again! Was Knightsford a retirement home for old Parkhurst screws? How many more of them would I find here? All thoughts of leaving my past behind me were fast disappearing.

I quickly searched my memory for what I remembered about Hall from Parkhurst. He had been a new screw, just starting. The cons had taken the piss out of him unmercifully. He had been a complete coward, too, wholly intimidated by the surroundings. This wasn't unusual at Parkhurst though. There were some very dangerous cons there, and the vast majority of the screws were intimidated to some extent. This one had given the impression of someone who would have liked to have been vindictive and nasty, but just didn't have the bottle.

I remembered him only vaguely. We had never spoken. He clearly remembered me though. That wasn't surprising because, what with my escape attempt and the subsequent riot, I had probably been the best-known con in the jail. And, as far as the screws were concerned, the most hated.

Yet the smile on his face and the manner indicated that he was pleased to see me. Was it my recollection that was at fault? Had it all been just good, clean fun back at Parkhurst? Was what we had thought was hatred and vitriol just been the passion of the moment?

Perhaps there was another explanation. I had already met the Chief, who had dwelt on Parkhurst as if it had been a golden era. Now this screw, who must have hated me six years previously, was welcoming me like an old friend.

Maybe there was something about Knightsford. Perhaps it was an enchanted place in that it transformed harsh and hardened attitudes into ones of forgive and forget. But I had been too long in the system to believe that. Screws, like leopards, never changed their spots. They could become older, or more tired; they could just be looking for a quiet time. But underneath, the vast majority of them would always hate a con just as a cat hates a mouse. It was the natural order of things.

It was all very confusing, but I was equal to this game. I had learned cunning. Not underhandedness or outright deceit. This dishonourable world would never taint me with its treachery. But I could be planning to kill you now, and you would never know it from my face.

'Hello, guv,' I replied, putting the heavy box on the floor. That left both of my hands free, and I dreaded him putting out his hand for me to shake. There seemed to be no cons about, but I inwardly cringed at the thought of anyone seeing me shake hands with him. Such a thing would never have happened in a long-term jail. And if it had, the screw would have met with hostility from his fellow screws, the con from his fellow cons.

Hall told me how he had become an SO at Parkhurst and moved to Knightsford two years ago. He sang the praises of the place, emphasising the facilities and the caring attitude of the regime. He hoped that I would settle in OK.

It was all done very pleasantly. I looked for underlying hostility and couldn't discern any. He looked directly at me as he finished, and I felt that I should reciprocate. I told him of all the trials and tribulations of the past couple of years. It was nothing he wouldn't read from my record, so I might as well get in with my version first. I didn't whinge about it, just told it matter-of-factly as if I was tired of all the trouble and was looking for some respite. And this wasn't far from the truth.

I could see him listening intently, staring at me as if he was looking for any underlying meaning. I could read his thoughts quite clearly. He was wondering if the years had broken my spirit, and whether he would be able to intimidate me now, as I and my fellows had intimidated him six years previously. Whatever his conclusion, his manner continued to be solicitous in the extreme.

Finally, he directed me to a cell and told me to unpack my kit. 'And if you're short of anything, Norm, come back and see me,' he concluded.

I picked up my box and walked away. I had gone only a few yards when Hall called after me. 'Oh, by the way, the Governor wants to see you. So can you get yourself back here for ten-thirty?'

'OK,' I shouted over my shoulder as I continued towards my new cell. Any reassurance I had gained from the friendly reception rippled and faded like a desert mirage. Governors didn't normally wait on the arrival of cons, no matter who they were. The routine was that receptions always saw governors the next day.

'Don't kid yourself, Norman,' I told myself as faint stirrings of alarm rippled the surface of my calm. 'You're still the Norman Parker you've always been.'

I found cell No. 6 just a short distance along from the office. I pushed the door open with the box and dropped it on the bed. I looked at my watch to check how long I had before I was to see the Governor. I was surprised to see that it was still only just after 10.00. We had started out very early from Lincoln.

By 10.25, I was standing outside the office waiting for the Governor. I wandered closer to the centre so I could see into A and B wings. They looked deserted.

Occasionally a con would appear from out of one of the cells like a mouse from out of its hole. There would be a short journey to the recess or the wing office, then he would scuttle back from whence he came. I guessed that they were wing cleaners. Clearly, there wasn't a tradition here of having large numbers of cons hanging about the wings all day.

Just after 10.30, there was a jangling of keys and the gate leading to the Admin area opened. I turned to see a tall, thin man in a dark blue business suit hurry through. He locked the gate quickly behind him and walked speedily towards me. All his movements seemed rushed, bordering on the frantic. His pace was that of a busy man torn between too many deadlines.

He came towards me but looked through and past me. He hurried by and let himself into an office next to the main wing office, leaving the door ajar.

Hall had appeared at the sound of the Admin gate opening, and he now hurried into the office after the Governor. He quickly reappeared again and waved me inside. As I entered, he closed the door behind me.

The small office, about half the size of the wing office, belonged to the wing PO, who was on leave that day. The Governor had already ensconced himself behind the PO's desk. He was leaning back in the chair, elbows resting on the arms and fingers pressed together in an almost prayer-like pose.

'Sit down, Parker,' he said without turning his head or otherwise moving. As I had already guessed, this was to be an 'I'm going to let you know who's boss' session.

Hardly had my backside touched the seat than he started. 'Parker, you are way outside the parameters for this place. I have agreed to take you here as a favour to a colleague in the Home Office because, it seems, you were wrongly displaced from Gartree. However, let me assure you right from the start that any trouble whatsoever and you'll be gone immediately.'

I looked across at him. He was in his late forties and still had a head of thick curly hair. His face was very red, and the redness continued down into his neck. I noticed that both of his ears were very red, too. I recalled that he had already been flushed when he came across the centre, so it couldn't be anger. And from his quick, fretful movements I could sense that he was naturally tense.

Here was a man under extreme pressure. The running of a long-term jail was enough to make the most well-balanced of men climb the walls in a very short time. And this governor didn't appear to be the most well-balanced of men. He was living on the edge. I would have to expect an irrational reaction.

For a second, I toyed with the idea of saying, 'Well, thanks for the warm welcome and the vote of confidence. I'm sure I'll be very happy here, Governor.' But a wiser voice cautioned me. He would be bound to say something back and it would go on from there. I could see myself travelling back through reception towards another dose of 'good order and discipline' in a local jail.

Instead I said, 'I'm just looking for a quiet time, Governor,' and left it at that.

There was a moment's silence as he stared at me intently. Then he quickly nodded, indicating that the interview was over, and stood to leave. I followed him out of the office and he locked it behind me.

That was my introduction to Governor Maypole. Analysing it afterwards, I realised that he was probably frightened of me and my reputation for violent disruption. The immediate interview had been an act, role playing, to let me know that he wasn't going to stand for any nonsense.

I took it to be a sign of weakness. A more experienced governor would have seen me the day after my arrival, as was usual. However, I took his point. I would have to tread very carefully indeed.

I returned to my cell to unpack my stuff and lay it out. Before I knew it, an hour had passed and I heard the sound of men coming in from work. I looked out to see fellas hurrying into cells and reappearing with their plastic cutlery and cups.

I collected my own cutlery and followed the throng. We walked across the centre and along a passageway that opened out into a large room lined with tables and chairs. This could only be the dining hall.

At one end was a counter behind which stood several cons in kitchen whites serving out food. Among them stood a kitchen screw, a burly man of about forty with a scrappy Mexican bandit-style moustache. He stood with his arms folded, looking out at the queue of cons that snaked along the counter and up one side of the dining hall. Now and again he would laugh and nudge one of the cons standing next to him. He seemed to do this only when a particularly inadequate-looking con came into his view. The majority of the cons in the queue could have fitted that category.

I looked more closely at the kitchen screw. On his muscular, folded forearms I could see a riot of blue tattoos – he looked like an ex-seaman. He clearly fancied himself, and I read the situation immediately. He was surrounded by a bunch of tame cons and was throwing his weight around. If he had tried taking the piss out of queuing cons at Albany or Parkhurst, he would soon have been wearing the food, not serving it.

This was a challenge I couldn't ignore. If I let him take the piss out of me, I might as well bend over and let him kick me up the arse, too. But I didn't think he would say anything to me.

Before leaving my cell I had put on tailored jeans and a pair of smart trainers. A white T-shirt clung snugly to my upper body. The pecs, lats and delts stood out in stark relief, testimony to many years of lifting weights. Just for good measure, as I drew close to the counter I stared straight at him.

Our eyes met briefly and he quickly looked away. Whatever he saw was enough to convince him that here was a con he had better not take the piss out of. That was enough for me. I didn't intend to push it. Our relationship was formed and he would leave me alone now.

I dropped my eyes to look at the food. It was better than in many jails I had been in, but the portions were rather small. I collected my meal and went to sit at one of the few empty tables left. I knew that most of the tables would have regular occupants who sat there every day. I didn't want to have the aggravation of someone coming along and telling me that I was sitting in his seat. It could show weakness to move, but if I told him to piss off, it could lead to trouble. However, I knew that first impressions are especially important among cons. If I was perceived to be weak, all sorts of berks could come on to me, and then I would have to chin one of them. At first sight, though, the occupants of Knightsford's dining hall all looked pretty light-weight to me.

I had a set way of behaving in new jails. I ate my dinner and stared fixedly in front of me as if I had been doing that for months. My behaviour said that I didn't want to be disturbed. The dining hall gradually filled and the hubbub of conversation increased. Still I ate my dinner as if oblivious to my surroundings. A couple of middle-aged fellas sat down at two of the three remaining seats on the table. I ignored them and carried on eating.

I had made some interesting discoveries about human interaction while travelling through the system. Everybody seemed to be into role-playing in one form or another. If you arrived at a new jail and immediately set out to talk to everyone in sight and be overly friendly, very soon you would gain a reputation as a berk. That which is easily attained, nobody wants. However, provided that you had some degree of physical presence and if you remained detached and even hostile, it would arouse people's curiosity. They would wonder how it was that you were so independent and self-assured. They would wonder at those inner strengths that allowed you to go your own way and not worry about the opinion of others. They would fear that you would soon become a force to be reckoned with in the jail. They would then go out of their way to be friendly and helpful. You could then pick your friends from among the strongest and soundest. And if you were really forceful and independent, you could walk your own path and stay on your own.

A voice suddenly interrupted my reverie. 'Hello, Norm, I didn't expect to see you here.'

I looked up to see a tall, slim fella wearing gold horn-rimmed glasses standing by my table. He had on a smart blue jumper and neatly pressed jeans. I remembered him vaguely from the Scrubs several years previously.

'It's Danny, Danny Fox,' he said as he sat down in the spare place opposite me.

I quickly checked him in my memory. I remembered him as a weak fella who hung around with an equally weak crowd. He came from one of the seaside towns and had killed an old lady in a tie-up. The 'chaps' didn't particularly approve of people who killed old ladies in whatever circumstances, so he had been largely ignored by most of the 'faces' at the Scrubs.

But I would have to talk to someone here; otherwise the screws would categorise me as being withdrawn and anti-social. Foxy was clean and tidy and reasonably intelligent. He hadn't had a heavy, gangster reputation at the Scrubs. Perhaps I could associate with him occasionally without the screws reading anything ominous into it.

As I finished my dinner, Foxy told me about Knightsford or, rather, his version of Knightsford. He emphasised that the vast majority of the cons couldn't be trusted. He was particularly vehement in denouncing the nonces and grasses, looking sideways at the other two diners at the table.

I guessed that this was as much for their benefit as mine and realised that Foxy, too, was acting out a role. As I studied him more closely, I noticed how tense and intense he was. The intervening years since I had last seen him at the Scrubs had taken their toll. He didn't look a lot different physically, but mentally he was showing the pressure.

He screwed up his face to emphasise passionately particular points. He moved his upper body and arms in short jerky movements to underline his disdain for people or events. If he had been an actor playing a part, the director would have stopped him for going right over the top. I had long recognised that a clear sign of mental illness was an individual's inability to monitor his own performance. Foxy was obviously mentally ill, but then so were a large percentage of the inmates in long-term jails.

The meal over, I walked back with Foxy to the centre. He invited me up for a coffee, and I climbed the stairs with him to his cell on the twos of B wing. It was fastidiously laid out. There were curtains and bedspreads and table-cloths draped around a cell that resembled an overcrowded bed-sit.

Foxy launched into a potted biography of his prison career to date and a detailed description of his painting. He got out his portfolio and I had to study about a score of watercolours. They weren't bad, but I had seen far better. In another jail, at another time, I would have got up and walked out. But this was the new, more tolerant Norman Parker. Usually I wouldn't have chosen someone like Foxy for a companion, but Knightsford, at first sight, seemed singularly bereft of suitable companions. And I had just spent three weeks in solitary at Lincoln.

As dinner-time ended and work-time approached, I left Foxy's cell and made my way back to my own wing. 'I'll see you this evening,' he called after me.

As I passed C wing office, Hall was lounging in the doorway. He called me over and told me I had an appointment to see the Welfare in the Admin block at 2.00. His manner was impeccably pleasant, but I couldn't help but feel the underlying antagonism.

I lay on my bed, reading. I heard the call to work and looked at my watch. It was 1.00. I was sleepy after the meal and could easily have dozed off. But I didn't want to miss my appointment at 2.00. I got up and sat in the chair to continue reading.

At 1.55, I went to the office. Hall came out and walked with me to the gate that led into the Admin block. He unlocked it and pointed to a room along the corridor on the left. 'Look for Mrs Frank's office,' he said.

The gate clanged shut behind me as I advanced along the corridor. Whenever I was in an Admin block, I always had the feeling of not belonging, as if I were a trespasser. But I was glad that I didn't belong because these were the phoney people, the governors and Welfare staff who pretended to care but didn't give a damn. I wasn't their type of con at all. They liked the obsequious crawler who was all contrition and deferred to their supposedly superior status. I was much too outspoken for them.

The door to the office had a glass panel set in its upper portion with a net curtain behind. A small name-plate bore the legend: 'MRS

FRANK'. I knocked and heard a high-pitched, little girl's voice call out, 'Come in.'

The woman sitting behind the desk hadn't been a little girl for thirty years or more. And from the size of her now, I doubted if there had ever been anything 'little' about her. Mrs Frank was a strapping thirteen stone or more. She was wearing a blue floral summer dress that was far too young for her.

'Oh you must be Norman,' she trilled, then pouted, simpered and finally giggled. 'Do take a seat.'

I was yet to meet one of Knightsford's staff who wasn't strange in some way. This woman's adopted persona was that of a young girl. Perhaps she wanted to come across as innocent and naïve, hoping that I would reciprocate.

'I'm Nancy,' she continued. 'John Deal is your regular Welfare officer but he won't be back until tomorrow. I just wanted to know if you have any pressing problems.' She simpered and giggled again.

I was certainly getting the red carpet treatment. I hadn't been in the jail a full day yet and everybody was queuing up to see me. Perhaps they were just very helpful at Knightsford and wanted to ensure that you settled in OK. But paranoia told me that they just wanted to have a look at me.

I assured her that I was settling in OK. Following this lack of input, she could hardly proceed further. She said that if anything did come up I should ask to see her immediately.

As I turned to leave, she waved goodbye, wiggling her fingers at me. I walked out of the office with her giggles ringing in my ears. *Well, whoever that was*, I thought, *that wasn't the real Mrs Frank.*

I walked back up the corridor to the gate. It was locked and there was nobody about. The centre was deserted. I rattled the gate loudly to attract the attention of the screws in C wing office.

Suddenly Hall lunged out of the office, a look of annoyance on his face as he glared at the gate. His mouth was twisted into a snarl as he prepared to bawl out the offender, but when he saw it was me, a startling transformation came over him. The angry face smoothed into a weak attempt at a grin. 'Oh, it's you, Norm,' he blustered. 'I didn't think you'd be finished so quickly.'

I smiled in return as he ambled over to the gate to let me through. I hadn't missed the first reaction though and it confirmed exactly what I had suspected. Hall was still a thoroughly nasty piece of work. A verbal bully who would enjoy browbeating someone weaker.

Clearly he was still wary of me, though. In that respect nothing had changed. It was the old, old story. You had to intimidate the average screw just to get a bit of respect. The trouble with that, though, was it bred resentment.

Most screws are nothing if not hierarchical. They defer to all superior authority and, in turn, expect to be deferred to by everyone of inferior status. It throws their world-view completely out of kilter when this *status quo* is challenged. On the positive side, it made my dealings with them easier. The downside was their resentment, which would be reflected in the reports they secretly wrote. I hated such treachery and insincerity.

Hall let me through the gate. I thanked him and walked away. If hypocrisy ruled here, then so be it. After the trials of the last couple of years I was beginning to learn to bite my tongue. Simple self-preservation demanded it.

All I wanted to do was to preserve my self-respect. To be spoken to with a basic courtesy and to respond in kind. For if I allowed myself to be humiliated, my spirit would die, my will would crumble and I wouldn't survive the long years.

Control was all to the screws. The slightest show of spirit or individuality was regarded as treasonous rebellion, to be crushed and the perpetrator punished and humiliated. And humiliation was an integral part of their response. They knew the cons had their own hierarchy and value system. Many of the lifers at Knightsford had been professional men before their convictions. Many had been the screws' social superiors. Most of the thieves had had money and possessions far in excess of what the screws now had. And it rankled.

But in this demi-world, the screws ruled. To be confronted by a proud, talented or spirited prisoner was a challenge to the meritocracy they believed in. It would cause them to examine their own self-worth. And often they found themselves wanting.

I would pull my horns in a bit at Knightsford. I wouldn't challenge the minor innuendo. But if I was confronted on a point of principle, I would stand my ground. Anyway, this problem didn't seem likely to arise. They were treating me with a healthy degree of respect that I had hardly experienced in other jails.

I had been lying on my bed for only a few minutes when there was a barely audible knock on the door. It was pushed gingerly open, and there stood two of the sorriest-looking cons I had seen for many a long year.

One looked vaguely familiar. He was in his early thirties, but his hair was prematurely grey and his skin pallid. He had a bony, angular face and a consumptive build — a sickly child who had grown into a sickly adult.

The other one was equally unwholesome. He was much younger, probably in his early twenties, and had a sturdier frame although he was prematurely stooped about the shoulders. His face was his ruination, though. He had the stupid, vacant look of the half-wit. A long nose and a permanent half-grin completed a startling resemblance to Alfred E. Neumann, the ginger-haired, freckled idiot who graced the covers of *Mad* magazine.

He looked the archetypal nonce. I couldn't conceive that he could be in for any sensible crime. And even if he wasn't a sex case, the old saying sprang to mind: 'If he isn't a nonce, he'll do until one comes along.'

I was on the verge of saying, 'Now what do you two pricks want?' when I suddenly remembered that I was supposed to be in Knightsford mode. From what I had already seen, the majority of the cons here were nerdy-looking. If I volleyed every wally who tried to speak to me, I would soon be very unpopular.

That prospect didn't particularly worry me *per se*. I had become something of a loner over the past couple of years. Perhaps it was the constant transfers and spells in solitary — necessity had made me emotionally self-sufficient. What did concern me, though, was that those I rebuffed would get their own back by running me down to the screws. And if enough of them did it, the screws would think that it was me who was nasty and anti-social. I wasn't going to stand for every clown in the jail, but I would be civil if I could.

'Yeah?' I said with as much good grace as I could muster.

'Hello, Norm, it's me, Porter,' said the pallid one timidly.

The name rang no bells. I couldn't conceive that I had ever been even remotely friendly with such an obvious wally. The other one remained silent, just grinning.

'I was at Long Lartin with you. I was on E wing,' continued the first one, seeing my puzzlement.

A brief glimmer of recognition stirred in my memory. A face swam through the myriad others. I recalled an anonymous inadequate who had been regarded as a joke, when he was regarded at all. 'Epileptic', 'poof' and 'mental patient' were bits of information I dredged up to complete the picture. He obviously knew me, but that was no surprise because I had had a high profile in most of the jails I had been in.

The second one still said nothing. He didn't indicate that he knew me and I was sure that I wouldn't have forgotten a face like his.

The silence hung in the air. It was rapidly turning into one of those nutty situations that you often get in jail. I suppose I could have made things easier by getting up and shaking Porter's hand. But I didn't want to encourage him to be a regular visitor. On visit No. 2, I was sure I would quickly tell him to piss off.

'I'm surprised to see you here,' Porter persevered.

'I'm surprised to be here,' I rejoined. It was still difficult to believe that Knightsford had accepted me.

'You won't like it here, Norm. Nothing ever happens,' Porter said almost conspiratorially. He looked briefly over his shoulder as he mouthed this half-criticism of the regime.

'Well, that will suit me just fine,' I came back immediately. 'Because if nothing ever happens, then they can't blame me for starting it.' My previous seven shanghais arose like spectres in my memory. It would be all too easy for me to get shipped out for absolutely nothing.

Here was an opportunity for me to do some public relations

work. The last thing I wanted was for Porter to tell all his mates what a hard-case and trouble-maker I was and how it wouldn't take long for me to start. That would get back to the screws very quickly.

Porter looked surprised, but just nodded in agreement. When I didn't say any more, he backed out slowly. 'Let me know if there's anything I can do for you, Norm,' he said.

Like some bizarre double act, he and Alfred E. Neumann disappeared from view in reverse. The door swung to behind them.

I lay back on the bed, thinking about my recent visitors. This was going to be the negative side of being at Knightsford. There would be very few spirited, sensible cons to associate with. I envisaged a lonely period before me.

I looked at my watch and saw that it was still only early afternoon. I hadn't been told that I had to see anyone else that afternoon, and guessed that the rest of my reception appointments would be set for the morning. It seemed like a good time to explore my new jail. No one had said anything about having to stay in my cell. Knightsford obviously wasn't like a local jail. There would be freedom of movement within the wings.

I left my cell and stood for a moment on the ones. I might as well start with my own wing, although there didn't seem much to explore. It was typical of all Victorian-style prison wings, if a bit shorter than most. The cell doorways on either side of the landing receded into the distance like some detail from an Escher drawing. Up on the twos landing, identical lines of cells marched away from me.

A steel staircase dog-legged up to meet a bridge that connected the two landings on either side. Other than two recesses at the far end, there was nothing else up there.

I walked along the ones, away from the centre. Half-way along, right in the middle of the landing, stairs led down to some kind of basement. I descended a dozen stone steps worn hollow in the middle by the passage of thousands of feet over many years. It was always in the subterranean parts of jails that the feeling of age was strongest.

I found myself in what was obviously the bath-house. There were several showers in a recess to my right, and as I walked along a darkened corridor, I looked into bare rooms that contained only a bath each. There wasn't a soul about. It seemed both eerie and strange to find myself in such an easily accessible place which was deserted. Violence is endemic to prison life, and this bath-house was an ideal place to attack an enemy. It spoke volumes about the low-key regime at Knightsford and its well-behaved inhabitants that such a place could be left unlocked and unsupervised.

I came back up the steps, feeling a niggling sense of relief to be in the bright light again. There was something of the tomb about the bath-house. No doubt, at some time in the past, it had been a punishment block. They were usually located in the basement. That would explain the eerie, oppressive atmosphere. Perhaps human suffering still resonated in the walls. And if it had anything in common with other punishment blocks, there would have been suicides – the human spirit at the end of its tether, tormented by the solitude.

I must have registered all this subliminally as I had walked through its depths. The body, certainly one as finely attuned to suffering as mine, would have felt it. No wonder I had suppressed a shudder as I returned to the light.

I walked along my landing to the end. There was little else to see. The windows of the recesses either side revealed two toilets with half-doors, two urinals, several wash-basins and a slops sink.

I walked back up to the centre. I decided to explore the other two wings. I had nothing else to do and I just might see something of interest. Although I was looking for a quiet time at Knightsford, if I did see an escape opportunity that was especially promising, then I would have to take it.

A wing was identical to my own, even down to the basement half-way along its length. The door at the bottom of the stairs was locked, though. I surmised that this could just be a real punishment block.

I crossed the centre again and started along B wing. There was no basement and at the far end there were doors that obviously led into workshops. Other than that, it could have been A or C wings.

Standing back at the centre, I noticed a large, glass-fronted room up on the twos. I climbed the stairs and walked across to the glass-fronted room. It was a large TV room. I had already seen another when I came up from reception that morning. A glass partition sectioned off an area of the basement.

But I had little interest in TV rooms. That way lay death of the intellect. I had seen too many men who had sat back, year in year out, to be passively entertained. In the end they watched anything and everything. It didn't matter, because it didn't register. Their minds had just switched off under the weight of so much trivia.

I descended to the centre again. I had hardly seen a soul when, suddenly, a white-shirted figure burst out of the office at the end of A wing. He bustled across the centre, heading towards the gate leading to the Admin block.

The face with its full cheeks looked familiar. The slicked-down jet black hair and the barrel chest rang a chord. The waist-line bulged beneath the white shirt, heralding the onset of middle age. But the overall impression was still one of youth and vitality.

His eyes met mine and, for a second, I read arrogance and hostility there. It was a glare that was used to throwing out challenges, and winning. Then, as recognition dawned, it flickered, wilted, then crumbled. The man suddenly stared at the ground and headed past me.

The name and face came back to me. It was Parkhurst again, but there the shirt had been blue and Wade had been only a basic grade screw. A flash, young Taffy straight from the training school. He had had a swagger and a passionate commitment to football that bordered on the hooligan. In other circumstances, he could have been wearing the prison grey, but only as a petty offender.

He had clearly fancied himself and would have liked to have thrown his weight around a bit. Parkhurst had been full of hard-cases, though. Men far fiercer and tougher than he. It had been enough to cow him. His adopted persona had become that of a 'man's man'. Beneath the surface though, the coward's resentment had seethed.

The white shirt said that he was either a PO or SO now. Knightsford, with all its tame cons, would be just his milieu. I could imagine that he reigned here unchallenged.

The heavy, barred gate of the Admin block clanged shut behind him. I walked past the covered snooker table to look at a large notice-board fixed to the wall. As I started to peruse the dozens of notices stapled to it, I heard the gate open again. This time it closed more gently.

Soft, light footsteps scuffed across the centre behind me. I continued to read the notices. As the footsteps started to ring on the steel stairs at the end of A wing, I turned slowly to look.

I was just in time to see a slight figure trip lightly up the first flight. Before it disappeared from view behind the second flight, the tight-fitting, black trousers had registered.

In a world where sexuality was generally obscured beneath shapeless, baggy clothes, the roundness of the buttocks stood out. The tightness of the material around the slim legs told me that the figure was wearing what looked like women's slacks.

I saw shoulder-length brown hair that bobbed up and down with the motion of climbing. It curled round and inwards and had clearly been styled.

My immediate reaction was that this was a member of the local gay fraternity. Admittedly, there were no exaggerated movements that parodied femininity, and the frame was small and definitely very feminine. But women were very few and far between in men's prisons.

More interested now, I waited for the figure to reappear on the centre gallery. Suddenly it bobbed into view. The brown hair framed a face that was boyishly pretty. It was pale and round and unmarked by any make-up. Even at that distance the eyes were bright and intelligent beneath a fringe.

It was definitely a woman, but she carried herself quite unpretentiously. There was no studied poise or exaggerated grace. She was wearing a brown cardigan, unbuttoned to reveal a plain white blouse done up to the neck. Perhaps it was this deliberate 'dressing-down' that had confused me. If she had been in a dress, there would have been no mistake.

She disappeared through a doorway half-way around the gallery, directly opposite my wing. It was the first time I had realised that it was there.

From below, I could see a long corridor gleaming in reflected light before it disappeared into the gloom. There was another wing there, although it definitely wasn't residential. I resolved to explore it in due course.

The image of the woman slipped from my mind. I had no interest in women while in prison. Those few female staff that there were were eminently unattainable.

There were those cons who fancied themselves as ladies' men, who would preen and put themselves in the way of some female. Perhaps they wanted to reassure themselves that they still had the ability to chat up a woman. It could lead nowhere, though, and to me, it was immature. Worse, it made any female staff arrogant and vain. The plainest office typist became a princess with many suitors. Their attitude towards cons in general often became condescending.

My response to that was simple. I treated them exactly the same as male staff. If a volley was called for, then it was delivered. I was a great believer in equality.

I returned my attention to the notice-board. The typed sheets stated rules, advertised jobs and warned of changes in the regime. It was all very low-key. Threats were veiled and delivered in a spirit of cajolery. I smiled to discover that I was now a 'resident'. 'Residents are advised . . .' or 'Residents are requested . . .' began most of the notices. In the past, I had been a 'prisoner', an 'inmate' and even a 'convict'.

I didn't envisage that my status would now change in any practical way. The term 'resident' smacked of a degree of volition. In the free world, residents invariably had the option of leaving. Yet the doors and bars of Knightsford were clearly not just for show.

Next to the notice-board were the double wooden doors that led to the dining hall. At the opposite end of the room was a raised stage and thick, full-length curtains. In front of the stage stood an old upright piano. No doubt the dining hall doubled as a theatre.

Both side walls had numerous wired-glass windows and doors set in them. But the wall to my right was almost all wired glass. It gave a refreshing sense of space, of freedom, with no sign of bolt or bar. Through the glass I could see bushes and shrubs and the grass of a football pitch. The escaper in me reflected that it would be all too easy to kick through the glass and exit on to the pitch.

It could have been a dining hall almost anywhere. If you had suddenly woken and found yourself in it, you would never have guessed you were inside a jail. These were positive aspects of Knightsford that I liked.

Once again I was in the shortest corridor, but now with the staircase on my left. I climbed two short flights and found myself in a longer corridor. The floor was covered in lino tiles, of a type and quality I had never seen in a prison before. The decor was bright and immaculate. The rest of Knightsford wasn't run down by any means, but this section clearly stood out in its smartness.

I walked along the corridor and peered through the first door. Thick purple curtains formed a backdrop for a plum-coloured carpet. Rows of stained-wood pews marched out of my sight. I pushed the door open and stepped into the chapel. I noticed an immediate change in the quality of sound. Everywhere else in the prison sound carried, ricocheting off hard surfaces. Here, the carpeting and drapes served to smother noise, giving the effect of hallowed silence.

In prison, where space and resources are at such a premium, I contemplated the waste of such a place. It would stand empty six days a week. On the seventh, it would largely serve the cause of hypocrisy. Cons, who never went to church outside, who never showed their fellows any Christian compassion through the week, would file in here on a Sunday for appearances' sake. The 'righteous con' was a common and patently transparent type in the nick. However, many screws seemed to be fooled by them.

I had my own faith, one that had been formed and fired in the long night of solitary confinement. Most men will find something there, if madness does not find them first.

I was born a Jew, but never practised the faith. My Jewishness now served to keep the prison priests and chaplains at bay. The screws had to have some religious label for you, so it served that purpose, too.

In my faith I didn't need the appurtenances of velvet curtains, stained-wood pews, priests, chaplains or even rabbis. It was an intensely personal thing that helped to sustain my spirit and give meaning to what was nearly a meaningless existence.

It was almost the equivalent of positive thinking in theological form. My goal would be to come to terms with the dark side of my nature, to curtail it and imprison the beast. Out of the ashes of my former personality would rise the phoenix of a new and happier person. My crimes troubled me more than people knew.

Through the windows of the next room, I could see a counter and, behind that, rows of household goods stacked on shelves. It looked like a school tuck shop, but I realised that it was the prison canteen. Men would queue up here once a week to spend the few quid they had earned.

At the end of the corridor, behind a locked door, I saw a large room with books on rows of shelves along the walls – obviously the library. To the right, a larger room opened out. As I stepped into it I stopped and caught my breath in surprise. All along two adjoining walls ran a picture window that reached from knee height to the ceiling. There were no bars or grilles. I had never seen anything like it in prison before. The free world seemed just to pour in unrestricted. And beyond the window lay a panoramic view of half of Dartville.

Trance-like, I shuffled forward, never once taking my eyes off the view. There were rows of chairs ranged in front of the window. I lowered myself into one and soaked up the vista. So that was where free people lived.

Prison is a process, a succession of imprisonments. At first it operates only on a physical level, restricting your movement. Later, it extends to the psychological plane, encompassing your very perception. You come to exclude all thoughts, all visions of the free world. Even in the short time I had been at Knightsford, I felt a growing, a widening of my perception. It was as if levels of experience that had been switched off for so long were now being activated again.

It was a pleasant feeling, but also a painful one. It served to remind me of what I had missed, and was still missing. I would have to be careful that it didn't awaken too much of me and disturb my carefully constructed equilibrium. A free-world mind had no place in an imprisoned body.

I sat for long minutes staring out at the houses, gardens and roads. I wondered what it would be like at night, when all the lights were on. I resolved to return and find out.

I turned to check what kind of room I was in. I was pleased to see shelves filled with paperback books. This was obviously some kind of overflow library that I could visit at will.

I retraced my steps until, once again, I stood on the centre. I crossed to the corridor opposite my own wing, below the door through which the woman had disappeared. I had a sneaking suspicion that this would be the education block.

A short corridor ran parallel to the main corridor. A sign saying 'HOSPITAL' was fixed to the wall pointing along it. I could see some chairs and, in the distance, a bed. It seemed very small for a prison hospital. No doubt, at the first sign of serious illness, you would be shipped out to one of the big jails. I resolved not to fall ill at Knightsford.

At the end of the corridor, I could see what was obviously a gymnasium. Basically, it was a large, oblong room with wall-bars all along one side. A badminton court was marked out, the side-lines barely six feet from the walls. Basketball nets were fixed to boards at either end. There was an alcove hidden by a roller-shutter beneath one of the basketball boards. Through a crack I could see a multi-gym. A door near the corner led into a shower room. Stacked against one wall were racks of dumb-bells. Against another wall were two weights benches.

I was a confirmed fitness fanatic, working out religiously at least once a day. It was how I did my time, my physical discipline having become the basis of my mental discipline. It looked like I would be able to get at the dumb-bells whenever I wanted to.

Just before entering the gym, I had noticed a staircase leading upwards on my left. Now I climbed the two flights to the top. I found myself in another corridor, directly above the one I had just explored. This was obviously the education block. Classrooms with students sitting at desks were on either side.

Trying not to attract their attention, I stared straight ahead and walked by. As I came abreast of the last classroom, I saw out of the corner of my eye the woman I had noticed earlier. She was standing in front of a class, writing on a blackboard. About a dozen inmate students sat at desks watching her.

The corridor dog-legged at the end and I found myself back at the centre, standing at the rail of the gallery. So that was it. The grand tour of my new home. It wasn't much, but more than I was used to. I would have a greater degree of freedom than ever before.

I looked at my watch. It was just after 3.00; the tour had taken less than an hour. I returned to my cell and lay on the bed. Suddenly I felt sleepy. I would have a short nap before tea.

2

Hardly had I closed my eyes than there was a knock on the door. The door eased open and a head poked around it.

The face was young and handsome, if a trifle blue from beard shadow. Jet black hair stood up in a spiky, yet tidy style. At first I thought it had been dyed in parts, but as he stepped into the light I saw that there were large patches of premature grey.

I looked again at the face to check the age. Bright eyes sparkled with the arrogance of youth. He could be no more than twenty-three or twenty-four.

"Allo, mate, you're a Londoner, ain't you?' he asked in a broad Cockney accent. 'I'm from the East End myself.' An impish smile crinkled the corners of his mouth.

I swung off the bed to face him. The experience of years weighed him up quickly. The calm confidence, the roughness of manner without being rude, the genuine friendliness. Nothing jarred in the performance. It just could be that he was one of my own kind.

He was a couple of inches taller than me, with an athletic build. He looked a sportsman and I guessed he was a footballer. He moved with a slightly exaggerated swing of the shoulders, but then so did many Londoners.

'My name's Tom,' he continued, stepping forward and holding out his hand.

'Pleased to meet you, Tom. I'm Norman.' I shook his hand. 'Come in and sit down.'

He sat in a chair by my table. I returned to sit on the bed. 'I'd make you a cup of coffee or something, but I still haven't unpacked all my stuff,' I said, nodding towards the box still standing in the corner.

'Don't worry about that.' Nodding towards the box himself, Tom continued, 'Haven't made up your mind whether to stay yet, eh?' The smile at the corner of his mouth widened into a grin.

I smiled back. Someone had obviously said something to him. There were probably quite a few fellas at Knightsford who knew me from other jails, even if I hadn't recognised them yet.

'Don't look too bad at the moment, but then I've been in some right pissholes lately. What's the form here?' I asked. One jail differed so much from the next that it was very easy to put a foot wrong, right at the start, and then you would antagonise the screws. Things that were allowed in one jail, might be anathema in another. It was handy if you could find someone sensible who could tell you what was what.

'You'll have to watch yourself here, Norm,' said Tom earnestly, leaning forward. 'The cons in general are a right bunch of wallies. Most of them have never been in the nick before. They'll do anything to get out a bit earlier. So don't let anyone see you do anything.'

'I don't intend to do anything, Tom. To be honest, I've had a bit of a rough time over the last couple of years and I could do with a bit of a rest. Just to gather my strength again.'

'Oh, it's quiet enough here, too quiet, in fact,' said Tom. 'The screws will leave you alone, but you'll stand out. Many of them will be frit of you, so if you're involved in the slightest incident, they'll over-react.' He wasn't smiling now.

Well, there was nothing I could do about my reputation and what had gone before. I resolved to be extra careful, especially for the first few weeks.

'What's the SP on Hall?' I asked.

'He's a right two-faced cunt. He'll pretend he's one of the chaps. He'll talk in that fake London accent of his and have a joke with you, but he hates us. He can get his own way with the wallies and bully them. But he's got no arsehole. Anyone with a bit of spirit intimidates him. Instead of showing his resentment he'll stab you in the back.'

I was pleased. Tom's assessment squared with the one I had already formed.

'And what about Maypole?'

A serious look came over Tom's face. 'You really want to watch him, Norm. He's completely fucking nuts. I mean, really unbalanced. He's a full governor, but he seems to have a bit of an inferiority complex. As if he fears that people won't take him seriously as a proper governor. If there's any challenge to his authority, he goes right over the top. Even over little things. You'll see him in action before too long.

'He's already had a couple of heart attacks at other jails. They say he has moved here because it's quiet and nothing ever happens. It would be funny if it wasn't so fucking serious. He's got a lot of power over us. One of his favourite threats is: "I'll put you so far back in the system that you'll never get out." And he means it, too.'

I hadn't read that in him when I had met him that morning. I had noticed the tension, the sense of living on the edge, but much of that I had put down to the fact that he was dealing with me. Perhaps it was his 'troublesome prisoner' mode.

My tenure at Knightsford suddenly looked very precarious. With my track record, I was automatically in trouble with even the most balanced of governors. An insecure nutter was a very serious threat to me. I would really have to watch myself around Maypole.

'The PO, Docker, he's an old dog. But he's so close to retirement, he can't be bothered now,' Tom continued. 'Basically, he's just a miserable cunt. He ain't in today, but he's back tomorrow.

'The other SO, John Gale, on the opposite shift to Hall, he ain't a bad fella. He's civil and will help you if he can. But don't expect any real favours 'cause he's very much by the book.'

Tom paused. Conscious of the fact that he was doing all the talking, he was giving me the chance to say something. But I was content just to listen. This was all valuable stuff, things it would take me weeks to learn myself. At least I would know where the dangers lay now. And forewarned was to be forearmed.

Tom continued: 'The rest of the screws on the wing won't bother you. You'll hardly see them unless you go into the office for something. We're a bit lucky in that respect. There are a few slags on the other wings, but they hardly come in contact with us.'

'What about the Chief?' I asked. 'I met him when I arrived. He knows me from Parkhurst. He was a PO there and a right slag, but strangely enough, he seemed pleased to see me.'

Tom laughed. 'He's another right nutter. I swear to God, Norm, he's completely round the twist. I get on with him really well. I have a right laugh with him. I think he likes my sense of humour. But I get away with things that no one else can.

'Everybody else is terrified of him, though, especially the screws. He's really hard on them. He lives just outside the gates. On his days off, he lurks and tries to catch them leaving early. He's nicked several of them and they hate him.

'He's near retirement, too. I think he's making the most of his power while he's still got it. He doesn't bother too much with the cons, but if he does see something, he really goes into one. He seems half asleep a lot of the time. But he loves to agg the screws.

'You should see him first thing in the morning. Hall and the others lounge across the snooker table supervising the move to work. The Chief comes in through the Admin block corridor, sneaks right up behind them. I've actually seen him tip-toeing. He unlocks that big, iron gate quietly, then slams it behind him with all his force. You should see Hall and the others jump.'

Tom laughed at the memory. 'They all spin round angrily, but what can they say? He's the Chief. Sometimes if I'm about on the centre, he'll give me a little grin, then walk past with a straight face. He's a right scream.'

I was laughing with Tom now. I could imagine big, fat Hall jumping in fright. Getting a bit of his own medicine, being bullied in turn.

'But he can turn, just like that. I get away with joking with him, but I've seen him rare up on others over nothing. Most people stay right out of his way if they can.'

I resolved to do just that. Mind you, the list of people I was going to have to avoid was growing longer by the minute. At this rate, I would have to spend most of the time hiding under the bed.

'Who's the bird?' I asked suddenly.

'Which one?' replied Tom.

I realised that I had seen two today. 'The small, boyish one.'

'Oh, that's Jane.'

There was something in his reply, something I couldn't put my finger on. Almost as if he was talking about something personal. He saw my look and smiled, half-embarrassed.

'No, nothing like that, Norm. She's a right good person, Jane. She's all for us cons. She's the assistant education officer. She won't allow the screws in the education block and refuses to spy on the cons. The screws hate her. They'd get rid of her if they could.'

Tom said all this with considerable passion. I couldn't help but feel that there was something between him and Jane. She wasn't a bad-looking woman. There was bound to be a lot of competition for her attention. All the usual preening among the fellas who fancied themselves. And from what I had seen of other female prison teachers in the past, she would probably love it.

I accepted what Tom said about her being all for the fellas. Perhaps she was some kind of gangster groupie. But then I was a confirmed cynic when it came to prison staff. I resolved not to become one of her acolytes. I would have to have some dealings with her over my Open University course, but I would keep it very formal.

For a while we talked about some of the people we knew, both outside and in other jails, and found that we had a couple of pals in common. He would be easy to check out, but I was already sure that Tom was a decent fella. He seemed the epitome of the young, staunch East Ender. There was a tradition of pride on that manor. I felt in my bones that I could trust him.

Suddenly I looked at my watch and saw that we had been talking for over an hour.

'Come on, Norm,' Tom said, standing up. 'It's nearly tea-time. There's an empty place on our table. You can sit with us. The other two fellas, young Jack and Bill, they're straight fellas really. But they've got a bit more spirit than most of them here and they're quite staunch.'

I picked up my knife, fork, spoon and cup and followed Tom outside. 'Just got to pick up my own eating irons and I'll be with you,' he shouted as he ran up the stairs to the twos. He quickly reappeared and ran downstairs to join me. We walked quickly towards the dining hall.

We joined the short queue waiting against the wall adjoining the counter. From time to time, fellas called out to Tom and he replied. It seemed that he was well known and quite popular.

We collected our meal and sat down at a table near the centre of the dining hall. By now, a large queue had formed, snaking its way along the side wall. Men of all ages, shapes and sizes shuffled forwards towards the counter. As I talked with Tom, I scanned the faces. There were very few tough- or aggressive-looking ones. Now and again I saw a face that struck a faint chord in my memory, but no names sprang to mind. I might have been in the same prison as some of them at one time or another, but there was no one I really knew. And that was surprising, seeing how many jails I had been in.

Two fellas sat down in the empty seats next to Tom and me. Tom introduced me to Bill and Jack. The latter was in his early twenties with an open, likeable face beneath a riot of black curly hair. His expression was singularly lacking in guile. He had a youthful innocence about him of the kind you would be pleased to see in any young man that your daughter brought home.

Bill, opposite, was altogether different. He was in his late twenties, with a shock of untidy mousey hair. Horn-rimmed glasses with thick lenses attested to poor eyesight. Whereas Jack's face had a happy-go-lucky openness about it, Bill's was pinched, with tension and stress written all over it. The high, bony cheekbones stretched the pale skin tight across his cheeks. Crow's feet were etched into the corners of his eyes and mouth. I got the impression that he would be unable to take too much pressure. And from the haunted look in his eyes, I realised that he knew it, too.

'Hi,' he said with a brave attempt at a smile. There was a breath of a North country accent. It wasn't that his greeting lacked warmth. It was rather that he seemed ill at ease, as if he felt that his position within the group might be challenged by this newcomer.

Tom, me and probably Jack were all Londoners. This might be the source of Bill's problem. There was a lot of rivalry between Londoners and Northerners in most nicks. Perhaps Bill felt well and truly outnumbered now.

'I was just telling Norm about the place,' said Tom over the sudden silence.

'Yeah, right bunch of fucking wallies here,' broke in Bill immediately with unnecessary passion. It was as if he wanted to distance himself from the rest and any suspicion that he might be a wally, too. Jack just grunted and nodded in agreement.

It occurred to me that 'wally' was a comparative term. If weakness and a general criminal naïvety were the qualities of the wally, then both Jack and Bill might well have struggled in some of the hard jails that I had been in. That wasn't to slander either of them. What they lacked was a viciousness and a courage that bordered on the self-destructive. It was definitely a non-rational quality, but was survival specific for jails such as Parkhurst. There, all values became inverted. Strength and viciousness were all.

I could see an edge of it in Tom. Young and undeveloped, naïve even, but still there in its raw form. I hoped that he could escape the system before it turned him into something nasty. There was honour and principle in Tom, and already I got the feeling that there was loyalty there too. Of the 'young 'uns' that I had already seen, Tom seemed to stand out from most of the rest.

There was always a lot of posturing between the young fellas in any jail. Even in Knightsford there would be a young group who considered themselves to be an élite, even if that éliteness only extended to those who were young and slightly rebellious. I would find that Jack had a bit of a swagger to him at times, and Bill often had a wild, angry look. But it was Tom who was the star of the show. He had both criminal background and East End kudos.

However, he was still unsure of himself in some ways, and in others he was quite immature. He was still very young though. On the outside, a man of twenty-four would have had all the worries of adult life to mature him – the responsibility of taking care of a wife, running a home and earning a living soon forced the youth to put away boyhood things. When a teenager came into prison, the maturation process stopped. He was dropped into the womb of prison living. The regime would do everything for him. His relationships with his peers would be characterised by the childish pranks that pass for humour in prison. And if the youth came into prison at seventeen, then that would be his emotional age when he left, whatever his chronological age.

As we ate, the dining hall slowly filled up. Soon most of the tables were occupied. There was no unruly behaviour and little shouting, but the combined effect of 150 voices produced a din that was quite awesome.

From time to time, I observed those sitting at nearby tables. Tom had already told me that many of Knightsford's lifers had been professional men and it showed in their demeanour. Tom discreetly pointed some out. There were several ex-bank managers, solicitors and architects. One bearded old boy, who could have been Hemingway's 'old man of the sea', had been a priest before his conviction.

A snapshot of dining inmates in most jails would have revealed a crowd straight out of central casting. Broken noses, scars and cauliflower ears would have been much in evidence. But Knightsford's diners looked so normal. It wasn't that they all had something in common, for a more disparate crowd it would have been hard to find. It was just that the majority of them lacked that air of ominous hostility you would expect from a crowd of murderers. In fact, if a stranger had suddenly found himself transported to sit amongst them in Knightsford's dining hall, he could never have guessed who his companions were.

A shadow fell across the table and I looked up to see Foxy standing there with his dinner tray. 'Oh, so you've found somewhere to sit then, Norm,' he said to me, ignoring the others.

There was an undercurrent to his tone, as if he resented the fact that I wasn't going to sit with him. And the way he had ignored the others made for a hostile atmosphere.

'Hallo, Danny,' broke in Tom with a smile. He had got it straight away and found it amusing. I was pleased to see that he wasn't intimidated by Foxy. Bill and Jack echoed Tom's greeting. There was wariness and deference in their tone.

'Hello, Tom,' replied Foxy, ignoring Bill and Jack. Looking at me, he said, 'I'll see you later, Norm. We'll have a cup of coffee or something, eh?'

'OK, mate.'

I was careful not to appear too enthusiastic. I had noticed the deference that Foxy received from some of the others and gathered that he had some kind of reputation as a local hard man here at Knightsford. There was a tense aggressiveness about him that clearly intimidated the average Knightsford lifer, but it meant nothing to me. I had known him several years earlier at the Scrubs, when he had been entirely different. He had hung around with a crowd of complete wallies and was a nonentity himself. As long-term jails went, the Scrubs hadn't been a particularly tough one. It had been far too tough for Foxy, though. He had slunk around in the background, intimidated into obscurity.

I had often seen such changes of persona from jail to jail. The real man was revealed by the lowest common denominator of his past actions. So either Danny had grown very tough over the past few years or he was putting on an act for the domesticated lifers of Knightsford.

'You know Danny then, Norm?' asked Tom with a quizzical look in his eye. I could see that he wasn't sure how friendly I was with Foxy. For all he knew, we might be close mates.

Bill and Jack had stopped eating to watch my reaction. I got the impression that they feared Fox acquiring a strong ally, who would give more power and influence to him.

'Yeah, I was at the Scrubs with him. We weren't pals or anything. He wasn't one of our crowd and, in fact, I think I only spoke to him about twice in the two years I was there,' I said between mouthfuls.

'What was he like there?'

'A right cunt really,' I replied, my answer partially obscured by a mouthful of currant duff.

There was an explosive hoot from Bill as he looked over his shoulder to confirm that Foxy was out of earshot. Tom and Jack joined in the laughter like schoolboys reacting to some scurrilous or sacrilegious remark.

I owed no loyalty to Foxy and I had already gathered that he was something of a bully at Knightsford. I didn't approve of bullies, especially ones who had been as frightened as Foxy had been when there was some real competition about. What also rankled was what I knew about his case. He had been a small town burglar who had tortured an old lady to death while trying to force her to reveal where she had hidden her savings. He had eventually given himself up and confessed in a thoroughly unprofessional débâcle.

The London 'chaps' at the Scrubs didn't particularly approve of people who tortured old ladies. The average armed robber put himself at considerable risk when he went up against security guards and armed police. Although there was no sexual element in his offence, Foxy had been regarded as something of a nonce at the Scrubs. It was quite funny, really, that here he was at Knightsford, swaggering about like one of the 'chaps'.

Having declared the extent of my non-relationship with Foxy, Tom, Bill and Jack seemed to relax somewhat. We had obviously been discussing a touchy subject.

'He's not like that here,' said Tom. 'He's very high profile. In fact, he's far and away Knightsford's most troublesome prisoner. He's rared up on several of the screws and a couple of them seem quite worried about him. He's volleyed a lot of the cons, too. People are quite wary of him.'

I listened with interest. When I had first considered Foxy as a potential companion at Knightsford, it was as the quiet, unassuming lifer I had known at the Scrubs. Foxy in tearaway mode was another prospect entirely. I resolved not to spend too much time with him.

As I walked back to the wing with Tom, he asked what I was going to do for the rest of the evening. I said that I had missed the gym while down the block at Lincoln and was dying for a good work-out.

'I've been meaning to do a bit myself, but I've never got round to it. If you don't mind, I'll come with you,' said Tom.

'Give me half an hour to let my tea go down and I'll come and find you.'

I spent the next forty minutes in my cell unpacking the rest of my kit. Now that my stuff was laid out on shelves and locker tops, the place looked a lot more hospitable. I knocked a couple of nails in the wall and hung up my posters. Suddenly, it looked just like my last cell.

I put on a gym vest and a pair of shorts, pulled a home-made pair of track suit bottoms over them and laced up my trainers. I buckled my weight-lifting belt loosely around my waist. Now I was ready for the gym. I set out to find Tom.

I climbed the stairs to the twos and walked along to his cell. 'Come in for a minute, Norm,' he said, waving me inside. I sat in a chair as Tom put on his gym kit.

'Like the bottoms,' he said, smiling.

My training bottoms were only a pair of cut-down overalls with elastic around the waist and the trouser cuffs. You weren't allowed to have track suit bottoms in jail, and it was an offence to alter prison clothes the way that I had, but it was only a minor thing. However, it did show a bit of individuality on my part.

'I've had them for ages,' I replied, shrugging. 'No one's said anything before. I'll take my chances here.'

'Oh, they'll notice,' Tom laughed, 'but I doubt if anyone will say anything.'

Two cons were playing badminton as we entered the gym. The taller one was an Asian with a surprisingly 'English' look about him. Clearly an excellent player, his tall, well-muscled physique moved easily around the court. His handsome face and confident manner held none of the usual Asian submissiveness. I reflected that murder wasn't a particularly passive crime.

His opponent was shorter and stockier. He carried some extra weight around his waist and his plump face was red and beaded with sweat. Greying hair above horn-rimmed glasses gave him a decidedly middle-aged appearance. He had a pleasant, avuncular look about him, like some particularly accommodating bank manager.

They stopped playing as we entered. The tall Asian stayed where he was, but the other one walked to meet us.

Tom did the introductions. The Asian fella was George and the other one, called John Brewer, was known by his initials JB. He and Tom seemed to be good pals.

'I'll have a talk with you some time, Norm,' called JB as he returned to his game of badminton. I waved an acknowledgement.

Tom and I walked into the shower room. The weights were just as I had seen them that afternoon. I quickly selected a couple of pairs of dumb-bells, pulled a bench into the middle of the room and started to work out. Despite the three-week lay-off, I still retained much of my strength. Soon I was flushed and pumped.

Tom struggled to keep up with me, but I was too strong for him. He worked to his maximum though and that was the important thing. I was confident that I had found a good work-out partner.

After the session, we climbed the stairs again to make our way through the education block and back to my cell. Some of the classrooms were lit. The first one was obviously a woodwork room. Several cons huddled around benches sawing and chipping at pieces of wood.

The classroom opposite doubled as a music room. An elderly, fat man was hammering away enthusiastically at an upright piano. Above a pasty moon face, great bushy eyebrows sprouted wildly like those of a mad, classical conductor. His eyes stared blankly ahead, and he was clearly transported by the effort. A small dribble of spit ran from one corner of his mouth.

Across the room, several more elderly men sat in a group, each with a different instrument. One old boy was pumping energetically at a trombone, his face red with the effort. There was a tuba, a French horn, a double bass and a couple of instruments I didn't recognise. Over in the corner, a young fella sawed away at a violin.

They made a very strange-looking group. Every single one of them had the weird, perverted, nerdy look of the nonce. Even the young violinist wouldn't have looked out of place in a mental hospital.

Yet, by Knightsford's standards, these were the cream of Britain's cons. The best behaved and, therefore, the most trusted. I couldn't help reflecting, however, that the average mother of young children would have instantly sussed them out and hated them with a passion.

The music reflected their looks. The discordant crashes of the piano acted as counterpoint to the shrieks of the violin. The cacophony ground on, the players seemingly oblivious to the resultant din. There was a frantic air to it all, as some struggled vainly to keep up. It sounded like a fairground hurdy-gurdy running out of control down a hill.

'Sounds like the "Broadmoor Ensemble" tuning up,' I remarked to Tom.

Tom laughed. 'You ain't seen nothing yet, Norm. We've got some right fucking nutters here. And the best part of it is that the screws love 'em. God forbid you ever bashed one of them – you'd be right in trouble.'

In another classroom, several young fellas huddled around a table, playing a board game. From time to time, they would split into small groups and mutter conspiratorially. None of them was more than thirty and, compared to the rest of Knightsford's 'residents', they looked relatively normal. Not that they resembled most inmates of other jails; there were no broken noses, scars, bulging muscles or cauliflower ears. In fact, they looked more like a group of students.

'I'll introduce you to this lot. They ain't thieves or tearaways or anything, but they ain't too bad. They think they're the young jet-set, but they don't ever do anything,' said Tom with a smile. He pushed open the door and walked into the classroom. I followed close behind him.

The players looked up from their board game. On a couple of faces, there was wary concern. They looked from Tom to me and their concern deepened. It was as if a group of boys playing marbles had been disturbed by an older, rougher group.

I stood there with beads of sweat still running down my face. My squat, densely muscled physique was still pumped from the weights, and the sodden gym vest stuck to my chest. I mused that I just didn't look like your average Knightsford inmate. I had too much of the aggressive, thuggish air about me.

I looked at Tom, but he just let the silence hang there. He could sense their discomfort, and it appealed to his sense of humour.

Suddenly he laughed. 'All right, fellas. I want you to meet a friend of mine, Norman.'

Several of the players relaxed visibly. Tom introduced them to me in turn. For the moment, the game was forgotten.

Richie was a tall and painfully thin young fella with curly, girlishly long hair and a hooked beak of a nose. Steve was shorter and prematurely balding, whose 'Pleased to meet you, Norm' was muttered timidly as if he expected me to punch him in the face. Sam, a large lump of a young fella who was also balding, loomed in front of me, a good three inches taller than me. Layers of fat wobbled as he stepped forward to shake my hand. On his florid, fat face was a large, red birthmark that looked as if he had been hit in the face by a ripe tomato.

Eric, a bearded fella with an athletic build, seemed calmer and more self-possessed than the rest. At his shoulder stood a short, stocky fella with greasy black hair. Pete's skin was sallow and he looked decidedly unhealthy. A clutch of blackheads struggled for space beneath one nostril. His face was young, but his eyes looked years older. They lacked the innocent naïvety of the others and shone like bright points. There was a hardness there, but one born of desperation rather than strength. He was definitely rodent-like and had trouble holding my gaze.

'And lastly,' said Tom, 'this is Eddie.' A short, gnome-like figure shuffled forward. His untidy, brownish hair ran into and merged with an equally untidy, bushy beard. Bright, intelligent eyes peered owlishly out at me through round National Health glasses. The voice that greeted me was definitely North Country. I felt myself wondering who on earth he could have murdered to get here.

'What game are you playing?' I asked.

'It's a war game called Diplomacy,' Eddie replied self-consciously as if he feared I would think it a childish pastime for fellas of their age. I glanced at the ship- and bomb-shaped counters spread out across the map of Europe. It looked far too complicated for me to ask a simple question about how it was played, so I just nodded and said nothing.

'Well, fellas, we won't hold your game up any longer. I'll see you about,' called Tom as he turned to leave.

As we walked back to my cell, Tom told me more about the fellas I had just met. 'Eric and Steve were university students. There was a row in a pub and someone got hit with a glass. It cut the fella's throat and he bled to death. Don't ask me how it happened. It was the first fight either of them had ever been involved in in their lives. Their brief must have been a right berk for them to have got life.

'Sam was partners with a fella in a car front. I think the fella must have had him over for the business, 'cause Sam killed him. He'd never been in trouble before in his life. Pete killed an old lady on a burglary. I think it was an accident, but he was such a smack-head that even he doesn't know what really happened.

'Richie? Well, you'll never believe it, but he mugged an old fella in a park. I think it was the first criminal thing he ever did in his life. Anyway, the old fella fought back. Perhaps he thought he could do the skinny fucker.' Tom laughed. 'Richie hit him and he fell over and smashed his head. Sure enough, he died and Richie got done for murder.

'And, last but not least, Eddie. He didn't get along with his stepmother and stepsister. One day, the mother told him to turn his record player down. It was the last straw. He took a hammer and killed them both. He's a strange fella is Eddie.'

As I listened to Tom, I said nothing. From my experience of prisons and prisoners, I had already realised that these weren't exactly hardened criminals. In fact, they were more unlucky than murderous. I wondered how many hundreds of thousands of similar incidents there had been that hadn't ended so tragically. However, murder was murder in the eyes of the authorities.

Tom and I finally reached my cell. He settled into a chair as I made some coffee. Now I had my kit sorted out I could entertain, after a fashion.

As we sat back with our drinks, I remarked that it seemed strange that so few people used the gym. At all the other jails where I had been, gym classes were always fully booked every evening.

'They've just got no go in them here,' explained Tom. 'The main criteria for getting into Knightsford is a passive nature. Anyone with any bollocks doesn't get picked. Even the young 'uns would rather watch the telly than do something active. You've just seen that lot playing fucking war games. That's how I've let myself miss out on the weights. I could never find a regular work-out partner.'

'Well, how about Jack and Bill?'

'Jack's all right. He plays football every weekend and five-a-side a couple of times a week, but that's it. He's not a thief or anything. He got involved in a fight outside a pub in Aylesbury. He didn't even start it. Just kicked a fella a couple of times and he died. He was out on bail right up to the trial. Really, it was a liberty giving him a life sentence. He was just unlucky. There are thousands of young fellas all over the East End who are far worse than he is.'

This also bore out what I had already surmised. Jack hadn't seemed to be particularly violent or vicious. There were plenty of relatively harmless young fellas who were doing life sentences because of a punch-up outside a pub.

'And Billy's even more harmless than Jack,' continued Tom. 'His girlfriend packed him in and he couldn't handle it. He killed her and he's never got over it. Eventually I think it will crack him up. He's half-way there already.'

Bill's tense face and haunted eyes rose up in my memory. Yes, I had booked him for a crime where he had lost control. He didn't have such good control right now. That was one of the reasons for the haunted look. He had lost control out of weakness, more as a tantrum than anything else, and he could lose control again. Then he would be transferred to one of the hard jails and never get out. That's what really worried him.

Tom and I had been talking for about half an hour when I heard the spy-hole cover suddenly swing back. As I looked towards it, the door swung open and Foxy walked in.

'Where have you two been? I've been looking all over the jail for you.' There was a grin on Foxy's face as he spoke, but wrinkles of annoyance underlined his eyes. I had already noticed that Foxy was very demanding of people.

'I told you he'd never find us down the gym,' I said deadpan as I turned to Tom.

Foxy's laugh was loud and false. You could see that he had been put out by searching for us unsuccessfully. He would have liked to have shown his annoyance, but he was wary of how I would react. However, the emotion was in him and he could hardly contain it. It was obvious that he had very little control.

'You will have your little joke, Norm.' Foxy bared his teeth in a toothy smile. He suddenly bent over, put both his arms around my chest and back and squeezed.

It was a playful hug, but it was something more. It was also a playful attempt at chastisement. Normally, I wouldn't allow anyone to lay a hand on me, even playfully. It was a severe invasion of personal space. But suddenly, it all seemed very funny and I found myself laughing in spite of myself. I could see a pattern emerging. My taking the piss out of the unbalanced Foxy, whom everyone else feared. Foxy not brave enough to do anything about it, but having to do something to save face. And him starting to lose control in a physical way, but sublimating it into a playful hug.

'All right, Foxy,' I gasped between bouts of laughter as he gently shook me. 'Put me down. Put me down.'

Tom was laughing, too. Foxy seemed satisfied that the whole situation had turned into a joke. He could even pretend that we were pleased to see him, as the bringer of mirth.

He took his arms from around my shoulders and sat down on the end of the bed. 'So where were you?' he persevered. 'You couldn't have been in the gym, because I looked.'

'We were in the shower room, using the weights,' answered Tom.

A look of understanding came across Foxy's face. 'Of course, I should have guessed you'd be looking for a workout, Norm.' He became thoughtful, and I knew what was coming. I could read Foxy like a book. 'Look, I've been thinking of working out myself lately. Do you think I could come down the gym with you?' he asked.

I looked at Tom. It was an awkward situation. I couldn't think of one good reason to say no, other than that I didn't want to be in Foxy's company. I wasn't slow to insult someone when the situation demanded it. But this was my first day, and I was in passive mode.

Tom shrugged noncommittally. He, too, was in a spot. But that just put the ball back firmly in my court. Perhaps it wouldn't be too much of a pain working out with Foxy. And we would be away from the public eye in the shower room. Maybe he would settle for that and not try to hang around with us on the wings.

'It's OK by me, but Tom's got a say, too,' I said.

'That's OK,' confirmed Tom.

'One thing, Danny.' I was serious now. 'If you're not ready on time, we start without you. And we do my work-out, not all sorts of things you come up with.' I took my training too seriously to let Foxy mess it up.

'No, that's OK, Norm,' said Foxy with the eagerness of a child promised a treat. 'You're in charge of the work-outs.'

I wasn't being pedantic here. I had already noticed that Foxy liked taking control. Having often got his own way at Knightsford, he had grown to like it. I was very strong-willed myself, and there was no way that Foxy was going to take over my life. I would keep him in check right from the start.

For a while, we talked about Knightsford, then other jails we had been in. I noticed that, whenever it was Foxy's turn to hold the floor, he became totally taken over by the role. He would act out all the parts, his face completely transformed by whichever emotion he was describing. For a man who was so stern and unapproachable in repose, he became positively possessed in conversation. It brought home to me just how close to the edge Foxy actually was. Beneath the stiff, stern exterior was a virtual whirlpool of nearly uncontrollable emotions.

I don't know how we came to it, but suddenly Foxy was talking about his case. It wasn't the sort of thing that the sophisticated con did in public. It was inevitably an intensely personal affair, one that still aroused strong emotions and memories of trauma. However well one handled it, it had been an excruciatingly painful experience. If nothing else, it had heralded the loss of freedom and the loss of a large part of one's life.

Perhaps Foxy suspected that we had heard something about his case anyway. He knew that he had been relegated to the fringes back at the Scrubs. Maybe it was an attempt to put over his side of the story. Anyway, before we knew it, we were deeply involved in the tale.

He took us back to Margate where he had been living in lodgings, looking for a job. He told how he and the fella he shared the flat with had gone to burgle a large house. He stood to demonstrate creeping about in the dark. His eyes widened in the make-believe darkness and his face tightened with fear.

Suddenly, his arms cartwheeled about as he blundered into the old lady. He lashed out at her scream, his mouth wide in a silent scream of his own. Then concern and contrition overcame him as he bent over the body, striking a match to see through the blackness. Horror etched itself in every line of his face as the realisation hit him. Every tendon in his neck stood out in stark relief, like wire bands.

Panic, sheer panic overwhelmed him. Stiffly, in pantomime slow motion, he acted out the flight. As he sat back on the bed, relief showed in his face as clearly as it must have done when he had got back to his room on that day.

There was a pause. It wasn't for effect. Foxy was gathering himself for the final catharsis. Tom and I sat completely immobile. Somehow we had become a part of the tableau. Against our will, Foxy had woven this tale around us so that now we were thoroughly caught up in it.

Then he was off again. Still seated, he related how he had been nicked several days later on a minor charge and remanded to Southampton for the weekend. He had been placed in a cell with an old tramp. As Foxy had paced the floor, the tramp had slept peacefully on the top bunk.

There had been some old newspapers on the table. Foxy sat to read them. He mimed turning them over, then suddenly froze. His whole body went rigid as his hands gripped the imaginary newspaper. Extreme anguish mixed with horror transformed his face. He screamed.

This was a truncated scream, cut off with difficulty. The original scream must have galvanised the tramp in his bunk. The headline before Foxy had told of the brutal murder of the old lady.

Head in his hands, he had wept. Absolutely and completely, he had broken down, and the story had poured out of him.

It was testimony to the sheer power of Foxy's performance that the humour of the tramp's situation didn't have more of an effect on me. I imagined, in passing, some old dosser, quietly sleeping the afternoon away when suddenly he finds himself in the presence of an obvious madman who wants to confess to a brutal murder.

With the confession made, Foxy had become strangely relaxed now. It had been almost a physical act and had drained him. He laid his head on his arms and slept. When he had awoken a couple of hours later, the tramp and the newspaper had gone. In my mind's eye I could see the old boy ringing for the screw as soon as he realised Foxy was asleep. I could imagine his relief as he got out of the cell.

Now Foxy was into the inevitable trial, but it was all anticlimax. Tom and I sneaked a look at each other, wondering how we had got into this.

Foxy's face was still frozen in a mask of grief, the gold-rimmed glasses, greying hair and high cheekbones giving him a manic and Germanic look. There was no doubt in my mind that he was quite, quite mad. I secretly reassured myself that I could handle him if he did go berserk.

As Foxy finished his story, Tom and I sat there in silence. Feeling that he should say something more, Foxy said, 'Look fellas. I've told you this because you're my friends. Don't tell anyone else.'

Tom and I both nodded.

After the trauma of the confession, conversation was stilted and difficult. In his heart, Foxy knew he had messed up another social situation. He had embarrassed himself and had compromised the chance of friendship. But he put a brave face on it. If he ever once had to admit, even to himself, that he wasn't the most balanced, the most controlled of persons, then he would have had to admit the rest. And Foxy wasn't quite ready yet to admit that he was mad.

Tom said something about it getting late and we all stood and made for the door. It was nearly 9.00, fifteen minutes before bang-up. Like ourselves, others were leaving their cells to do whatever they had to do before they were locked up for the night.

Foxy now seemed to want to get away. He made a quick farewell and stalked off towards his own wing. He walked with a jerky stiffness, testimony to the tension that gripped him. His shoulders square and upright, fists clenched, his arms bent and pumping as he walked. He looked like a cross between Popeye and John Wayne, a walk that one could be remembered for. 'All part of the rich, Foxy persona,' I mused.

As he disappeared from view across the centre, I looked at Tom. 'Did that really fucking happen?' I asked in fake amazement.

He shook his head in disbelief, a serious look on his face. 'Norm,' he said, 'I've never spent much time with Foxy before. I've spoken to him in passing and also in the dining hall, but I've never sat down in a cell for an hour and talked. I always knew he was a bit crazy, but he's absolutely mad.'

'Yeah, well, I won't want too much of Foxy around me, I can tell you,' I replied.

As we stared after Foxy, both of us momentarily lost in thought, JB's tubby figure came around the corner. The badminton kit was gone and in its place was a pair of overall jeans and a T-shirt. He carried a steaming hot cup in one hand.

Tom's face broke into a grin as JB joined us. We quickly told him about the recent session with Foxy. From his reaction, I gathered that Foxy was quite a character and his doings were greeted with great mirth. JB laughed along with us.

Then he turned to me and asked how I was settling in. We chatted about Knightsford and then about other jails. Within a couple of minutes, his pleasant, good-humoured personality had put me at my ease. He was intelligent and prison-wise, too. It was reassuring to me that here was someone else I could talk to.

Suddenly, a voice spoke from behind me. 'Yahn, Yahn, I bang up now.'

The accent was strongly German, the sound throaty and weak. I turned to see a frail old man, standing as though he were about to fall. His face was incredibly old, his skin parchment yellow. White wisps of hair hung down his forehead. He must have been at least seventy and was obviously in poor health. In fact, he carried himself with the long-suffering air of a permanent invalid. I got the impression that he made a habit of overdoing the sympathy bit.

'OK, Otto,' said JB, for the old man had been addressing him. He made an effort to appear interested, although I sensed that he wanted to get away from him.

'Hello, Otto,' said Tom, smiling broadly.

The old fella screwed up his eyes and stared in the direction of the voice. Then, for the first time, he noticed him. His face broke into a wide smile. 'Ah, 'ullo, Tom,' he said.

Now he stared at me. 'Otto, this is Norm,' said JB, pointing to me.

"Ullo, Norm.' The husky, Germanic tone twisted the consonants as he spoke to me. He was clearly senile, smiling and nodding incessantly, his head cocked to one side.

'Yahn, Yahn, saw war film tonight. Saw Panzers und soldiers. Then Panzerfaust go *boom*.' He spoke suddenly with force, making me jump.

Now, as he warmed to his subject, there was passion in his voice. The German words that interspersed his speech rang out in the clipped, shouted fashion reminiscent of a hundred wartime newsreels. Otto was a living, walking cliché. A Second World War German trapped in a time warp.

I suppose I was surprised, but not greatly. My first concern was whether he was potentially dangerous to me. Once I had confirmed to my satisfaction that he wasn't, I promptly relegated him to the category of 'sundry nutters'.

I had been in dozens of jails, but I was quickly developing a healthy respect for Knightsford's psychiatric flora and fauna. My new jail had some class acts all of its own. I reflected that if I was fated to meet a Second World War German, then Knightsford was as likely a place as any.

'OK, Otto, I'll see you in the morning.' JB ushered him away, Otto still muttering about 'Waffen SS und Panzers'.

'He's a right pain, but he's an interesting fella,' said JB, turning back to us. 'His father was chief martial arts instructor to the Japanese Army, and Otto was a master of unarmed combat himself. And, although he says he wasn't, I'm sure he was in the SS in the war.'

I turned to watch this shadow of a former Nazi shuffle away. 'If only Adolf could see him now,' I said to no one in particular.

'He's only been like that for the past couple of years,' continued JB. 'He used to be a stocky, powerful bull of a man. When three yobbos attacked him in Soho, he killed two of them with his bare hands and cabbaged the third. He's been in nicks all over Europe. He used to carry a card explaining about how he had been trained to kill in the special battalion he was in. It didn't do any good this time. He got two life sentences.'

A memory sparked deep in my subconscious. I went back eight years to the Scrubs. I pictured a stocky, powerful man who resembled a burly Austrian innkeeper. He had been sixty then, but was still strong and dangerous.

What a transformation! I would never have recognised him. He had been all of sixteen stone then, but now he was barely half that. Whatever the wasting disease he'd contracted, it must have been a serious one.

But now the screws were coming along the landing. I saw Hall pulling doors to and calling out 'Goodnight, boys' in his phoney London accent.

I didn't like screws locking me up. I didn't want them to have the satisfaction. It was only a little thing, but I always banged my own door. I said 'Goodnight' quickly to Tom and JB, walked into my cell and banged the door behind me. My first day at Knightsford was at an end.

As I stood alone in my cell, I was in familiar territory again. Whatever the jail and whatever the regime, there was always one unchanging constant: every night I was locked up on my own. The hours between now and the following dawn stood as a silent challenge that I would have to deal with by myself.

But I had dealt with it before and would deal with it again. I undressed, turned out the light and got into bed. It had been a long time since I had woken in the chokey in Lincoln that morning. Suddenly I was exhausted, both physically and mentally.

As I drifted away, I mused on my new surroundings and some of the weird people I had met. I didn't know yet if I was going to be happy at Knightsford, but one thing I was sure of. It was going to be different.

I awoke early the following morning, and when the screw opened my door, I was already up and dressed. I hurried towards the wing office to apply for a reception letter and a visiting order. My mother would want to visit my new jail as soon as possible.

There was another SO standing behind the desk. There were always two SOs to a wing so this had to be the one on the opposite shift to Hall. He looked a definite improvement.

A boyishly handsome face smiled out from under thinning, fairish hair. He must have been in his mid-thirties, yet had the trim figure of a man ten years younger. There was an amused sparkle to his eyes. Not in a sarcastic way. More as if he could see the humour in a way of life that was characterised by so much trivia.

'Oh, you must be Parker,' he said before I could speak. 'I hope you're settling in all right, Norman.'

He said it with concern, if not deep sincerity. He continued to smile pleasantly, showing me that he wasn't being sarcastic. The use of my first name further confirmed it.

I opened my mouth to speak, when I suddenly noticed a con standing behind him in the corner of the office where there was a kettle and some cups on a table. The idiot features of Alfred E.

Neumann grinned at me over the SO's shoulder.

I wasn't surprised that the unctuous half-wit was making the tea for the screws. He certainly didn't look like a prison rebel. What did surprise me, though, was the speed with which he had got to the office. To my chagrin, I had discovered that he lived in the next cell to me. I thought I had been quick off the mark, but he must have started on running blocks.

Before I could regain my composure, there was a rush of feet behind me. Another con hurried past me to join 'Alfred' next to the tea table.

'Hello, Mark,' said the SO as he passed.

'Morning, sir,' muttered the con as he started sorting the cups out. He was a man in his late thirties, but almost completely bald. A few wisps of hair were combed over his scalp in a vain attempt at a cover-up. He was quite stocky, but had a pronounced stoop. His manner was utterly deferential. He hung his head as if fearing to give offence by making eye contact. I realised that his stoop could also be an act of self-abasement. Here was a man who had been completely broken by prison. He looked as if he depended on it for his every need. That dread word 'institutionalisation' sprang into my mind.

It seemed as if there was some competition to make tea for the screws. I wondered if this little scenario was being played out in the offices on the other wings.

A flare of anger seared me. These weaklings were all that I despised. That way lay death of the spirit. In another jail, I would have given them both a volley. Knightsford mode made me bite my tongue. Suppressed anger would have to suffice.

Taking my hesitation for uncertainty, the SO spoke to me again. 'My name's John Gale. I want to remind you that you have to see the doctor this morning. Go to the hospital immediately after work-call. Then, when you're finished, go up to the education department. They want to see you.' He paused to let the instructions sink in. 'What else can I do for you, Norman?'

Suddenly, realising what I was there for, I asked for the reception letter and visiting order.

The SO fumbled on the desk before him. He picked up a pen and wrote on something. He handed me an envelope with a letter and a VO inside.

I was surprised that he had given it to me right away. He was certainly going out of his way to be helpful. 'Thanks, SO,' I said, smiled at him and walked out of the office. I returned to my cell.

The next priority was to wash and shave. With my towel and toiletry bag, I headed for the recesses at the end of the landing.

I picked the one on the right. I stood at a sink to the left of a large window that looked over the landing. As I shaved, I could watch the comings and goings of others as they passed.

There wasn't much movement. I realised that many of the others must be late risers, although I did see a couple of fellas go into the other recess and empty their pots down the slops sink.

I had been shaving for about five minutes when the German suddenly came into view, shuffling along the middle of the ones like a man just awakened from a deep sleep. As he saw me, he veered to the right and entered my recess.

''Lo,' he said in a sing-song voice full of self-pity.

'Hallo,' I said peremptorily and continued to stare into the mirror.

I had long ago discovered that the vast majority of nutters were lonely. People avoided them because of their infirmity. To encourage them at all was virtually to invite them into your life. And I had enough problems of my own. I would keep conversation with the German to a minimum.

Then there was the problem of my Jewishness. Not that I was particularly Orthodox, because I had never been in a synagogue before coming into prison. However, that didn't mean I made a habit of fraternising with ex-Nazis. Even one as old and decrepit as the German.

He would notice the blue card on my door sooner or later, or he would find out I was Jewish in some other way. If I kept my distance, it would cause no trouble. I didn't want a situation to arise where I had to chase him away. I imagined that he must fawn on the screws in the same way that he fawned on everybody else. No doubt he was a favourite with some of them.

He went into one of the two toilets behind me and closed the door. In the mirror I could see the top of his head above the half door. I heard him rustling the toilet paper.

I returned my attention to the act of shaving, but hardly ten seconds had passed when I was suddenly aware of the most awful smell.

The smell of shit is unavoidable in prison, most commonly as you wait in line to empty your chamber pot in the mornings. It's not that you become a connoisseur of excrement, rather that you become no stranger to noisome odours. But the smell coming from the German was of a different order of magnitude to anything I had ever experienced before.

It was a gut-churning smell that was impossible to ignore. It had a strong, chemical smell, but at the same time reeked of everything that was foul and decaying. Whatever illness beset him, it was obviously centred on his gut.

I could hardly leave the recess as I was only half-way through shaving. There were no windows to open to the outside either, and even if there had been, I wasn't at all sure that would have had any effect on the smell. I would just have to put up with it. However, I resolved to shave in the other recess in future.

I returned to my cell, finished dressing, then went to the dining hall for breakfast. I collected a bowl of porridge and some bread and butter. Ignoring the others seated at the tables, I returned to eat in my cell. For me, breakfast wasn't a communal meal.

Before long a bell sounded, followed by a loud shout of 'Down to labour', repeated several times. I came out of my cell and headed for the centre. Scores of others were hurrying in the same direction. Ahead of me, Tom clattered down the stairs, struggling to pull on his overall jacket.

SO Gale and half-a-dozen other screws were standing on the centre. They were gathered around the snooker table, marking names off on a board resting on its top. I crossed in front of them and went into the hospital.

At the end of a short corridor, two elderly cons were already sitting on a bench outside a closed door. I sat down next to them but didn't speak. I noticed a small name plate with the word 'SURGERY' fixed to the door.

I had been sitting there for about five minutes when it opened. A short, rotund man bustled out. He wore a well-pressed white jacket, tightly buttoned over his ample belly. His fat face was a deep brown and his skin was sleek and oily. Thinning strands of black hair were slicked down to his scalp. He had an unctuous appearance, but his tone was far from that.

'First one, in to see the doctor,' he said in a high-pitched, pompous tone.

I guessed that the two old fellas before me were regulars, because they were both dealt with very quickly. Then it was my turn.

'Next,' called the medic, poking his fat face around the surgery door. I stood and walked into the room.

The doctor was seated behind a large, leather-covered desk. A name plate with the words 'DR GOLD' was displayed prominently near its front edge. A small forest of pens stood tidily in a glass holder. A folder lay open on a large blotter. Next to it stood a telephone.

It was a neat and tidy desk, and from what I could see of Dr Gold, he was similarly neat and tidy. At the moment, he was bent over the folder, writing.

'Take a seat,' he said without looking up. 'I'll be with you immediately.'

I sat in a chair directly in front of the desk. I settled back and studied the doctor unobserved.

He was a small, dapper man in his late forties. His well-groomed hair and neatly trimmed moustache spoke of a fastidious manner. A smart blue blazer with silver buttons set off a spotlessly white shirt. His red patterned tie was done up to the neck in a small, neat knot.

His face would have passed for handsome except for the thin, pointed features, which made him resemble a mouse. For a second I could almost imagine him with long whiskers.

The final touches were two large gold rings on his left hand and an equally ostentatious gold watch around his right wrist. Clearly, our Dr Gold was something of a dandy.

He finished writing and screwed the top on the pen and placed it beside the blotter. He closed the folder and, turning in his chair, put it on a shelf behind him. Taking another one, he twisted back to face the desk and set it in front of him. Each task was done in a slow and methodical manner. Then he looked up. I was the next task to be dealt with.

'Ah . . . Parker,' he said, reminding himself who I was with a quick look at the folder. 'Arrived here yesterday, eh?' His speech was clipped and precise, his tone mellow and middle class.

'Yes, Doctor,' I replied, sitting up in the chair and folding my hands in my lap.

'Travelled about quite a bit, eh?' His eyes flitted back and forth between the folder and my face.

I nodded. He was a medical man. I didn't feel I owed him an explanation of my disciplinary record.

He looked at me more intently. He made a mental note of my reticence. He was used to his prisoner patients answering all his questions. For a second, our meeting was in the balance. He toyed with the idea of repeating the question.

Coming to a decision, he suddenly smiled. His lips parted to reveal small, neat white teeth. The resemblance to a rodent was now very marked indeed.

He placed his elbows on the desk and put his hands together in an almost prayer-like pose. I recalled that the Governor had done the same. I wondered if he had copied the mannerism from the doctor or vice versa. His eyes met and held mine. Unspoken words passed between us.

Then the moment was past. He unclasped his hands and sat back in his chair. 'Any pressing medical problems, Parker?' His manner was brisk and business-like now.

'Not really, Doctor. Just a bit of psoriasis and I've got some cream for that.' I was equally business-like.

'OK,' he said and nodded. It signified the end of the interview. 'Mr Patel,' he called out, turning towards a doorway on his right. I looked to see the chubby Asian hurrying out of a room lined with bottles and jars. I was clearly forgotten. I stood and walked out of the room.

I knew I hadn't handled the interview very well, but I didn't care. Keeping out of trouble was one thing, but to kowtow to every pompous upstart official was something else entirely. I intended to keep my dignity no matter what.

I crossed the centre and headed towards my cell. I wanted to collect details of my Open University courses before I went to the education block.

SO Gale was standing outside the wing office writing names on a notice-board. He turned at the sound of my footsteps.

'Norman,' he said pleasantly, 'the PO is in his office. He'd like to see you for a minute.'

I hesitated, not knowing whether to mention my appointment at the education block. Realising that I had all morning to go there, I looked around for the PO's office.

SO Gale pointed to a plain wooden door, a dozen feet from the wing office. It was the same office where I had met Governor Maypole the previous day. I walked over to the door and knocked. Just above my knuckles was a small nameplate that said: 'P.O. DOCKER.'

There was a pause, then I knocked again. A muffled voice called out, 'Come in.' I pushed open the door and entered the office.

The air was smoky and foul. The PO sat behind his desk, a lighted cigarette in his hand. The remains of several more lay in an ashtray like crushed insects.

PO Docker looked like a man who over-indulged in everything, except exercise. He was in his fifties, but his face was lined and furrowed like a man ten years older. The skin was blotched with patches of red. Tiny red veins ran down either side of his large nose. He looked like Walter Matthau on a bad day.

Above everything else, he gave the impression of being very tired. Not just physically tired, but tired of the mundane business of being a PO. There was prickly bad temper below the surface, but he lacked the energy to indulge it. From his age, I guessed he wasn't far from retirement. No doubt he was just going through the motions now.

He motioned me towards a chair. Closing the door behind me, I sat. Docker cleared his throat.

'Parker,' he began. I instantly wondered what had happened to the 'Norman'. I gathered that this was going to be one of those 'I'm going to tell you the way things are going to be' sessions. 'I believe the Governor spoke to you yesterday. Well, I'm going to emphasise what he said. This is a quiet little jail. Any trouble and we move the offender out. You're coming up for your first full parole review shortly. It would pay you to keep out of trouble here.'

He stopped suddenly. It was as if the effort of speaking had taken it out of him. He took a long drag of his cigarette. The lined face disappeared behind a cloud of smoke.

'As I told the Governor, PO, I just want a quiet time.' I peered through the smoke to gauge his response.

'OK, Parker,' he said, then dissolved in a paroxysm of coughing. He gasped for breath as he tried to recover, but the coughing continued. 'That's all for now,' he wheezed, nodding and pointing at the door. As I walked out, I could hear him still coughing and spluttering behind me.

It was hard to assess how the interview had gone. He had given me the gipsy's warning, but without the oppressive threatening of Maypole. My input had been negligible. I concluded that I had done nothing to antagonise him further.

I returned to my cell and collected the record of my OU courses. I climbed the stairs to the gallery and entered the education block.

A couple of classrooms were empty and in darkness. Two others had just inmate students in them. I recognised Richie, Pete and Sam from the previous night. I guessed it was a period of private study.

About half-way down the corridor a door was open. The room inside was carpeted and I could see books around the walls on shelves. Directly opposite the doorway, Jane, the woman I had seen the day before, sat at a desk, engrossed in writing. She didn't notice me as I entered.

To my left was another desk, bigger than hers. A large man sat behind it. He wore thick glasses and had an enormous, bushy grey beard that hung down his chest. He peered at me like a myopic Father Christmas.

'Hallo, my name's Mr Camber. And who are you?' he said in a hearty, friendly manner. He rose to his feet and held out his hand.

I took his hand and shook it. I hated rudeness and always reciprocated good manners, even though, unfortunately, good manners were often interpreted as a sign of weakness in prison. Out of the corner of my eye I was aware that Jane had quickly lifted her head, then looked down again.

I explained to Camber that I was partway through my sixth Open University course. I had all the set books. The only help I required from the education department was to send and receive my assignments, arrange a tutor for me occasionally and give me a day off work each week to do some studying – the usual OU arrangements.

It was all very straightforward. Camber said that he would arrange everything and wished me luck with my course. As I turned and left, Jane still had her head down, writing diligently. I reassured myself that here at least were two people who knew nothing about me.

3

I n that I was quite wrong, at least as far as Jane was concerned. She had heard all about Norman Parker two days before I arrived at Knightsford.

It had been at the Knightsford Board meeting. She had grown to hate these meetings. Increasingly, she was the odd one out. The lone voice crying in the wilderness.

She had been the first woman to work in the prison. At first, they had disliked her merely because of her gender. They had made it clear that they thought there was no place in a men's prison for a woman. Later, when they realised that she had an opinion of her own and wouldn't be swayed by theirs, they hated her for that. Now, it was a constant war of attrition.

Board meetings increasingly followed the same pattern. All the men would gang up against her. At best, they patronised her. More commonly, they rubbished everything she said. Eventually, she had come to be regarded as anathema to everything the establishment held dear. She posed a real threat to those officers who, in their weakness, feared the very principles she stood for. Somehow she had managed to emasculate them by not sharing the same sense of humour, the same politics, the same values, the same opinion of prisoners or women or blacks.

For a while, she had thought it might be different when Nancy Frank had arrived. Her field was probation, but they shared the common perspective of being women in an institution that embodied male power. But Jane was to be disappointed: Nancy Frank continually followed the company line.

Monday's Knightsford Board had started the same as all the others. The board room was large and decorated in the Adam style. A massive mahogany table filled most of its space. Around its sides were set twenty-two carved-wood chairs. A cut-glass chandelier hung above its centre. Golden sconces adorned each wall. It was a very tasteful room. Far too tasteful for its present function, that of assessing the progress, or lack of it, of particular lifers over the past few months.

Jane arrived early. She was always before time, not wishing to give the others any further excuse for criticising her. She took a seat at the foot of the table, opposite from where Maypole would sit.

Deal and Mrs Frank were already seated side by side, the Probation Department presenting a united front. They were deep in conversation, but raised their heads briefly to acknowledge her. Then they continued to whisper together conspiratorially.

Further up the table, PO Docker was laughing with Mr Mann, the SO from B wing. They turned towards her and smiled, before carrying on with their joke.

Opposite them sat SOs Wade and Hall, old friends from Parkhurst. Both pointedly ignored her, with Hall actually turning his back. He hated her with a passion. She wondered what she had done to inspire such loathing. It didn't particularly worry her, though. She had seen through his two-faced manner long ago. She had heard him talking to the young lifers in his false London accent, as if they were all mates together, yet he was their fiercest critic at these meetings.

As she unpacked her briefcase and arranged the papers in front of her, the door opened again. PO Jones, Wade's superior, came in, followed by Mann's No. 2, SO Terry. Both smiled at her and muttered, 'Morning, Mrs Roman.' Then they turned and said loud 'Good mornings' to all the rest of the table before sitting down.

Jane still sat alone at the bottom of the table, with seats either side of her remaining unoccupied. This isolation was symbolic of her position in the meetings. It no longer hurt her, but the way they all greeted each other warmly, while merely acknowledging or ignoring her, was so very obvious.

Again the door opened. The tall, cadaverous figure of Mr Waters, the Security PO, hurried in. A quiet, dignified man in his late fifties, he had the manners of an old-fashioned gentleman. Of them all, he was the only one Jane felt any warmth for. Yet he was utterly professional, bordering on the aloof. Not just with her, but with everyone. She often felt that he would have liked to side with her occasionally, but no doubt the massed hostile ranks of his fellows deterred him.

He wasn't deterred from sitting next to her, though. Perhaps it offended his sense of good manners for her to be left sitting all on her own. He settled into the seat next to her, muttered a few pleasantries, acknowledged the greetings of the rest, then stared directly in front of him, looking nowhere in particular.

It was 9.30 and time for the meeting to start. As if on cue, a door at the far end of the room opened and in came Governor Maypole, Chief Hughes and Deputy Governor Bone. They were the senior staff of the jail and had been sitting in a private room just outside the board room. They continued their private conversation as they entered, laughing together over some shared joke, oblivious to the others in the room. It was, Jane noted, their way of emphasising their seniority.

As they took their seats at the head of the table, it was as if they suddenly became aware of the rest. Shouting loud and hearty 'Good mornings' to the room in general, they noisily lowered themselves into their chairs and spread their papers out in front of them.

Maypole picked up a small wooden gavel from the table in front of him. He rapped three times on the mahogany and called the meeting to order. His face assumed a stern expression, firmly in governor mode now.

Jane had observed on many occasions how uneasily the mantle of power settled on him. He certainly lacked confidence. All those present were aware of his humble origins, and he clung to the trappings of power — the rules, the ceremony and the points of order — like an immature NCO to his stripes. It was as if, without them, he would be found wanting, not a proper governor at all.

Maypole cleared his throat and picked up the first sheaf of papers in front of him. All around the room, others did likewise. He opened his mouth to speak, when suddenly the door swung open and in swept Dr Gold, late as usual. He always made a point of coming in last.

'Sorry I'm late. Sorry I'm late. Good morning. Good morning,' he said as he sat as near to the top of the table as he could.

Jane barely suppressed a smile. Maypole's face wrinkled in annoyance as he muttered 'Good morning' in return. He made no criticism though. That was another thing that Jane had noticed: he was weak with his staff and lacked authority.

Gold settled himself in his seat and removed some papers from his case, a smug, self-satisfied look on his face. The silver buttons on the front of his smart blue blazer winked in the light. He cut a fine figure sitting there and he knew it. It was clear that he considered himself some way above all the others. He was, after all, a member of the medical profession and, by definition, something of a gentleman. Also, he was appointed by the Home Office and so remained outside Maypole's authority on a whole range of matters. He didn't flaunt this to the point of being disruptive, but he liked to take his little liberties.

Deputy Governor Bone picked up his pen again and added Gold's name to the minutes. Maypole always made him or the Assistant Governor keep the record. It was a sop to Maypole's pride and a way of emphasising a superiority that he didn't really feel.

As much as he tried to hide it, it rankled Bone. He was a big, distinguished-looking man in his late forties. He had greying hair and perfect white teeth that made for a dazzling smile. It was one of his strongest points. He smiled often. An Oxford graduate, Bone had an educated, if pompous manner and a singularly upper-class accent. He was by far the social superior of all those present and hid the fact with difficulty. He was simply marking time, waiting impatiently for the day when he would be a governor in charge of his own prison.

'The first case to be considered today is that of John Brewer,' said Maypole, reading from the papers in his hand. He looked around the table to see who would begin. He knew none of the 'residents' personally; he just met them in passing as he moved about the prison.

Jane knew John Brewer well. He wasn't in any of her classes at the moment, but had been in the recent past. He often came up to the education block to talk to her. He was mature, sensible and stable, and in her heart, she felt he would never re-offend.

John had been quite a successful sales rep, and had never been in trouble before. When he had found out that his wife was having an affair, he was devastated and, taking a pistol from the gun club he belonged to, had shot the lover dead. Then he had given himself up. Now in his late thirties, he was philosophical about his ruined life; there was no hatred or bitterness in him. He realised that the use of a gun had made the offence that much more serious. He also accepted that, even though he had done ten years, he wasn't out of the woods yet.

Docker cleared his throat and stood up. As Brewer's wing PO, it was his place to speak first. In truth, though, he hardly ever saw the man. However, he did have the reports of the other wing staff to go by.

Using the broadest of generalisations, he spoke of Brewer's progress, using bland phrases like 'no problem on the wing' and 'seems to have come to terms with his sentence'. All straightforward stuff that could have applied to scores of other lifers on C wing. Almost as soon as he had started, he was finished. He had said little of substance.

Now, as his second in command, it was Hall's turn. C wing's SO was more in touch with the day-to-day running of the wing. He personally came into contact with everyone.

Hall hoisted himself upright and pursed his lips, savouring the moment. This was the part he enjoyed. He would indulge his vitriolic nature to the full, wounding those he disliked and patronising those he could barely tolerate. The latter were always the ones he could insult without reply. The ones who ran to do his every bidding.

'Yes . . . well, Brewer,' he began, letting the sentence hang in the air. Jane cringed inwardly. She knew this beginning well. It wasn't going to be an all-out assault on Brewer's character, but with a combination of sarcasm and innuendo, it would be damaging enough.

It was all so unfair. Didn't they ever stop to consider that these were men's lives they were dealing with? The Board should be a forum for sound argument and cold logic. After all, the Home Office in London relied on its assessment for, to them, each lifer was only an impersonal number and a name on a file. The Board served to put flesh on the bones. However, the approach at Knightsford lacked professionalism.

'Brewer's one of Knightsford's "jet-set", of course,' Hall continued. 'Just to refresh your memory, that's made up of some of the younger residents, the footballers and the "education block intellectuals".' He shot a sideways glance at Jane. 'He's not a core member and doesn't hang around with them all the time, but he's on the fringes. He's quite independent and only comes to us when he wants something. Also, we think he was one of those involved in drinking hooch at Christmas . . .'

There was more in a similar vein, but after a couple of minutes, Hall ran out of things to say. Jane mused that there was only so much you could make out of trivia and innuendo. However, Hall had given the impression that there were things about Brewer's conduct that he disapproved of.

Just as he was about to sit down, he stopped. Something else had caught his eye on papers he held. 'Oh yes,' he said, 'I've a work report from the kitchen PO here. Says Brewer works well, is no trouble and can be trusted.'

This positive report had been added almost as an afterthought, and the grudging way it had been delivered detracted from its weight. Jane was always amazed at how, when he disliked someone, Hall invariably tried to make positive things sound negative and vice versa.

Hall lowered his enormous bulk back into his chair, signalling that he was finished. There was a moment's pause, then Deal stood up.

Jane could never really weigh up John Deal. A nondescript man in his late forties, with curly black hair shot through with grey, he had spent most of his life in the Services, yet had no military bearing. Everything about him was anonymous. He would live and die in his plain, grey suit, with which he always wore the same tie. His black shoes were scuffed and in need of polishing, and his white shirts were always frayed around the collar and rarely clean. He had a seedy air about him.

On his own, he could be quite pleasant. However, his natural timidity tended to make him agree with whoever was the strongest. There was never any chance of his becoming an ally of Jane, even if he had passionately agreed with her point of view. Increasingly, he had come under Mrs Frank's influence. She firmly laid down the 'probation line' and he dutifully followed it. The rest considered him a team player — Deal could always be relied on not to rock the boat.

All eyes were now turned to him. He stood there, blinking nervously behind his thick-rimmed glasses. He shuffled the sheaf of papers he held in his hand, coughed, then started to speak.

'Well, I don't see as much of Brewer as Mr Hall.' He turned and smiled at him. Ever the diplomat, he didn't want to undermine what the SO had said. However, he didn't have it in his nature to be nasty and vindictive. His sins were those of omission rather than commission.

What followed was a rambling account of the four meetings he had had with John Brewer over the past six months. Again, there was little of substance that you could draw any conclusions from. Anonymous words like 'polite', 'friendly' and 'well-mannered' peppered the report. Concluding that Brewer was making good progress, Deal sat down again.

Almost immediately, Dr Gold was on his feet. He straightened his tie, made sure he was showing the appropriate amount of cuff, then read from the pages he held out at arm's length. His report was based on one twenty-minute interview he had had with Brewer three days previously. Jane listened with interest. She knew that John had a strong personality. The doctor wouldn't have had it all his own way.

This was reflected in the report. Gold spoke of Brewer as being stubborn and argumentative. Jane knew that this meant that, instead of agreeing with everything the doctor said, Brewer had tried to put over his own point of view. When Gold said that Brewer had been guarded in his answers, he looked around the table to make sure this had sunk in. The implication was that the inmate had something to hide.

Once again, there was little factual substance to the report. It consisted mainly of what Gold had read into Brewer's seemingly innocuous replies.

'And of course, a firearm was used,' he concluded with some force.

Next he waved a bundle of photographs. As the medical officer, Gold had access to the autopsy photographs of the victims, and Jane was always mortified at the way he used these to sway the argument one way or the other. Also, a few of the men seemed to have a sick fascination for them. They would pass them from one to another, like naughty boys with pornographic photos. Sometimes, a particularly horrific one would cause faces to be screwed up. Occasionally, ones showing explicit details of a woman's private parts would be greeted with barely stifled laughter. Jane often thought that, had the prisoners who were being assessed been seen to behave likewise, they would have been called 'morbid' or 'insensitive'.

Once, in the early days, she had allowed the photographs to be passed to her. It had been done more out of a sense of duty than from curiosity. After all, if she was to attain a sense of balance, of fairness, then she should see the crime in all its awfulness.

The photographs were of a young woman who had been stabbed several times. The skull and body had been shaved to better reveal the wounds. Jagged rips showed in the skin where the knife had entered. Close-ups detailed the torn tissue. The woman's dead face had stared out at Jane like a shop window mannikin. So smooth and lifeless, yet so obviously human.

She had slept badly that night, and the photos haunted her for weeks. That aspect of the case had taken over her mind completely, obscuring all other details of the perpetrator. Afterwards, if she saw the man about the prison, his face would suddenly dissolve, to be replaced by the nightmarish death-mask of his victim.

She decided never to look at autopsy photographs again. Far from giving her a sense of balance, they had tipped her over into horror. Let others look at them; she would make do with the description of the offence.

Gold now placed the bundle of photos on the table in front of him. Hall stood to reach over and pick them up. He scanned them, then passed them to Wade. They went round the table, some passing them straight on, others pausing to look. Jane averted her eyes as they reached her and passed them straight on to Waters.

Now that this ritual was over, Gold's part was at an end. He sat back with a satisfied look.

For a moment, there was some confusion around the table. This was the point when the Board became an open forum. The wing PO and SO had spoken. The relevant probation officer had said his or her piece. The doctor had delivered his view. Now anyone who had any further comment to make could speak.

Jane indicated to Maypole that she wished to say something. He nodded almost imperceptibly and she rose to her feet. Every face at the table turned to look at her. There were ironic smiles on the faces of some. Others glared at her with open hostility.

At this point, Jane often wondered if it would be better if she just sat down again. Whatever she said in a man's favour only served to antagonise those around the table. She feared that her support often did damage to the man she was defending.

'John Brewer isn't taking education classes at the moment, but he used to be in my English class,' she began. 'He sometimes still comes up to see me, so I feel I know him quite well. I find that he is a mature, intelligent man who deeply regrets the offence which brought him here. He has considerable insight into his previous state of mind and feels that, in a similar situation, he would act differently.'

Hall turned to Wade and whispered something. Wade smiled. He turned back to face Jane, but stared up at the ceiling, as if in bemused amazement.

Jane ignored him and pressed on. She spoke of John's devotion to his elderly mother with whom he intended to live when he was released. She told of his intention to work as a sales rep again, emphasising that he had never been in trouble before and had always been in employment.

'I am confident that John Brewer, if released, will not offend again,' she concluded.

There was a loud 'Harumph' from Hall to indicate his disapproval.

'Please, Mr Hall,' implored Maypole in a soft, weak tone.

He so disliked unpleasantness and, with his lack of authority, found it difficult to deal with. Increasingly, he was becoming more like a mother of boisterous children than the Chairman of the Board.

Jane glared at Hall, then sat down. He was such a disgusting hypocrite. She knew that in a few hours' time, as he stood on the centre at dinner-time, he would greet Brewer with his usual 'How you going, JB, me old mate?' and smile disarmingly.

There was a protracted silence. Jane's pronouncements were

greeted with either instant and violent argument or a polite silence, depending on the strength of feeling against the particular lifer. Polite silence meant that they didn't agree with her and her opinion wasn't going to prevail, but Brewer wasn't one of those they really had it in for, so they weren't going to get excited about his case. They disliked his strength of character and his insufficiently deferential manner. If he had ever been outwardly rebellious, he would have roused their passion. As it was, they would do enough damage to prevent him moving forward, but they hadn't done anything serious that would put him back.

Maypole sat to sum up the proceedings. His function was to collate all the reports and deliver an opinion. Inevitably, it would agree with that of the majority of his staff. He rarely had any intimate personal knowledge of the man being discussed.

'Well, I think it is quite straightforward,' he began. 'I think we should recommend that, for the time being, no recommendation should be made as to any progress on Brewer's part. No recommendation for a move to open conditions. Just let him carry on the way he is going and we will have another look at him in six months' time.'

And that was it. Jane knew that, with those few words, Maypole had condemned John Brewer to serve several more years in prison. Several unnecessary years.

Now, Brewer forgotten, it was the turn of the next. Maypole picked up another sheaf of papers from the table and stated, 'The next case is David Rogers.'

All around the table, others shuffled their papers. Jane had hers set out in neat piles in front of her and she reached straight for the appropriate file.

David Rogers was a tragic case. He had raped and murdered a young boy when quite young himself, and had done the past ten years very hard indeed. He wasn't a strong man by nature and that was where the problem lay — he hadn't been strong enough to dismiss his sick fantasies.

The years had totally broken him. His cowed spirit, combined with the nature of his offence, had made him an outcast among the other prisoners. He thought that the staff were his friends and he had become totally dependent on them.

They despised him, but tolerated him. He was useful to them. He made their tea, ran errands for them and was the butt of their jokes. He never got annoyed, just grinned foolishly and hung his head. He always did exactly what they told him, even when they were wrong. He never disagreed with anything they said. He never challenged their control in any way. *Ergo*, he wasn't dangerous.

Well, not to them anyway. After all, David was in for young boys and there weren't any young boys in Knightsford to test him. Somehow, that always escaped their attention. Their main criterion was obedience: the compliant were rewarded.

Docker rose to his feet again. 'We are all aware of the shocking nature of this man's offence,' he began, 'but he seems to be making a determined effort to better himself. He is no trouble to the wing staff. On the contrary, he goes out of his way to assist them . . .' Within three minutes he was finished, his report vague but positive.

After Docker, Hall again held the floor. This time, though, it was 'Dave' this and 'Dave' that. Rogers was no threat to him. He did everything he was told. Hall was full of praise for 'Dave's quiet and respectful manner. Not only have we come to trust Dave on C wing, we have come to rely on him. I feel sure that he is a changed man from what he was before.'

This time, Hall went on for a full five minutes. He detailed the minutiae of David Rogers' obedience and deference over the past six months. 'In my opinion, Dave is a quiet and stable young man who deserves some reward for the progress he has made,' he concluded.

Jane stifled her own 'Harumph'. She had only spoken to David Rogers on a couple of occasions and had found him weird and creepy. She thought he had an obvious mental problem, but psychiatry wasn't her field. She had nothing to back up her opinion except her intuition. But in spite of her gut feeling, she couldn't bring herself to condemn the man. She just didn't know him well enough.

As Hall finished, Mrs Frank hoisted herself to her feet. Gone was the little-girl simpering. In its place was a cold and vindictive adult. She didn't like David Rogers. There was nothing unusual in that, though. She strongly disapproved of the vast majority of Knightsford's lifers. However, she had a finely attuned understanding of the politics of these Boards. Certain staff had their enemies for whom they put in the poison; they also had their favourites whom they wished to reward. Mrs Frank had no desire to thwart their plans.

Her assessment of David Rogers was suitably vague and insubstantial. After all, there were no foolproof indicators of how a man would behave on release. However, she didn't want to go on record as arguing for Rogers' release. She repeated words such as 'polite' and 'well-mannered' that had been in both Docker's and Hall's reports. She concluded without reaching a conclusion but, on balance, the report was positive.

Gold's report was similarly vague. He recalled the pale, cowed individual who had slumped in the chair as he had interviewed him. He hadn't looked like he had the drive to do anything aggressive. He had certainly been intimidated by the doctor's questioning. Gold had difficulty arousing any interest in a man like this. His report said nothing detrimental, so it counted as a positive assessment.

As he finished, he placed a bundle of photographs on the table in front of him. This time, no one picked them up. Rogers' supporters had no desire to be reminded of that side of his nature, fearing the trauma of having to look at the body of a murdered child for no pressing reason. Gold replaced them in a folder.

The open-forum stage brought no takers this time. Other than making tea for the screws in C wing office and sitting in his cell, Rogers was hardly seen about the prison.

Maypole drew all the strands together. 'We must be seen to encourage those who make progress,' he droned. 'The recommendation is that David Rogers be recommended for open conditions.'

Jane had a strong interest in the third case. Neil Bowen was one of her best students. He had passed several Open University courses and was almost a permanent fixture in the education block. For this last reason, she could expect some opposition from the others.

They had a curious attitude towards education in prison. Some of them resented the fact that prisoners had access to resources that they themselves had never had and that their children had to struggle for. Others felt that prison was a place for punishment and that to educate a man simply made for a more intelligent criminal. A few were just jealous. It upset their view of things if a prisoner was shown to be more intelligent than they were.

Jane would have to tread carefully here. She knew Neil well and liked him. In the circumstances, it was her duty to give a report, even more so since she was as sure as she could be that he would never re-offend.

Neil had talked to her often about his offence. He had been a shy and naïve young man, desperately in love with his young wife. Her affair and desertion had shattered him, especially when she had left him with their only child. He swore he hadn't set out to kill her. The hurtful things she had said to him when he had finally tracked her down had pushed him over the edge. He was adamant that he didn't remember strangling her. However, he was equally adamant that he accepted full responsibility.

Jane didn't doubt that he still loved his wife, 'though dead these past ten years'. As for remorse, he regretted his actions every day of his life. He wasn't unnaturally maudlin about it, but maintained a quiet but dignified air of grief.

The experience had unquestionably matured him. He would never fall in love so deeply again and he had better control over his emotions now. It had left him a sad young man, who seemed older than his thirty years. Jane pictured the long, lank hair that hung to his shoulders, framing a pale but sensitive face. With his tall, angular physique, he reminded her of an impoverished poet, starving in his garret. His gentle nature belied the circumstances of his offence. If anyone was a good prospect for release, then Neil Bowen was.

Luckily, he wasn't on Hall's wing. But A wing was the fiefdom of his ally and co-conspirator PO Wade. She could expect some stiff resistance from him.

PO Jones' report was succinct and to the point. He employed all the well-worn phrases — 'no trouble on the wing', 'quiet and respectful', 'has used his time to try to better himself' — and, like clichés, they had become devalued, bland and unconvincing.

Sometimes Jane wished that there was some empirical way that lifers could demonstrate that they were no longer dangerous, if they ever had been. Some pragmatic test to show that, in similar circumstances, they would now act differently. But there were no such tests. That was why they were reduced to this bizarre charade. Banal repetition of trivia and personal prejudice.

PO Wade finished his private conversation with Hall and rose to his feet. In many ways, Wade was quite sharp. He was aware of what impressed his superiors and went out of his way to cultivate such attributes. He was a stickler for formality in settings like Board meetings. He gave the impression that he was a man who abided by the rules and was, therefore, reliable and dependable.

'Mr Chairman, ladies and gentlemen,' he began with just a ghost of a Welsh accent whispering at the ends of his words. 'I don't see as much of Neil Bowen as Mrs Roman . . .' He turned to acknowledge her with a slight nod. The sarcasm was in his manner rather than in his voice, but his meaning was clear. Everyone on the Board would be aware that Neil Bowen was one of the education block regulars. '. . . But I know him well enough. It is true that he is a quiet, well-mannered individual whose time at Knightsford has been free of any trouble or upset. However, there is evidence to suggest that he was this same, quiet, well-mannered individual when he brutally strangled his wife some ten years ago. So perhaps we should be looking for something else.'

Wade paused, then continued in a way that suggested that he had found that elusive something else. 'Neil Bowen's problem is that his goals aren't realistic. We have heard before of his success in the academic field, of exams sat and passed. But exams aren't everything. In fact, in Bowen's case, they may even be counterproductive.'

Here he turned a page theatrically, and read from the text. ' "His parents are lower working class. His father is a milkman and his mother is a cashier in a butcher's shop." ' He put the sheaf of papers back on the table to make it plain that what followed would be his own words. 'In my opinion, Bowen's academic achievements will put a barrier between him and his parents. They will no longer be able to communicate with him at his higher level. It could well lead to frustration and friction. He would have done better to concentrate on learning a trade. For this reason, I consider that his expectations are not realistic.'

Wade sat down. Hall gave him a playful nudge that said, 'Well done.' Both looked across at Nancy Frank. As Neil Bowen's probation officer, it was her turn to speak next.

Suddenly, there was a knock at the side door, and it swung open to the accompaniment of rattling cups and saucers. A tea trolley appeared in the opening, pushed by a florid-faced, matronly woman in her late forties.

'Ah, Mrs Owens,' purred Maypole, 'what a timely interruption. I'm sure we could all do with some refreshment.' He beamed at her approvingly.

Mrs Owens was one of the parole clerks who worked in the office downstairs and doubled as tea lady when the Board was in session. She was a cheerful type, who fussed over the men like a mother hen. She was always accommodating. Nothing was too much trouble. She always did what she was told and she never, ever argued.

'Well done, June,' said Hall. 'Always pleased to see *you*. Coffee with milk and two sugars, please.' He smiled broadly at her and she smiled back.

Others called out their orders from around the table. The meeting was forgotten as they collected their drinks and bantered with June.

Jane sometimes thought that she must be growing old and cynical. Was it her imagination or did they deliberately overdo Mrs Owens' welcome? Implying that here was a woman they could relate to, while there were some women, not a million miles away, who were not at all welcome.

Cups and saucers were passed around the table. Teaspoons rattled against china, creating a musical cacophony. There were gasps as hot tea and coffee burnt eager lips.

Her job done, Mrs Owens backed out of the room the way she had come. She was instantly forgotten, her role fulfilled. Only the cups and saucers remained, silent testimony to her visit.

'Now where were we?' asked Maypole. He looked round the table bemusedly, searching for inspiration.

'Ahem.' Mrs Frank loudly cleared her throat and raised her hand.

'Yes?' said Maypole eagerly, pleased for any help.

'It's my turn, Governor,' she said quietly.

Maypole nodded in approval. 'Carry on, carry on.'

Pushing her cup away from her, Mrs Frank stood up. Holding her sheaf of papers in both hands like a hymnal, she looked directly at Maypole.

'I tend to agree with SO Wade.' She paused and looked across at the senior officer, who smiled at her in return. 'You all know my opinion on the role of education in this establishment. It should act as an adjunct to the rest of the work we do here and not as the sole goal.' The unintended rhyme made her hesitate for a moment.

'There are many areas to be considered when we recommend a man for eventual release. Conduct within the prison. Attitude to both staff and the original offence. Maturity and the growth of self-control. Home circumstances and family background. All these things are important. Not one of them can stand in isolation from the rest.'

She flicked a quick glance at Jane. 'Education and educational achievements are important. Much of our resources, some would say too much, are diverted towards education. However, it is not the be-all and end-all of everything. Other criteria must be given equal weight.

'I have spoken to Bowen on several occasions over the past six months. It seems to me that he has become increasingly argumentative. When I have tried to point out other areas of concern, he has insisted that his future depends on his getting his degree.

'In this instance, I truly think that too much knowledge can be a dangerous thing. He has learned a great deal, but he has forgotten how to listen to those he should be listening to. I think Neil Bowen should return to basics and concentrate on a realistic plan to enable him to fit smoothly back into his family on his eventual return to society.'

Clutching her papers to her chest, Mrs Frank sat down. Both Wade and Hall were smiling broadly, and Hall twisted vigorously in his seat to stare at Jane.

The unexpected exertion, coupled with his usual large and greasy breakfast, caused him to fart quietly but audibly. Instantly he went very red and dropped his head to stare at the table in front of him like a naughty schoolboy. 'Beg your pardon,' he muttered. It served to detract from his own performance. Mrs Frank closed her eyes and also lowered her head towards the table. Jane smiled inwardly at this unexpected windfall.

Mrs Frank's attack on the role of the education department had come as no surprise. Increasingly, Jane had found herself engaged in an ideological battle against the others. She wondered if they ever took any notice of the Home Office's regular pronouncements on the important role of education in prisons.

It was again the turn of Dr Gold. He rose to his feet, an enigmatic smile playing around the corners of his mouth. He was well aware of the political interplay between the various Board members. He had sat in on enough meetings over the past twelve months to know that. In the main, he liked to think himself above it all. He wouldn't lower himself to the petty squabblings of those he considered his social inferiors. He had his own agenda, that of maintaining his own exalted position. At times he would descend into the fray when confronted in interview by a particularly disrespectful inmate. But above all else, he was determined to be seen as his own man.

He remembered the Bowen individual quite well. The man had been intelligent as well as respectful. He had seen nothing in either his conduct or attitude to suggest that he was anything other than a model prisoner. He for one didn't feel threatened by the fact that Bowen had passed several credits towards an Open University degree. He had a degree himself, as well as several medical qualifications. He well knew the value of education, not only for passing exams and gaining better employment, but also for personal improvement. He didn't doubt that, through his studies, Bowen had come to know himself better.

'Bowen presented himself as a stable, intelligent and well-behaved young man who has come to terms with his sentence better than most,' he began.

Mrs Frank's face was a picture. Petulance played around her mouth, while her eyes blazed with anger. At times, she despised and detested the pompous doctor, but he was a powerful man and she couldn't afford to alienate him and drive him into the enemy camp. She would have to hide her disapproval. Normally, he was either an ally or remained neutral. She would have to treat today's performance as a temporary aberration.

'He seems to retain good relations with his family, with whom he intends to live when he is eventually released. I am treating him for a rheumatic condition, but there is no sign of any other illness, either physical or mental.'

The doctor paused. It seemed as if he was on the verge of saying something, then changed his mind. He pursed his lips and continued. 'My opinion of Bowen is that he has made good progress and has a realistic attitude to his future. I do not consider him to be dangerous at this present time, either to himself or to others.' As he sat down, Gold placed a bundle of photographs on the table in front of him.

Once again, Hall was the first to reach for them. They showed a young woman, her face swollen and distorted as the result of strangulation. Her eyes bulged and her mouth gaped in an eternal scream. Traces of blood could be discerned beneath one nostril.

Ritually, the photos went the rounds of the Board members. Jane passed them on without looking, but Mrs Frank examined them closely. She passed them on, but leaned across to whisper to Hall. When they finally came back to him, he handed them again to Mrs Frank. Then he leaned across to whisper to Dr Gold.

Jane had been looking at her notes, waiting for the photos to complete their rounds. She indicated to Maypole that she wished to speak and he signified his approval. With Gold on her side, she felt a lot more confident.

'I have known Neil Bowen for close to eighteen months now, seeing him for several hours most weekdays.' Her voice was low but clear and she looked straight at Governor Maypole. 'As we have already heard,' Jane briefly turned her head towards Mrs Frank, 'Neil is something of a scholar. Lacking any formal education, he has applied himself well and passed four credits on the Open University.

'We have also heard, and I am the first to agree, that academic achievements aren't everything. In Neil's case, though, his progress has transcended the educational. He now has far greater insight into his own personality. He understands where he went wrong before and feels that he was emotionally immature at the time of the offence. He also feels, and I agree with him on this, that he now has the emotional maturity to handle a similar situation in a more acceptable way.'

There was an audible snort from Mrs Frank. Jane looked towards her, then at Governor Maypole. Maypole, with a look of resignation on his face, shook his head slowly and deliberately at Mrs Frank. She reciprocated by lowering her head in an exaggerated nod.

'In my opinion,' Jane was coming to her conclusion now, 'Neil Bowen is a changed man. He is a talented individual who still has much to contribute to society. I consider that the death of his wife came as a result of a domestic situation that provoked him beyond endurance. I do not consider Neil Bowen to be a violent person in the accepted meaning of the phrase. Nor do I consider that he ever was.'

Jane shuffled the papers in her hands, then sat down. Immediately, Mrs Frank was on her feet. 'Governor Maypole, Governor Maypole,' she cried, waving the sheaf of photos in her outstretched hand.

Maypole raised his own hands in an attempt to calm her. 'Mrs Frank, Mrs Frank, *please*,' he said, his tone almost beseeching.

Taking this as permission to speak, Mrs Frank remained standing. 'We are dealing with very serious matters here,' she began, her voice raised in passion and anger. 'It's all very well Mrs Roman defending her favourites, but it's the public who will inevitably suffer. We have all noticed that she refuses to look at the autopsy photographs. I do not like to look at them myself, but I do so out of a sense of duty. It helps to remind me of the enormity of some of the crimes we have to deal with.' She fanned out the photos and held them up. 'Look at the poor face of this young woman, cruelly snatched from this life at such an early age. Who would not say that the man who perpetrated this crime was a very violent man indeed?'

She paused and, for a second, Jane thought she was finished. But there was more to come. Drawing herself up to her full height and inhaling deeply until her chest was puffed out, Mrs Frank presented a picture of righteous indignation. At that moment, she looked a very large lady indeed. 'I fear that, at times, Mrs Roman allows her personal feelings to overrule her professional responsibilities,' she concluded with as much dignity as she could muster.

The Chief had been lolling drowsily in his chair. Mrs Frank's outburst now brought him fully awake. He was a traditionalist of the old school, and the idea of women working in a man's prison was anathema to him at the best of times. He could remember the old days when these meetings were run solely by men. The strident tones of the clearly overwrought Mrs Frank had startled him. And anyone who startled Chief Hughes had better watch out.

He had no time for Mrs Roman. Entirely too sure of herself and possessed of strong opinions. He didn't believe the many rumours he had heard about the various liaisons between her and certain inmates. The sheer volume of them defied belief, and she didn't look like she had it in her. Perhaps that's what got up Mrs Frank's nose. That Mrs Roman was attractive but didn't flaunt it.

He wasn't taking sides. He had too little interest in either of them for that. But he wasn't going to stand for shrieking women disrupting the proceedings. Especially when he had nearly been in a state where he would have been totally oblivious to them.

'Governor, Governor,' he muttered gruffly, shaking Maypole urgently by the arm.

Maypole was taken completely by surprise. Usually, the Chief took no part in the proceedings. It was rare that he had any intimate personal knowledge of individual lifers. It was even rarer that he roused himself to speak out either for or against them.

There had been meetings when the Chief's quiet snoring had been a source of embarrassment to him. It seriously detracted from his authority to have the Chief Officer of the prison fall asleep in a meeting chaired by himself. But all he could do was ignore it.

He couldn't ignore the grip on his arm, though. Holding up his hand to silence Mrs Frank for, still standing, she looked like she might continue, he announced, 'Chief Hughes has something to say on the matter.'

Like two people on either end of a see-saw, Chief Hughes rose as Mrs Frank sank into her seat. Every head turned to look at him, for this was something of an unusual event.

The Chief wobbled unsteadily for a moment as sleep-drowsed legs strained to hold his fifteen stones aloft. His big head rotated slowly to fix everyone at the table with his steady gaze. In the old days, he had been a man to be feared by con and screw alike. Now, in the twilight of his career, he was content merely to harass incompetent and lazy staff. He had handed out several 'half-sheets' in the past few months, so the old lion still had some teeth. He was a man to be avoided.

'It seems to me,' the deep and lilting Welsh tones rolled around the room, 'that certain people are getting far too excited. The debate is becoming far too personalised. I know Bowen. Knew him when he started his bird at Cardiff. Not a bad lad at all. Never any trouble, even if he was a bit green and immature.'

He stopped and deliberately ran his eyes over them all again as if daring anyone to interrupt him. 'I still speak to him regularly here. Great change in the lad. He's older, but he's grown up a lot, too. Much more mature and nowhere near as green. I can't see what all the fuss is about. He's just a Welsh lad from the valleys who went wrong.'

Again he surveyed the room, daring anyone to disagree with him. There was a deathly silence. Mrs Frank sat, mortified. She had badly overplayed her hand. First, she had misread Gold's position on Bowen. Now she had stirred the normally somnolent Chief.

The Chief sat down and, after what seemed like an age, the Governor cleared his throat and spoke. In a reedy tone, as if reluctant to stir the volcano that sat at his side, he summarised the argument. 'It seems that there are two clear shades of opinion on the case of Bowen. Fortunately, it isn't a pressing case, as he will have another Board before his LRC in seven months' time.' He hurried on before there could be any more interruptions. 'For the meantime, I am going to recommend that Bowen be recommended for open conditions. Should there be any change for the worse over the next six months, we can always rectify matters at his next Board.'

Maypole quickly put Bowen's folder to the bottom of the pile and read from the cover of the next. 'We now come to the case of Howard Dobbs.'

There was a rustling of papers as the others prepared themselves. Jane was secretly jubilant. For once she had carried the day.

She had no knowledge of Howard Dobbs and, to the best of her recollection, had never spoken to the man. It was the same with the case of the next inmate. She sat, playing no part, as PO Mann and SO Terry from B wing became involved for the first time.

The sharp rapping of Maypole's gavel brought her out of her reverie. He was saying something about having heard the last case for the morning. Jane looked at her watch. It was just before 11.30. Almost two hours had passed since they had started.

She was on the verge of rising when she realised that Maypole was saying something else. She sat back to listen.

'Just one more thing before we break up for the morning.' Maypole was in jovial mood now, the worst was behind him. 'I have been advised that there is a lifer on his way here, by the name of Parker, who would not normally be accepted. He has been involved in trouble in various jails over the past 12 years. In fact, he seems to have been almost constantly on the move.

'I've accepted this man as a favour to Head Office because it seems that he was wrongly moved from his last prison and is at present in the punishment block at Lincoln. Let me assure you all that, should he misbehave here, that's exactly where he will return to. I thought I had better advise you of his imminent arrival.'

'Governor.' Hall had his hand up. He had been in animated conversation with Wade.

Maypole acknowledged him.

'Is this man's name Norman Parker?'

'Yes, it is.'

Hall clapped his hands over his face in exaggerated horror. He looked sideways at Wade who was shaking his head.

'I know him, Governor. And so does Mr Wade.'

Maypole looked at Hall with interest now. It was unusual to be warned about a man by the Home Office. If Hall had any personal knowledge of this Norman Parker, then he wanted to hear it.

'We were at Parkhurst with him in 1975. He was nothing but

trouble there. He made an escape attempt, then triggered off a riot. He's an animal. A very nasty piece of work indeed.'

Jane was surprised. Hall actually sounded quite worried. His normal bully-boy bluster was gone. Jane wondered what sort of man this Norman Parker was that he could instil such fear in Hall.

'Well, don't worry about it,' said Maypole unconvincingly. 'As I've just said, should he start his nonsense here, he'll be on the first escort out.'

With this, the meeting broke up. Waters and Bone left immediately. The rest stood around in small groups talking. Jane made her way gingerly around the table and left the room.

'Jane, Jane.' The words seemed to come from far away. Suddenly she realised that someone was calling her name. She had been miles away. Lost in the remembrance of Monday's Knightsford Board.

She was still staring at her desk, pen in hand. She had been staring blankly at the paper in front of her and hadn't written anything for several minutes. It had been Norman Parker coming in that had prompted the reverie.

She looked up and her eyes widened in surprise. Neil Bowen was standing in front of her. How strange when she had only just been thinking about him. She noticed Camber sitting at his desk staring at her. She really must have drifted away.

'Oh, sorry, Neil, I was thinking about something,' she said briskly, then stood up. 'I'll start the class right now.'

She left the office and walked with Neil to a classroom further down the corridor, where five other inmates were already seated at their desks. Silently she ran through their names in preparation for filling in the register she carried beneath her arm. There was Tom, Niven, Graham, Anwar, Pete and Bill. Together with Neil who walked next to her, all her regulars were there. Mentally she prepared herself for another class.

4

ack on the wing, I returned to my cell and pulled the door to
behind me. If I were seen hanging about, I was sure someone
would arrange for me to start work. I would be in the workshops
all too soon. For the present I was content to lie on my bed and read.

I must have dozed off. I woke to feel a dull pain in my chest. I
had rolled over on to my book. I looked at my watch. It was nearly
11.30, time for dinner. I picked up my cutlery and headed for the
dining hall.

As I passed the wing office, SO Gale called to me. 'Norman,
you start in the electrical shop this afternoon. It's at the end of B wing.
When the work-bell goes after dinner, just follow the rest and you will
find it.'

'OK, guv.'

I carried on towards the dining hall, where a small queue had
already formed. Tom was there, together with most of the 'young 'uns'.

'How ya going, Norm?' he said, strolling over to join me.

'Well, I've seen the doctor and didn't really get on with him.
Then I saw Docker and he gave me another warning. After that I saw
Camber, and your pal Jane blanked me. And lastly, I've been told that
I start in the electrical shop this afternoon.'

'Jane's all right, Norm, you'll see,' said Tom. 'Watch out for the
electrical shop though. The instructor in there is a right nasty bastard.
They call him the "poison dwarf". He's all for capital punishment and
he tells you so.'

I had my own opinion of capital punishment and defended
anyone's right to have theirs. However, that didn't extend to telling a
lifer that you were in favour of it. It was insensitive in the extreme. It
was the same as telling him that you felt he should have been
executed.

'Well, he better not tell me,' I said.

Suddenly Tom waved to someone behind me. 'Here, Norm. I
want to introduce you to someone.'

I turned to see a young fella in his early twenties. He was about
the same weight as me, but slightly taller. He was well made, but not
quite stocky. Sandy-ginger hair crowned a florid chubby face liberally
sprinkled with freckles. He walked up to us with a rolling gait that was

almost a swagger. He seemed to move carelessly, but with a distinct litheness and fluidity.

'Niven, I want you to meet Norman,' said Tom.

'Hello, Niven.' I stuck out my hand. As I looked into his face, I saw he was quickly weighing me up. I saw wariness in his eyes, and arrogance, too, and got the impression that he was used to getting his own way. It was strange with bullies. I always saw in them a predatory self-confidence, as if they were about to roll right over you.

'Hallo.' He shook my hand, but there was no warmth in the greeting. I immediately felt that he viewed me as a rival. There was a sulkiness in his expression that you would expect of a child who had been told that he would have to share something that had previously been exclusively his.

'Niven's captain of the football team,' added Tom in a determined attempt to make this introduction go as smoothly as possible. I could sense that he felt there could be problems between this Niven and me.

'Do you play?' asked Niven. There seemed more to this query than mere politeness.

'I've played in a couple of nick teams, but I'm not that good,' I replied with a smile. I was quite relaxed. I didn't know who he was and I didn't really care. From the way Tom had gingerly introduced us, he could well be the local nuisance. But if I had survived the rigours of Parkhurst, I was unlikely to find much to fear in Knightsford.

First impressions were so very important, often irrevocably establishing the parameters of a relationship. Prison was all about pecking orders. If you didn't portray a strong enough presence in the beginning, someone could well come on to you and you would have to act.

I wasn't worried about Niven. I would get on with him if I could, but if it had to be, then I felt I could handle him. If nothing else, his immaturity worked against him.

'We'll have to get you a game then,' he said, the wariness plain on his face now. I guessed that the football team was his personal territory and he feared a strong rival.

With that, the conversation seemed to be at an end. He drifted away to join the crowd of young 'uns and I continued to talk to Tom.

'Niven's all right, but he can be a bit of a fucking nuisance at times,' said Tom, as if an explanation were necessary. 'He doesn't have a go at me and he won't bother you, but he bullies most of the other young 'uns. He's absolute murder on the football pitch. He screams and shouts at them and even chucks them off. He's a brilliant player, though. The best I've ever seen in prison. He could easily have been a good professional. He's got so much talent. He never trains – it's just natural. He's good at all sports, it sickens you really. Whatever he turns his hand to, he's good at it.'

Tom looked quickly over his shoulder to check where Niven

was before continuing. 'I was nicked young myself, so I understand him better than most people. His trouble is that he was nicked at fifteen. He'd only been in this country a few days from Ireland. Him and an older fella stabbed a fella in a café. The fella died and they did Niven for the murder. He's still a young kid really. He hasn't grown up. He doesn't know anything and he hasn't seen anything. He's got a terrible temper, though, and it will get him into trouble.'

'It seems like it already has,' I said. 'Mind you, I'm not that interested in football to fall out with him over it.'

'Look, as I said, Norm, he won't bother you. He tends to pick his mark, does Niven.'

I was grateful to Tom for filling me in on the people and customs of Knightsford. I didn't doubt that I would have eventually found my own way, but with Tom's advice, I could do it with a minimum of friction.

The settling-in period was always difficult. The more dominant cons invariably had things set up the way they wanted them, and any new arrival was bound to be viewed as a threat to the *status quo*, especially as the whole set-up was based on dominance and submission. What they had claimed by force could be taken from them in the same way.

Suddenly, I heard a commotion behind me. Someone was talking, almost shouting, in a strong Cockney accent. And it was a very exaggerated one. People only talked like that in Sid James comedies.

''Allo, Tom, me old son.' The voice was right in my ear now.

I turned to see a little old boy in National Health glasses. What little remained of his hair was brushed over the top of his head in a forlorn attempt to cover the bald pate. His small nose was viciously hooked into a beak, and he seemed to do all his talking out of the side of his small, thin-lipped mouth. He moved with quick, bird-like motions, as if he were perpetually in a hurry or on the verge of important matters. He fired off barrages of words at everyone he came in contact with, sometimes stopping, but more often sweeping by like some marauding pocket battleship. And all in that exaggerated London accent.

I understood the accent. The vast majority of men in prison weren't professional criminals, but once in the system, they were hardly likely to admit that they were there through foolishness or spur-of-the-moment opportunism. Some even tried to adopt an alternative persona. As most professional crime was carried out in and around London by born-and-bred Londoners, a Cockney accent was almost *de rigueur* in certain criminal circles. Therefore, mugs who happened to have a London accent and little else going for them sometimes developed overnight a strong Cockney accent, adding any rhyming slang they might know.

I guessed that the little old boy was in this category. Either that or he was doing an enthusiastic impersonation of 'Cheerful Charlie Chester' meets Max Wall.

'Hallo, Derek,' replied Tom to the noisy, cheery greeting. Then he introduced us.

Derek stepped forward quickly and shook my proffered hand vigorously. I could feel a surprising amount of strength in the bony old hand.

'Norm, me old mate, we was at Parkhurst together, don't you remember?'

I stared into the old face, examining it more closely.

'I was on A wing. Pals with Big Bert,' he added.

There was a glimmer of memory. I saw the great bulk and shaven head of Big Bert, an image that was hard to forget. Then in the background, like the moon appearing from behind a mountain, swam an old face. Now I remembered him, but only vaguely.

He had been just an anonymous old boy then, who had followed Bert about like a stray dog. Heaven knows where Bert knew him from. None of us knew him, not even his name. There had been no noisy, exaggerated Cockney accent then. He had been just a frightened old man, thoroughly intimidated by the violent professional criminals who surrounded him. I couldn't recall him ever speaking. Just huddling close to Bert, as if for safety.

I mused again on the peculiar nature of Knightsford's residents. What an amazing transformation had come over Derek. Here he acted like some archetypal, elder villain strolling through his territory.

'Oh, yeah, I remember now. I've been through a lot of nicks since then, Derek.' My reply was more truth than lie. 'How is Big Bert?'

The question caught him off guard. Whatever his connection to Bert, I couldn't see the latter keeping in contact with him.

'Oh, he's OK,' he blustered, thinking on his feet. I saw him look at me closely, wondering if I knew the latest whereabouts of Bert. 'He's out now. Sent me a card about a month ago.'

With that, the conversation was over. We had nothing else in common and the longer he talked about Big Bert being in touch with him, the more likely I was to catch him in a lie.

'Oh, well, Norm,' he said suddenly, breaking the silence, 'must be getting on, must be getting on. Hope you settle in all right here. Let me know if there's anything I can do for you.'

He turned and hurried away up the queue. As he went, he fired noisy, almost aggressive greetings at people he knew. There were responses from them all, though many seemed quite half-hearted. I surmised that, to them, Derek was a pain, but that it was better to acknowledge the fiery old sod than risk the rough edge of his tongue.

Tom and I collected our dinner and went to sit at the usual table. Before long, we were joined by Bill and Jack again. Talk was mostly about football and the coming league match on Saturday. There were all the usual complaints about wrong tactics and the team not being picked fairly. Niven's name was constantly mentioned, although very softly by both Bill and Jack.

It seemed that Knightsford FC was very much a one-man show, with that one man being Niven. They were top of the league, but enjoyed a considerable advantage in that they only played at home. Outside teams were always intimidated when they came to play inside a prison, surrounded by scores of baying home supporters, with none of their own.

Niven was the top scorer in the league. In fact, he had already broken the league record. It seemed that it was nothing unusual for him to score ten, eleven or even more goals in a game.

Tom, Bill and Jack were all agreed that he was greedy. Tom even went as far as to say that it was impossible to get a return pass from him. He should have known, playing right wing to Niven's centre forward. I resolved to watch the game this coming Saturday. I had seen some good footballers in prison, but Niven seemed to have something extra. Also I was interested to see the interaction between Niven and the rest of the team. The weekly match seemed to be the main social event for Knightsford's young 'uns. To be in the team was to be someone. To be dropped was social death.

'I know you, don't I?' The harsh, grating voice was almost in my ear.

I turned quickly to see a very old fella wearing a long grey overcoat standing next to our table, his face twisted in a scowl. Rough, reddened skin showed through grey, grizzled whiskers. Pure white hair receded from a washboard forehead. His eyes, although squinting and dim, had a bright, shiny hardness in their depths. The prison-wise should take heed of eyes like that.

He must have been all of seventy, frail and stooped, but amid all the decay there was a vitality that belied the years. It wasn't a positive or healthy force, though. Rather, it was born of bitterness and hatred. For someone so old and feeble, it was surprising that he exuded so much hostility.

'What?' I said warily, now very much on my guard. I had known old boys who could be very dangerous indeed. It didn't take much strength or agility to creep up behind someone, reach over and stab them in the eye with something sharp. Just an insane viciousness.

''Allo, Arthur,' said Tom. Without ever taking my eyes off the old boy, I saw him smile.

'Hallo, Tom,' the old fella replied. His smile was more of a grimace. There was a brief flash of teeth, but it was gone when he turned back to me.

'Albany, wasn't it? I knew you at Albany,' the grating voice demanded. The tone reminded me of the elder Steptoe without the histrionics. There wouldn't be too much emotion from this old boy. 'Brown, Arthur Brown. Don't you remember?' He thrust his face forwards as if closer examination would stir my memory.

I didn't like his manner at all. In fact, if it had come from a younger man, there would have been an aggressive response from me. But what could I do? I couldn't clump the old bastard for lack of respect. I would have been universally condemned for taking a liberty with an old man. And, whatever the circumstances, it would be me who was moved out. So I thought I had best humour him.

'Albany was a long time ago and I've been in a lot of nicks since then, mate. You do look a bit familiar, though.'

I said this in the most unpatronising manner I could, but he was on me immediately. He might be old, but his mind was razor sharp. 'I remember you,' he growled, 'just starting off, you were. We were both on A wing, the reception wing.'

Deliberately, I cast my mind back. Once again I walked the landings of Albany, meeting old acquaintances and staring deeply into their faces. But I couldn't see this old boy who now stood in front of me.

The fact that he could remember me didn't mean that his memory was better than mine. I had been going through a particularly rabid phase in those days and had had a very high profile. There had hardly been an incident that I hadn't been involved in, one way or another. He would have been in his sixties and just another old boy anonymously pottering about on the wing.

'Perhaps it will come back to me,' I said a bit lamely. Being on the defensive was an unusual experience for me.

'Pah!' he said, fixing me with a hard stare. Then he turned away and was gone.

As soon as he was out of earshot, Tom, Jack and Bill started laughing.

'Who *was* that old bastard?' I asked, laughing myself, but with a humour I didn't really feel. I could see the funny side of it, though. After all, a supposedly tough fella doesn't get bullied by a seventy-year-old man every day of the week.

'That's Arthur Brown. We call him "old poison bollocks". He's doing life for his second murder. He's a right bitter old bastard. He knows he's never getting out,' Tom said, still laughing.

And then I remembered the case and the man. He had been sentenced to life in the late Sixties for murdering his wife. He had served just over ten years when they let him out. The fact that he had turned sixty helped to convince the parole board that he wasn't still dangerous.

He had been out just over a year and had married again when he had murdered his second wife. Again he had used a shotgun, but this time he had severely wounded his father-in-law as well. When they had got him in the nick, the local police had been shocked to find that this harmless-looking old boy's only regret had been that he hadn't killed the father-in-law as well. He had sworn to come back one day and finish him.

In sentencing him to his second life sentence, the judge had recommended that he never be released. Not surprisingly, the judge had taken the view that, as long as he was capable, Brown was dangerous.

I remembered someone pointing him out to me back at Albany, and I could recall talking to him in passing a couple of times. He had been a staunch old boy who had hated the screws. Such had been the conditions there that any ally against the screws had been welcome. He had been quite dangerous, too, in spite of his years. Vaguely, I could remember an incident where he had stabbed another old boy with a pair of scissors. He hadn't been a man to provoke for no reason.

We finished our meal, still laughing about Brown from time to time. 'Have you seen outside yet?' asked Tom as we stood up from the table.

'Not yet,' I replied. 'I don't know how or when to get out there.'

'It's open now,' said Tom pointing behind me.

I looked over my shoulder to see a single glass door set in the glass-panelled wall of the dining hall standing ajar.

'Let's drop our eating irons off in our cells, make a cup of tea and go out.'

I nodded in agreement and headed back to the wing with Tom.

Ten minutes later we were back in the dining hall, both carrying steaming cups of tea. We walked to meet the bright sunlight, streaming in through the open door.

I squinted, the glare temporarily dazzling me. Through a blur I could see several conifer-type trees, each higher than a man, standing among various kinds of shrubs. These, in turn, were set in multi-coloured flower beds, and here and there, more flowers blossomed in big, green tubs.

It was like another world. It was so beautiful. The sweet scent of the flowers bathed my nostrils. The late-summer sun warmed my face. A gentle breeze caressed my neck.

I stopped involuntarily and breathed in deeply. All my senses seemed to come alive at once. I wanted to see, smell, touch — all at once. Deep inside me, I felt part of this manicured nature as a distant race memory stirred. I had never felt at home within the bricks and concrete of my prison home, and this had served to remind me of the unnatural state of my existence.

In the security jails, foliage was kept to an absolute minimum: trees and shrubs could shield illicit activity and dangerous contraband could be buried in flower beds. The authorities there had coerced and disciplined nature itself.

'Come on, Norm.' I glanced up to see Tom looking at me, a puzzled frown on his face. I had stopped just outside the doorway, standing with my eyes half-closed.

'I didn't realise you had Kew Gardens here,' I said, making a joke of it.

'Oh that,' said Tom, as if noticing the plants and flowers for the first time. I had forgotten that he was still very young. His set weren't interested in the beauty of nature. That was for older, more boring people.

I walked on a dozen paces through the swathe of garden to join him on the edge of the football pitch. Directly opposite, beyond the other touchline, stood the prison wall. At one end, behind the goal, there was a large greenhouse, and at the other I could see the corner of what I guessed was the visiting room. The all-glass walls gleamed with reflected light.

Without the football pitch, it would all have seemed very natural and pretty. But from a footballer's perspective, the towering wall hugging the touchline – with barely six feet between them – was positively claustrophobic. There was a significant danger of running to keep a ball in play and carrying on to crash into the wall.

Even stretched to these extremes, the pitch was far from regulation size. It was only about eighty yards long and the width couldn't have been more than fifty. No doubt the league made an exception because this was a prison. I mused that it would be a bit crowded with all twenty-two players on the pitch.

Tom and I crossed to sit on the ground with our backs to the wall, facing the dining hall. There were other groups spread out along the wall, and I recognised several of the young 'uns.

Sitting close to the touchline, I could appreciate the difficulties of playing on such a pitch. 'A bit small, ain't it?' I remarked.

'It's fucking ridiculous, Norm,' said Tom with passion. 'With everyone on the pitch it's like five-a-side. You've got no room to run with the ball.' I realised I had touched on a sore point.

Suddenly he stood up and raised both hands above his head. 'You can see what it's like to take a throw-in from this side. You're so close to the wall you can't take the ball back behind your head.'

Eventually, however, the tranquillity and beauty of the surroundings soothed even his savage breast, and flopping down next to me, we soon lapsed into silence. We sat there, eyes half-closed, sleepily soaking up the sun.

Occasionally, other cons came out from the dining hall and went to sit in various parts of the grounds. A full ten minutes after Tom and I had come out, a screw appeared and sat on a bench by the opposite touchline. I was impressed by the apparent lack of security. Clearly, it wasn't a priority here.

All too soon, the screw stood up and called out, 'Nearly time for labour, boys! Nearly time for labour!' Men reluctantly climbed to their feet and made their way back into the building. The cool gloom of the dining hall seemed like a tomb after the warmth and light of the outside.

Tom and I returned to our cells. I put on an overall jacket in readiness for work. Soon there was the deep resonance of a gong being struck. The cry of 'Down for labour!' was taken up by several screws.

I walked towards the centre, along with scores of others. Above me, dozens more hurried along the twos. The centre was like an ants' nest as everybody made their way to work.

'See you tonight, Norm!' called Tom as he hurried down the stairs from the twos. He turned to the left and headed towards the end of A wing and the Works Department, while I turned right on to B wing and followed the crowd towards the workshops. SO Gale and a group of screws stood around the covered snooker table and marked off our names on lists as we passed.

I climbed a flight of steel stairs and entered a short corridor. There was a doorway to the left, but another flight of stairs led upwards.

'Where's the electrical shop, please, mate?' I asked a passing fella.

'Through that door there,' he said.

Going through it, I found myself in a large room. It was a typical factory workshop. Plain, undecorated walls ran nearly to the ceiling, with small, cantilevered windows at the top. A small, prefabricated office stood in one corner. Several large wooden work tables were dotted about the room, each surrounded by wooden chairs. Overhead, rows of strip lights glared down unrelentingly. A radio was playing softly in the background.

There were already half-a-dozen men spread around the tables. In front of them were large, blue plastic boxes containing electrical components. They were busily emptying them on to the tables. Some were fixing components to small black circuit boards.

A couple of fellas looked up at me as I entered. They seemed embarrassed, almost demoralised. This was the 'reception' shop that everybody had to pass through. The work was dull, boring and poorly paid, and the instructor was known to be a nasty piece of work. 'Here's another poor sod,' I read in their eyes as they looked at me.

I knew that settling into a job was probably the most crucial test in any jail. The screws always made sure that everyone passed through a 'reception' shop where the working conditions were poor. It was their way of telling you that, in their eyes, we were all the same. It was almost a ritual humiliation.

A few years previously, I would have enjoyed myself here. A chair would have gone through the office window, the electrical components flying across the room like plastic hail. It was amazing how a bit of violence grabbed their attention and earned their respect. Rudeness and arrogance dissolved in the face of physical intimidation. It was a savage indictment of the system that, unfortunately, this was all they seemed to understand.

But, a dozen years into my sentence, I no longer had the same strength. Slowly, inexorably, it had leached away until I had reluctantly come face to face with my own mortality. The passing years had etched lines on my face and thinned my hair. Four thousand, identical, boring days had numbed my imagination until there were no new experiences for me in prison now. My spirit, which had burned with such a fierce intensity that it had catapulted me into situations almost involuntarily, now just sustained me. In the face of endless years to come, I was satisfied to survive each day.

I was far from broken, though. My spirit was still relatively strong, my head still held high. I was like a fighter in the twelfth round of an endless contest. I had taken a lot of punishment and sustained some damage, but I had also handed it out. However, I could no longer charge in as in the early rounds. I was content to counterpunch now. Action had now been superseded by reaction. Provided they didn't go out of their way to humiliate me, to try to break me, then I would leave them alone.

I sat at an empty table. I knew I wouldn't be left idle for long. Sure enough, a white-coated figure hurried over from the office, like a spider across its web.

The 'poison dwarf', as his nickname suggested, was a small man. He stood less than five-and-a-half feet tall and was weedy with it. Although encroaching middle age had sprinkled his jet black hair with grey, enough of it remained for him to grease it back like some ageing rock star. This was his only concession to style though, for the rest of him was unrelievedly dull.

His eyes moved constantly, like a hungry bird searching for grubs. He walked with his hands clasped together, fingers intertwined. Passive though most of Knightsford's lifers might be, this gesture revealed his inner tension at working among murderers.

'Your name is . . . ?' The unfinished sentence hung in the air as he stopped in front of me.

I waited deliberately before answering. 'Parker, guv'nor,' I said curtly, looking deep into his eyes.

He hesitated, examining me more carefully. Perhaps it was the lack of deference, of respect. Most Knightsford 'residents' would have addressed him as 'sir', rather than the slangy 'guv'nor'. On the other hand, I didn't look like most Knightsford inmates. There was too much of the thug. Aggression was too near the surface.

'You'll be . . . be in here for a few weeks,' he stuttered as he began, still not completely sure of himself. I wondered if they had briefed him on my past record. 'The average stay is about six weeks, depending on vacancies in the telephone shop upstairs.' He seemed to have more control over himself now. 'The work is quite straightforward, if a bit tedious. We assemble circuit boards for industry.'

He paused, as if waiting for some reply. I sat there, saying nothing. As he had said, it was straightforward. What was there to say?

'If you have any problems, let me know. My orderly will be out in a minute to show you what to do.' He unclasped his hands, putting them behind his back. I took this to be a sign that he had finished. I nodded to show that I had understood.

He turned and walked away. Almost as an afterthought, he stopped by a table where men were industriously fixing components to boards. He snatched a handful of finished boards from a box and quickly examined them, before throwing one on the table in front of a stockily built fella. 'Too loose,' he barked. 'They're too loose,' then stalked away into the office.

Just like one of those Swiss clocks, as he entered the door of the office, so his orderly came out of the door of a nearby storeroom. No doubt they had practised it many times before.

The orderly was elderly and bald, with just a fringe of pure white hair running above his ears. Whether he walked with a stoop or was merely cowed, I couldn't tell. He hung his head as he approached me.

'Hallo,' he said in a thin reedy voice. 'This is a finished circuit board.' He held out a black oblong of plastic. It was about six inches by four and was as thick as several credit cards. Fixed to its surface was an array of multi-coloured components, some in bright, primary colours, others a riot of coloured lines and squiggles. They all had a short length of fuse-type wire attached to each end, by which they were fixed to the board. The finished article looked as if a child had stuck coloured sweets to a card.

'This is a silicon chip,' the orderly said, holding out a small piece of black plastic. He thought I would be interested, and I was. This was part of the new technology I had read so much about.

I turned it over in my hand, noting the rows of small sharp metal teeth on the bottom. It didn't look particularly sophisticated. I handed it back. 'I've heard they're going to start putting these in screws shortly,' I said deadpan.

I thought it was funny. He obviously didn't. He looked quickly over his shoulder before continuing as if I hadn't spoken. 'You can take your time for the first week, because you're on learning wages. The second week you start piece-work.'

'And how many will I have to do then?'

'The easiest way to think about it is about one every two minutes.' He was already walking away from me. No doubt he had been volleyed before over such a steeply set rate, although setting it had nothing to do with him.

I began to fix components to the plastic boards. With steady, deliberate movements, I copied the sample board he had left with me. It was quite relaxing, really, something like occupational therapy. The task only held half my attention: another part of my mind listened to the radio and daydreamed.

When I had finished three boards, I decided to time myself. Clumsy fingers, working at speed, fumbled with small components. Nevertheless, I ploughed through it smoothly enough. I checked my watch for the new world record and found myself looking at something over fourteen minutes.

This immediately told me something: it definitely wasn't my type of work. I was no quitter and had worked long and hard in the past to improve on personal bests. But there's improvement and then there are miracles, and I had never aspired to the divine. I realised I would never be able to do them fast enough to earn a decent week's wage, so there was no sense in driving myself mad.

I continued to do the circuit boards, but with no sense of urgency now. I would do enough not to be nicked for being 'idle at labour', a catch-all charge. But I wouldn't be working to any harsh deadlines.

At 3.00, a siren went. It was time for afternoon tea. There were eight others in the shop, and from somewhere, each of them produced a cup with a little silver-coloured spoon sticking out the top. They filed through a door at the back of the shop and came back with steam rising from each cup. The hot water urn was obviously next door.

'What's through there?' I called to a big Scots fella who had come over to speak to me a couple of times during the afternoon.

'It's the design shop. We get our hot water from their urn.'

His answer caused me to wrinkle my brow in thought. I was sure Foxy had said that he worked in the design shop.

'How long we got for tea-break?' I called across to the Jock.

'Fifteen minutes.'

I walked through into the other shop. Whatever I expected, it wasn't the high-tech drawing office I encountered. It was massive, fully twice as big as the workshop I had just left. A section was partitioned off at one end.

In the first part there were rows of benches, each with sophisticated electronic measuring and testing machines on them. Strange-looking devices stood near sloping drawing boards. Intelligent-looking cons bent over them, working away quietly.

I walked in and out of the rows, peering over shoulders at complicated blueprints. I saw one or two faces I recognised from around the prison, but no one took any notice of me.

Occasionally, I came upon a prison-related project, which I studied with interest, just in case it might give me an edge in the future. I was especially intrigued by the design for a cell door that could open inwards or outwards. That would soon put a stop to fellas barricading themselves in their cells.

As I neared the partitioned section, I saw it was purely a drawing office. Foxy stood, deep in thought, among the inclined desks. I crept up behind him and poked him gently in the ribs.

'What the . . . ?' He spun round suddenly, startled, his arms raised, the voice nearly a shout. It was a typical Foxy overreaction. Heads turned from nearby benches.

I wasn't concerned. It was funny to see Foxy jump and it served the double purpose of showing others that, whatever his reputation at

Knightsford, it didn't particularly bother me.

'Oh, it's you, Norm,' he said, instantly turning from anger to supposed good humour. He laughed maniacally. Like an overgrown child, he threw his arms around me and shook me playfully. This served to show the others that we were sharing a joke. 'You're a fucker, Norm, creeping up on me like that.'

'Put me down, Foxy,' I said, laughing now in spite of myself. He was phoney as hell. With someone he wasn't intimidated by, he would have turned on him and bawled him out. He wasn't known for his sense of humour. However, I had no fear of him and was finding his antics increasingly funny. I didn't intend to drive him mad, but there were some laughs to be had from the old Fox.

He promptly set about making a fuss of me. Seeing I had no tea-break drink, he offered to make me a cup of coffee. I didn't particularly want one but, remembering that Tom had told me Foxy was quite mean, I accepted. He scurried about and, within a few minutes, I had a steaming cup of coffee in my hand.

'I'll show you around the shop.' Foxy was waxing expansive now, offering to show me his domain.

I followed him out of the drawing office, back into the main shop. Around one corner, dozens of alarm-type clocks were piled up on a bench. A bright light shone down on them and each clock emitted a low-pitched '*beep*'.

'These are light-sensitive alarm clocks,' chirped Foxy. 'You can set them at night and when the appropriate amount of daylight strikes them, they start beeping loudly and wake you up.'

I found this all very interesting, in spite of my nutty guide. This was the most useful and innovative workshop I had ever seen in prison. Light years away from the tedium of sewing mailbags or even making circuit boards.

'Come on,' said Foxy, tugging at my arm. He was clearly getting carried away with the guided tour bit.

He led me into an office where four civilian instructors were sitting, drinking cups of tea. Totally ignoring them, Foxy took me to a desk behind them.

'This is the main shop computer. We work out models for all the projects on this.' He began tapping at the keys.

Computers were new and unfamiliar territory to me. I watched with growing interest.

'Excuse me, Geoff,' he said gruffly to a civvy whose chair was close to the bench. He said it as if he shouldn't have been in the way.

Geoff quickly moved his chair. 'Sorry, Danny,' he said softly, averting his eyes. I could see that Foxy had the shop civvies thoroughly intimidated.

He passed further along the bench and returned with a disk. He put it in the computer and tapped several more keys. Complex designs sprang on to the screen. It was fascinating, but I didn't have a clue what I was looking at.

Suddenly, I glanced at my watch. It was 3.15 and time for me to get back to the 'poison dwarf'. I didn't want to get on his wrong side on my first day.

'Must be getting back, Danny,' I called as I passed him the empty coffee cup. 'See you at tea.'

Foxy was now engrossed in the computer. He set the cup down beside it and continued to tap at the keys. 'Yeah, see you later, Norm,' he called over his shoulder.

I returned to the electrical shop and was once again in a world of components and Radio 2. I realised that there had been no music in the draughtsmen's shop.

The rest of the afternoon passed in a drawn-out blur. I had spent less eventful periods, but mostly when I was asleep. Eventually the siren went for 4.30 and tea-time.

I headed back towards my cell, joining up with streams of men coming from the telephone shop upstairs, and metalworking and joinery shops downstairs. The centre was again awash with hurrying bodies.

I rinsed my hands and face quickly in the recess and headed for the dining hall. Tom, Jack and Bill were already sitting at our table. After collecting my meal, I told them about my encounter with the 'poison dwarf', which set them laughing. They laughed even louder when I told them about the startled Fox and the guided tour.

Bill was beside himself. His face was flushed and he was gasping for breath. My rendition had been funny, but surely not that funny. Then I noticed that he was looking beyond my shoulder.

I swivelled to find the Fox standing right behind me. He had caught me telling them about creeping up behind him.

'He is a fucker, this Norm,' he said, laughing maniacally and setting his tray down beside mine. He grabbed me around the shoulders with both arms and shook me gently in my seat.

He was just like a big kid. Bill shrieked at the incongruous sight of a grown man wrestling so publicly with me while I was trying to eat my tea. Tom and Jack were laughing heartily. The joke was on me now.

Again, I laughed in spite of myself. I had left such messing about behind me in my teens. So it was ridiculous, but quite funny. 'Fuck off, Foxy,' I said, laughing all the while.

'And don't forget, I'm coming to the gym with you and Tom tonight.' Foxy got that in while I was on the defensive.

'Well, we're going down there at 5.30, and if you're not there, we're starting without you.' My tone was serious now.

'I'll be there, I'll be there,' he said as he walked away.

'He's a right nutter, that fucking Foxy,' wheezed Bill, still laughing uncontrollably. I guessed that he was both amused and intimidated by Foxy. He found it a relief to be able to laugh at him innocently while in my company.

At 5.20, I was outside Tom's door in my gym kit. To my surprise, he was ready. He dropped a paper he had been reading on to his bed, paused briefly to comb his hair in a mirror high on his wall, then stepped outside to join me.

We walked together towards the centre. The cover was off the snooker table and two fellas were playing, while another two sat on chairs waiting for a game.

''Allo, Dougie, having a game then?' Tom called out as we passed.

A well-built fella in his fifties spun round and peered myopically over the top of his glasses at us. He was almost completely bald, but had combed a few dozen long strands across the top of his large head in an attempt to compensate. His fat face was unshaven, the whiskers grizzled and grey. Knightsford was no fashion parade, but his clothes looked particularly ill-fitting and uncared for. Out of the corner of his mouth protruded a short, fat dog-end that seemed to have gone out hours ago.

Suddenly, his face split into a grin, revealing a set of badly stained teeth. He puffed energetically on the dog-end and, to my surprise, clouds of smoke poured from it. He threw back his head and laughed a raucous, hacking laugh.

''Allo, Tom mate,' he roared, at the volume you would use for shouting across King's Cross station. I assumed he was a little deaf. Spittle flew from the corners of his mouth and he roared with laughter again. 'Where are you fucking off to?'

His snooker opponent and those waiting were all smiling now, and there was a broad grin on Tom's face. I realised that I was in the presence of another of Knightsford's star nutters.

'We're off to the gym, mate,' Tom called, on the move again.

''Ave one for me.' Dougie held the dog-end now. 'I'm just going to give this old cunt a seeing to.' He gestured towards his opponent and roared with laughter again.

'Tom, Norm,' a voice called to us from along B wing. We looked around to see Foxy walking towards us.

He was certainly dressed for the occasion. Whereas Tom and I had on light blue prison gym vests and blue prison shorts, Foxy looked like he was ready to lead out the British team at the Olympics. The bright red singlet clung tightly to his slim body. Shiny white shorts with a red stripe either side fitted snugly around his hips. White ankle socks and white trainers with neatly tied bows graced his feet. The finishing touch was a large, snow-white bath towel draped around his neck, where a gold St Christopher medal hung beneath his Adam's apple. He still had his glasses on.

'Expecting to meet a few birds down there, are you, Danny?' I asked, smiling.

He walked up and punched me playfully on the arm. 'You've got to look the part, Norm,' he said.

Well, that was one thing we didn't agree on before we had even started. I was one of the old 'sweat and snot' brigade. A work-out wasn't a social occasion for me. I believed in getting stuck in and damn what I looked like. I didn't have a lot of time for posers in the gym. I said nothing, though. I didn't really care how Foxy was dressed, just as long as he got stuck into the work-out.

As the three of us entered the long corridor leading to the gym, I glanced back at the snooker table, just in time to see Dougie patrolling around the table, holding the cue at waist height with both hands, like a geriatric hunter creeping up on a small animal. Suddenly, he moved quickly to the table. Bending only slightly, he struck the cue ball smartly, then jumped backwards. The white flew along the table, cannoning first into one ball, then several others. Soon there were upwards of a dozen balls flying in all directions.

The white careered around the cushions, dangerously clipping the jaws of a pocket. At one moment, it seemed as if every ball on the table was in motion. Miraculously, none dropped into the pockets, and eventually, they all came to rest.

There was a moment's silence, then Dougie threw back his head and brayed his raucous, hacking laugh. Everyone laughed with him. Dougie's style owed more to ten-pin bowling than snooker.

'There's an interesting story about Dougie,' said Tom as we started down the corridor.

'I thought there might be,' I replied, but my sarcasm was lost on him.

'He was a tramp before he was nicked,' he continued.

'He still is.'

'Yeah, I know he's a nutter, but he's got a good heart.' Tom obviously had a soft spot for him. 'He's very straightforward, doesn't pull strokes and sends his wages every week to his brother who's still in a nut house.'

I held my peace now. I regarded loyalty as the finest human quality. If Dougie sent his wages to his brother each week and went without himself, he was a loyal and principled fella indeed. It was hard enough to get by in the nick on the few quid they gave you as wages, which allowed you to buy sugar, jam, tobacco and those few creature comforts that meant so much. Yet Dougie willingly went without all this.

'He used to get about around East Ham.' As Tom said this, the beginnings of an explanation dawned. That was Tom's own manor.

'Knew him on the out then, did you, Tom?' The sarcasm was in the enquiry and not my innocent tone. Foxy laughed, causing me to join in.

'Fuck off, Norm,' Tom laughed. 'I'm trying to tell you an interesting story.' He was just as partisan about East Ham as I was about Notting Hill, my own manor. There was nothing nasty about it, just friendly rivalry. I suppose I started it when I jokingly asked him if they still had outside khazis in the East End.

'He was an outpatient at a local mental hospital,' Tom continued regardless. 'He killed an old lady tramp in a derelict building. That's what he got his life for. The interesting thing is that, if you listen to him carefully, he's an absolute ringer for Alf Garnett. He doesn't put it on at all. They say he's always been like it.'

Tom paused for breath, but then hurried on before I could get in another sarcastic remark. 'Well, Johnny Speight, who wrote the series, always said that he based the character on an old tramp he'd seen hanging around East Ham. Local people swear it was Dougie.'

This didn't surprise me. It was only my second day, yet I had already met a mad governor who had started off as a screw; a Second World War German; an old butcher who did a passable impersonation of 'Cheerful Charlie Chester'; a homicidal pensioner who had murdered twice and only lived for the day when he could finish off his father-in-law; and now the personification of Alf Garnett. All part of Knightsford's rich tapestry, I concluded.

'It wasn't you who taught him how to play snooker, was it, Tom?' Foxy guffawed again.

'Bollocks,' said Tom with a laugh.

By now, we had reached the door of the gym. It was immediately obvious that some sort of function was about to take place. Four table tennis tables had been set out lengthwise across the gym. Standing self-consciously in a group were six 'residents'. It was obvious that they were dressed in their best gym kit. White T-shirts neatly complemented well-pressed white shorts. Spotless white ankle socks rose above cleaned and polished trainers. It was evident that this was as much a social occasion as a sporting event. A hint of sweat would be an embarrassment tonight.

Standing at the other end of the gym was a small group of civilians, both men and women, similarly attired to the cons. They were gathered around a short, stocky fella, wearing the sort of track suit that prison PTIs usually wore.

'Oh, no,' said Tom out of the side of his mouth. 'They've got an outside table tennis match tonight. Bob's brought in some of the birds and fellas from his local pub. It's going to be a right posing session. Our lot will be all politeness and good manners. Bob will walk up and down like a big, tough prison PTI making sure that none of his lot is murdered before they get back to the pub. While, behind his back, that little fat bird will flirt with young Rob, the little fella with black hair.'

Tom's account sounded par for the course. The usual nonsense that went on when cons met civilians in prison. Men with damaged egos, desperately projecting some false persona. The civilians, equally desperately, trying to show that they weren't going to hold it against them that they were prisoners. It was all so false. Why couldn't they just be themselves, relax and enjoy the evening? That was why I never attended these 'outside' functions.

'Well, the multi-gym's open,' said Tom. 'I suppose I'd better just make sure it's open for us.'

He walked towards Bob, calling out the PTI's name. The subsequent discussion was all very polite. Bob smiled and gestured for Tom to carry on.

Bob was a short, stocky fella in his early thirties. If you hadn't been told he was an ex-Marine, it wouldn't have been hard to guess. The close-cropped hair, upright stance and plain appearance spoke of years of acting on other people's orders. If anyone had told me that he was imaginative or creative, I would have been surprised. The deadpan, morose manner militated against him having much sense of humour either. I suspected he would be rather gauche in social settings.

The multi-gym was set in an alcove about fifteen feet wide by nine feet deep. It had several stations and enough space beside it for an Olympic bar and a bench. We were the only ones there. That didn't surprise me. The vast majority of Knightsford's lifers didn't seem to have a good work-out in them.

As the most experienced, I structured the work-out. I had been training for years and knew what I was doing. Soon the three of us were working our way through the various stations.

I quickly assessed my two work-out partners. The gym was a good place to find out at least something of a man's character. Confidence, arrogance, self-discipline, commitment – these were all qualities that could be revealed.

Tom was a game kid. He listened to what I told him, pushed himself to the limit and got on with his work-out with a minimum of fuss. I could see that there would be some rivalry between us when he improved, but at the moment I was too strong for him.

Foxy was different altogether. He opened by walking up and down, flexing his muscles. Sharp grunts came from between clenched teeth, yet he was doing nothing more strenuous than thinking about the work to come. I cringed inwardly. I hated posers in the gym. The fellas who grunted and roared like circus strong men in a performance that owed more to show business than to weight-lifting. It was embarrassing. The sport already had a poser's image anyway. It wasn't difficult to look ridiculous.

By the time Foxy was half-way through his first set of bench press, the grunts had risen through three octaves, and the outside visitors were looking over in the direction of the guttural shrieks. Foxy wrestled beneath the bar as if in mortal combat with an alligator. Tom looked over at me, then raised his eyes to the ceiling in disgust. I stood there saying nothing, embarrassed myself.

The performance wasn't over by any means. A final, orgasmic shriek signalled the final rep, then Foxy was up off the bench. He strode up and down, grunting and puffing, both arms akimbo, like

King Kong about to attack. It was quite a performance and one I felt worthy of his bizarre personality. I now knew that Foxy liked to attract a bit of attention and show off.

'Are you all right, Foxy?' The sarcasm was thick as I stood with my hands on my hips, watching him.

'What's the matter, Norm?' He paused from grunting to stare at me, his attention returning from those he had been trying to impress.

'You ain't had raw meat for tea, have you?'

Foxy knew what I meant, but still he prevaricated. 'You've got to put a bit of effort into it, Norm.'

'I put plenty of effort into it, Danny, but I don't make all that noise. I ain't down here to entertain the fucking visitors, mate. Let's just get on with it, eh?' There was anger in my voice now. Work-outs were deadly serious for me, and I didn't want any distractions. And Foxy making a fool of himself, and possibly us as well, was a major distraction.

'OK, Norm,' said Foxy, dropping his eyes from my glare. 'I'll try not to make so much noise.'

We carried on working and the table tennis match started. Foxy's grunts could still be heard above the clicking of the returns, but they weren't so intrusive now. I resigned myself to the fact that Foxy was one of those gym grunters.

Although I was lost in the work-out, from time to time I looked out into the gym. Our fellas were gently stroking the ball back to their opponents, politely chatting between points. Nothing so unseemly as a sweat stain showed on their antiseptically clean kit.

Bob was patrolling up and down the gym, like a sinister Butlin's Redcoat. His expression said that nothing untoward would happen while he was about.

Fifty minutes in, we were finished with the multi-gym. All had not gone smoothly. While Foxy had reluctantly deferred to my advice, he had then taken every opportunity to correct Tom's lifting style. Often it had been nit-picking and only served to put Tom off. 'For fuck's sake, Danny,' he had said angrily after the umpteenth interruption, 'you're doing my head in. Shut up and leave me alone.'

'I'm only trying to put you right,' Foxy had argued.

From the depth of Tom's anger, I could see that there was going to be some rivalry between them. 'Oi, Foxy,' I had interjected, 'this is my work-out. It only needs one of us to give advice.'

'OK, Norm. I was only trying to help him,' Foxy had replied. After that, there had been sullen silence.

'We'll finish off with some stomach work,' I now said as we stood sweating heavily.

There was a separate incline board, but no room to use it in the alcove. I dragged it out into the main gym and set it up alongside the nearest table tennis table, but a good yard away. We wouldn't be in their way and would hardly distract them. In fact, they would only really see us when we got to the top of each sit-up. For the rest of the time, we would be below the level of the table.

The two nearest players were oblivious to our presence anyway. Bennett — a tall, light-skinned coloured fella whom Tom had introduced me to on the way in — was now playing the little fat bird. She was very young and quite pretty, but a superabundance of puppy fat coarsened her appearance. As she jumped about in pursuit of the ball, large portions of her moved in the other direction. She was peaches-and-cream nice, though. She simpered and giggled at all of Bennett's jokes. He returned her shots, rather than trying to get them past her. He gallantly ran to retrieve most of the loose balls. He deprecated his own game, while politely praising hers. They were both enjoying a social interaction that was a model of zest and propriety.

Foxy excused himself from the sit-ups, saying, 'I do my sit-ups in my cell every night,' but I suspected that he was just tired. 'I'll see you both later,' he called out and walked, stiffly but deliberately, out of the gym.

Tom and I got stuck into the sit-ups. We were already running with sweat, but the intensity of the exercise caused small rivulets to cascade down our faces and arms. We pumped out sets of twenty, one of us on the board, the other standing behind the upright holding his feet. There was a rough cadence to the exercise. A low grunt would escape me as I reached the top of the movement. Out of the corner of my eye, I could see the brightly lit vista of the gym. I glimpsed the tables, the players, Bennett and the little fat bird, all before I sank from view below the level of the table.

Suddenly, I felt a pressure low in my abdomen. A thrill of alarm ran through me as I recognised the familiar feeling of wind.

Normally, it would have been no problem. Prison gyms were usually all-male environments and loud farts were part of working out. But this wasn't a normal occasion. It was one of Knightsford's set-piece social functions and there were women present.

As I rose in the sit-up, I desperately tightened my buttocks as I contracted my abdominals. Muscles strained with effort to bring me to the top of the movement. Then, as I relaxed my abdoms for the easier downward arc, I must also have subconsciously relaxed my buttocks. As I sank below the level of the first table, an explosive, ripping sound thundered against the incline board and reverberated around the gym. There was no mistaking its nature.

I heard a clatter against the surface of the table as Bennett dropped his bat in surprise. I couldn't see his face, but I could imagine his embarrassment. All other play stopped as 'residents' and visitors alike spun around to look for the perpetrator of this social outrage. There was an extended silence.

At the first rip, Bob's head had spun around, too. He glared in the direction of the noise and looked straight at Tom, who was still standing, holding my feet. I had stayed down, lying motionless on the board with only the toes of my trainers in view.

Tom immediately flushed bright red. He stood there, staring straight ahead, as if nothing had happened. He could hardly start shouting out that it was me who was responsible.

'You cunt,' he muttered under his breath. 'You've put it right on me.'

I felt a nearly irrepressible urge to laugh, but smothered it just in case Bob was walking over to investigate.

All eyes were still on Tom. He remained, standing erect, staring into the middle distance.

Suddenly, I saw his nose wrinkle in disgust. 'You dirty bastard,' he muttered again as the smell hit him. He was committed now, though. He could only stand there and pretend that nothing had happened.

Gradually, play restarted on the tables. But there was only the sound of balls striking bats. All conversation had succumbed to the collective embarrassment.

I unhooked my feet from the top of the incline board and clumsily rolled on to the gym floor. On my hands and knees, I crossed the few feet into the alcove, crawled into the corner and remained out of sight. After a minute, I stood up and walked out again. The players were chatting together, but now in a much subdued fashion. I suspected that I might well have ruined the evening for some of them. Bob was pacing angrily up and down, occasionally glaring across at Tom. He still stood behind the metal upright of the incline board, his face still red.

We carried on with our sit-ups, but not nearly so energetically now. 'You'll be all right, you cunt,' he growled to me under his breath. 'You'll be all right.'

I smirked at his threats, well knowing that he wouldn't be doing any farting this evening. He would have to wait for another time to get me back.

We finished the sit-ups, replaced the incline board in the alcove and headed for the door.

'Thanks, Bob,' Tom called out as we left. Bob stared straight ahead and ignored him.

Tom moaned about my farting all the way back to my cell. 'You've done it to me before, Tom,' I said, laughing. 'In fact, you farted several times during our work-out last night.'

'Yeah, but that was different. There were no birds present,' he retorted.

'No, Tom, what was different tonight was that I did it to you. Be fair, mate, it was a blinder, wasn't it?'

Tom wasn't really annoyed about it. It was just that tonight the joke was on him. 'It's all right for you, Norm, but Bob takes us for football training. He's like a little kid. He'll sulk about that for weeks now.'

Back at my cell, I made us both some coffee. Tom sat back on my bed, his head resting against the wall and was strangely silent. For a moment, I thought he was still thinking about the incident in the gym.

'Norm, I want to say something to you.' His tone was serious now, not at all like the irreverent Tom I was coming to know. I looked over at him. His face was stern, and his eyes, fixed on mine, were full of emotion. I waited for him to begin.

'I know you've known Foxy longer than you've known me, Norm, but I just can't work out with him. He's so domineering, so bossy. He wants to take your life over. I've seen him with other people, Norm. He starts off OK with them, but he's just got to have his own way. Eventually, he totally dominates the fella and drives them away. He can't keep a friend. He won't do it to you, but he's already started with me. Every time I picked up a weight tonight, he was on me. I just can't handle that. I can't concentrate. It puts me right off.'

Tom paused for a second before leaning forward. 'Look, Norm, I really like working out with you. But you've known Foxy longer than you've known me, so maybe it would be best if I dropped out and just you and Danny work out together.'

I heard the words he was saying, but knew his heart wasn't in them. Some people might have taken this emotion as a weakness. To me, it was a strength and to his credit. It showed that he was a proud and principled young fella, passionately committed to his beliefs. I was flattered that he thought so much of our fledgling friendship.

With friends, I was a very emotional person, too. Long years of living alone and being moved from jail to jail hadn't destroyed this trait in me. It just lay deeper now. I had made good friends so many times, only to leave them behind in my wake. It was death by a thousand emotional cuts and was the only way that prison could hurt me now.

Now I felt that there was at least one person in Knightsford whom I could trust. Who would stand with me if I was in trouble and would sacrifice himself to help me. It was more than just reassuring. I felt a warmth from the shared friendship.

A wave of emotion swept over me. My eyes grew hot and moist. I felt the beginnings of a lump in my throat. Much of the past year I had spent in solitary. Strong emotion had been no part of my life. Now I felt it overwhelm me.

'Look, Tom, I don't give a fuck about Foxy. I hardly ever spoke to him back at the Scrubs. He was a right cunt. Half a nonce really. I'm not too impressed with him here either. I know he laps me up, but only because he's afraid of me. He's a bit of a bully, is Foxy. The only people he laps up are the ones he's a bit frightened of. In another jail, I'd probably have told him to fuck off right from the start. But there's not a lot to choose from here and I'm trying to keep a low profile. If he wants to talk to me, then I'll talk to him. But he's not a friend, Tom. Just 'cause he tells me he's my pal don't make it so. He's just a prison acquaintance, that's all. We work out all right together, Tom, so let's keep it like that. In fact, Foxy can't work out with me any more.'

There was a charged silence. 'Thanks, Norm. I enjoy our work-outs, too. I'd have been gutted to have to drop out.'

Suddenly, it was all a bit embarrassing. It was time for a change of mood. ''Ere, we both sound like a pair of poofs,' I said. 'You ain't gonna cry, are ya?' My sarcasm was heavily overstated.

'Bollocks, you're the one with tears in your eyes.' Tom was right back to his old, piss-taking self.

The mood had passed. But our relationship was irrevocably changed. Things that we had only felt had been spoken. We were good pals now.

'Who's going to tell Foxy?' asked Tom.

'Don't worry about it,' I replied. 'Tomorrow night I'll tell him I'm not going to the gym, but you and I will go anyway. He'll soon get the message and it will probably be better than telling him to his face. From what you've said, it must have happened to him before. Anyway, fuck him. If he says anything, I'll chin him.'

The subject was closed now. Tom and I began to talk of other things.

'Hello, boys.' We both looked up to see JB standing in my doorway.

I waved him towards a space on my bed. 'Do you want a cup of coffee?'

'No thanks, Norm,' he replied. 'I just want to duck in here out of the way for a minute. Otto's hanging about outside my cell, waiting for me.'

Otto was the old German. 'I don't know why you don't just tell him to fuck off,' I said.

JB smiled and pulled a face. 'I know I should, but I've got a bit of a soft spot for the old fella. I suppose I feel sorry for him.'

'Tell Norm what happened the other morning,' interjected Tom.

JB laughed but looked embarrassed. 'Well, he can be a bit of a pain, the old German,' he began reluctantly, then paused.

'Go on,' encouraged Tom.

'Well, I was sitting in my cell eating my breakfast,' JB continued, 'when in shuffled the old German. He sometimes comes in in the mornings. I didn't even look up. Just kept on reading a paper as I ate. Usually, he'll chunter away in that broken English of his for a few minutes, then shuffle out again.' He stopped and looked over at Tom.

'Well, tell him the rest of it,' Tom encouraged.

Reluctantly, JB went on. 'Suddenly I heard him say, "Yahn, my piles. They bleed." I looked up and he was holding out a tissue to show me. It had blood on it.'

'Aaargh.' I rocked back in my chair, screwing up my face and laughing. 'And you have the dirty old bastard in your cell?'

JB laughed self-consciously. 'He's an old man and shot to

pieces. He just can't help it.'

Tom had said that JB was a nice fella, and it was obvious that he was very kind-hearted. However, my personal philosophy was that you just couldn't allow every nutter to walk into your life and drive you mad. I had enough problems trying to get through my own bird. I would be loyal to my close circle of friends, but welfare work I'd leave to the professionals.

'Well, thanks for telling me anyway,' I said. 'I think I'd better find a way of falling out with the old bastard, so that he doesn't keep coming in here.'

'You'd be wasting your time, Norm,' said Tom. 'I've tried everything short of setting about him, but he's so fucking mad, he just takes no notice.'

'Don't worry about that, I've got an MA in rudeness. I'll find some way to discourage him.' While I said this with conviction, I was wondering how I was going to do it. I couldn't go too strong, otherwise he might go to the screws and say that I'd had a go at him.

We had been talking for another twenty minutes when, suddenly, the German shuffled into view down the landing. He was moving very slowly, and every dozen paces or so he would stop and look about him in a lost, confused fashion. It was just my luck that one of his stops occurred right outside my door. Perhaps it was because he heard JB's familiar voice that made the old head slowly swivel until he was looking at us.

'Oh no,' muttered Tom under his breath.

'Well, talk of the devil,' mumbled JB, laughing, then, more loudly, said, 'Hello, Otto.'

''Allo, boyis.' The old voice was slow and tired and full of self-pity. He shuffled into the cell.

I knew I had to do something. But what?

Suddenly, I jumped to my feet and ran over to the nearest wall. Forcing my face up against it, I began moaning and grunting as if in some kind of fit. The old German stopped in his tracks.

Acting had never been my strong point, but what I lacked in the thespian arts, I made up for in effort. Tom and JB's laughing didn't help. My performance must have been quite convincing, though, because the German backed slowly out of the cell. He stood in the doorway looking at me, then at the two others. He pointed his index finger at his temple. ''Im fokkin' mud.'

The gutteral accent twisted the words almost out of all recognition, but his meaning was clear. Tom and JB burst into fresh gales of laughter, and they were still chortling after the German had shuffled away.

'That's quite an accolade if he thinks you're mad, or rather "mud",' said JB.

'It did the trick though, didn't it?' I retorted.

'You just wait and see,' came back JB. 'He'll have forgotten all about it by the morning. I've tried a few things myself and nothing's worked.'

The gong for bang-up reverberated through the prison. We said our goodnights and both Tom and JB left. I slammed the door on my second day in Knightsford.

5

I was up and ready when the screws unlocked the next morning. I wasn't one of those who could lie in bed in the mornings. I liked to get up, wash, shave and have breakfast. It put me in the right frame of mind to face the new day. To me, a man without self-discipline was no sort of man at all.

With my towel and toiletry gear, I headed for the recess. Both were empty, but I chose the one on the right. I was aware that the German had used this one the previous morning, but that had been before my attack of madness last evening.

I went in, closing the door behind me. The recess hadn't been used since the evening before so it smelled fresh and clean. I positioned myself at the sink, directly in front of the window. Once again as I shaved I looked out on to the landing through the window.

Sure enough, the German appeared, shuffling along the middle of the landing. He looked first at one recess, then at the other. The left-hand recess was empty, the door standing wide open. He looked towards the right-hand recess and saw me through the window. He smiled at me and headed towards the door to it.

Two things were immediately apparent. First, JB had been right when he had said that the German would have forgotten all about my seizure the previous evening. Second, it seemed the German liked to have a bit of company when he had a crap. Perhaps communal shitting was an act of comradeship among Nazis.

'Oh, no,' I said out loud. He was going to stink out the recess again. There was no way I could stand for this every morning. Apart from aesthetic considerations, it was likely to affect my health.

As the German moved past the window, heading for the door, I rushed in the same direction and reached it a split-second before him. Our eyes met through the wired-glass panel as I reached down and seized the door handle.

A confused look passed across the German's face. He couldn't understand what I was doing standing directly behind a door through which he was about to enter.

His hand reached out and grasped the door handle. He pressed down on it, his eyes fixed firmly on my face. Consternation appeared when the handle wouldn't move. He looked down at it, to see what the matter was.

Suddenly, it dawned on him. Me, standing behind the door, and the handle that wouldn't turn. With a grimace of determination, he threw all his strength into pressing down the handle. His face contorted and his lips drew back, revealing clenched teeth.

Now it was a trial of strength. Both hands of the master race vied with the right hand of the chosen people for access to the khazi. It was no contest.

A few years earlier, I would have had a struggle on my hands. But now he was a sick old man. The handle wouldn't budge.

'Fokkin' bustad, yo fokkin' bustad,' he called over his shoulder as he shuffled away towards the other recess.

'Yeah, fuck off!' I shouted in return. 'This is one Jew you ain't gonna gas with your Zyklon B turds!'

As I walked back to the sink to continue shaving, I found myself giggling. I was used to the bizarre, but the sheer ridiculousness of the situation suddenly struck me. It occurred to me that, should anyone walk by and see me standing in a recess at 8.00 in the morning, laughing to myself, they would surely think me mad.

Day three at Knightsford was largely uneventful, and I realised that this would be the pattern for most of my days here. I collected my breakfast and ate it in my cell. When the work bell rang, I headed towards the electrical shop, calling 'Morning' to Tom as he clattered down the stairs, still pulling on his overall jacket.

I fixed components to circuit boards through the morning. I had brought my own drink for break-time and stayed in the shop to drink it. At dinner, I sat with Tom, Bill and Jack as usual.

The afternoon seemed to drag interminably. I contemplated the lot of those who were destined to fix components to circuit boards for a living. I preferred prison.

At tea, Foxy appeared at the table and asked if we were going to the gym. Tom looked a bit sheepish as I curtly told Foxy that we weren't. As he walked away, I was sure he knew.

At 5.30, Tom and I crept along the twos and peeped along B wing towards Foxy's cell. He was nowhere to be seen. We quickly scampered across the centre gallery and disappeared through the door into the education block.

'Ain't it nice what you have to do to have a decent work-out?' I muttered to Tom, making a joke of it. I was beginning to feel a bit sly.

'Be all right if he's already down there,' said Tom in reply. We both laughed, but a thoughtful look came into my eyes as I contemplated this possibility.

'Don't worry, Norm. He's never had a work-out on his own before.' Tom's reassurance was welcome. It would be best if there wasn't any unpleasantness.

We passed well-lit classrooms with several students already

taking their seats. In one, Jane was writing on a blackboard.

'She does some hours, don't she, Tom?'

'As I told you, Norm, she's very committed.'

The gym was completely empty. Not even the badminton court was in use. 'Must be a good night on the telly, eh?' I said.

'Every night's a good night on the telly for this mob.'

'How about a circuit, Tom?' I asked.

'Yeah, that will do.'

I had seen a lot of stuff stored under the stairs just outside the gym. We carried the buck in and the low parallel bars. We scattered several medicine balls about. I pulled the beam out, while Tom arranged the benches. Soon, we had a passable assault course laid out.

This time, I had brought my radio. I set the big Hacker down over by the wall bars and turned it on. The sound of rock music reverberated around the gym.

For half an hour, we charged around the circuit. It wasn't a particularly difficult one, so we took it nice and steadily, going for stamina. When we had finished, we took a five-minute breather, then put all the stuff away. The apparatus seemed much heavier, so we took our time.

We started in on some sit-ups on the gym floor, and lost all track of time. When I looked at my watch, it was after 7.30.

Suddenly, we were aware that someone was in the doorway watching us.

There was an amused smile on Jane's face. She regarded us like an adult who had caught boys in a childish game.

'Mind you don't do yourselves an injury,' she called out. I instantly suspected the pure academic who never took any physical exercise. 'I heard all the noise as I was coming down the stairs and wondered what you were up to.' The innuendo hung in the air, her amusement showing more clearly now.

Tom rose to his feet a bit sheepishly and walked towards her. 'Hallo, Jane. Just finished classes, eh?'

I climbed to my feet behind him and walked over. I was well aware of how many academics regarded physical exercise. However, I was intelligent enough to know that they were wrong. Judiciously pursued, physical development went hand in hand with mental development. And for me it was an absolute safety valve.

'Jane, I don't think you've met Norm.' Tom gestured towards me.

'Hello, Norman.' Her greeting was polite and friendly, but amusement still played around her mouth.

I felt a fledgling anger stir in me. My incipient paranoia flared. I didn't much care for people taking the piss, even if they were diminutive lady teachers.

Tom's manner was puzzling me, too. I had suspected that there might be something between the two of them, even if it was only that he was one of her favourite suitors, but I would have expected him to be more forward, more intimate, more in charge of the situation.

But it was Jane who was in charge. Tom, usually garrulous and irreverent, was suddenly awkward and unsure of himself.

'So you're one of these muscle men, too, are you, Norman?' There was a definite smirk on her face now.

The barb struck home. Who did this bird think she was? She might have most of the young blades dancing to her tune, but as far as I was concerned, she was just another prison official. I didn't give a damn about her one way or the other.

'Just think of it as another perk of your job, ma'am.' Anger had provoked me into uttering a remark that was right out of character. I instantly regretted it.

Anger now flared in her eyes, and the strength of it surprised me. I saw her whole body stiffen. 'I suppose you think that's why I do this job,' she said with a calm that belied the tension in her. Tom was just a bystander now. The interchange was between Jane and me, fury flashing between us like lightning.

As far as I was concerned, verbal arguments were the province of the middle class. My working-class experience told me that, at some stage, there would be violence. If Jane had been a man, I would have been measuring him up for a right-hander by now. But I was stymied. There was not the remotest chance that I would punch her and I had no desire to continue the acid banter.

'Is that what you think?' she demanded.

Secretly, I was amazed at her spirit. Anyone else in the jail would have thought twice before challenging me in such a way. Certainly, none of the screws would have done it. Yet here was a mere slip of a woman giving me a hard time. She forced the retort out of me.

'Whatever turns you on, ma'am,' I said almost sullenly.

'I'm surprised at you.' She had her hands on her hips now, a classic school teacher's pose, and I knew I was in for a lecture. 'I know that you've done several Open University courses, and I hoped that you would have a better understanding of things. Have you any idea at all why some women want to work in men's prisons?'

She took my silence for ignorance.

'It isn't the reason that the screws give you, you know. Or even the reason fashioned out of most prisoners' starved fantasies. Yes, I've heard the rumours about me and the favours I'm supposed to offer. All that serves to do is to make it difficult to establish any credibility with the blokes coming up to the education department.'

She paused for breath. Her face was flushed with both anger and exertion. There was no chance of either Tom or myself interrupting her now. I stood there in the face of the onslaught like a man before a firing squad. I really had touched a nerve.

However, I had sufficient detachment to see that it was all becoming quite funny now. She was obviously a feminist and a committed one at that. She had my deepest sympathy. I, too, was a committed feminist, though I had arrived at that position by a different route. It was not that I had finally come to recognise the worth, the undeniable equality, of women. I knew so little about them, having spent most of my adult life in prison. No, it was just that I had become completely disenchanted with the average male.

I had lived cheek by jowl with men in prison since I was eighteen. Instead of being impressed by supposed male strength in all its forms, I had been disgusted by the general weakness. On their own, away from their women, many men were quite lost. And when it came to courage, strength, tenacity – all supposed male attributes – so many had been found wanting. Only a small minority of men were reasonable examples of the myth of male superiority.

That was how I had come to discover my own comparative strength. Not so much in a positive way, by heroic achievements. But more from observing the weakness in others. By comparison, I was strong.

If only women could see some of their heroes in the prison context, observe the selfishness, the vanity, the dirty habits, the weakness, the gossiping and the deceit. I was pleased I didn't have a daughter. I would have despaired of her choosing a worthy mate.

Jane wasn't to know all this, though. To her, I was probably just another thug who had educated himself in prison. She knew nothing of my conversion from extreme right-wing politics to my present socialist position, my current espousal of most of the left-wing causes that had previously been anathema to me.

I had become disgusted by the futility of violence, although I was forced to continue to employ it merely to survive. There had been a sea change in my personality, and most of it unobserved. And as far as I was concerned, it would largely remain so. The change was for my personal benefit and not just for show. Now I was a more complete and happier person.

'Maybe you need to know something about Pablo Freire's work in South America, something about the factory workers and peasants in Italy in the Twenties, or even something about the women's movement to understand why I see my role as essentially a political one.' Now she was being patronising.

'It has nothing to do with revolutions or challenging tangible power structures, but rather it's to do with empowerment.' Jane paused for breath, and possibly, effect.

'Paulo,' I said suddenly.

'Pardon?' she barked at me, puzzlement twisting her features.

'It's Paulo Freire. He wrote *The Pedagogy of the Oppressed*. You said "Pablo".' I spoke matter of factly.

Jane glared at me, then physically gathered herself to continue, but she had lost some of her momentum. She was determined to finish, even though she felt she had already said too much.

'Empowerment isn't about getting inmates to rebel, Norman, or about subverting prison regimes. It's about subverting a much wider, deeper system of which prisons and inmates are only a part.'

Realising she was in danger of going on too long, she plunged towards the end. 'What I try to do is to encourage people to take control over their own lives.'

Then she was finished. She had definitely lost control and knew it. She had been carried away by the passion of her own rhetoric and it had taken a lot out of her. She stood there, still angry, but slightly embarrassed and deflated.

Suddenly I felt very sorry for her. I realised that I had provoked her. She must have known something of my background and my standing among the cons. She had felt compelled to impart her own personal philosophy to me.

I felt flattered, but at the same time disconcerted. I had seriously misjudged her. This was no gangster groupie, acting out her fantasies by working in a men's prison. My instinctive aggressive response had been way out of order. I had heard that Jane had great compassion for the prisoners she worked with, and I had just had proof that she was ferociously committed to her point of view and had incredible courage. Never, in all my years in prison, had I met a prison employee who hadn't sold out in some small way. This Jane was the first.

I had to make amends. This woman was as much 'one of my own' as any of my criminal comrades. And not because she wished to subvert the established order, but because she believed in truth and justice and all those hackneyed values that the establishment purported to embody, yet constantly devalued by conniving at their breach.

Jane still stood there, hands down by her sides now, her fists clenched. I saw that Tom, just standing there with his mouth open, was going to be no help. The argument had gone right over his head.

'Look, Jane,' I began, 'I think we've got off on the wrong foot here. From what Tom tells me, you always go out of your way to help the cons here. We've got enough enemies among the screws, without falling out with each other.'

It wasn't the best speech I had ever made. I stood and observed its effects.

The anger still burned strongly in Jane though. What was worse, it was apparent now that she felt slightly ridiculous for having blurted out the lecture.

'Well, it's very good of Tom to sing my praises like that.' Her sarcasm was thick and bitter. 'But perhaps my reputation should have impressed you more.' She shook her head vigorously as if shaking free of the argument, her hair dancing at the sides of her face like curtains in the wind. She pressed her lips tightly together, then looked down at her watch. 'Well, I must be going. My family will wonder where I am. See you both tomorrow,' and with that she was gone.

I looked at Tom and pulled a face. He shrugged and shook his head. 'What the fuck was that all about?' he asked.

'It must have been something I said.' I was laughing now. 'She's a bit stroppy, your Jane, isn't she?'

'Well, she's always been all right with me.' There was genuine puzzlement in his voice.

We walked back to the wing in silence. Jane was in both our thoughts. I regretted upsetting her, but in a way she had asked for it, even if I had misjudged her badly. I wouldn't lose any sleep over it.

Jane handed in her keys at the gate-lodge and hurried over to the rack in the carpark to collect her bike. It was a long ride to her home, but she enjoyed these late summer evenings. The dying sun in her face and the wind in her hair eased the tensions of the day. She hated to take the pressures of the prison home to Robert and the children. But she was under attack from so many sides.

Virtually every official in the jail hated her. Or, rather, hated the way she did her job. Just because she didn't spend every moment in class worrying about spelling, reading and sums but, instead, got people to use their brains. More was learned as a result of discussion and argument than from poring over reading and writing.

She could understand the authorities' concern. People who develop the capacity to think for themselves are less easy to control.

But the authorities weren't her only concern. There were those inmates keen to be noticed for their partisanship by those responsible for writing reports. This fifth column was harder for her to deal with, because she liked to be fair and open with all the prisoners. The moment she started to be devious with some, she would be acting just like the screws.

She found that she was breathing hard. Trickles of sweat ran from her armpits. She realised that she had been pedalling much faster than normal. She was still angry. She made a conscious effort to relax.

The image of Norman Parker sprang into her consciousness. She realised that he had been lurking in her mind for a while, and that that was what had been fuelling her anger.

But it wasn't his fault really. She was angry with herself. How had she allowed herself to lose control like that? She must have sounded like some dogmatic party ideologue running off at the mouth with that set-piece speech. Normally she kept her political opinions to herself while at work.

And he had laughed at her, too. The way he had caught her out over the mistake about Paulo Freire had particularly incensed her.

She realised that she had tried to impress him. Heaven knows why. He certainly didn't look very impressive himself. From what she had heard about him, she had been expecting a strapping giant, but he was short and bald and not particularly good-looking. However, it was undeniable that he was viewed with some awe by many of the inmates. No doubt much of that was due to his potential for violence. His record was disgraceful. But it wasn't only that. He clearly had a good intellect and was something of a leader. She had heard that he had led disturbances in other jails.

It occurred to her that they had certain things in common and she didn't like these parallels. She smiled when she realised that they were probably the two most hated people in the jail as far as the staff were concerned. Yet they were worlds apart. She hated violence in all its forms; he was violence personified.

In mitigation, he had spent nearly all of his adult life in prison. He was truly a product of the system. It had created him in its own image. Who was to say that she wouldn't have become violent, having to deal with swines like Hall?

That brought a fresh smile to her face. Hall had definitely been frightened by Parker's imminent arrival. For that alone she ought to forgive this surprising inmate.

She was surprised to find that she had forgiven him already. The conclusion was inescapable. They were unlikely comrades, but comrades all the same.

I awoke the following morning with the severe hump. It was nothing to do with the events of the night before. Social trivia hardly touched me nowadays.

I swam up to consciousness and instantly regretted the dawning of the new day. I closed my eyes against the early light filtering through my curtains. I tried to hide in the darkness against the impending reality of another day in prison.

A psychiatrist would have called it depression, but it was merely an understandable reaction for someone in my position. Nearly twelve years into my sentence and still I had no idea if and when I would ever be released. The criteria used to decide that were so blurred and so changeable. I felt powerless to influence my future in any positive way.

The frustration bred rage. I felt it seething at the back of my still slumbering brain, like a catalyst just waiting to trigger a violent chemical reaction. I longed to indulge the feeling, knowing that the catharsis would purge me of the incessant itch.

But the results would be catastrophic for me. Yes, I could punch Hall up in the air and kick Maypole around the centre. I could tell them to stick Knightsford and all its hypocrisy and move me out. And they would, but it would cost me eight to ten years, if not for ever. I would probably be sent to Dartmoor, where it would be instantly off with the screws. I would keep going backwards until I ended up in the dispersals again, no further advanced than the day I started, almost twelve years ago.

And that would mean death. I knew that my strength wasn't infinite. Sooner or later it would wear me down, just as it had done to so many others. You could count on the fingers of one hand those men who had survived twenty years or more without serious deterioration.

I hand-cranked my willpower into life. I knew from past experience that, just as long as I put one foot in front of the other, I would get through the day – provided that I could make that first step.

But rationality dictated that there was no alternative. Life was the only game in town. I climbed out of bed and switched on the light.

When the door opened, I marched down to the recess, ignoring everybody and everything on the way. I was in just the right mood for the German this morning. If he tried to shit in my recess, I would teach him a lesson that even his fragmented mind wouldn't forget.

The German duly appeared, shuffling along the middle of the landing. He looked to the right and then to the left, the usual self-pitying expression on his face. Big doleful eyes pleaded over an appeasing smile, his head bowed in supplication. When he reached the recess, he started to turn to the right, then his eyes caught mine through the window. He immediately veered to the left. I saw his mouth moving with unheard curses.

I felt no great pleasure that I had antagonised him, just relief that a confrontation had been avoided. I didn't want to take my mood out on anyone. I had little respect for those who indulged this weakness. I would just keep myself to myself until my mood passed.

Hall was by the office when I went down for breakfast.

''Allo, Norm, how you going, me old mate?' The phoney Cockney accent perfectly complemented the false sentiments.

I couldn't handle his hypocrisy this morning. I toyed with 'Bollocks' as a riposte, but managed to substitute 'All right, guv,' as I swept past.

He was still next to the office, waiting for me, when I returned with my breakfast.

'Norm, Norm, can I have a quick word?' he pleaded, concern showing clearly on his face.

I stopped right in front of him.

'Norm, you don't look too happy this morning. Is something wrong?'

I looked into the bloated face. Of course something was wrong. I had spent the last dozen years getting up every morning to face the mind-numbing boredom of another day in prison. It was a pointless existence and I was finding it ever more difficult to motivate myself. No doubt I would pull out of it as the morning progressed. But at the moment, I, very understandably, was pissed off with all things prison.

Would Hall understand that, though? He undoubtedly had his own swings of mood, but then he was a 'normal' person while I was a convicted murderer. By definition, my feelings could only be abnormal. And any deviation from an even, pleasant mood could possibly herald trouble.

I had no wish to be referred to the psychiatrist for so-called depression. I didn't want the screws going on red alert every time I walked about with the hump. It seemed that, at Knightsford, I couldn't even allow my emotions to show.

'No, I'm all right, guv. Just didn't sleep too well last night, that's all.' The lie slipped smoothly off my tongue.

'Oh, that's all right, Norm,' said Hall, relieved. 'If ever there's anything wrong, you just come and let me know.'

As I walked away, I could feel his eyes boring into the back of my head. I lived in the land of the emperor's new clothes. Hypocrisy ruled. No one ever said what was truly on their minds.

The boredom of fixing the components to the circuit boards drained most of my ire. I worked away on my own, not speaking to anyone, and by mid-morning I was back in full control again. I consoled myself that I was lucky to be in a relatively well-resourced jail like Knightsford.

Just before 11.00, the 'poison dwarf' strolled over and informed me that I was wanted back at the wing office.

Hall was standing behind the desk when I entered the office. 'John Deal, the probation officer, would like to see you, Norm. I'll let you into the Admin block.'

Just past Mrs Frank's office, I saw a door with 'JOHN DEAL' written on it. I knocked and heard a voice shout, 'Come in!'

Deal was sitting behind a desk reading a newspaper. 'Oh, you must be Norman Parker,' he said, waving me to sit in the chair in front of the desk. He put the paper in a drawer.

Deal had a worn, dishevelled look. The grey hair, lined face and crumpled appearance spoke of a man who had settled for less than his original ambitions.

'Sorry I wasn't here the other day when you arrived, Norman.' His speech was clipped and precise. 'I believe you saw Mrs Frank?' I nodded.

Deal leaned forward, putting his elbows on the desk and clasping his hands together. I guessed this was candid mode, and I wasn't to be disappointed.

'Norman,' he said, looking me straight in the eye, 'I want to be completely frank with you. I was a petty officer in the Royal Navy, so it's impossible to pull the wool over my eyes.'

This *non sequitur* temporarily confused me. What possible connection could there be between being a naval officer and having the ability to discern whether inmates were being truthful or not? For a start, he was operating in a totally different milieu.

The Royal Navy is an élite organisation, with high self-esteem and motivation. The men are all volunteers who are well fed and cared for. They are trained towards one particular aim, that of working with their officers to carry out warfare at sea. Their mutual safety depends on their level of expertise.

None of us prisoners was here voluntarily. We were far from being an élite body of men and were universally castigated and condemned. Our officers were, by and large, rejects from other occupations. They regularly lied to us and assessed us by such narrow criteria that to tell them the truth could be distinctly dangerous to us. In short, there were absolutely no parallels at all.

I realised that I was in the presence of a monumental prick. The problem was that he was quite a powerful prick, *vis à vis* myself and my future. I would have to be very careful in what I said.

He opened a folder that lay on his desk and questioned me about the various moves I had made in the previous fourteen months. There had been nine of them, including to Knightsford. I explained about the court case, knowing that all the details were there in front of him.

'Well, Norman,' he said as I finished, 'that's all behind you now, and you're at Knightsford. What do you think of it here?'

'The facilities are very good, much better than anywhere else I've been,' I answered truthfully.

'And what do you think of the other residents?' He studied me closely, awaiting my reply.

What could I say? What was he looking for? If I told him that they were the most dispirited, demoralised, spineless bunch of cons I had ever seen in my life, would he be pleased at my honesty? I very much doubted it.

'They're . . . they're . . .' I hesitated, searching for an answer.

Luckily, Deal answered the question for me. He leaned forward with a knowing smile on his face, as if, at long last, I finally understood. He shared this revelation with me. 'They're ordinary people, Norman, ordinary people. Knightsford's lifers are just like anyone you could meet in the street.'

Well, whatever I had expected from him, it wasn't that. If he had said that they were all Martians, I wouldn't have been so surprised. I realised just how close I had come to putting my foot in it.

I nodded as if in agreement as my mind raced to come to terms with such a ridiculous statement. I didn't doubt that there must be a few normal people among Knightsford's cons, but was he really speaking about the bizarre collection of nutters I had observed over the past few days. The German, Dougie, Brown, Foxy, Alfred E. Neumann, Harold the hunchback in reception and scores more. Were these even remotely normal?

I was sure that they weren't. What he meant was that they were well behaved and sufficiently subservient. Obviously, the ultimate sin at Knightsford was to have a rebellious spirit.

Thankfully, the interview was over now. I ached to get away

from this fool before I spoke my mind. I would have plenty of physical freedom at Knightsford, but little psychological freedom. They would leave me well alone, but I would have to be careful about expressing my opinions. They could murder me with a line of writing.

I wandered back to the centre and rattled the gate. A passing screw let me through. I collected my cutlery from my cell, but it was still too early for dinner. I climbed the stairs to the twos and went to stand in the gallery that overlooked the centre. Leaning on the railing, my eyes scoured the landings, searching for all those normal people Deal had just told me about. Obviously, one of us must be wrong.

Hardly had I started looking, when Tom came along A wing. He saw me up in the gallery and climbed the stairs to join me.

'What are you doing in the "crows' nest", Norm?' he asked. 'That's what we call this, you know. Where all the fellas stand each evening, leaning on the railing and watching people go by.'

'I'm looking for ordinary people, Tom, just like you find in the street.' I told him about the conversation I had just had with Deal.

Tom laughed. 'Yeah, he's a right silly bastard, but unfortunately he's the probation officer for our wing. He's not too bad really. You're lucky you haven't got Mrs Frank.'

Suddenly, I saw Harold the hunchback from reception walk crab-like across the centre. 'Look, Tom,' I said pointing, 'he looks ordinary enough.'

Tom laughed again. 'There's a story about him, you know, Norm.'

'I thought there would be,' I replied.

'He's a terrible nonce . . .'

'Now that *is* a surprise,' I interrupted.

'He dragged a young girl away from a cricket match, raped her, strangled her, then hid the body in a cave.' Tom ploughed on before I could break in again. 'He actually took part in the search parties, even though he kept returning to the cave over the next week to fuck her dead body.'

Tom paused. It was enough to make anyone pause. But there was no chance of my interrupting him now. I had guessed Harold was a monster when I had first seen him in reception. Such a monstrous form could only have perpetrated a monstrous crime.

'He's the only surviving lobotomy case who isn't in the nut house,' Tom continued.

'Then perhaps he should be.' Now here was something I knew a bit about. I had read a couple of books and articles on psycho-surgery. The original pre-frontal lobotomies had been very crude, and virtually every patient had been left a cabbage. Harold didn't look much like a success either.

'Here's another nutter,' said Tom, interrupting my train of thought.

I looked down and saw Porter hurrying across the centre.

'And another two.' Tom was pointing at two fellas I hadn't seen before. 'They're both ex-Rampton.'

As the shops turned out, so scores more people crossed the centre beneath us. A very high proportion were either mentally ill or so eccentric that there was little difference. I didn't need any further proof though. I had already been sure that I was right and Deal was wrong.

Tom and I carried on the conversation over lunch, with Bill and Jack joining in. We picked out people in the queue to back up our side of the argument. There was no shortage of examples.

Then I told Tom about my getting up with the hump and Hall asking me what was wrong.

'They don't miss much here,' he said, suddenly looking serious. 'They call Knightsford "The Goldfish Bowl", you know. What the screws don't see for themselves, some of the cons will tell them. You have to keep a low profile here, otherwise you won't reign.'

It was all very depressing. We finished the meal mostly in silence.

That afternoon was our shop's turn for the gym. I changed into my kit and worked out on my own for an hour.

At tea, talk was mainly about the match the next day. It was one subject that seemed to bring the normally taciturn Jack alive. He vigorously argued with both Tom and Bill.

Tom and I returned to his cell for coffee. We decided to go to the gym, even though no PTI would be there and I had already had a work-out that day. There was little else to do, other than sit in our cells talking or go to watch the telly.

I was just about to leave to put on my kit when Foxy appeared at the door. If he was aware that Tom and I had slipped down to the gym without him the previous evening — and he must have been — he gave no indication of it. In fact, he was even more pleasant than usual.

'Hallo, boys,' he said, breezing in. 'Look, I was thinking of making a meal on Sunday evening and I was wondering if you both would like to join me.' Foxy looked at us, eyes wide with expectation.

Suddenly, I felt sorry for him. He was a nutter and a bully, but he had always been friendly to me. I knew he was trying to buy my friendship and it made me feel guilty. I hated bullies and bullying. The thought that I might have intimidated him into offering the meal bothered me. I desperately wanted to refuse, saying that he didn't have to buy my friendship. But I feared that would hurt him more. Behind the façade, Foxy was a desperately lonely fella.

Tom was embarrassed, too. I knew he was feeling guilty that we had slipped down the gym behind Foxy's back. He looked over at me for guidance.

'Well, the old Fox ain't been among the chickens, has he? It ain't roast chicken is it, Danny?' I thought it best to make a joke out of it.

'Well, as a matter of fact, it is,' he said, shaking his head and laughing. He grabbed both of my arms as I sat on the bed and shook me playfully.

It had been an educated guess on my part. We were allowed to buy meat from the canteen, paying for it out of our wages, and chicken was cheap and popular.

'Well, I suppose we'd better have some of that, eh, Norm?' said Tom, joining in.

'What time do you want us there, Danny?' I asked.

Foxy was well pleased. There was a broad smile on his face. 'It will be ready at six o'clock,' he said. 'Don't be late, fellas.'

'All right, Mum,' said Tom laughing.

Foxy shook him playfully, too. The unpleasantness of the work-out was forgotten now. For a terrible moment I thought that Foxy was going to ask about the gym again, but perhaps he didn't want to push his luck. Not after just making friends with us again.

'I've got a visitor coming in tonight who wants to look at my paintings, so I can't stop,' said Foxy. 'Goodnight, Norm. See you at the match tomorrow, Tom.' And with that, he was out of the door and gone.

Tom and I looked at each other and shrugged. We both felt embarrassed, knowing that we had taken the easy way out.

'There wasn't much we could do, was there, Norm?'

'No, not really. He seems determined to be on the firm with us. We've just got to make sure that he isn't round us all the time.'

'That won't be so easy once we encourage him.' Tom looked doubtful.

'Oh yes, it will,' I said with conviction, 'because I'll soon tell him to fuck off again.'

We went to the gym. Two fellas I didn't know were playing badminton while Tom and I did some sit-ups in the corner. It was a short work-out. Barely forty-five minutes later we were crossing the centre again.

Dougie was standing by the snooker table, a cue in his hand. Next to him stood a nun. She was very small, just a shade over five feet. Dougie towered above her.

His attitude had changed considerably. Not only was he quieter, but all the expletives had been deleted. He padded around the table taking occasional shots, returning to stand beside the nun. He was like a small boy with his Sunday school teacher.

'What's the nun doing here?' I asked Tom out of the corner of my mouth.

'Oh, that's Sister Anne. She's in here every Friday.' He waved across at her and she waved back. 'You wouldn't believe all the people who come in here on a Friday.' He paused. 'Here, Norm, come with me. I want to show you something.'

We walked round the snooker table and went through the door

leading to the dining hall. I immediately heard a hubbub of many voices, some raised in an attempt to be heard above the din. We turned the corner, and through the open doors I could see a huddle of people. The smell of civvy cigarettes and the fragrances of women's perfume assailed my nostrils simultaneously.

There were both men and women, dressed in civilian clothes. An equal number of cons were dressed in prison gear, although I didn't recognise any of them. The crowd was gathered in bunches in front of several dartboards fixed to the wall. Some of the people were throwing darts.

'Well, I'll be fucked,' I said in amazement. Except for the absence of drinks, it was a scene from any one of a thousand pubs up and down the country.

'You ain't seen nothing yet, Norm. You won't believe this place.' Tom pulled at my arm, leading me back the way we had come. 'There's more people here of a Friday night than there are left in Dartville. There's darts players, chess players, bridge players, lay visitors. And then there's the religious mob. The nuns, priests, vicars, monks, Jehovah's Witnesses – in fact, one of almost everything. All visiting Knightsford's poor "residents".'

We were back on the centre. 'Come on,' said Tom. 'Just stand up here a minute.'

We climbed the stairs to lean against the railing of the gallery again. There were several 'crows' already there. A couple waved to Tom, then me.

'What are we looking for?' I asked after a minute or so.

'Hang on, I'll show you,' said Tom.

Another couple of minutes went by. 'There you are.' Tom pointed. A middle-aged man in a brown monk's habit was walking along the landing. He stopped at a door, knocked, then went in.

Half a minute went by, then Tom spoke again. 'Look, Norm, down the end of A wing.'

Down on the ones, just past the recess, a tall man wearing a dog-collar was going from cell to cell. Several paces behind him followed another nun.

'What did I tell you?' Tom looked at me quizzically.

'Hypocrisy heaped on hypocrisy,' I intoned. 'There can't be a cleric left in Dartville tonight. Mind you, this lot need some fucking saving.'

Half an hour later, we had both showered and were sitting in Tom's cell. It was still only 7.00 and we had over two hours to kill.

'Where's Jack tonight?' I asked. He was usually to be found hanging around Tom's cell.

'Probably watching the telly.' Tom stood up. 'Come on, let's go over to Bill's cell. He'll probably be sitting in there with Steve. You haven't met him yet.'

Bill's cell was on the opposite side of the landing and we had to cross over the bridge to reach it.

'They're both nice kids these two, Norm,' said Tom as we walked, 'but they're a bit strange. They're absolutely inseparable. They go everywhere together. They sit in Bill's cell night after night. Often they won't even talk. Just sit there reading or listening to music. Don't expect a lively evening, but it'll make a change.'

Tom knocked on the cell door and pushed it open. I followed him in. Bill was sitting back on his bed, his back against the wall, reading a paper. He looked up slowly as we came in. I got the impression that he hadn't moved for quite a while.

He had a bored, sleepy look on his face. As he saw Tom, his face broke into a smile and he sat up. He looked pleased at the distraction.

'Hallo, Tom. Hallo, Norm,' he said. He didn't seem quite so sure of me, but there was no hostility. He quickly looked around his cell to make sure everything was tidy and that we would have somewhere to sit. It reminded me of friends' wives outside, when I had made surprise visits. He moved to the end of the bed to give us room to sit down.

'Hallo, Steve,' said Tom to a young, fair-haired fella sitting on a chair in the corner. He had been reading a book and was slumped down in his chair as if he, too, had been there for a long time.

Steve sat up and lowered the book to his lap. 'Hello, Tom.' His smile said that he was genuinely pleased to see him.

Steve and I exchanged 'Hallos' and I sat down on the bed, facing him. I realised that I had seen him a couple of times around the prison and resolved not to confuse him with the 'Steve' I had met in the education block.

He was slim to the point of being thin. His chest was completely flat like that of a pre-pubescent youth. Long fair hair hung down to his shoulders, framing a smooth, hairless face that was almost girlish. He wasn't effeminate, insofar as he didn't make feminine gestures, and his voice was deep and manly. But he was definitely a late developer. I reflected that, in one of the harder, long-term jails, Steve would have excited some interest.

He was pleasant enough, though, and quite intelligent. In fact, he was far sharper than Bill. If Tom made a joke at Bill's expense, he would be slow to grasp it, taking it seriously at first. Steve, however, would be right on it and would immediately come back with his own riposte.

They began to talk about the match the next day. They all played in the team. But as soon as I got the chance, I turned the conversation around to the subject of Foxy. That always seemed to get a laugh.

Sure enough, Steve and Bill were both enthusiastic Foxy-watchers, although I got the impression that they were a bit afraid of him. But in the privacy and safety of Bill's cell, they could indulge their interest. Soon I had them both laughing, Bill almost hysterically.

They were easy enough company. We chatted mostly about trivia, but spent a pleasant couple of hours. Before we knew it, it was nearly 9.00.

I rarely, if ever, asked about what people were in for, and certainly not to their faces. It wasn't the done thing. However, as I returned with Tom to his cell, I asked him what Steve had done.

'You wouldn't believe it, really, but he was a soldier in Northern Ireland. His sergeant was a right bastard who kept picking on him. One day Steve just snapped and shot him stone dead with his rifle.'

I tried to picture Steve in army battledress and the image just didn't gel. The smooth, girl-like youth could never have looked war-like. No doubt that had provoked the sergeant to pick on him. I guessed he would have been picked on by the other squaddies, too.

The gong went for the end of evening association. As I went down the stairs towards my cell, I saw the German slide up to a tall, fussy screw called West. He had a reputation for being pedantic and petty, but was easily intimidated.

The German tilted his head up to look up at him, almost beseechingly. West stared straight ahead, trying to ignore him.

'Gud nate, sir.' The voice was soft, pleading and full of self-pity. He reminded me of a cat rubbing up against someone's ankles.

'Good night,' said West peremptorily, still staring straight ahead.

I felt angry that any con should belittle himself by going to such lengths to ingratiate himself with a screw. Especially one so weak and arrogant as West. Where was the German's pride?

Then it occurred to me that perhaps his training had conditioned him to respond to the uniform. Maybe his confused mind had mistaken the screw for a German officer. *Obersturmbanführer* West. The very idea brought a smile to my face. Hitler wouldn't have conquered too many countries with the likes of him in the ranks. With that thought in my head, I slammed my door on another day in Knightsford.

6

When I awoke on Saturday morning, I felt quite positive about the coming day. There was no work, so I wouldn't have to put up with the 'poison dwarf' and the electrical shop until Monday. And I was quite looking forward to the football match in the afternoon too. So much more would become plain about Knightsford's pecking order. Then, tomorrow, there would be the visit from Mum and Dad, followed by dinner *chez* Fox in the evening. It wasn't an itinerary to impress a socialite, but it was quite stimulating by prison standards.

I washed and shaved in the recess as usual. I made a habit of shaving every day, even though there was little reason to. If you feel scruffy and seedy, it is all too easy to sink into a negative state of mind. Many cons allowed themselves to become undisciplined and unkempt, but this was the first step down the slippery slope towards personal deterioration and decay. Many of the lifers at Knightsford wore scruffy, dirty clothes and had a couple of days' growth of beard. Their self-respect had leached out of them until they looked as unkempt as their surroundings.

After breakfast, I decided to catch up on my washing. Working out twice a day or more meant that I got through a lot of training gear. I had a bucket crammed full with shorts, T-shirts, socks and sweatshirts. I filled several sinks in the recess, washed and rinsed the lot, then hung the clothes on lines strung across the basement stairs that led to the bath-house.

I was pleased that I now had this little routine down pat. The official, once-a-week kit change only dealt with prison-issue gear. Your personal stuff you had to wash yourself, as best you could. The actual washing wasn't the problem; it was the drying. There was little room in a cell to hang wet clothes. The lines across the basement stair-well were ideal.

Settling into a new prison was all about setting up routines like this, which allowed you to live decently. I was nothing if not a survivor. I was confident that it wouldn't take me long to get Knightsford sussed.

Unlike myself, Tom wasn't an early riser. He was also permanently grumpy in the mornings, whereas, usually, I was quite bright. At just after 9.00, I climbed the stairs to his cell with a mischievous smile on my face.

I rapped sharply on his door. 'Oi, Harris, you going to lie in bed stinking all day?' My voice was loud and abrasive.

A throaty 'Bollocks. Fuck off' came from out of the darkness.

I pushed the door open and walked in. 'Cor, it fucking stinks in here, Tom. You haven't shit in your pot, have you?'

After a few years in prison, most self-respecting cons managed to control their bowel movements so that they only used their pots for pissing in when they were locked up. Only the lazy and the low-lifes shit in their pots.

'No, I fucking ain't,' came the outraged reply. He knew I had been joking, but he was angry to think that I might have suspected him of such a thing. It was enough to damage a proud young con's reputation. 'Anyway, what time is it?'

'Nine o'clock and work-out time,' I answered. 'Come on. Let's get down there before all the bars are gone.'

There wasn't much danger of that, because few of Knightsford's 'residents' took advantage of the gym sessions. However, there was only one Olympic bar and the first ones in always grabbed it.

'Turn the light on, Norm,' the disembodied voice said from the darkness. I switched it on. Tom swung out of bed, screwing up his eyes against the light.

''Ere, ain't you got hairy legs for a young fella.' My tone was serious and I tried to keep a straight face, but a smile curled at the corners of my mouth.

Tom looked at me quickly to see if I was joking or not. Quite a few young fellas had become pals with older fellas, only to discover that the latter had ulterior motives. A few had even been raped. Predatory homosexuals were a problem for young fellas in prison.

As I saw the concern in his eyes, a broad grin split my face.

''Ere, fuck off. I ain't ready for this first thing in the morning,' said Tom, reassured now. 'You'll be all right, you cunt. There's got to be a time when you're not at your best. That's when I'll start on you.'

'You've got no chance, son. I'm right on the ball twenty-four hours a day.' I was determined to have the last word.

'You weren't the other morning, though, when Hall pulled you,' Tom came back at me.

'That was absolutely a one-off. You'll have to go some to catch me with the hump.'

Tom stood in front of his mirror, combing his hair. Then he started to pull his gym gear on. 'I'll have a shower when I come back.'

'You don't have to explain about getting up and not washing, mate.' The sarcasm was thick in my voice again. 'You're from the East End. They've still got tin baths and outside khazis over there, ain't they?'

'Yeah, but we ain't got all those spades that you got over in West London.' His laugh was loud and false.

We arrived at the gym bang on 9.15. Ted, the senior PTI, was on duty. He was a short, stocky, middle-aged man who had worked in the Australian prison service for many years. He was easy-going enough, if a bit lazy. However, he didn't have the swings of mood that Bob had.

We worked out for just over an hour, avoiding any leg work that might tire Tom for the afternoon's game of football.

I showered when I got back to the wing, then played pool on the small table at the end of A wing for a while.

Saturday dinner-time was different. Young fellas walked about the dining hall with parts of their football kit on, even though kick-off was still two-and-a-half hours away, with a bang-up in between.

There was an air of excitement, of expectation. Chests were stuck out, walks became swaggers. The football kit was a badge of pride, a personal statement. Here at least, it said, were a body of spirited men. Men to represent the prison and do battle against the invading enemy this coming afternoon.

It was all a bit adolescent for me, but I knew Tom took it very seriously, so I refrained from taking the piss. For me, there were other areas in which to demonstrate one's manhood.

The meal was dominated by talk of football. Tom, Bill and Jack all called out to various members of the team, some of whom came over to the table. There was plenty of back-slapping and mutual encouragement as they psyched themselves up for the coming game.

However, underneath all the cheeriness was an underlying tension, a nervousness. Tempers were short. It was like the strained calm before a battle. All the pressures that had built up through the week were going to be discharged in the afternoon game. I mused that, for some, organised sport was warfare by another means.

At 1.00, everyone was locked away. The screws went off duty for their dinner. I lay on my bed, dozing.

An hour later, the screws came back and unlocked us all again. I strolled along the ones to go to the toilet before watching the game. Now there were fellas walking about in full football kit. The dreary greys and blues of normal prison garb would suddenly be replaced with flashes of bright red football strip. The air was full of the harsh *clack clack* of studs on the hard floors of the landings.

I waited on the ones as Tom, Jack and Bill clattered down the stairs. They seemed serious now, minds fixed on the imminent contest. They all greeted me, but their thoughts were of the coming game.

They stopped just before the centre and looked back down C wing. JB was 'clacking' awkwardly along the ones like an overweight lady in high heels, his attention more on the act of walking in football boots than on looking about him.

'JB!' called out Tom. 'Where's Niven?'

'How the fuck do I know?' asked JB. 'I've just been unlocked like you have. Don't worry, he'll show up. He always does.'

As if on cue, Niven appeared up on the twos. He bowled along unhurriedly, looking straight ahead.

He descended the stairs towards us. A cascade of greetings followed in his wake. He hardly acknowledged them, walking up to and through the group. There was confidence mixed with arrogance on his face. This was his day and he knew it. Not only was he the captain and star player, he picked the team and virtually *was* the team.

Seeing him in football kit, I could discern the athlete, the powerful, well-muscled legs of the footballer. He walked with a rolling, but agile gait. Even though wearing studs on the hard floor, he seemed sure-footed.

Like courtiers around their king, Tom, Jack and Bill formed up behind Niven as he swept by. Richie, Eric and Foxy hurried to catch up as the group headed towards the dining hall. I noticed that Foxy was wearing the goalie's kit. A smile came to my face. This should be good for a few laughs.

I let the 'warriors' push ahead, as I waited for JB to catch up. 'Arrogant little prick,' he muttered as he joined me, nodding towards Niven's back as he disappeared through the doorway. Being that bit older, he wasn't at all overawed by him. I gathered that there was more than a little ill-feeling within the side.

It was bright and sunny outside as we left the dining hall. All the footballers ran on to the pitch, collecting several footballs from a nearby bench as they went. I strolled over to the far side and sat down with my back to the wall.

More footballers appeared from out of the darkness of the dining hall. Steve emerged with Pete and another fella I didn't know. Finally, George came strolling out.

There were about forty or fifty inmates sprinkled around the pitch in groups of twos and threes, and a bunch of screws had gathered around the bench. Hall leaned against it, his enormous bulk making it look like a child's toy. Around him were Ted the PTI, West and, of course, Wade. I wasn't surprised at the latter's presence. I guessed that the Welsh football hooligan longed to be in the team.

Out on the pitch, the serious business of warming up and looking good was taking place. Foxy was ambling back and forth in the goal, like some mechanical, robotic goalie. I couldn't imagine anyone as tense and stiff as Foxy being agile enough for the job.

Fellas were frantically calling for the ball to take shots at him. Aware of watching eyes, players lashed the balls unmercifully. With everything sacrificed for power, most flew harmlessly wide of the goal.

Richie, who was thin enough when fully dressed, looked

positively Biafran in football kit. With his permanent stoop, his hooked nose and long thin limbs, I feared that one strong tackle would leave him in a heap of component parts.

Bill was like a man possessed, clearly out to do or die. He made kamikaze dashes down the left wing to cross the ball, before plunging over the line and stopping just short of the wall. I was sure that, if the situation called for it, he would cross a ball, then run full tilt into the wall.

Even in the bright red football kit, Pete looked decidedly seedy. The game hadn't started, yet his socks were already down around his ankles. He was unshaven and his skin had an unhealthy pallor. This would have told me that he was a druggie even if I hadn't already known.

I saw him gather a ball just outside the penalty area. He rolled it to just in front of the penalty spot, then walked to the side of it like a golfer addressing a golf ball. He rose on the balls of his feet, his elbows sticking out like chickens' wings, and ran several short steps towards it, like a prima ballerina with her laces tied together. With a final flourish, he struck the ball viciously with his right foot.

Or, at least, that's what he intended to do. If he had been watching the ball more carefully instead of being concerned with how he looked, he might have noticed that the ball was resting in a slight depression, one of scores dotted about the pitch. Suddenly his right toe came into sharp contact with the mound in front of the ball. Instead of flying towards the waiting Foxy as everyone expected, the ball stayed right where it was. The effect on Pete was far more dramatic.

As his toe struck the ground, you could see the shock wave run right through his body. He seemed to freeze in exactly the position he had adopted, still on the balls of his feet, elbows out at his sides, his eyes looking down his body. Then he slowly crumpled to the ground, clutching at his leg just below his right knee. Without uttering a sound, he rolled in agony in the dirt.

Niven immediately burst out laughing. It was a loud bray, designed to maximise Pete's discomfort. Not the sort of supportive behaviour one expects from one's captain, I thought.

Richie and Eric ran over to help Pete to his feet. With him hopping on one leg, they half carried him to the touch-line where he sat with his back to the wall, gingerly and painfully rubbing his toe.

'That's all right, he's only the sub,' shouted Niven, still laughing.

JB and George, older than the others, seemed to be taking everything much easier. They were standing close to each other, bending and stretching, and only bothering to kick the ball when it came near them.

Tom, Steve, Jack and Niven were knocking a ball about

between them, setting each other up for shots at Foxy. I noticed that Niven took as many shots as the other three put together. However, he lashed the ball with either foot and with little or no effort. They all screamed past Foxy into the net.

'Good shot, Niven,' called Foxy each time, as he sheepishly collected the ball from the back of the net. Niven just looked at him with contempt, the beginnings of a smirk on his face. I couldn't tell if he was pleased that his shot had gone in or was contemptuous of the abilities of this goalie on whom the match could depend.

The identity of the one fella I didn't know was soon revealed to me. He had been knocking a ball about with Bill when Niven suddenly screamed out, 'Starling!' He looked up like a child caught misbehaving, fear in his eyes. He scrambled to kick the ball over to Niven, then, embarrassed, looked down quickly. Niven, grinning, collected the ball, showing a child's pleasure at being obeyed so quickly. He was quite a bully, I concluded.

Suddenly, there was a flash of colour at the far end of the pitch as the outside team in all-yellow kit appeared. At the same time, I saw Maypole and the Chief stroll along the opposite touch-line to join Hall and the rest of the screws. It seemed that the weekly football match was quite an occasion.

A referee appeared, dressed all in black. Niven walked forward to shake hands with the opposing captain and to spin up. The two teams then lined up. Tom and Bill were playing to the right and left of Niven's centre-forward. JB, George, Starling and Richie were spread out across the mid-field. Jack, Eric and Steve were the last line of defence in front of an increasingly anxious-looking Foxy.

Suddenly, the pitch looked very small indeed. With all the men on the field, it seemed incredibly crowded. There would be no room to run with the ball. It would be like five-a-side football, but played by twenty-two. The whistle went and the game started. Our lot surged forward, eager for the tackle. Bodies crunched into bodies as a full week of prison tension expressed itself as sport. Soon, the whistle went again and there was an opposing player on the floor.

This, then, was to be the recurring pattern. Either the ball ran out of play off the small pitch or someone was injured. The whistle went with sickening regularity as the ref struggled to keep control of this demolition derby of a match.

With no room to run with the ball, most of the players just seemed to lash at it as it appeared through a forest of legs. Niven's skill, though, immediately became apparent. With his powerful legs pumping, he twisted and turned past the opposition. He pushed one, then elbowed another, with the ball at his feet all the time. His close control was amazing. It was a precocious talent, far above anything I had previously seen in prison. He was certainly good enough to be a professional.

He was constantly calling for the ball. And he always got it immediately, even if he was surrounded by opposing players. The rest of the team existed only to feed the ball to Niven's feet. And if they didn't do it quickly enough or accurately enough, his voice could be heard above all the din, roundly abusing the offender.

Suddenly, he called for the ball. Starling passed it to him immediately. There were three players between him and the goal. He elbowed one out of the way and sprinted past him. His speed was amazing. He showed the ball to the next, then swept it by him. He juggled it between his feet and got the remaining defender going the wrong way. He lashed the ball with his left foot and it flew like a bullet into the roof of the net. The goalie didn't have time to even move.

A ragged cheer ran around the pitch, and Richie, Bill and Jack all ran over to congratulate him. He ignored them as he walked back towards the centre spot. It was as if it had been his achievement and his alone and their praises were no more than he deserved. His arrogance was almost as impressive as his talent.

The screws on the touch-line were all cheering too. Maypole was clapping enthusiastically. I guessed that Niven was something of a favourite with them.

The game resumed, but it was all exactly as before. The ball came to Niven and he jinked and turned, the ball sticking to his feet like glue. Suddenly, he burst out of a knot of players again and fired the ball into the corner of the net.

By half-time, we were leading 6–0. Every goal had been scored by Niven out of situations that had demanded a solo effort.

If I had expected his mood to improve as he put more goals in the net, I was to be disappointed. Instead, he seemed to be increasingly losing control. He screamed and shouted and cursed the length and breadth of the pitch, his speech full of 'cunts' and 'fucks' and 'bastards'. Where he should have encouraged, he abused. Where praise was called for, he grudgingly held his peace.

At half-time, he sat alone on the bench, eating his piece of orange and ignoring the others. If there were any tactics to discuss, he was discussing them with himself. As spectators walked by and congratulated him on his goals, he pointedly ignored them. He only looked up to smile when Maypole and Hall walked over to him.

Within ten minutes of the start of the second half, Niven had scored three more goals. By now, though, his mood was completely out of control. He screamed like one demented every time he wanted the ball. If anything wasn't to his liking, he roared abuse at the perpetrator. It was a virtuoso performance of zero self-control.

Maypole, Hall and the other screws seemed oblivious to all this. They cheered or applauded whenever Niven did something skilful, but took no notice whenever he cursed, screamed or threatened.

I observed all this with interest. Niven was a young and

immature murderer, who had stabbed someone to death during an argument in a café, and one would have thought that Maypole and company would have shown concern over his clear and continuing lack of self-control. But not a bit of it. They smiled like indulgent fathers at the performance of a favourite son.

Tom had already told me that Niven sucked up to the screws, and that one particular Irish screw had taken him under his wing. It was suspected that Niven told him things he shouldn't have — a couple of things only he had known about had come on top.

I realised that I would have to be very careful in any clash with Niven. I wasn't particularly worried about the physical outcome, but, whatever the circumstances, official sympathy would be with him.

I didn't mind a game of football, but I didn't kid myself that I was very good at it. I had played in several prison teams before and would probably play at Knightsford. But I wouldn't put up with any of Niven's abuse.

I noticed that he reserved his particular ire for certain players. To Tom, JB and George, he said very little. And when he did abuse or criticise them, he got some abuse back. This grudging respect had no relationship to the way they were playing either. They weren't the best players on the pitch by any means. Clearly, it was because Niven was physically more wary of them. Yet more evidence of the bully in his nature.

To the other players, though, he was merciless. He seemed particularly incensed by Starling, who was quite skilful. He was nowhere near as good as Niven, but was head and shoulders above all the rest. Yet Niven criticised him incessantly. He took it all without a word in reply.

Suddenly, when we were 9–0 up, Starling burst through the mid-field and fired a useful-looking shot towards the top right-hand corner of the goal. It went just wide. Niven immediately bawled him out for not passing to him.

When the same thing happened five minutes later, the shot barely missed the left post. Niven screamed as if in pain. He ran towards Starling, pupils dilated, his face as red as flame. 'Get off, you cunt, get off!' he screamed, grabbing him by the neck with one hand. He dragged him to the touch-line and bodily threw him off the pitch. He motioned angrily to Pete, who was still sitting against the wall, to come on to the pitch. Pete hurried to obey.

If anyone was outraged by Niven's behaviour, they didn't let it show. Even the ref, who one would assume should have been put out by this novel form of substitution, waited patiently for Pete to come on to the pitch. I looked across at Maypole *et al*. They were still smiling.

It spoke volumes about the nature of the regime at Knightsford. It had nothing to do with absolute types of behaviour. The staff weren't career professionals observing their 'residents' with a detached objectivity in the interest of the general public. Rather, they were incompetent buffoons who indulged their prejudices by playing favourites. Providing you deferred to their authority, you would be all right, but if you showed any spirit, any wilfulness in directing your own life, you would earn their undying enmity.

With two minutes to go, the score stood at 12–0. The visiting team had all but given up in the face of this rout, and our players, too, were just going through the motions now. No one chased loose balls, and there was no urgency in closing down opposing players.

Suddenly, a long ball came through the middle. Its pace was too much for JB's tired legs. He watched as it went through to the opposition's centre forward, who ran with it to the edge of our penalty area. With both Eric and Jack coming to challenge him, there seemed to be no real danger.

Without looking up, the forward lashed at the ball. He caught it awkwardly and it flew between Eric and Jack, bobbling and skidding unevenly across the penalty area towards the right-hand corner of Foxy's goal.

The Fox, who had had virtually nothing to do so far, and had been standing stiff and immobile for a long time, looked surprised as the ball appeared in the penalty area. You could see the thought register that he would have to dive for this one, but it was already too late.

He fell to his left, like a cut tree. On the way down he extended his arms. He cringed in anticipation as the ground rushed up to meet him, his face showing the pain as he landed heavily. But at least he had got down for the ball, even if the move had resembled the slow-motion action replay. The only problem was that the ball was now behind him in the net.

There was a roar from our supporters, the noisiest I'd heard from them all afternoon. People were pointing at Foxy and laughing.

Niven had been standing idly by the half-way line, his hands on his hips, his interest in the game largely over. He now bellowed with rage as he saw the ball in the back of the net. He ran to the edge of the penalty area.

'Well, fuck me, Foxy,' he shouted in a very Irish voice. 'Me fucking Granny could have got that. You're fucking useless.'

Foxy made no reply as he gathered the ball sheepishly from behind him and threw it overarm towards the centre spot, his face a white mask of tension and anguish.

As the final whistle went, the score stood at 12–1, all of our goals scored by Niven. The fellas filed back into the dining hall. From the looks on their faces, you could have been excused for thinking that they had lost by that score. Niven's abuse and shows of bad temper had robbed them of any feeling of triumph, and it was clear that many, if not most, hadn't enjoyed the game. Yet I was sure that they would all be there again next week.

I walked with JB back to our wing. 'That's the last time I play with that Irish prick,' he said angrily. I said nothing, not wishing to make the situation worse.

Suddenly, there was a lot of shouting behind us on the centre. We turned to see Foxy waving his arms in the air, his face red with rage. His eyes bulged, the sinews in his neck standing out like ropes, his mouth wide open.

A tall, rangy fella stood about a yard away, cringing in the face of this verbal onslaught. I recognised him as one of the nonces that Tom had pointed out to me. This was a particularly bad one, though – he had raped and killed a young baby.

'Don't talk to me, you fucking nonce!' Foxy was screaming at the top of his voice. 'Don't talk to me about the football or anything else! If you ever talk to me again, I'll fucking kill you!'

By now, all the screws had run out of B wing office and were standing in a semi-circle a few yards from the Fox, not quite knowing what to do next. It seemed as if Foxy was about to go berserk.

All at once, he became aware of their presence. With a final roar of rage, he spun round and walked past them on his way to his cell. 'Fucking nonce, I'll break his fucking neck,' he muttered audibly as he went.

Jack, who had been standing close to the argument, now caught up with JB and me. 'What happened there, Jack?' enquired JB.

'All the fella said to him was "Good game, Danny",' replied Jack. 'He was congratulating him, but maybe Danny thought he was taking the piss.'

'Well, threatening to kill him in front of all those screws won't look so good on Foxy's record,' I remarked.

'It will only go down alongside all the rest,' said JB, shrugging.

After tea, it was time for bang-up. As the doors closed, I mused that it was probably for the best – an hour's solitude would give tempers a time to subside. I lay on my bed, listening to the radio, waiting for the football results to come on. The first item was about several players being sent off in a big London derby. I reflected that perhaps there *was* a place for Niven in professional football after all.

We were unlocked again at 5.30. I went up to Tom's cell and found Jack already there. Tom looked up quickly as I came in, alarm showing briefly in his face. He was fiddling with some paper on his table.

'Do you have a puff, Norm?' he asked.

I paused before replying. Until I came into prison, I had never seen a drug, and I had quite old-fashioned views about them. I still retained many of these. In the main, I felt they sapped the will. And while it was all very well to go away to that nice, rosy, drug-induced world to escape the awful reality of prison, each time you came back, that same reality would be waiting for you, but now it would be even harder to handle.

Then I had been told by solid, down-to-earth people that cannabis relaxed you. I wasn't a man to be swayed by someone else's opinion, however, and I decided to try it for myself.

I found that it did relax me, but more importantly, it gave me a different perspective, albeit a temporary one, on the events of the previous week. It was almost like looking through another person's eyes. I could discern where I had been over-paranoid. I could critically assess decisions I had made. I was now the voice of reason when, normally, reason wouldn't have got a look in. I felt it was a positive experience that could help me to survive.

After that, I puffed occasionally, and only at weekends. I hadn't had a puff for quite a while, though.

'Yeah, occasionally I do, Tom,' I finally answered. 'Why?'

'Well, me and Jack usually have a puff on a Saturday evening, I wondered if you wanted one, too?'

I considered the situation. The screws always made a right fuss about cannabis in the nick. Sanctions far outweighed what you would get in a court outside. Having observed the way Knightsford was run, I was sure they would take a very dim view if I were to be caught.

Tom saw my hesitation. 'Look, Norm, don't worry. We take plenty of precautions. One of us goes out on the landing to keep watch while the other's puffing.'

I must not have looked convinced. After all, I'd just had nine shanghais, and I didn't fancy a tenth.

'There's no way we want to be caught, Norm,' Tom continued. 'And we know the risks. There's a slag here called Lewis. He was passing a mate's cell and he smelled him smoking cannabis. He ran straight down to the hospital and lollied him. When the hospital screws ran up, they found nothing, but they swore they could smell cannabis. They shipped the fella out to Dartmoor the following day, just on the strength of that.'

I listened to this tale of treachery and it did nothing to reassure me. It seemed that there was a fifth column among us.

'What I'm saying, Norm,' Tom said, determined to convince me, 'is that we know it's a serious thing, but we take plenty of precautions.'

'OK, mate,' I said, deciding to rely on his advice, 'but if I'm caught, I'm going to say you made me do it.' There was a smile on my face now.

'Yeah, that's right. You can say I bullied you,' said Tom, laughing too.

He made a small pipe that was basically just a tube of paper. He cut four small spots for each of us off a brown lump of hash the size of a sugar cube. He placed a box of matches on the table and, next to this, a tin of talcum powder.

'You go first, Norm. Me and Jack'll keep watch outside for you.

If I come in and say, "It's on top," you squirt some of the talcum about and I'll throw the gear out of the window.'

They disappeared out the door. I prepared to use the pipe, hoping that my usual rotten luck wouldn't intervene tonight. I did the four spots as quickly as I could, then went outside to find Tom and Jack.

They were standing several feet along the landing, leaning on the rail. As he saw me come out, Tom broke away from Jack and walked towards his cell.

'All right?' he asked out of the corner of his mouth as he passed me.

'Better than all right.' I went to stand next to Jack.

Five minutes later, we repeated the process while Jack took his turn. Then we all went back to sit in Tom's cell.

'We usually go and watch a bit of telly on a Saturday night,' said Tom. '*Buck Rogers in the 25th Century* is on. It's a right lot of shit, but when you're out of your nut, it's quite funny. So are some of the residents in there. Come on, there's nothing else to do.'

I followed them to the big TV room that overlooked the centre. There were a dozen rows of seats, with an aisle down the middle, and about three quarters of the seats were occupied.

A game show was on as we entered. Tom walked down the aisle, then stopped as he saw Bill and Steve sitting in a row on the left. We squeezed through and sat in three empty seats next to them.

Normally, I couldn't stand to watch TV. It was a sure way to achieve brain death in prison. But my altered perception made it a novel experience. Also, I was relieved to be out of the way of the screws. The last thing I wanted tonight was Hall to stop me and ask if I was all right.

Buck Rogers eventually came on and I tried to lose myself in the make-believe world of the 25th century.

Suddenly, Tom nudged me. 'Watch this,' he whispered. He indicated a tall, thin fella who was walking down the aisle. He was elderly, with thinning grey hair that barely covered his pate. He had that anaemic, washed-out look that can come from long years spent in prison.

He paused next to an empty chair near the front. He bent to pick up a pair of spectacles from the seat. He held them up to the light to look through them, put them on and sat down.

A couple of seconds passed, then he stood up. On either side of me, Tom, Jack, Bill and Steve stood up, too.

The elderly fella beat both thighs with his hands as if brushing crumbs off his lap. Beside me, Tom, Jack, Bill and Steve brushed away the same imaginary crumbs.

With a final slap of his hands on both thighs, he sat down again. Behind him, the four mimics repeated the gesture and sat down simultaneously.

They laughed quietly among themselves. 'That's Warris,' explained Tom. 'He's totally fucking institutionalised. He does that every single time he comes in here. He's like clockwork.'

'I suppose there's a story about *him*, eh?' I asked sarcastically.

'You'd better believe it. Warris has been away twenty-seven years. He's one of Britain's longest-serving lifers. They done him for killing his second wife, then found that his first wife had died in suspicious circumstances, too. They never tried him for it, but it's on file.'

'Well, then, it ain't surprising that he's institutionalised, is it?' I commented. I looked over at Warris and vowed that I wouldn't end up like that, however long I had to do.

Another game show followed *Buck Rogers*, and as Tom wanted to watch it, I stayed, too. By the time that had finished, we had had enough TV for the evening, and the three of us returned to Tom's cell, made some coffee, then stood drinking it outside on the landing, leaning on the rail.

Observing Knightsford's 'residents' while wrecked gave me a whole new perspective on them. It was amazing how the mind tended to accept as normal bizarre things and events that had become commonplace. But if the bizarre is commonplace, does that make it normal? I didn't think so.

The effects of the puff seemed to strip away the layers of hypocrisy to reveal the reality underneath. Mental barriers that once separated types, categories and classes melted away. Everything stood out in stark relief and was assessed accordingly. The answer was very clear. Knightsford was a false and twisted world. I felt like shouting out at the top of my voice, 'The emperor ain't got no new fucking clothes! He's stark, bollock naked, so there!'

But I didn't. It was enough to know that I was right. I would play their silly games, just the same as everyone else. I wouldn't compromise my principles in any way, if I could help it, but I couldn't afford to fight everyone else's battles, too. Let them stand on their own two feet. The screws seemed to be leaving me alone now, but I had earned that through the trouble I had been in during earlier years. I would stand by Tom if he was in trouble, but the rest of the cons would have to look after themselves.

'Here comes Warris,' said Tom, interrupting my reverie.

I looked down to the ones and saw Warris hurrying along with a clear plastic jug of hot water in his hand.

'Just watch his next trick,' said Tom. 'He's collected his hot water for his cup of tea at nine o'clock. He'll go up to his cell, put the jug of water on the table outside, go in and come out with his pint mug, lift the jug up to the light and look through it, pour half of the water into the mug, leave the mug on the table while he goes into the recess to throw the rest of the water away, come out, pick up his mug from the table, then go into his cell and bang up. He does exactly the same thing every single night.'

I watched in amazement as Warris did exactly as Tom had predicted, his face expressionless as he went through his nightly ritual. I repressed a shudder. They had sentenced Warris to life, but his mind and spirit had died. Dead as any zombie, he just went through the motions now, as oblivious to the higher forms of thought and emotion as the beasts of the field. Surely death was a more honourable end than Warris's condition.

For a moment, I felt guilty that we had made fun of him, albeit behind his back. But it was the only way to deal with it. The reality was too awful to contemplate seriously. That way lay depression, madness and death. We would laugh in the charnel house to better protect our besieged sanity.

I said my goodnights to Tom and Jack, walked carefully downstairs and banged up.

I awoke Sunday morning feeling mildly exhilarated. I would be seeing my mother in the afternoon.

'Love' had almost become a word of weakness in my world, because there was no place for it. The rational must always triumph over the emotional. Yet I still loved my mother dearly. And she loved me.

I had given her little reason to be proud of me. My capacity for violence might have endeared me to my friends and comrades, but she would have been content with a far less macho son.

However, we shared a deep and caring relationship. She was totally devoted to me and wouldn't hesitate to sacrifice herself. She was truly my best friend. I fully reciprocated her feelings and longed for the day when I could be with her in her declining years.

I was no mummy's boy, though. I had spent too many years on my own in prison for that. But in this emotional wasteland, I well knew that she was the only person I felt love for, and that she was the only person who loved me. She was like an emotional anchor. It warmed my soul to know that, somewhere in the world, there was at least one person who cared for me. The bitter chill of loneliness had almost penetrated to my core, and she was the fire that prevented its further advance. My constant fear was that she would die while I was in prison. For all my strength and resilience, I didn't think I would be able to carry on if that happened.

But that fear was far from me today, for in a few short hours, I would be in her company.

My father would be there, too, but we had no emotional attachment. The rift between us was too old and too deep. I didn't love him, but I would honour him as my father. I would honour the office of father rather than the man.

I went through my usual morning routine of visiting the recess and then breakfasting. I rousted a reluctant and sleep-dazed Tom from his bed to drag him down to the gym. Afterwards, we walked through the dining hall and out into the early morning sun to cool off.

As we circuited the football pitch, a crowd of people came down some back stairs from the main building and then stood talking in the kitchen yard. There were about thirty of them, though fewer than half were 'residents'. The outsiders wore civilian clothes and were evenly split between men and women. They all looked very smart, and although the colours they wore seemed bright by comparison with the greys of the inmates, their dress was prim and proper.

'Who's that lot then, Tom?' I asked.

'Oh, they're the Christians, mate,' he replied, laughing. 'The lions will be out in a minute.'

'No, really, who are they, Tom?' I was interested now.

Tom examined the crowd more carefully. 'Oh, that's the Roman Catholic mass coming out,' he said. 'They have it every Sunday morning.'

'Look, Tom, there's Jane,' I said.

He waved to her until he caught her eye. She waved back to him, then to me, and motioned for us to come over.

I wasn't looking forward to this. It was the first time I had seen her since the episode in the gym, and I didn't much fancy the surroundings either. If she had another go at me, I could hardly volley her right outside the church and in the midst of freshly prayed Catholics.

'Hallo, Tom, hallo, Norman,' she chirped brightly as we drew close. Her face was open and friendly with a total absence of guile. It was as if the cross words on Friday had never happened.

I reflected on how nice she looked, standing there in the bright sunshine. She had on a bright red coat, with a tiny CND badge partly hidden by the lapel. Her dark brown hair seemed almost black this morning and glistened as it fell around her shoulders. Her pale, girlish face looked particularly innocent and pretty.

At times, there was something almost child-like about Jane. She seemed to exude a mixture of goodness and naïvety. I reflected that she wouldn't thank me for the remark.

She looked at our sweaty gym kit and was about to say something. But then she clearly thought better of it.

'Isn't it nice to be out in the sunshine on a morning like this?' she said blandly.

'Very nice,' we replied in unison. Obviously, this was to be a very proper exchange.

'Do you come to mass every Sunday?' I asked, deciding to take the initiative.

'Whenever I'm not doing anything with my family,' she replied, regarding me quizzically. 'Do you attend mass yourself, Norman?' I could swear that there was the beginnings of a smile at the corners of her mouth as she asked the question.

Tom laughed, and Jane looked at him sharply.

'Unfortunately I'm Jewish,' I answered quickly to explain Tom's laughter.

'Why "unfortunately"?' she asked as she turned to me again.

Now she had me. It had been a mistake and I couldn't think of a worthy reply. 'Well, perhaps I meant "fortunately",' I said. 'It serves to keep the chaplains and priests away from me.'

Jane smiled politely, but I could see that she was less than impressed by my irreverence. I reflected that, with her, I seemed to have a talent for putting my foot in it.

As I examined my motives more deeply, though, I suspected that perhaps I couldn't resist having a sly dig at her. For at the back of my mind, I found that I still considered her a prison official and the local 'belle'. I knew that this was unfair of me, and I resolved to eradicate such thoughts from my mind in future.

We all said goodbye and Jane drifted back into the crowd. As we walked away, Tom poked me in the ribs.

'You certainly have a way with words when it comes to Jane, Norm,' he remarked.

'Yeah, I know. It must be something to do with the chemistry between us.'

'I've got a visit this afternoon,' I said to Tom as we walked back to our wing after dinner. 'I'll see you at tea-time.'

'OK, Norm. Have a nice one,' he replied. We both banged up for the dinner hour.

When we were unlocked at 1.30, I went to stand by the wing office. They would tell me when my visitors arrived.

As usual, scores of people were milling about the centre, among them a number of men wearing an old blue football strip. To my experienced eye, this lot didn't look much like footballers. Great fat bellies vied for space alongside weedy, skinny frames. Many were quite elderly, some wore spectacles, and all wore bandages on one part of their bodies or another. It was a veritable 'Dad's Army' of footballers.

As I stood there watching, JB came along.

'Who's this little firm then, JB?' I asked.

'Oh, they're the "Wallies",' he replied. 'They have a match on this afternoon. Anyone who can't get in the first team and wants a game can take part. It's not a serious match, even though they've got an outside team coming in to play them. It won't be very skilful, but it's very funny to watch.'

Suddenly I noticed Sam, Eddie and Steve among the throng. They had looked much more at home in the education block, gathered around their board game. They seemed quite out of place in their football kit, like career academics reluctantly dragged from the classroom.

'Well, it's reassuring to know that there's life after the first team, JB, just in case we get too old for it,' I remarked.

'You speak for yourself, mate, you speak for yourself,' laughed JB as he walked off. 'Have a nice visit.'

Just before 2.00, a young screw came out of the office. 'You've got a visit, Parker,' he said to me. 'Do you know where to go?'

'Yes, thanks, guv.' I headed off along the ones.

Right at the end of our wing, a gate set in the gable wall stood open. I passed through and crossed an open space into the visiting room.

This was housed in a separate building, something like a miniature community hall, with toilets and a cloakroom in the foyer. Beyond was a large room with tables and chairs.

As I walked in, I was struck by the feeling of light and space. All four walls were constructed out of glass panels. There was plenty of room between the sixteen tables, all of which were empty.

I passed a screw sitting just inside the entrance and went to sit at a table in the far right-hand corner. I sat with my back to the glass, facing into the room. It was a pleasant surprise not to have a rub-down search before being allowed on the visit.

Within seconds, my mother appeared in the doorway. Following close behind, as if on a lead, was my father.

She hurried to meet me as I stood up and stepped away from the table. She threw her arms around me and we hugged each other.

'Oh, son, son.' Her voice was thick with emotion. 'I hope you'll be all right here.'

'It's OK, love,' I replied. 'Come and sit down.' I found public displays of emotion embarrassing and I didn't see why we should entertain the screw with our domestic dramas.

I sat my mother down opposite me, then turned to shake my father's hand. He gazed at me through age-dimmed eyes — at seventy-five his sight was fading fast.

'How are you, son? How are you?' he asked earnestly. He pursed his lips and wrinkled his nose as emotion threatened to bring tears. The irony was that he now appreciated the family that he had largely ignored before.

I had caused too much grief myself to be unforgiving. 'OK, Chas, OK, Chas, come and sit down,' I cajoled.

My mother had visited me in some truly awful jails, and she was full of questions about the conditions at Knightsford. When I reassured her that it was the best I had ever been in as far as facilities were concerned, she visibly relaxed.

'If it's all right here, boy, please try to settle down for a while.' She gripped my hand across the table. 'I'm not as young as I used to be, and this last year of travelling about has nearly finished me. And I've got your father to look after, too.'

I squeezed her hand. So often in the past I had got involved in trouble out of loyalty to my mates. And so often they hadn't turned out to be the mates I had thought they were. Yet I was betraying this, my best mate, every time I had a tear-up.

'Don't worry, Mum. Everything will be all right now. I'll be able to stay out of trouble here.' As I said it, I resolved to keep my promise. I would ignore Hall and Deal and the institutionalised hypocrisy, and put my mother first for a change. For the same reason, I wouldn't try to escape from Knightsford, even though security wasn't very impressive. With me on the run, the pressure would be all on my mother, and I didn't doubt that it would kill her. As it was, I could well do with a rest myself. Perhaps I could sit back for a couple of years and just see what fate sent me. At a later date, I could always change course.

As we settled into our visit, other 'residents' entered the room and sat with their visitors, but I took little notice of them. I was sure each person valued their privacy and didn't particularly want prison friendships intruding into their family life. However, I couldn't help noticing Foxy and his visitor.

He had come in soon after me and had sat at the table in the far left-hand corner. Now, as an attractive, dark-haired woman hurried across the room, he rushed to meet her. They embraced passionately in the middle of the room, then stood there, clinging to each other. For long seconds, they kissed and hugged each other in a public display that would have embarrassed teenaged lovers. Yet Foxy was my age and the woman was not in the first flush of youth. I smiled at the thought that, even in love, just as in everything else, the Fox went right over the top.

Blissfully unaware of anyone else in the room, they finally disengaged and went to sit at the corner table. Here they continued to cling to each other like reunited lovers who are soon to be parted for ever. I reflected that so much of Foxy's life was high theatre.

However, it was none of my business, and for a second, I felt guilty for looking. But I could hardly have missed such a public demonstration of passion. I turned my attention to my own visitors.

We were allowed to eat on visits at Knightsford, so my mother had brought me a chicken salad. We talked as I ate, with my father mostly staring over my shoulder and out through the glass panels.

I turned to see what he was so interested in and smiled when I saw the 'Wallies' running about the pitch in pursuit of the ball. My mother gestured for me to leave him alone. He lost track of conversation so easily now that dialogue with him was difficult. I continued to chat with my mother.

Suddenly, Hall walked into the room and went to stand by the screw. He looked over to me and, when he had caught my eye, nodded and smiled.

I nodded and smiled in return. My mother looked around, then also smiled at him.

'Who's that?' she whispered as she turned to face me again.

'That's Hall, the SO in charge of my wing,' I said, keeping my voice down. 'He's a two-faced bastard, but he's all right with me. He knew me at Parkhurst, so he leaves me alone.'

'Oh,' said my mother, but there seemed more to that single syllable than just a simple exclamation.

'Why's that?' I asked.

She leaned forward to whisper even though Hall was several yards away. 'He was on the gate when they let us in. I heard the other officer tell him that the outside football team had arrived and were standing out there in the rain. The fat one, Hall, he said, "Well, if they've come here to play with these animals, then they deserve to stand out in the rain." Then he shut the gate and left them outside.'

It only confirmed what I already knew. Hall was such a monumental hypocrite. I could already picture him after the game, standing on the centre as our players came in, saying, 'Good game, boys,' in his 'We're all lads together' manner.

From the look on her face, I could tell that my mother was regretting telling me about Hall, so I quickly changed the subject.

The two hours passed very quickly. From time to time, I couldn't help but notice Foxy and his lady, still wrestling passionately in the corner. It must have been very frustrating for them and should have been embarrassing. People at nearby tables certainly looked uncomfortable. But the couple seemed oblivious to anything but each other. At the risk of sounding prudish, at their age they should have known better.

As the screw shouted for us to finish our visits, I stood and embraced my mother. In the corner, Foxy pinned his lady to the wall in his passion. I shook hands with my father and hugged him, then waved as the two of them walked slowly and reluctantly out of the room.

Foxy's goodbye was a lingering one. Slowly, they prised themselves apart, then made their way, hand in hand, to the door. The woman moved away from Foxy, still holding his hand in hers. At the extremity of their reach, their fingers briefly clutched, then the bond was broken and the woman walked away quickly without looking back. Foxy turned sharply and went to stand at the window, looking out on the now deserted football pitch, his face a mask of despair.

I was lost in my own thoughts. The visit from my mother would sustain me until she came again in a fortnight's time, but I still felt her loss. Everybody else felt the same. There had been six of us on visits, and we all now stood silently on our own, waiting for the screw to say that we could go.

I filed out of the room, again surprised not to be searched before being allowed back on the wing. Clearly, there was a high degree of trust at Knightsford.

The serving of tea was already in progress. I collected mine and carried it back to my cell. I waved to Tom and Jack as I passed our table and called across that I would see them after bang-up. I was in no mood for company.

As I lay down in my cell for the tea-time hour, I felt that, with the visit behind me, I could now settle into Knightsford more easily. My mother knew now that I was all right, and that would take the pressure off her. And knowing that, it would take the pressure off me. Provided that the likes of the German didn't drive me mad, the future, for a change, looked quite rosy.

Just before we were unlocked, I put on a freshly pressed pair of denims and one of my better T-shirts. If Foxy had been good enough to invite me up for a meal, the least I could do was to make myself presentable.

When my door was unlocked, I went straight up to Tom's cell. I was pleased to see that he also had dressed for the occasion.

'How was your visit?' he asked as I walked in.

'Good,' I replied. 'Now my mum knows the place is OK, it's put her mind at rest. It's handy being able to have something to eat, too.'

'Yeah, the visits ain't bad here,' Tom conceded.

'Glad to see you've dressed for dinner, by the way,' I said. 'Coming from the East End, I expected you to have your overalls on and a three-day growth.'

'Don't worry about us East Enders,' Tom came back at me. 'We can show you Notting Hill mob a thing or two when it comes to being smart.'

'Who's the bird who was up visiting Foxy today?' I asked, sitting down.

Tom looked at me knowingly and laughed. 'Now that *is* a story,' he said.

'Well we've got half an hour before we're due at Foxy's, so you've got time,' I said.

'Nosy fucker, ain't ya?'

'Yeah, nearly as nosy as you, mate. You're dying to tell me about it.'

'Do you know what a KV is, Norm?'

'No.'

'Well, "KV" stands for "Knightsford Visitor". Those cons who don't get visits from family or friends can apply for a KV. They're all people picked from the local community. They volunteer to come in as often as they can and visit someone.'

'So Foxy's visitor is a KV then,' I said.

'No, not exactly,' replied Tom, smiling again. 'Her husband's Foxy's KV.'

I sat there, looking puzzled. 'What you've got to realise, Norm, is that we're dealing with the Fox. He's slippery and devious. Nothing's ever straightforward.'

Tom settled down on his bed, reaching for the pillow and placing it between his back and the wall. I guessed this was going to be a long story.

'You've seen the Dep, Bone?' he asked.

'Yeah, JB pointed him out to me.'

'Well, he's a personal friend of Foxy's bird's husband. He asked the fella to become a KV, and Foxy ended up with him. Now, by all accounts, he ain't a bad fella. He teaches photography at the poly and he plays in a local pop group, even though he's about forty-two. So he ain't exactly dead wood.

'He started to visit Foxy twice a month. Then, he started to bring his wife up with him. She's a bored housewife, a small-town girl who's never been out of Dartville. And, like most middle-aged couples, their marriage was going through a crisis.'

Tom paused. I had no intention of interrupting him, though. I was captivated.

'After a couple of visits, Foxy got very friendly with both of them. Next thing you know, he's playing footsie with the bird under the table every time the husband goes to get the teas. Fuck knows how he didn't tumble something was going on, but then maybe he thought the Fox wouldn't do anything like that to someone who was being kind to him.'

'He obviously didn't know the Fox,' I interjected.

'Well, the fella could only come up every second week,' Tom continued. 'Foxy said that he would like a visit every week, so the bird volunteered to come up on those weeks her husband couldn't make it.'

'Had to be a get-up between them, surely?'

'Probably,' replied Tom. 'Anyway, that's what happened. One week, they come up together and Foxy and the bird play secret footsie under the table. The next week, she comes up on her own and they pull each other about for a couple of hours. It's the scandal of the nick, Norm. Everybody knows about it except the husband. The Dep's got the right hump about it. Not only is the fella his mate and he introduced him to Foxy, but you can bet your life he's terrified it'll all end up in the *News of the World*.'

I sat there shaking my head, partly in amazement, partly in disgust. There was no doubt about it: the Fox was a right liberty-taker. I was pleased that Tom and I had decided to keep him at arm's length, and now I didn't feel the least bit guilty about occasionally having a go at him.

But it was none of our business if Foxy decided to break up his visitor's marriage. The majority of Knightsford's cons would do the same if they had the opportunity. I wouldn't have done it and I was sure that Tom wouldn't have either. But we were among the few in the place who had any honour or pride.

'Come on, Tom,' I said, looking at my watch and standing up. 'It's about time to go and have dinner with that cad Foxy.'

'For fuck's sake, don't let on I've told you about the bird,' Tom said earnestly.

'Don't worry,' I replied. 'If I said anything, I would probably have a go at him. Let's just go and have a laugh.'

We walked along the twos of B wing and stopped outside Foxy's door. Normally, I would have just knocked and walked in. However, I knocked loudly three times and stayed on the step.

The door opened slowly and there was the Fox.

'Er, excuse me, is this Chez Fox?' I asked in my most formal voice.

Foxy's face split into a grin. He ran out, grabbed me in his arms and playfully shook me. 'Always taking the piss, Norm, always taking the piss,' he said, laughing.

We followed him in. The cell had been very neat and tidy the first time I had been up there, but now it was immaculate. I guessed that Foxy was obsessively fastidious. On each of several little tables, a neat table-cloth was precisely arranged to reveal the polished wood corners, and set in the middle was a small plate of biscuits. On a larger table was a white lace table-cloth with settings for three. The plates were all different patterns, but the cutlery matched. Next to each plate stood a china mug.

Foxy pointed to two stools alongside this table. Tom and I sat down.

'Bit of a piss-hole this cafe, ain't it, Tom?' I suddenly said.

Foxy grabbed me around the shoulders and wrestled me about.

'Now don't start, Norm,' he said, laughing.

'All right if I blow me nose on the table-cloth, Danny?' asked Tom.

Foxy spun round and grabbed him by the shoulders. 'And don't you start either.'

We were both finding it difficult to keep a straight face. Foxy in 'mine host' mode was too ridiculous for words. The formal setting of the meal was evidence of the difficulty Foxy had with social situations. No doubt he felt that, if there were clearly laid-out rules, he could follow them and everything would be all right.

'Would you like a cup of coffee before you start?' asked the Fox.

We both shook our heads. 'OK then, I'll just pop down and get the food.' He hurried out of the door.

He must have run all the way, for barely a minute later, he was back. He bustled in, breathing heavily, carrying a large tray. On it were several small saucepans and a baking tray containing a sizzling chicken surrounded by a dozen or so roast potatoes.

I moved back from the table lest, in his eagerness to please, the Fox dumped the lot in my lap. 'That looks nice,' I said.

Foxy's face lit up with pleasure. He had never been known to do anything for anyone else at Knightsford, but he was certainly going out of his way to make a fuss of Tom and me.

Setting the tray down on a locker, over by the window, he began carving the chicken. 'Do you want a wing or a leg?' he asked, looking up at us.

'A wing, please, Mum,' said Tom.

Foxy shot him a hard look, but he had his hands full with the chicken.

'I'll have a wing, too, please,' I said quickly. I shot Tom a look that told him to leave off until after we had eaten. I could see the chicken ending up on the floor.

Foxy set plates piled with food in front of us and sat down himself, and we started eating. It was as good a dinner as you could have got anywhere in Dartville that evening and too good to waste time talking. Within ten minutes, we were done.

As Tom and I sat back on our stools, Foxy reached for the flask of coffee. I saw him looking at some spots of gravy that had splattered the cloth next to Tom's plate, but he said nothing.

Over coffee, we talked. Foxy spoke about his painting and how he hoped to become a commercial artist when he got out. We discussed the football, the regime at Knightsford and the lifer system in general. For after-dinner conversation in prison, it was reasonably erudite. Foxy could be quite sensible sometimes.

After a while, though, the conversation flagged. I looked at my watch and saw that it was 7.30. We had been with the Fox for an hour and a half.

As Foxy saw me look at my watch, he stood up and began to clear the table. Tom and I stood up, too, intending to help him.

'It's OK, fellas. I can do it,' said Foxy.

'We ain't gonna let you wash up on your own, Danny, so don't bother to argue,' I said firmly. Good manners dictated that we didn't take advantage of him like that.

We carried all the pots and plates down to the kitchenette next to the centre, put them in a big sink and washed them. Then we carried them back up to Foxy's cell.

'Do you want some biscuits before you leave?' asked Foxy.

'Not me. I'm full up,' I replied. Tom nodded in agreement.

'Look,' said Foxy, 'do you fancy doing this every week? We could divide the cost between us and have a meal every Sunday?'

I looked over at Tom. Foxy had us here. It would sound most ungrateful if we said no. He had trapped us into being in a foodboat with him.

Tom shrugged and nodded to me. 'All right, Danny,' I said smiling. 'Let us know what to get before pay day.' Foxy looked as pleased as punch.

As we walked back towards the centre, I heard Tom laughing behind me. 'He certainly trapped us into that, didn't he?' he said.

I chuckled with him. 'Yeah, but if he's satisfied with that, it'll be a cheap price to pay for avoiding him the rest of the week.' With that thought in our minds, we went back to Tom's cell to spend the final hour before bang-up.

7

On Monday morning, just as I had mentally prepared myself for another long day of mind-numbing boredom in the electrical shop, I had a pleasant surprise. As I passed the office on my way back from breakfast, SO Gale told me that I had two call-ups. The first was with the chaplain, then the education department wanted to see me.

When the call for work went, I went up the stairs to where I had seen the chapel on my first day. On a plain door set in the wall just before it was a tiny name-plate reading 'CHAPLAIN'. I knocked, heard a muffled voice from inside and went in.

I was in an office the size of a large broom cupboard. Behind a large desk that took up almost a third of the space sat the chaplain.

I had a very low opinion of prison clerics, based on past experience. The vast majority of them were weak men whose first duty was to the Home Office and then, if the former allowed it, to God. I had been in jails where brutality and cruelty had become institutionalised, yet the chaplains and priests walked about as if nothing was amiss. They were in an ideal position to report official wrongdoing, yet rarely, if ever, did. They betrayed the very prisoners they were meant to serve, epitomising the maxim: 'There are none so blind as those that will not see.'

Of course, they were bound by the Official Secrets Act, which they had been forced to sign, and no doubt they used this as an excuse when they saw things that contradicted their Christian principles. But by putting man's law before God's, they earned the contempt of the vast majority of prisoners who despised them as hypocrites and weaklings.

This chaplain sitting in front of me didn't look much like a strong character either. Wispy fair hair hung over weak, shifty eyes that never once held mine. The lined, care-worn face seemed washed out and lifeless, holding not a vestige of hope for a prisoner asking for his help. He puffed maniacally at a cigarette in a way that suggested that smoking was a greater support to him than Christ.

'Oh, you must be Parker,' he said in a thin, reedy voice. He waved me to a chair in front of the desk.

'That's right, Chaplain,' I replied as I sat down.

'You're Jewish, aren't you?' he asked. I nodded. 'Oh, so you're not really one of mine.' I nodded again.

For a moment, he seemed at a loss for words. No doubt he had a set-piece for the regular punter. 'There's no resident rabbi here,' he finally said. 'I know there's a synagogue in Dartville, so I'll get on to them. I hope to be able to fix you up with someone.' A weak, wheedling smile crossed his face and I cringed inwardly. Here was another prison chaplain who would be more at home with the nonces and monsters.

Suddenly, I just wanted to get away from him. It was almost as if his weak spirit was sucking energy from mine. I fidgeted in my chair.

'That will do fine, Chaplain,' I said, standing up.

He seemed quite surprised that I had taken the initiative. He stood, too, and hesitantly held out his hand. I shook it reluctantly. It felt cold, limp and weak in my grip, and I resisted an urge to squeeze it tightly. 'Thanks for your time, Chaplain,' I said briskly and walked out the door.

I shook the memory of the chaplain from my mind. It was like a clammy, unhealthy thing that had no place in the bright sunlight that flooded in through the windows of the corridor. I headed in the direction of the education block and was surprised to discover that I was looking forward to the possibility of meeting Jane again.

I wasn't to be disappointed. As I walked into the office, she was sitting behind Camber's desk, with no sign of the usual incumbent.

'Hallo, Norman,' she said brightly, looking up and smiling.

'Hallo.' I was reluctant to use her first name for fear of seeming over-familiar.

'I've got some news for you about your OU course.' She reached for some papers on the desk. 'I've informed Milton Keynes of your presence at Knightsford and they will send your units here in future. If you hand in your finished assignments to me, I'll send them off for you. And I've arranged for a tutor to come in at regular intervals.'

She studied the papers more closely. 'I see that you've passed six credits already, Norman, so that means you've got your Ordinary degree. Congratulations.' She glanced up and smiled at me again.

She actually looked like she meant it. So many education staff just went through the motions. I remembered what Tom had told me about her commitment.

Unusually for me, I couldn't think of anything to say. There was a short silence, then she continued.

'Norman, the Governor won't allow full-time study here, so your study day is Wednesday. You can do your private study wherever you like. In your cell, in one of the classrooms or in the library. If you have any difficulties finding a suitable place, come and see me. In fact, come and see me if you have any difficulties at all.'

I felt that some response was called for and wondered why I felt intimidated by this woman. Perhaps it was because I now realised that she was on my side and I didn't want to say anything that might upset her again.

'I should be able to get on with it now, thank you.' I managed to smile. 'Thanks for all your help.' I turned to leave.

'Norman,' she called after me. I stopped and turned round. 'Have you met Sam, Eddie and Steve?'

'Yes, Tom introduced them to me the other evening.'

'Oh, good,' she said. 'They're nice boys and they're all on OU courses, too, although they're not as far advanced as you are. You'll find them in a classroom just down the corridor. It might help you to speak to them about the OU here.'

'Thanks, I will. And thanks again for your help.'

I went along the corridor as directed and found Sam, Eddie and Steve. They seemed genuinely pleased to see me, and Jane's assessment of them as 'nice boys' appeared quite accurate.

We chatted for a while about the OU, and they filled me in on the details of studying at Knightsford. From their account, I gathered that there was a high degree of official hostility to education, especially from the ordinary screws. But this was as it had been in every jail I had ever been in, so there was nothing unusual in that.

The more I talked to the three of them, the more I realised just how 'straight' their backgrounds had been. All well educated, they were polite to the point of being timid. I wouldn't have chosen any of them as regular companions, but that was more a reflection of my robust approach to living in prison than any serious criticism of them. However, they were trustworthy enough and easy company.

I wasn't surprised to discover that I shared something of the same politics with Eddie. With his beard, long hair, scruffy appearance and National Health glasses, he was the epitome of the trendy lefty. All that was missing were the sandals, and I later found out that he wore those about the wing.

Steve and Sam were completely different. They could truly be described as 'Thatcher's children', enthusiastic advocates of unrestrained market forces and let the Devil take the hindmost. Steve was the more reasonable of the two, his ideology incorporating strands of 'welfare capitalism'. Sam, though, was somewhere to the right of Ghengis Khan. I envisaged hours of interesting political debate with them. Tom was an interesting companion and good friend, but he wasn't in the least cerebral.

All three of them assured me that Jane could be trusted and had the best interests of the cons at heart. Eddie went further, saying that she would never grass anyone and referred to her as Knightsford's 'earth mother'.

As I left their company, I noticed our 'earth mother' in the classroom opposite. She gave me a quick wave as I passed, then returned her attention to her class. I noticed Tom and Niven sitting in the front row. I headed towards the workshop and prepared myself to spend an hour or so with the 'poison dwarf'.

Jane was pleased that Norman had taken her advice and had consulted Sam, Eddie and Steve. She hoped some of their 'niceness' would rub off on him. She had been alarmed when she had found that Tom had become friends with him. Tom was young and impressionable and easily influenced by the sorts of role models who were regarded with awe in the East End.

However, following the few encounters she had had with Norman, her opinion of him had somewhat mellowed. He certainly wasn't the animal that Hall had described. He was intelligent and proud and, from what Tom had told her, fiercely principled. But the aggression was so close to the surface. At times he seemed to almost bristle with hostility.

Suddenly, she felt guilty. Who was she to condemn him for that? Tom had told her of some of the terrible jails that he had been in. Survival had been all. And it was surprising how well he *had* survived.

All the same, she hoped he would settle down here. He certainly wouldn't be able to act up like he had elsewhere; they would ship him out immediately. But no doubt he knew that and would act accordingly. She fervently hoped he wouldn't lead Tom astray.

She turned her attention back to her class. The six of them, murderers all, sat waiting for her to begin. She often marvelled at how she had come to be here.

There was nothing in her background to suggest she might find a career in prison education. She had got a good honours degree in English from Sussex University, but her first love had been politics, and for a while she had worked for the local MP as his personal assistant. But she had felt unfulfilled. She wanted a more personal sort of contact with the people she wished to help. She trained as a social worker.

It was purely by chance that she had seen the advertisement for an assistant education officer at Knightsford. She knew absolutely nothing about prisons, except that they enjoyed an unsavoury reputation. The idea of working in one was a challenge to her. She had applied for the job and was more than surprised when she got it.

Now she had mixed feelings. She was under so much pressure from so many quarters. The punitive and uncaring outlook of the rest of the staff was totally at odds with her gentle nature. She would never claim to be a saint, but she found it impossible to connive at their official indifference.

The prisoners, too, had put her under a lot of stress. Their loneliness would often almost overwhelm them. They seized on her kindness and attention like drowning men to a raft and, in some cases, had come to depend on her totally.

To the younger ones she was a surrogate mother, or perhaps an elder sister. They would come to her and discuss their problems and their fears. To the elder ones, her role was more blurred. Some treated her like a surrogate wife, while others behaved as if she was a surrogate lover.

The ones who had killed their own wives were the most dependent. The event had shattered their lives and severely damaged their egos. What they saw as their wives' betrayal had undermined their self-confidence. The terrible question that troubled them was: did their wives' rejection imply rejection by all women? Were they so unlovable that they would be rejected in the future?

Jane's empathy towards them was often misconstrued. Or, rather, was over-reacted to. They so desperately wanted to believe that someone could care for them that some felt they shared a secret romance with her. That it was unreciprocated didn't seem to trouble them, but short of her being downright rude to them, it was virtually impossible to convince them otherwise.

However, as long as they were only secret romances, figments of their imaginations, there would be no harm done and no problems. The trouble was that, increasingly, some of them were starting to act out their fantasies.

Niven, sitting in the front row next to Tom, was a case in point. He had been little more than a child when he had first come into prison. He had welcomed Jane's kindness and concern, and she had taken the place of the mother he had left behind in Ireland. However, his immaturity, combined with a childish streak of selfishness, had quickly turned this into something else. He was now convinced that he was in love with her, and what's more, he was convinced that she was in love with him or, at the least, had led him on.

On several occasions, he had got her on her own and confronted her. He had protested his love and, when she had politely and diplomatically rebuffed him, he had become angry. Only two days before, he had demanded that she go down with him to the dining hall and get behind the stage curtain – a place where they wouldn't be disturbed.

Such a sordid scenario might have seemed funny to her if the situation hadn't been so serious. And there was no one that she could talk to about it. If she reported it to the staff, Niven would get into serious trouble, almost certainly resulting in him being shipped out. If she spoke to any of the other residents about it, there might be trouble between them and Niven or the rumour might spread. If she spoke to her husband Robert about it, he would only worry and think that the job was too much for her. Inaction seemed to be the only action open to her.

Tom, sitting next to Niven, was comparatively much more mature. He still had a childish desire to win the approval of his criminal peers, but he was far more worldly where women were concerned. He was a good-looking boy, the twinkle of devilment in his eye making him look every inch the handsome rascal. He handled his relationship with her well enough. There was no untoward overfamiliarity and certainly no thoughts of romance. Sometimes she found his rough East End humour disconcerting. He had once accused her of farting in front of the class. He had just been winding her up, but she had been dreadfully embarrassed. In time, though, she had come to regard him as both a comrade and a friend.

The thought of Dougie, sitting further across the classroom, brought an instant smile to her face. Part simpleton, part mental patient, he had a heart of gold. His rough manner and foul language belied a nature that was honest and caring. Dougie was a child in a man's world and was constantly bemused by its duplicity. She didn't doubt that he had come to depend on her and regarded her as his best mate. But he wasn't demanding of her and was content with simple friendship.

She had an especially soft spot in her heart for Neil, sitting near to the back. With his quiet, introspective ways, he was the least demanding of them all. He still carried the death of his wife like a cross, and Jane knew he secretly pined for her. He had come to find himself through study, though, and she had helped and encouraged him all she could. He was rapidly becoming a fine student.

However, he wasn't strong enough, and he never complained, about anything. Suffering with pains all over his body, he had continued to endure them until she insisted that he go to see Dr Gold, who had said that it was just rheumatism. She had her doubts, but there was little else that could be done in the circumstances. She continued to exhort Neil to take more care of himself, but she feared that he might lose the will to live.

Graham troubled her. He sat right at the back, never taking his eyes off her. He was one of those who, having killed his wife, had now transferred his affection to her. He wasn't demonstrative about it, but from the way he acted whenever he was alone with her and from some of the things he said, she knew that she would have to be very careful that she didn't encourage him.

She was surprised at him really. He had been a major in the army and was now in his early forties, and she had expected a more disciplined man. But perhaps his wife's infidelity had destroyed his emotional stability. Jane hoped that he would be content to worship her from afar.

Part of the trouble, she was sure, were the lies and innuendo that some of the staff spread about her, which were enthusiastically promoted by those residents who wished to curry favour with them. Small wonder that many prospective students came up to the education department expecting favours of a decidedly uneducational nature.

It made her job so much more difficult. It wasted so much time having to explain that they had been misled into believing that anything other than behaviour of a professional and educational nature would be achieved through any relationship with her. At first, she had found this very embarrassing. The thought that some of her prospective students might expect sexual favours from her had caused some sleepless nights. But she had dealt with it head on and was now constantly surprised about how very little embarrassed her.

Anwar Hamid, sitting over by the window, was never any trouble. A Bedouin from Saudi Arabia, his behaviour towards women was never less than completely proper. His wife and children were nomads back in his own country. Jane had brought in an Arabic-speaking student from the local polytechnic who had spent hours teaching Hamid how to read and write in his own language. Jane herself had spent hours writing out letters for him to laboriously copy. He had had to pay an interpreter/agent to deliver them to his wife and read them to her. Every month he sent all his prison earnings to a bank in Saudi for her. Often they were stolen or, for other reasons, never reached her.

He was eternally grateful to Jane and revered her to the point almost of worship. But her support wasn't enough to prevent severe bouts of depression.

This was his second indeterminate sentence: he had stabbed a man to death in similar circumstances before. His chances of ever getting out were slim and he knew it. The pressure on him was intolerable, and he often quarrelled with other residents back on the wings.

There were only six students in this, her most regular class, but they were such a diverse bunch. Their educational needs were just as diverse, too. They ranged from the most basic English, maths and social skills for Hamid and Dougie, to quite advanced sociology and creative writing for Neil and Graham. Somewhere in the middle were Niven and Tom.

And now they were all waiting patiently – or, in Niven's case, not so patiently – for her to begin. She stood up and started to write on the blackboard.

That dinner-time, I decided I had better get back into my running. I was a reasonable middle-distance runner, and running had been a regular part of my physical regimen. In the close confines of security prisons, though, it wasn't always easy to find a suitable course.

The yard surrounding the football pitch wasn't especially big, and the course I would have to run went up and down steps and around sharp corners. But it was all that was available.

It wasn't a circuit I would be able to sprint over, so running shoes weren't particularly suitable. I put on a pair of leather work boots. The extra weight would compensate for the slower speed. Three miles around the compound would still be a good work-out.

I collected my dinner and got one of the orderlies to put it in the hotplate for me to pick up later. Wearing just a T-shirt over my training bottoms, I went out into the yard.

The first couple of circuits were quite tricky as I had to concentrate on where I was placing my feet. I strode out across the open space in front of the dining hall, then pounded up the steps next to the visiting room and skipped round the ornamental pond. At the base of the wall surrounding the prison was a narrow concrete path. I ran along it to the first corner, turned through ninety degrees and opened up along the next, longer stretch. A turn through sixty degrees brought me to the end of the path. I jigged down a short flight of steps and was back on the open space in front of the dining hall. In all I had run about 250 yards. Tom had told me that twenty-one laps represented about three miles.

Soon the concrete was singing beneath my boots. I ran around the circuit, only breaking my stride for the steps and sharp corners. The sun burnt my head and shoulders, and the wind blew refreshingly in my face. Warm rivulets of sweat coursed down my neck and poured from underneath my arms.

As I ran, I felt a blissful sense of freedom. The mental shackles seemed to fall away, and the enclosing walls melted from consciousness. I could have been running across the sands of a deserted beach.

I finished with a galloping sprint and stood for a few seconds in the garden outside the dining hall to get my breath back.

I collected my dinner from the hotplate, dropped it off in my cell, then went down the steps into the bath-house for a quick shower.

When I got back to my cell, I saw that I had twenty minutes to eat my dinner before the call for work went. It would be a tight schedule, but if I were quick, I would be able to get my dinner-time run in all right.

That evening, Tom and I went to the gym as usual. Afterwards, I went for a shower, then joined Tom in his cell for a cup of coffee.

'You know, they're a strange couple, Bill and Steve,' he said with a puzzled look on his face.

'Why do you say that?' I asked as I settled back with my coffee.

'Well, I went over to Bill's just now and they've got the door wedged up.' He looked at me quizzically. I sat there, saying nothing.

'It happens quite often,' he continued. 'I saw them going off together for a shower earlier. Now the door's wedged up and the spy-hole's blocked. When I asked Bill about it before, he said they were drinking some hooch. But I knew that was a lot of bollocks because there was no hooch about.'

As I looked at him, a cynical smile played about my lips.

'What are you laughing at?' he demanded.

'You're really naïve, you know that, Tom?' I said.

'Why? Why's that?' He looked perturbed as well as puzzled.

'They're at it, that's why.'

' "At it"? How do you mean, "at it"?' Exasperation tinged his voice.

I leaned forward in my chair. 'They're fucking rumping each other, you doughnut,' I said forcefully.

'*Pah!*' said Tom explosively, rocking on the bed. 'You're such an old fucking cynic. You always think the worst. You've done too much bird, you know, that's your fucking trouble.'

'Have I?' I said, sitting back again and smiling. 'I don't think so. It's as I said: you're naïve.'

'OK,' he said, crossing his arms and trying to show a patience he clearly didn't feel. 'Why am I naïve?'

'All right, Master will explain to Pupil where Pupil has gone wrong,' I said patronisingly.

'Bollocks,' said Tom laughing. 'Just get on with it.'

'Do you know what a woodsman is?' I asked.

'Well, yeah,' he said hesitantly.

'A woodsman walks through the forest and countryside noticing all sorts of little things that we townies don't ever see, Tom. A twig broken here, a few tufts of fur there – they all tell him about the secret habits of the local wildlife. The likes of me and you walk right past these clues and don't even notice them.'

Tom looked at me, interested but puzzled as to where this was all leading.

'Well, take me,' I said, pointing to myself with both hands, 'I'm a woodsman of the prisons. Over the years, I've observed little things about people's behaviour, insignificant events that seemed quite innocent in themselves, yet later it turned out that something quite devious was going on. Now, I've got a kind of sixth sense. I can read the signs. I don't say that I'm always right, but mostly I'm not far wrong.'

'Well, OK, Mr Woodsman,' said Tom in parody, 'what's fucking going on here?'

'Let's just read the signs, Tom,' I said, quietly confident. 'We've got two young fellas who spend all their spare time together. They go everywhere together. Sometimes, they just sit in the cell together, not even speaking for long periods, just reading or staring into space. The youngest one, Steve, is very effeminate.'

Tom suddenly snorted in disagreement.

'No, I don't mean he minces about,' I said hurriedly. 'What I mean is that he's got a smooth, hairless body just like a bird and a face that's almost pretty. Often, that's nature's way of telling you that he's got a lot of female hormones in him. All us men have both sets you know, male and female.'

Tom laughed abrasively. 'You know, you're too much, Norm. You sound just like one of them nature programmes.'

I laughed too. 'Yeah, but it's all true, Tom.' I waited for him to stop laughing before I continued. 'Then you tell me that they go off for a shower together, then immediately afterwards wedge up together. You say that they aren't drinking hooch, they don't puff, and I'm pretty sure that they're not sawing the bars trying to escape. So what else is left? What illegal activity could they possibly be up to that they need to wedge up over?'

'Lots,' said Tom petulantly. He clearly did not want to believe such a thing about two people he liked and spent time with.

'Well, name some,' I challenged.

Tom sat back on the bed, deep in thought. Several seconds went by. He shook his head.

'You know what Sherlock Holmes said, Tom,' I said. 'Eliminate the impossible and what's left is the probable.'

'Yeah, well, you're not Sherlock Holmes.'

'We'll see,' I said, smiling. 'We'll see.'

Tom thought for a moment. 'Mind you, there were some queer goings-on at Maidstone when I was there,' he said. 'It was weird. Older geezers who seemed just like your dad would try to pal up with you and next thing you knew they were trying to get hold of you.'

'I know,' I said. 'I had it myself when I was your age.'

Suddenly, Tom smiled. 'I ain't being funny, Norm, but when we first palled up together, I wasn't too sure about you.'

'Oh, thanks very much!' I cried, throwing my hands in mock anger. 'Why don't you just call me a fucking nonce?'

'Oh, I soon realised it wasn't like that.' Tom hurried to reassure me, mistaking my pretend anger for the real thing.

I decided to take advantage of his mistake. 'Well, seeing as we're both being honest, Tom,' I said, 'I must tell you that I did fancy you at the beginning.'

Now it was Tom's turn to look upset. His eyes widening in surprise, a look of consternation spread across his face.

I savoured the moment, knowing that I couldn't let it go on for too long.

'However, once I got a look at those fucking hairy legs of yours, it put me right off.' I burst out into a braying laugh.

'You cunt!' shouted Tom, laughing now. He knew I had got him.

I looked at my watch. There was still an hour to go before bang-up.

'Do you fancy some beans on toast?' Tom asked.

'Wouldn't mind.'

'Come on then,' he said, jumping to his feet. He went over to his locker and took out a tin of beans. Then he picked up a plate with several slices of bread and a couple of knobs of marge on it and left the cell.

I followed as he went down the stairs, across the centre and through a doorway next to the hospital entrance. I found myself in a large room, the size of four cells. Set around the walls were two large gas stoves with ovens underneath, two commercial sinks, a large commercial toaster and several formica work-surfaces – a well-equipped kitchen by prison standards.

There was an elderly, grey-haired fella using the toaster. Another old boy, short and very fat, was standing in front of the stoves.

'You do the toast, Norm,' he said, handing me the plate with the bread and marge. 'I'll take care of the beans.'

As I waited my turn behind the fella using the toaster, Tom chose a small saucepan from among several on one of the work-surfaces. He rinsed it under the tap, opened the beans using the can-opener fixed to the wall, poured the beans into the saucepan and walked over to the stove.

The short, fat fella stepped to one side as Tom set the saucepan on the stove next to the one he was using and lit the gas. Then he came over to stand beside me.

He gestured towards the back of the fat old boy. 'Very bad nonce,' he mouthed silently, then made a wanking motion with his right hand.

I studied the fella more carefully. He was only about five feet tall, but enormously wide. He wore a huge pair of stained bib-and-brace overalls and beneath them, thick rolls of fat hung like folds in a curtain. With his thick, powerful arms and broad, square shoulders, he must have been quite a handful in his younger days. I pitied the poor woman or child who had fallen into his clutches.

As if he had become aware of my staring, he turned slowly around. It was a waddling movement, as he transferred his bulk from foot to foot. An enormous face came into view, hung with great fleshy jowls. He peered over the top of a pair of wire-framed glasses perched on the end of his nose. It was a sleepy, dozy face. He reminded me of Sleepy, one of the Seven Dwarfs, but blown up to massive proportions.

I glared back at him. He stood there for a moment, seeming puzzled by my hostility. Then he shook his head, as if suddenly realising that he might be in danger, and quickly looked away. Again, waddling from foot to foot, he slowly turned back to the stove. I felt an overwhelming urge to run over and kick him up the arse. I resisted the temptation with difficulty.

The toaster became vacant, so I stepped up to it with the bread. Tom walked over to the stove and stirred the beans. Soon the short, fat fella gathered up the two pots that were on the stove in front of him and waddled out of the room.

'That's Alf Walker,' Tom said out loud now that we were alone. 'They say he's done over thirty years. He killed a little girl during the war. He was due to go before a firing squad, but they reprieved him at the last moment. When he got out, he immediately killed another kid. He's been in ever since.'

'Fucking slag,' I said vehemently.

'Yeah, but Maypole doesn't think so,' said Tom brightly. 'He's the only lifer who's allowed to work outside the jail.'

'Where does he work?'

'With a civvy electrician. When he goes outside to work on the screws' quarters, he takes him with him. And that's not all. Once a week the civvy takes him down to the beach to paddle, and buys him a stick of rock.'

'You're fucking joking?' I said incredulously.

'I'm fucking not,' said Tom emphatically.

'Is there any chance of him getting out soon?'

'No chance. He's not up for his review for another eighteen months and he's not got much chance then,' Tom replied. 'I told you, Norm, you won't believe this place. If your face fits, you're all right.'

'Yeah, well, so much for the Home Office ruling that you can't work outside without a date or a D Cat,' I said angrily. 'You know, I'd like to write to the local papers just to let the local mums and dads know that Maypole is letting a terrible nonce out among them every week. But unfortunately I don't do things like that. What's so special about that slag? Why does Maypole like him so much?'

'I don't know,' said Tom, shrugging. 'He's very childish and always laps Maypole up. Perhaps he feels sorry for him. Mind you, he's a right fucking grass. I've seen him run when an alarm bell goes and point out to the screws where the trouble is.'

'So that makes him all right, eh? These people are such fucking hypocrites.' I shook my head in disgust.

Now the toast was ready, Tom and I headed back to his cell. Beans on toast would make a much better end to the evening than thinking about Alf Walker. We split everything between us and sat down to eat.

As Tuesday's daily round began, I reflected that it seemed as if I had been at Knightsford for far longer than just a week.

When I got to the shop, I was pleasantly surprised to find that we had another gym session that morning. Another surprise came at dinner-time when Arthur Brown spoke to me. We had been crossing the centre, with Tom a yard or so in the lead, when I saw the crusty old bastard coming towards us, his usual sour expression fixed on his granite face.

'All right, Tom?' he said as his face split into what was meant to be a smile but looked more like a carnivore about to feed.

''Allo, Arthur,' replied Tom cheerily.

'All right?' he barked as he came abreast of me.

It sounded almost like a challenge and caught me completely unawares. I had already dropped my eyes to the floor, thinking he was going to ignore me. 'All right,' I parroted in reply.

Brown swept past without a further word.

'What's up with him then?' I said to Tom. 'From the way he

performed the other day, I didn't think he liked me.'

Tom laughed. 'He's a sour old fucker, but he's very staunch. He hates the screws. He knows you're one of his own so he wouldn't ignore you. But don't expect too much from him.'

'I won't,' I replied.

Suddenly, Tom nudged my arm and pointed to a fella who was already half-way down our wing. 'Come on. We'll have a laugh here, Norm. I want you to meet this fella.'

He started to walk faster. I hurried to keep up.

'Chris!' he shouted. 'Chris!'

The fella stopped and turned around. A smile lit up his thin face as he saw Tom hurrying towards him.

'Hallo, Tom,' he called out as we drew closer. He seemed friendly enough, with no gross behavioural disorder that was immediately apparent. I would reserve judgement, though.

He did seem a bit stressed out, however. He was probably no older than his late thirties, but his thin face was lined and drawn, making him look ten years older. His hair, long and lank, hung untidily around his narrow shoulders, and he resembled an ageing hippy who had been overwhelmed by his drug problem.

'Chris, show Norm here your soft toys,' said Tom.

'OK,' replied Chris, turning into a cell. It was a mess. It had so much stuff in it that the eye had trouble taking it all in. Any serious inventory would have taken a month. Dotted all around, on chairs, tables, shelves, the bed, perched on top of books and lying on the floor was the weirdest assortment of soft toys I had ever seen.

There were several strange pigs in various sizes, a couple of lions and tigers, a giraffe, a gorilla, a bright yellow duck and a long green crocodile with white, sharp-looking teeth. The *pièce de résistance*, though, was an enormous bumble bee hanging from the ceiling, its broad yellow and black stripes catching the light as it turned slowly in the breeze from the window.

It was an incongruous setting in which to find such a collection, and I laughed heartily. Chris chuckled alongside of me. 'Good, eh?' he said.

'Yeah, terrific,' I replied enthusiastically. 'Do you sell any of them?'

'Only to people I like and *never* to the fucking screws,' said Chris forcefully. 'You can have any of them you like for a half-ounce.'

That seemed reasonable enough. 'Let me decide who I want to send one to and I'll come back to see you,' I said.

'Did you see that fat cunt Hall standing on the centre?' Chris asked Tom. Tom nodded. 'Well, I gave that cunt a coating this morning. He told me I couldn't send money out to a pal of mine. I told him it was none of his fucking business. I hate that bastard.'

It was all spoken with great vehemence, and the transformation from his previous mood was remarkable. For a second, Tom looked embarrassed, then made an excuse about having to see someone and ushered me out the door in front of him. As we walked away, I could still hear Chris chuntering back in the cell.

Tom was smiling now. 'He's all right, is Chris, but he's really fucking bitter. In fact, that's what I call him, "Bitter Chris". He's doing a recall and he's got the right hump over it. He hates the screws and goes on about them all the time. He ain't violent, but he does give them some agg. None of us like screws, but he goes on about them all the time.'

I added 'Bitter Chris' to my list of Knightsford's eccentrics.

8

Wednesday was my OU study day. It was a relief to be away from the 'poison dwarf' and his components for a while.

As the call for work went, I wandered up to the education block. Eddie, Sam and Steve were already sitting in a classroom. I went to join them.

At first, we talked about academia and politics. Then we got on to a subject that was dear to us all. It came as no surprise to me that they were all ardent 'Fox-watchers'. We shared a few stories and spent an enjoyable hour. I came out, almost dizzy from laughing.

I had decided that, although I enjoyed their company, I wouldn't get much work done if I stayed with them, so I repaired to the library annexe. With the houses of Dartville spread out panoramically before me, I settled down to study.

I got down to dinner early. As Tom and I sat at our table, there were only thirty or so people in the hall. We were so early that even the screw wasn't at his usual post by the door.

Suddenly, I saw the Fox striding purposefully into the room. His face looked pale and angry, his jaw muscles standing out in stark relief as he gritted his teeth.

At first, I thought he was heading towards us, and I mentally prepared myself for a confrontation, while wondering what I had done to upset him. However, at the last moment, he veered to the right and disappeared out of my sight behind a pillar. I craned my neck and saw him stop at a table right in the middle of the dining hall. He pulled out a chair, climbed up on it, then on to the table itself. Heads started to turn.

'Right!' he roared and stamped his foot on the table. Two inches of daylight appeared underneath the cruet set, as it skittered dangerously near the edge. There was immediate and total silence. Men stopped talking, the clinking of knives and forks ceased and servers at the hotplate paused from serving. For a long moment, all that could be heard was the gentle steaming of the coppers from within the kitchen.

'Right!' shouted Foxy again. 'I've just about had enough! This is the second week on the trot that I've gone down for my clean laundry and some bastard's taken it!' He glared around the room as if looking for the culprit.

'I'm not a nonce, I'm a fucking man!' roared the Fox, beating at his chest with his right hand. He stamped his foot again. The cruet set rose, then clattered to the floor. 'If anyone wants to have a go at me, then let them come and see me personally and not have a go at me behind my back!'

Suddenly he seemed to have run out of things to say. He stood there in stony silence, his body rigid with tension. In an effort to save the situation, the threw his arms in the air. '*Aaagh!*' he roared at the ceiling. He jumped down from the table, cannoning into a nearby chair. He kicked it out of his way and sent it clattering across the hall. Arms pumping, he stormed between the tables, past the open-mouthed screw who had just come on post, and out of the dining hall.

The silence was almost palpable. Men stood or sat in a mixture of shock and embarrassment. Some gazed at the now-empty table as if they didn't believe what they had just seen.

I looked across at Tom. His eyes were closed and his head was bent. His lips were pursed as if he was dying to say something but had thought better of it.

Around us, the dining hall started to come to life again. Men talked in whispers, almost as if they feared the imminent return of the Fox. Some were seen to shake their heads disbelievingly. The servers started serving again.

My own mood swung between anger and amusement. But the over-riding emotion was anger. For a while I had been in a potentially dangerous situation in which there had been a significant chance of violence. The resultant adrenalin rush had brought me to red alert. I could feel it still coursing through my veins.

'What a cunt,' said Tom, his eyes open now. 'Now do you see what a lunatic he is, Norm?'

'Yeah, Tom,' I replied, 'but it's all bollocks really. I was at the Scrubs with him and he was never like this. Someone would have knocked him spark out. It's gone to his head being among all these wallies.'

We ate in silence for a few minutes as the dining hall filled up around us.

'By the way, Tom,' I said suddenly. Tom looked up in surprise. 'Thanks for falling out with Foxy on the weights – otherwise he could be wrapped right around us all the time.' We both laughed. 'Mind you, if he keeps on the way he's going he'll be eating on his own on Sunday night.'

We returned to the wing and headed for Tom's cell. As we neared it we saw the Fox, his face fixed in a sombre expression, his brow deeply wrinkled as he paced up and down, deep in thought, outside Tom's cell, obviously waiting for us.

'Oh shit,' said Tom. 'I wonder what he wants.'

As we drew close, he saw us.

'Hallo, boys,' he said, his face breaking into a strained smile.

Neither of us felt like smiling back, the memory of his recent seizure still fresh in our minds. We both grunted a grudging, 'All right.'

Foxy followed us into Tom's cell. 'Look, boys,' he started, 'I just wanted to tell you that, when I had a go at those cunts down the dining hall, it wasn't directed at you.'

'Oi, Foxy,' I interrupted, 'let's get one thing straight right from the start.' My right index finger was approximately six inches from his nose. 'If I had thought for one moment that you were having a go at me, I would have jumped up and hit you right on the chin. Then we could have taken it from there. So never mind about coming round here to apologise.'

Now it was my turn to stand there with my jaws clenched and my face white and angry.

His mouth firmly closed now, the Fox dropped his eyes from my stare and hung his head. There was nothing like a bit of good, old-fashioned intimidation to put the Fox in his place.

'Look, Norm,' he said, his voice was almost a whine, 'you and Tom are my mates, I wouldn't want to upset you.'

'Well, I might as well put you right on that while you're here, Foxy.' I couldn't pass this opportunity for me to let him know exactly where he stood. 'I have very few mates in prison, mostly acquaintances. Now personally, I don't give a fuck what you do. If you want to make a cunt of yourself and get yourself shipped out, that's your business. Just make sure you don't get me shipped out, too.'

'Oh, no, I'd never involve you, Norm.'

'You've already involved me. People see you hanging about with me, then you go into one. The screws are already worried about me. They're just as likely to say that I've put you up to it. I've been shipped out for less.'

Foxy stood there like a naughty boy who has just been scolded.

'Look, I went up to that dining hall screw afterwards and apologised,' he said. 'I told him that I'd just had enough of someone nicking my laundry.'

'And you think that makes it all right then?' My sarcasm was scathing. 'All that does is make them think you're very unstable. Saying sorry afterwards don't erase it from their minds.'

'I know,' said Foxy reluctantly, dropping his head again.

'Well, as I said, it's your funeral. You do what you like. But do me a right favour.' Foxy lifted his head and looked at me. 'Don't fucking do it while I'm about.'

'All right, Norm,' he said softly, 'I'm sorry.'

Now I started to feel guilty as I saw the hurt look on his face. 'Look, Danny,' I said, 'we're all under a lot of pressure here. It's just a matter of handling it in the right way. Now I want to speak to Tom about something, so I'll see you later, eh?'

'OK, Norm. See you later, Tom.' It was a thoroughly crestfallen Fox who walked out of the cell.

'Well, you certainly told him, Norm,' said Tom, beginning to laugh.

'It's the only way with him,' I replied, straight-faced. 'I won't stand any bollocks off the Fox. I know him of old. I'll defend any man's right to self-destruct, but not if he's standing right next to me.'

'Well, if nothing else, we shouldn't see too much of Foxy for the rest of the day,' said Tom. As it turned out, it was a couple of days before we saw him again.

If I had thought that unstable behaviour was reserved solely for the 'residents', then an event the following day quickly disabused me of this notion.

We were sitting in the dining hall and it was packed. There were a lot of men sitting down and as many still standing in the queue. The noise level had risen steadily until there was quite a din.

'Khan, Khan, is Jack Khan in the room?' The loud voice cut right through the hubbub. I looked up to see an A wing screw standing several tables away.

The room went quiet. Every head turned.

'Has anyone seen Jack Khan recently?' shouted the screw.

Still there was silence. Some began shaking their heads and looking around the room. But no one spoke.

The screw turned around and walked quickly out of the room.

'Who's Jack Khan, Tom?' I asked, just as he took a mouthful of duff.

Good West London manners should probably have prevented me from speaking to him while he was eating. Good East London manners should certainly have prevented him from answering. But with a mouth full of pudding, Tom began to tell me the saga of Jack Khan. As usual, he knew all there was to know.

'You know that little fat Paki with the deed-box on his foot. The one always limping about?' he mumbled almost incoherently.

I remembered a short, tubby Indian fella about my age. I had seen him limping and noticed the thick-soled orthopaedic boot he wore. He had a permanently sad expression. 'Doleful' certainly described the long, drooping jowls, the elongated nose and the sad eyes.

It seemed he had fallen in love with an English girl, but it had all gone wrong. He was devastated. He decided to kill the girl and then himself. That evening, he strangled the girl in her flat, then went to the nearest railway lines.

Although quite educated, he was unfamiliar with things that most Englishmen would regard as commonplace. It came as quite a shock to him to find that the middle rail was electrified. There was a flash and, unconscious, he fell partially on to the tracks. He could have felt little as a train passed right over him and sliced off half his right foot.

When he had come to, it was debatable whom he was the more surprised to see – the doctors or the police. Within a day, he had been taken to a prison.

He had ended up with a life sentence, an orthopaedic boot, an occasional stutter and a permanent place as a figure of fun in Knightsford. By any other standards, his was a tragic story, but in the cynical world of Knightsford, such ineptitude could only be mocked.

'Well, he can't have escaped, not with that boot, surely?' I said. Bill and Jack laughed.

'Oh, he'll be tucked away somewhere and they'll have forgotten him,' Tom advised, still munching on the duff.

As we came through the doorway leading to the centre, on our way to Tom's cell, I saw Maypole and the Chief standing beside the snooker table. Several screws seemed to be hurrying about on various missions.

I always came on red alert when Maypole was about and if possible, stayed out of his way. My reasoning was that, if he didn't see me, he might, in time, forget about me. It was a vain hope really, but a sensible policy.

Maypole was not a happy man. His face was swollen and blood red. He had a wild look in his eye and his body movements were quick and jerky. He looked as if he was on the verge of an explosion.

The Chief stood beside him, pale-faced and concerned. He had his hand on Maypole's elbow as if trying to calm him down. He might well have succeeded if, at that moment, Jack Khan hadn't come strolling up the passageway leading from the Admin block, an impassive, dull expression on his face. He took so little interest in life now, mundane things held no interest for him. He had retired into a personal cloud of numbing grief and hid from life as best he could.

Maypole stood transfixed, his pupils dilated and his fists clenched. His chest swelled as he seemed to gather himself for some great effort.

'Khan!' he screamed. 'Where have you been?' The Chief let go of his elbow in surprise.

Khan looked up when Maypole screamed and the situation began to register on his face. However, he was still a long way from speaking.

'Khan!' screamed Maypole again. 'I asked you where you have been!' The scream tailed off into a ragged gurgle. The Chief clutched Maypole's elbow again in alarm.

With concern on his face now, Khan hurried to the gate. A screw ran to open it – there were several standing around now. In fact, everyone within fifty yards was standing and staring.

Maypole was oblivious to it all. As Khan stood timidly in front of him, he raised both arms above his head like a conductor about to strike up the band.

'WHERE . . . HAVE . . . YOU . . . BEEN?' Each word was loudly and deliberately roared into Khan's face.

The Indian's occasional stutter now let him down. As he waved one arm towards where he had just come from, his lips worked furiously but no sound emerged.

'WHERE?' screamed Maypole in a final, climactic, full-throated roar.

The blast of sound seemed to release whatever it was that had been tying Khan's tongue. 'Welfare, Welfare,' he cried. 'I've been to the Welfare.'

Maypole paused to let this quite reasonable explanation sink in. After all, if Khan had been to the probation department, someone must have let him through the gate. And that someone should have made a note of the fact that that was where Jack Khan was.

It was clearly a mistake. But the officer's mistake was as nothing compared to Maypole's. He had completely over-reacted and had called a state of alert.

He became aware that everyone was looking at him, and for a split second, he began to feel very foolish. But foolishness is not something that absolute dictators have to suffer.

'*Why didn't you tell someone?*' he shouted, but quieter now.

Khan shook his head in confusion. It was a nonsense question. It wasn't Khan's responsibility to inform anyone.

'But I was told . . .' he muttered.

'WHY DIDN'T YOU TELL SOMEONE?' Maypole shouted louder.

Something inside Khan seemed to snap. As if becoming aware of the ridiculousness of the argument for the first time, he shouted back: 'I was told to go!'

Maypole reacted as if struck. He stepped back, throwing his arms wide, narrowly missing the Chief, who moved aside with surprising speed. I reflected that he must know Maypole's habits of old.

'*Chief, get this man down the block!*' Maypole roared.

Khan stood there, frozen into immobility. So did everyone else. The order had taken everyone by surprise.

Maypole was incensed by the inaction. 'GET HIM DOWN THE BLOCK!' he screamed, looking around wildly.

Several screws hurried over. The Chief stepped forward and shooed a quivering Khan away with his hands. The screws formed up around him and ushered him away in the direction of the block on A ones.

Tom and I began to move away. We realised that we had seen enough of this little scenario and had better be on our way before Idi Amin noticed us.

'What a fucking nutter!' I said out of the corner of my mouth as soon as I thought we were out of earshot.

'And that's the prick who's going to assess us,' Tom muttered back.

As we walked in silence, I mused that, had Maypole been one of us, his little outburst would have put his release date back by several years. But then, he was the Governor.

Late on Friday evening, I was told that the rabbi was coming on Saturday morning. At 9.30 the following morning I entered the deserted visiting room, and sat at a corner table.

Several minutes passed, then a tall, well-built man came into the room. He had a bushy black beard and the familiar black hat, but from his face and manner, he could have been a priest.

He was immediately at his ease, and tried to put me at mine. I had found that, with quite a few rabbis, as soon as they knew that I had killed someone, a part of them immediately disowned me. That a Jewish boy had committed murder was quite unacceptable to them. But this rabbi wasn't like that. He asked me where my family was and if I wanted him to phone them. He asked if I was settling in OK. He told me that he had never visited the prison before, although he lived in Dartville, but assured me that he would come every fortnight.

I didn't want anything from him. Too many prison Jews belittled themselves by demanding too much of rabbis. I didn't particularly need him to reinforce my faith either. I had become my own rabbi many years previously.

But it was courteous of him to come and see me, and I would be courteous in return. There would have to be a report written on me by some cleric, so better him than either the chaplain or the priest.

He left me a bag of fruit. I resolved to try to do something for him in return.

In the afternoon, I watched the football again. I wouldn't have missed it for the world. There was a new, burly fella in goal in place of Foxy, but other than that, it was a re-run of the week before.

Niven quickly scored eight goals and the opposition had largely given up by half-time. The second half was distinguished only by a blazing row between Niven and JB, standing toe to toe, noses only inches apart. For a second it looked like they would come to blows. But the game flowed on and the incident was lost in the general mayhem.

I walked back to the wing with Tom and JB.

'Well, I know I've said it before,' fumed JB, 'but that's absolutely the last time I play with that little Irish cunt.'

'Don't worry about it,' said Tom consolingly. He looked thoroughly pissed off, too. I decided that I didn't really care if I got into Knightsford's first team or not.

The following day there was a 'Wallies' game, this time between two inmate sides. Tom told me not to play, because the standard of play would be too low and it would be demeaning to play as a 'Wally'.

I had little reputation to lose as a footballer, though. I didn't kid myself that I was anything more than an enthusiastic trier. However, I would run until I dropped, and while there might not be too much skill, I could never be faulted for effort. I looked forward to a run-out with the 'Wallies'.

I almost had second thoughts when I saw the assembled 'athletes' gathered on the centre, who looked as if a hundred-yard sprint would kill the lot of them. I noticed there were several well-known mental patients kitted up, too. With a shout of 'Go on, you Wally' echoing in my ears, I made my way out on to the pitch with the rest.

Before we kicked off, I noticed Niven and the rest of the first team sitting against the wall. I realised that some of them would be watching my performance with interest. Competition for places was fierce, and if I was to join the team, someone would have to be dropped.

The whistle went and the game began. A forward kicked the ball and it flew into the opposing team's ranks. As it came to their player, he immediately lashed at it with his foot. It flew back into our ranks.

This was to be the pattern then. As no one had the skill to trap the ball, then pass it before the opposition was on him, everyone just lashed at it the second it came near them. No one ran with the ball. The proceedings resembled one of those amusement arcade games where just the leg of each wooden footballer moves.

Suddenly, the ball flew into an open space near the touch-line. Immediately nineteen players chased after it. A pack of dogs would have had superior tactics.

Hoots of derision sounded from the touch-line. Pete seemed to be the most vociferous, closely followed by Richie. I reflected that the worst of the first team players were being the most critical.

I shouted at Eddie as he took a throw-in, and almost as a reflex, he threw the ball to me. The pack wheeled and headed towards me.

I made as if to run across the pitch, then checked and headed the other way. Several 'Wallies' collided as they tried to imitate the move. As I ran, the thunder of boots sounded behind me. I pushed the ball ahead of one of our players who had run into the opposing half. He pushed it in front of him, then trod on it. He fell heavily and several 'Wallies' fell on top of him. There was a roar of laughter from the touch-line.

But my move had been good enough. I would settle for running about and laying some decent balls off, even if the moves never came to anything.

Towards the end, a loose ball came to me at the edge of their penalty area. There was a ruck of players between me and the goal.

They turned and headed towards me.

The ball bounced awkwardly and rose to about knee height. I jumped in the air and, with both feet off the ground, volleyed the ball towards the goal. It was a passable bicycle-kick, but there was no power to it. It looked quite good, though, and sailed just past the post. There was an '*Oooh*' and a smattering of applause from the touch-line. They didn't know it, but they had just witnessed my one and only footballing trick. They would see nothing better from me.

It was a fitting end to the game for me. As I walked off, Tom came up beside me. He was laughing, but he assured me that I had had a good game.

As I went out for my run at Monday dinner-time, I was surprised to see Steve warming up. He had on boots like mine, but wore shorts and a singlet. The boots looked quite out of place on the end of his long, thin, hairless legs.

'How many laps you doing?' I called over to him.

'Twenty-one,' he called back.

'I'll run with you then, OK?' I asked.

'Sure.'

Soon we were pounding round the yard. I let him lead, being content to stay behind. I was quite a good runner and didn't want to humiliate him. We were going for a run together, not a race.

The early pace told me that he wasn't a bad runner himself, and suddenly his big boots didn't look quite so out of place. I opened up with him.

I was always a slow starter. I liked to gradually build up the pace until I was on a charge. Once I reached the speed I liked, I could hold it. My last lap would always be my fastest, which was just as well, because I was weak on sprinting. Any average runner could beat me in a sprint and I didn't have a sprint finish.

Steve's early pace stretched me to the limits. Soon my lungs were bursting, as I strained to keep up with him. There was no doubt about it, he was out to test me.

With half-a-dozen laps behind me, my lungs started to catch up with my legs. Breathing was still painful, but I knew I could hold the pace. If it was hurting me, I knew it must be hurting him. And I could handle extreme levels of pain.

We clattered up and down the steps, swerved around corners and thundered along the straights. I would stay with him now, provided he didn't have a sprint finish.

As we started the eighteenth lap, he suddenly checked. He must have been running near to his limit for a couple of laps, but now it had got too much for him. The pace slowed appreciably.

A yard behind him, I was under pressure but had got used to the pace. For a second I contemplated going past him. After all, he had tried to run away from me. But maybe that was his usual pace. I would give him the benefit of the doubt.

I slowed to match him, stride for stride. It was easy for me now. I was running well within my limits. We cruised for two laps.

At the start of the twentieth, Steve suddenly increased the pace. This took me completely by surprise, and I realised that he was building up to a sprint finish.

The slippery little bastard. He *was* out to race me. And I had let him off the hook when he ran out of steam on the eighteenth.

But it was too late now. I would never build up to his speed in time. I sprinted with him, but was ten yards behind when we finished in front of the dining hall.

In the closed world that was Knightsford, I knew it would soon go round that he had beaten me. I smarted at the defeat, but felt reassured that he'd had to kid me to achieve it. I would show him no mercy next time.

'Well done, Steve, good run,' I called over as he bent double, breathing deeply.

'Good run,' he gasped.

'When are you out again?' I asked, breathless myself.

He thought for a second, then said, 'Friday.'

'We'll do it again Friday, Steve.' I walked into the dining hall, leaving him still breathing deeply.

That evening, Tom chipped me about Steve's victory. Obviously, the young 'uns had been talking among themselves. I didn't want to make an excuse; it would sound too much like sour grapes. 'We'll see what happens the next time, mate,' was all I said.

Over these first weeks at Knightsford, I had been keeping a weather eye out for the Chief. You didn't see him about much, but apocryphal tales circulated, telling how he had caught someone doing something and had thrown the book at them.

Mostly, though, it seemed to be the screws he was after. One day, he had hidden in the bushes opposite the gate and jumped out on a screw who was slipping out to dinner early. He put him on a charge immediately. The fact that it was the Chief's day off only added insult to injury.

The fellas got a good laugh out of it, but it only added to the Chief's reputation for instability and danger. Received wisdom was that he certainly wasn't a man to mess with.

I didn't hide from him, but if I heard he was in a particular part of the jail, I would avoid it until he had gone. On those occasions when we did meet, he would always smile and look genuinely pleased to see me. Sometimes he would even reminisce about our days at Parkhurst, his perception of which regularly differed from mine.

But I could never forget his previous persona as 'God'. This was a strange jungle I was living in. The old lion might be purring like a pussy-cat now, but I was sure he could still bite like the king of cats if he wanted to. I avoided him when I could, and humoured him when I couldn't.

One morning, just before the call for work, I heard a thunderous, resonating *crash* as the Admin gate was slammed shut. I ran to my door to see what had happened and was just in time to see the Chief walking past the snooker table. He had the beginnings of a smile curling at the corners of his mouth as he looked straight ahead.

Hall and the other screws leaning on the table had anything but smiles on their faces. The shock of the sudden noise had done nothing for their early morning liverishness. If looks could kill, the Chief would have dropped dead on the spot. He was a powerful man, though, and all they could do in return was to glare at his retreating back.

I walked back into my cell smiling to myself, remembering what Tom had told me. The Chief must have crept up the Admin passage again.

Five minutes later, the call for work went. I came out of my cell and called up to Tom. Within seconds, he was clattering down the stairs to join me. We headed towards the centre on our way to work.

As we got near the table, the Chief came out of Docker's office. He was half-a-dozen paces in front of us when he suddenly looked over his shoulder. 'Hallo, Harris, you poof,' he said to Tom out of the corner of his mouth and laughed. He winked at me.

Now Tom could have his cranky moments at times, and didn't need a lot of encouragement to go right over the top. He had told me that he got on well with the Chief and had a laugh with him, but I wondered how he would deal with this. Especially so early in the morning and him not the best of risers.

'Oh, a poof am I?' he said loudly in his best East London uncouth. He suddenly held both arms out in front of him, hands crooked like claws. 'Well, let's have a quick reef of your arse then, Chief.'

The Chief had been looking away, but now he glanced behind him with some alarm on his face. From Tom's tone, it had sounded like he meant it.

With a roar, Tom ran towards the Chief, his hands reaching out for the ample behind, fingers wriggling ostentatiously in anticipation.

'Get away, Harris!' squealed the Chief, surprise mixing with consternation and the beginnings of a laugh. He scooted away from Tom, around the corner of the snooker table.

'Give us a reef of your arse, Chief!' roared Tom in hot pursuit. His fingers scrabbled against the serge encasing the Chief's rear.

'Get away!' squealed the Chief, again, his words ending in a high-pitched laugh. Tom still pursued him.

Hall's face was a picture. Here was the chief officer of the prison, a man who regularly terrorised all the screws and personally tormented him, and one of the lifers was chasing him around the centre trying to grab his arse. No screw in the jail dared to have even a mild joke with him.

Hall smiled a sickly smile, as if he found it all quite amusing. The other screws smiled with him. Like us, they always humoured the Chief, and now none of them had the nerve to say anything about the undignified spectacle before them.

Tom could have caught the Chief easily, but he had had his fun. 'I'll give you, call me a poof,' he called over his shoulder, laughing as he walked away along A wing.

The Chief was leaning against the wall, breathing heavily. The unaccustomed exertion had winded him. Between breaths, he was laughing. The screws still stood round the table, smiling discreetly.

As I made my own way along B wing towards the electrical shop, I was amazed. Tom had told me that he joked with the Chief, but I certainly hadn't thought it extended to this.

It wasn't something I was about to try myself. And I wasn't quite sure whether I should be relieved that the Chief had a sense of humour, or worried that he was obviously more unstable than I had first thought. I resolved to continue to stay out of his way.

There was one institution at Knightsford that I had, so far, managed to avoid. The weekly five-a-side session took place on a Wednesday. It was nearly as important an event in the social calendar of Knightsford's young 'uns as the Saturday league game. In fact, it served as both a training session and a trial. A bad performance on the five-a-side under Niven's eagle eye could lead to a spell on the subs bench on Saturday. Similarly, if any talent, old or new, put on a particularly spectacular performance, he could find himself among the chosen few at the weekend.

I had heard Tom talking about the five-a-side session, but was under the mistaken impression that it counted as one of our two official shop gym periods each week. The criterion for attending was, in fact, membership of the first team squad. And since Niven picked the team, he also picked the squad.

I came out of the electrical shop just before 10.00, and headed for my cell to get kitted up. I saw various members of the team hurrying along the usually deserted landings. There was excitement in the air as they called to each other.

'How's the leg?' shouted Richie to Eric.

'Oh, it'll stand up to it, I think. I've got it strapped.'

Tom came bustling along the twos, arms pumping, shoulders swaying, like a man on a mission. 'You ready for this?' he barked at Bill.

'Right I'm fucking ready!' shouted Bill, the tension thick in his voice.

Anyone watching this could have been forgiven for thinking that we were about to rumble with a hostile firm. The way our lot were gearing up for combat, surely it couldn't be just for a game of football between ourselves?

At 10.00, we were all assembled in the gym. Niven stood on his own, staring surlily at the floor. The rest looked warily at each other. Very shortly friends could be on opposing sides.

The Fox was conspicuous by his absence, no doubt sulking over being dropped from the team. JB hadn't showed either. Tom concluded that he must have meant what he had said after the last game about not playing with Niven again.

A surprise appearance was put in by Porter, he of the weedy physique and epileptic fits. He seemed to have qualified simply because he was one of Niven's most constant sycophants. One of the crumbs that fell from the team captain's table was an occasional game with the squad. *Ergo* Porter.

A second surprise was Jeff West. Bob, the PTI, was on leave. As a trained 'games officer', West would take the session.

This was something of a joke. A more 'unsporting' type than West was hard to imagine. In his early thirties, he was a compact, well-muscled man of medium height, but was totally unco-ordinated. He had absolutely no background in sport and was especially useless when it came to ball games. Coupled with his natural timidity and fussy nature, he was lost in the rough-and-tumble world of prison sport.

He also happened to be quite a nasty piece of work. His personal views had got him on the local Prison Officers Association committee, and he was a staunch member of the give-'em-nothing brigade. Unfortunately, his lack of courage curbed the open expression of his views. Therefore, he tried to achieve his goals by a mixture of cunning and deceit. He was universally disliked by the young 'uns, and he fully reciprocated their feelings.

His appearance in shorts was met by sniggers and an open hoot of derision from Niven. It was obvious that his legs were usually hidden by his long, serge trousers. They were milk-bottle white.

If he had thought that he was going to take control of the situation, then he was quickly disappointed. Niven nominated Tom to pick one team, while he picked the other.

West's second disappointment was that he wasn't going to need the whistle he wore around his neck. He had clearly envisaged a steady trot up and down, just pausing occasionally to whistle up a stoppage. However, when it became apparent that there were only eleven of us who wanted to play, West was drafted in as one of the goalies, much to his chagrin. But to refuse would have smacked of cowardice and a reluctance to be one of the boys.

We went out of the back of the gym into a small yard about forty yards long by thirty wide, bounded on three sides by the wings and on the fourth by the wall. Faded white lines could barely be discerned on the tarmac. There wouldn't be a lot of room to manoeuvre. There was also every possibility of colliding with a wall or crashing to the tarmac.

I awaited the start of the game with interest.

I wasn't to be disappointed. It was every bit as insane as I had expected.

Everyone immediately charged about as if their lives depended on it. Tackles were ferocious and executed without quarter. Two charging bodies would meet head on like battling stags. One, and sometimes both, would be sent sprawling to the tarmac. Soon, half the team carried battle wounds of scuffed knees and bleeding elbows.

Niven was in his element. His short, powerful legs carried him into the thick of the action, where he twisted this way and turned that. Explosive tackles invariably left him with the ball. In the heat of the moment, he screamed at his team and browbeat them into obedience.

On the other side, Tom had been similarly transformed. He charged into the fray, eyes wide, elbows akimbo, with no thought for anything but connecting with the ball.

Bill had completely flipped. He screamed down the wing in pursuit of every ball, even the impossible ones. He went sprawling several times and soon carried more wounds than anyone else. Seemingly oblivious to the blood pouring down on to his socks, he got up each time and re-entered the fray with renewed frenzy. So committed was he to getting stuck in that Knightsford nearly had its first footballing fatality.

The pitch had no free-standing goals, only white lines painted on brick walls. Bill charged into the goal area in pursuit of the ball. He struck it at full speed and it ricocheted off the goalie. Bill, however, was no longer concerned about the whereabouts of the ball: he had just noticed that he was bearing down on a brick wall at maximum sprint. He managed to turn his head to one side just in time. His shoulder and hip collided with the wall with such force that he bounced a good yard off it, falling to the ground like a log.

Only Steve went to help him. Bill limped about painfully as the game continued to rage about him, and made a few tentative runs down the wing. As soon as he realised that nothing was broken, he charged back in, but with a slight limp now.

At first, I had been content to run into whatever space there was and hit first-time passes. The madness was infectious, though, and before long I was as demented as the rest.

I was much better at five-a-side than full-sized football. This wasn't too much of an accolade really. It just meant that my squat, powerful, eleven stones of muscle on muscle were better suited to close-quarters combat on the tarmac than sliding about in the mud.

I had always suspected I had a death wish. Certainly, some of the things I had done in prison had been carried out with no regard for my personal safety. With the phrase 'war by another means' running through my mind like a stubborn song, I made kamikaze dashes into the action.

For Jeff West, it had all turned into a nightmare. The

footballing young 'uns were the group he most disapproved of in the whole prison, and now he was in the midst of them as they raged about the yard.

Although he had taken a short course as a 'games officer', he had never had any love for contact sports. Not only was he thoroughly inept at all games, he hated the pain and discomfort of the knocks and scrapes. At first, he had been pleased that he was in goal where, he thought, he could avoid the mayhem involved in passing and tackling. However, he soon made an alarming discovery. Although it was only a plastic ball, it hurt like hell when it hit exposed flesh.

At the start, the fellas had been intent only on the game. As they broke through to shoot, though, they suddenly realised that the detested West was lined up in their sights. Soon, vicious, full-blooded volleys were rebounding off the wall all around him.

West cringed away from one well-struck shot, only to have it crash into the fleshy part of his thigh. The pain was incredible, like an electric shock that burned on and on. He jigged up and down and rubbed his thigh in a vain attempt to make the pain go away. But by then another player was bursting through with the ball. The shot cannoned off West's hand, bending it backwards, and it felt as if he had broken his wrist.

It did nothing for his composure to notice that the fellas were laughing at him. But with the pain still burning in his thigh and wrist, he no longer cared about his reputation. He would be satisfied to get through the game in one piece.

Suddenly, Tom ran on to a ball close to goal and lashed at it in a first-time shot. The ball rocketed straight at Jeff West, who just had time to see it coming. He threw up his hands and turned his head away in a frantic effort of self-preservation. The ball flew between his outstretched arms and struck him in the side of the face with a resounding *thwack*. The force of it knocked him sideways as his glasses went skittering across the tarmac. He fell to his knees and put his head in his hands.

For the first time that day, the game stopped. Fellas stood with hands on hips and smiles on faces. No one went over to help him up.

He spent a full minute on his knees, then climbed slowly and painfully to his feet. He blinked blindly as his water-filled eyes tried to focus. There was a blood-red mark the size of a dinner plate on the side of his face. He touched it gingerly, then pulled his hand away quickly as the pain became too much. He picked up his glasses and, without a word, went to sit on a patch of grass over by the wing. He had clearly had enough for the day.

That left the teams uneven. 'OK, I'll go off, too. My fucking leg's killing me,' said Bill. He limped into the gym and disappeared. I reflected that the injury must have been bad for him to go off.

The game continued, with Niven screaming abuse at his team every time they failed to pass the ball to him quickly enough, and

Tom still charging about as if it were a cup tie. But now much of the pace had gone out of the match. Tackles were still homicidal, but the initial flood of adrenalin had been dissipated. Tired legs began to take their toll.

As I walked back to the wing with the fellas, they seemed strangely quiet, almost as if some deep need had been sated. They had withstood the fury of battle for another week and proved their manhood, and now they could retire, honourably, from the field to lick their wounds. And next Wednesday, they would be back for more.

'Good game, eh, Norm?' said Tom as he walked beside me.

'Yeah, good game,' I replied. It was all right for Tom and the rest of the young 'uns, but I was thirty-seven. One of these days I would have to grow up.

Now that I had been at Knightsford for a couple of weeks, I was right into the routine of the place. Days began to merge into identical days and weeks into identical weeks. Living in Knightsford was like watching a river. Great stretches of anonymous water flowed by with just the odd piece of flotsam to enliven the view. Looking back, there was little out of the ordinary to single out a particular day. Memory began to drown under the weight of so much routine trivia.

By now, Tom and I had relaxed into a strong, easy-going friendship. We made no great demands on each other and didn't spend every second of our spare time together, but we were mates.

We were both strong people in our own right, but together we were a force to be reckoned with. In some ways, this made us a rallying point. Other 'residents' went out of their way to befriend us and seek our opinions. I watched this situation carefully, though. I didn't want Maypole to think that we were taking over the place.

Fortunately, Tom handled it all with admirable maturity. If anything, he had become more level-headed since we had met. Other young 'uns now looked to him for a lead.

He told me that he had got his life sentence at seventeen for stabbing a fella in a row outside a club. It wasn't unexpected – that was the sort of life he had been leading.

He was the eldest of five brothers, who all considered him the leader. In the rough-and-tumble of teenaged life in the East End, fights and stabbings were commonplace. Tom was young and game and often the first to steam in. Perhaps the surprise was that it hadn't happened sooner.

Now, seven years into his sentence, he could see the futility of it all. His brothers were still doing the same things that he had done, and he feared he would get involved again if he returned home. There was a sadness in him, too. Always ready to sacrifice himself, he felt hurt that others didn't reciprocate. He saw none of his former friends and his brothers visited only rarely. This in itself had matured him.

Another power centre in the jail was Niven and whichever sycophants he was surrounded by at the moment. However, as Tom got on well with him, there was no friction between us. In fact, we rarely came into contact with each other, except when playing football.

As I watched Niven playing a variety of sports and games, I could see where the source of his power lay: he was absolutely brilliant at everything. I watched a game of basketball where he was far and away the best player, soaring to catch the ball safely, dribbling with mesmerising skill and shooting with unerring accuracy. Just as with the football, though, he was very greedy. Everything was an individual effort, but he did score the baskets.

At table tennis, too, he was virtually unbeatable. Often he would allow the opponent to build up a big lead. Then, with little or no effort, he would whip winners off backhand or forehand and win with consummate ease.

He was also excellent at volleyball, cricket and snooker. He rarely practised and often could go without playing for weeks. But when he did play again, he would invariably thrash the opposition. His talent seemed inexhaustible.

Unfortunately, his personality didn't match his talent. He was consistently moody and immature, and despite his own incredible skills, he was childishly jealous of others. This was the basis of his selfishness and greed. He would intimidate to get his own way. He was civil enough to me, though, so there was no problem. My days of playing the Sheriff of Dodge City were long past. As long as I and my close friends were all right, the rest would have to look after themselves. I had enough problems trying to survive my own sentence.

I continued to see Jane about the place, but usually only in passing. Tom saw her in class most days and he kept me regularly informed. The more he told me, the more impressed I became. She really was as he had first described her, and I wondered at her strength of character. However, I held back from getting too friendly with her. I didn't want to be thought of as another of her many 'suitors'.

It was plain that she was guided by her own conscience, too. One evening, Tom was annoyed to the point of disgust about her latest student.

'Norm, she's only teaching that fucking hunchback Harold,' he complained plaintively.

'Well, if he's put down for classes, she probably can't refuse him,' I replied.

'But he ain't, Norm. He won't even go in the education block. She takes him up into the overflow library to teach him English.' He threw his hands up in disgust.

'Tom, she ain't out of the East End. She ain't one of the "chaps". She don't believe in what we believe in. So you can't expect her to blank nonces,' I explained.

'But she's up there on her own with him,' he said with exasperation.

I paused. Harold the hunchback was as evil and unstable a nonce as I had ever seen, and I was sure that Jane could not comprehend the nature of his mind. Her natural honesty, goodness and belief in God would make her see him as one of the afflicted. But I could look through his eyes. In his ugliness, he would resent her beauty. Her kindness would strike no chord within him, who had known only cruelty. His evil nature would be repelled by her goodness. And then there was his psychotic sex drive. Like some rogue program that had run once, the urge to rape and kill could run again. The thought of her being on her own with him was worrisome. The analogy of 'Beauty and the Beast' immediately sprang to mind.

'There's nothing we can do about it, Tom,' I said after several seconds. 'We can't slip away from work to hang about the library. Anyway, she's a big girl now, I'm sure she knows what she's doing.' This last was said to reassure Tom, but I wasn't so sure of it myself.

'If that fucking nonce hurts her, I'll kick his fucking head in,' said Tom with passion.

'Oi, Sir Lancelot, just mind you don't go getting yourself into a whole lot of trouble,' I cautioned.

The sarcasm did nothing to calm him. 'I swear I'll do him if he touches her,' he said. I decided to let the matter drop.

The next time I ran with Steve, I was ready for him. I walked into the fresh air with the dinner smells strong in my nostrils to see him limbering up at the edge of the pitch.

'Doing twenty-one again, Steve?' I asked. He nodded. 'OK, let's go,' I said.

Once again Steve went off at a gallop. Soon my lungs were screaming for air as I struggled to keep up with him. I focused on the pain and lied to myself that it was manageable. I willed myself to ignore the pressure in my chest.

We passed the ten-lap mark and Steve increased the pace slightly. I felt a flicker of alarm as I wondered if he had not run his fastest last time. I clung on like grim death.

By the sixteenth, I wasn't comfortable, but I knew I could continue at that pace, providing that Steve didn't increase it again. Then, at the start of the eighteenth lap, Steve did exactly as before. As he ran out of steam, the speed slackened within three paces, and I had to check myself to avoid running into him.

But I wouldn't stand for it again. He had caught me out with that the last time. I would have to pull every last bit of energy out of him to drain his legs before the final lap. I surged past him, and as the gap widened between us, I increased the pace. The extra speed would damage me, but not nearly as much as it would damage him.

Out of the corner of my eye, I saw him try to stay with me. He increased his pace only to fall back after several strides. He knew he couldn't keep up. I had broken him.

I showed no mercy. I strode out as if I were running against the clock, and sprinted to halt just outside the dining hall. Steve was 150 yards behind me. When he finished, he bent double, deep breathing wracking his body. I walked over to him.

'Good run, Steve.' I struggled to keep any inflection out of my voice. I didn't want to take the piss, but the situation demanded that I say something.

'Yeah,' he gasped, still bent over.

'Are you OK?' I asked, concerned now.

'Yeah, yeah, I'm all right.'

I walked in, leaving him still breathing deeply by the side of the pitch.

I didn't say anything to Tom, but that evening he asked me about it. He was all the more impressed that he had heard it from Steve.

'So you done him dinner-time then?' Tom asked with a smile.

'Yeah, I suppose you could say that,' I replied, smiling myself.

'So that's one each. Who's gonna win the next one?' he challenged.

'I'll win 'em all now, mate,' I said matter of factly. Then I explained what had happened the first time. 'To tell the truth, I don't think he'll try to race me again. He knows I've got the beating of him now, and even if he does pull a stroke to win one, he knows I'll punish him the next time out.'

Sure enough, each time Steve and I went out after that, he set a healthy pace but made sure we finished together. We both grew to enjoy running together.

My first game for the prison team was something of an anti-climax. There was a thrill as I came out of my cell after the dinner-time bang-up with the kit on, a feeling that I was now one of Knightsford's élite. But I was experienced enough to know that this wasn't much of an achievement. I would need something more to sustain my interest than whatever buzz I got from wearing the first team kit.

True to his promise, JB wasn't playing. He came out to watch the game and couldn't resist remarking to me that they'd replaced one old boy with another.

The game went as all the previous ones. The rest of us were just a machine to feed the ball to Niven's feet, while he cajoled, blustered and intimidated his way to glory. I found the pace of the game very fast. No sooner had I collected the ball than someone was on me. Consequently, my game was hurried and some of my passes went astray. A fair number found their way to Niven, though. I had been ready to respond to any criticism from him, but he never said a word to me.

We won by a ridiculous margin, Niven scoring all but one of the goals. Again, this hadn't improved his humour, and he had regularly bawled out half the team.

I walked off the pitch at the end of the game and joined in the mutual congratulations, but I hadn't much enjoyed myself. Niven's bad humour had affected everyone, and I felt that I should have said something, even though he hadn't had a go at me. I realised that first team football at Knightsford would always be like this, and I resolved to drop out as soon as the pain outweighed the pleasure.

Sunday evening dinner with Foxy was rapidly becoming an institution. Now, though, Tom and I bought some of the ingredients and assisted with the preparation. It helped to pass the time on what would otherwise have been a boring Sunday evening.

When we ate with him, we would discuss the events of the week, and would check his version of any Fox stories that had come our way. Often he would tell us of some that we hadn't heard. He was rapidly becoming an observer of his own life.

There had been two incidents during the previous week, both in the shop. In the first, Foxy had gone into the office to get something out of the cabinet, and as he went through the drawers, he happened to look up. Lewis was standing at his workbench, watching him out of the corner of his eye.

The Fox had immediately lost control, perhaps remembering the time when Lewis had reported his mate for smoking cannabis and got him shipped out. Foxy ran out of the office and over to Lewis.

'Are you spying on me, you fucking slag?' he screamed, his finger hovering an inch from Lewis's nose.

Everybody in the shop stopped working and turned to watch.

'No, Danny, no, Danny.' Lewis's fat jowls quivered in fear as Foxy towered above him.

'I saw you looking at me in the office.' The tip of the Fox's finger lanced towards his victim's eyes.

Lewis jerked his head back. 'I just happened to look up, Danny,' he whined.

Foxy, now aware that all the activity in the shop had ceased, looked around and saw that every eye was on him. But as he looked, everyone looked away and began to carry on with what they had been doing. His face still a mask of rage, the Fox turned away and returned to the office.

'I might have made a mistake,' said Foxy across the table, 'but I hate that bastard Lewis.' He laughed.

Tom and I had already heard the story from another source. We looked at each other and raised our eyebrows. It was another nail in the Fox's coffin.

The second incident had come two days later. The Fox had been standing in the drawing office trying to fight off a fit of early morning pique. In the background, the light-sensitive alarms were beeping away insistently.

Suddenly, like a man at the end of his tether, the Fox roared and ran out into the main shop. He rushed over to where the alarms were being tested and switched off the light.

'How the fuck are we supposed to put up with that?' he shouted at a nearby civvy instructor. The man froze where he stood. All the civvies were wary around the Fox.

He turned and walked back towards the drawing office. Then he stopped. The other five occupants were now standing in a group looking over at him. In their midst was Starling, a smile on his face.

'What the fuck are you laughing at?' roared the Fox as he ran over to Starling again. Again, the finger was thrust into a frightened face. 'You think it's funny, you cunt? I'm the only one who's got the arsehole to come out and say something about all the noise, and you take the piss.'

'I wa-wasn't taking the piss, Danny,' stammered Starling.

'Then what was you fucking laughing at?' screamed the Fox.

'I d-don't know,' whinged Starling, on the verge of tears.

Rage had drained the blood out of Foxy's face until only his eyes burned brightly in the pallor. He glared at the cringing Starling. 'If you ever take the piss out of me again, I'll break your fucking jaw,' he threatened.

Starling said nothing, relieved that it was a threat rather than action.

Tom and I had also heard this story from someone else. Again we looked at each other and raised our eyebrows. I smiled and looked at the Fox.

'What's the matter, Norm?' asked Foxy politely.

'What's the matter?' I repeated. 'You do want to get out some day I suppose, Danny?'

'Of course I do, Norm,' he replied, looking at me as if I were stupid.

'Well, you don't think that the reports that they must be writing about you will help your cause, do you?' I was trying hard to keep the sarcasm out of my voice.

Foxy sat there for a second, thinking. 'No,' he finally said, dropping his head. 'I don't suppose they will.'

He was silent, and I thought that was the end of the matter.

'But I can't help it, Norm!' he suddenly blurted out, clenching both hands into fists and gritting his teeth.

I looked over at the manic Fox and concluded that he was right. No, he couldn't help it, and I realised that it was a waste of time to even talk about it. I changed the subject.

As we sat back after the meal, the Fox suddenly, and for the first time, started talking about his girlfriend. For that was how he described his female visitor. I reflected that her husband might have something to say about that, but held my peace.

'Caroline's told me that she intends to leave her husband,' he said gravely.

I was dying to make a funny remark, but this was a very sensitive subject with him. Instead I said, 'Do you think that's wise, in view of your situation?'

'But I love her, Norm,' said the Fox emotionally. Again his hands clenched into fists and his face twisted with passion. I wondered if there was any subject that the Fox didn't get excited about.

Presumably, he thought that this last remark answered my question. 'She just can't stand living with him any more,' he continued. 'She can't stand him touching her.' He thumped the table lightly with his fist.

'What about the kid then, Danny?' interjected Tom.

Foxy hung his head. 'She's going to take her with her.' Now he sounded embarrassed.

It was the first I'd heard about any child. The Fox, in his selfishness, was breaking up a family.

'How old's the daughter, Danny?' I asked.

'Twelve,' he replied. There was no arrogance in him now. 'I intend to marry her, boys,' he hurried to assure us as if that made it all OK.

'Well, I suppose you know what you're doing,' said Tom in a tone that said he was sure he didn't. There was a protracted silence and then we changed the subject again.

The following week saw a major change in my employment. I was told that I had served my time in the electrical shop, because now there was a vacancy in the telephone shop.

The 'poison dwarf' looked surprised when I didn't look pleased at the news. He looked even more surprised when I told him that I was content to stay where I was. Usually, 'residents' couldn't wait to go upstairs. The pay was much better and the job more interesting. But I had been to have a look a week or so previously and I hadn't been impressed.

The telephone shop was big, fully three times the length of the electrical shop. In it was situated a production line for making children's telephones. These were no toys, but quite sophisticated smaller versions of the real thing. Obviously, the prison had a contract with an outside company.

The production line was spread all around the shop. Each product was passed from table to table as pairs of cons added parts and adjusted them. Finally, the telephones were placed in boxes and two obsequious-looking cons registered them in a book.

It was all too regimented for me. They looked like galley-slaves chained to their benches. There would be no freedom, no originality in the task, each man under pressure from the men behind and those in front. Perhaps it was an affront to my socialist soul. This looked like a thousand capitalist sweatshops, exploiting the downtrodden worker. Or perhaps it was just an affront to my arrogance and individuality. I didn't want to become a slave, in spite of the extra money.

It was all apparent in their eyes as they looked up at me. They saw another victim who would soon be joining them in their misery. Their own lack of spirit would not seem so abject if everyone had to go through the process.

But I wouldn't be joining them. At least, not if I had the slightest choice in the matter. I had been pleased to discover that there was no compulsion to leave the electrical shop. But the work was so mind-numbingly boring and so poorly paid that no one had ever wanted to stay.

'I'll stay here in the electrical shop, I think, guv'nor. I don't think I could handle working on that production line.'

The 'poison dwarf' was stunned. Grudgingly, he had brought me the good news – so many others had been delighted to escape his clutches – yet here I was, saying I didn't want to go.

'I'll have a word with them upstairs,' he blustered. 'Maybe they can work something out.' He hurried away.

Ten minutes later, I was called upstairs. All eyes were fixed on me as I went into the office.

Four civvies were waiting for me. The oldest one motioned for me to close the door behind me.

'So you don't want to work in the telephone shop, Parker?'

'To be honest, I couldn't handle that production line, guv,' I replied.

'Well, how about if we gave you a job cleaning?'

'What would I have to do?'

He stood up. 'Come with me and I'll show you.'

As he led me through the shop, curious eyes followed our progress. Most new recruits got no further than the first table of the production line.

He unlocked a door at the back of the shop. It opened to reveal a small toilet containing a WC, a hand basin and a bench against the wall. It was spotlessly clean and didn't look as if it had been used for ages.

'This is a spare officers' toilet that is never used,' said the oldest civvy. 'You can use this as your office. You can sit in here and store your cleaning gear in here, too.' He turned round to face the shop. 'You would be responsible for cleaning this whole area,' he continued. 'You won't be paid as much as those on the production line, but there won't be a lot in it.'

I sized up the offer. It sounded like a good number. 'OK, guv, I think I could do that,' I said, trying not to sound too enthusiastic.

'You can start as soon as you like. By the way, my name's

Howie. What's yours?' He was certainly going out of his way to be pleasant.

'Norman, guv,' I replied, preferring 'guv' to 'Howie'.

If he was taken back by this mild rebuff, he took pains not to show it. 'OK, Norman,' he said. 'I hope you'll enjoy working up here.'

I immediately retired to my office-cum-toilet. It had definite possibilities. The bench, covered with cushions, would double as a bed where I could sleep away some of the long hours spent in the shop. I also resolved never to use the toilet.

I had quickly weighed up my new bosses, and a more spineless bunch I hadn't seen in a long time. Howie, the oldest one, looked like one of the old boys out of the *Muppet Show*. Grey hair stuck up in riotous confusion around his bald pate, which was a deep shade of red. A long pointed nose and recessed chin added to an appearance that bordered on the bizarre.

His three companions didn't have a lot going for them either. In their late twenties, they were all of a type. Narrow shoulders and sunken chests complemented vacant faces and eyes that could never meet and hold yours. They certainly weren't managerial material.

They were, however, held in some esteem by the 'residents', plenty of whom were willing to debase themselves to win favour with them. In any other place, the civvies would have had trouble commanding even a modicum of respect, but, in the telephone shop, a regular crew of grovellers constantly polished their egos for them. They would get none of that from me, but I thought I would be able to handle them easily enough.

However, first I had to create the right impression. If I just disappeared into my office and wasn't seen again, they would soon come and roust me out. I decided to attack immediately.

Broom in hand I sallied out into the shop, and approached the first bench in the production line. I began to sweep around the legs of the benches and chairs. Most production-line workers stop only for tea-breaks, especially if they are on piece-work like this lot were. However, the first two got the message right away. Reluctantly, they stood up and walked out into the aisle, carrying their chairs with them. There were also boxes of components on the floor, which I moved, and swept the floor.

I repeated the process with the second two, but with these, I had to rap the legs of their chairs with the broom a couple of times before they got the message. Then they, too, stood and shuffled out into the aisle.

Within twenty minutes, I had finished. All the dirt was swept into a neat pile and thrown into the bin by the recess. The production line settled down again and was in full swing.

There was some consternation when I reappeared with a mop and bucket. Once again, they were all forced to stand, then move into the aisle. Mopping quickly, but without rushing, I worked my way along the line. There were no audible complaints, but several faces seethed with resentment at this second interruption.

The civvies had been watching my progress with a mixture of dismay and amusement. Out of the corner of my eye, I saw them nudging each other and pointing. I suppose they couldn't make up their minds whether to be pleased that they had an efficient cleaner or concerned that I was disrupting the production line.

I soon helped them make up their minds. Immediately I finished at the last bench, I appeared in their office doorway armed with mop, bucket and broom.

'Excuse me, gents, this won't take a minute,' I announced.

Reluctantly, they climbed to their feet and shuffled out of the office. No doubt the previous cleaner had appeared at set times on set days. I moved in with my cleaning paraphernalia and pulled the door shut behind me.

That effectively prevented them from getting into their office for a good ten minutes. When I finished, Howie was waiting for me outside.

'Very good job, Parker,' he said grinning weakly. 'Just a word, though. Cleaning is important, but we try not to hold up the production line for anything. So if you just do your bits and pieces as best you can, everybody will be pleased.'

This was exactly what I wanted to hear. In fact, it was the whole object of the exercise. I immediately retired to my office retreat. I now had licence to spend a bit of time in there. I closed the door, spread out a blanket on the bench and settled down for a quiet doze.

Over the next days and weeks, I established a pattern that everyone got used to and seemed satisfied with. Twice a day I would appear and work my way around the production line, rapping the odd ankle with my broom in the process. The rest of the time I spent in my office/toilet either dozing or reading, and regularly slipped out for gym sessions. Soon, no one even noticed my comings and goings. I had become just another part of the ecology of the telephone shop.

It was unusual for Tom and I to be 'crows', but on this occasion, we were trying to kill an hour at the start of a long and boring evening. We leaned on the rail of the gallery and gazed down on the various inhabitants of Knightsford as they passed beneath.

Suddenly Maypole and the Chief appeared from the corridor leading to the gym. They walked out on to the centre and stood surveying the wings. I surmised they must be on one of their evening tours.

As if by magic, dozens of the most abject sycophants appeared in the vicinity of the 'centre'. They would hover self-consciously, then, when they thought there was an opening, head across the centre to engage Maypole and the Chief in conversation.

A couple of weeks had passed since I had first seen Alf Walker in the kitchen. I had noticed him a couple of times since, always hurrying back and forth with little pots and pans. It seemed he had a full-time job just keeping himself fed.

Suddenly, Alf Walker waddled through the door from the direction of the reception, accompanied by a tall, elderly man in brown Works overalls.

'Who's that with the fat nonce?' I asked Tom.

'That's the civvy electrician he works with,' he replied. 'The one who takes him down the beach. In fact, you can bet that's where they've just been.'

Tom's guess was right on target. There was a small stick of rock sticking up out of one of the pockets of Walker's voluminous overalls.

Maypole had noticed his arrival and turned to face him. Tall and slim, he towered over Walker. The latter gazed up at him like a half-witted child seeking approval from a parent, an idiot grin on his face.

Maypole clasped his hands behind his back, bent forward and smiled broadly. 'And where have *you* been, then?' he asked in exactly the manner you would use to a young child.

Walker jiggled from one foot to another. He smiled and, in his excitement, shook his head from side to side. 'I've been to the beach . . . and I've paddled . . . and I've had a rock and some candy floss . . .' He grinned broadly as he recalled his experiences.

Maypole grinned in return, and for a moment, I thought he was actually going to pat Walker on the head and say, 'Good boy.'

They exchanged a few more words of infantile banter, then wandered off, Walker and the electrician in the direction of the former's cell on A wing, Maypole and the Chief towards the dining hall.

Tom and I looked at each other and shook our heads. If we hadn't heard the exchange ourselves, we wouldn't have believed it. Maypole had made a personal pet out of the most dangerous child-killer in the jail. To let him loose on the unsuspecting inhabitants of Dartville smacked of recklessness in the extreme. But if anything went wrong, it wouldn't be Maypole who suffered.

Even though I was now a first team player, I didn't change my work-out routine. I still continued to run, lift weights and do circuits. As a result, I was far and away the fittest player in the team.

A couple of weeks after I had first played, Tom asked if I would take the team out on a training run.

'What's Niven got to say about this?' I asked, fearing that the juvenile egomaniac would think it was a bid to take over the team.

'It was his idea, Norm.' Tom's expression showed that he was as surprised as I was.

'Are you sure?'

'Yeah, Norm. I think he was impressed when you ran the legs off Steve.'

'How many will there be?' I asked.

'Only about half the squad. Niven's told the rest that they'll have to go running on their own.'

The following evening was fine and dry. A light breeze rustled our hair as the eight of us stood stretching in the centre of the football pitch.

I had abandoned my bottoms and boots for shorts and trainers. This was going to be a sprint. The rest were similarly attired.

Niven smiled at me good-naturedly as he waited for me to start. Richie stood with Bill and Steve, the three of them impatient to begin. Tom, Eric and Jack stood in another group, grinning like mischievous schoolboys.

'Right, fellas, we're going to do some grid sprints,' I began. 'This will improve your fitness and lung power. We'll trot along three sides of the football pitch and then sprint along the fourth.' I indicated the touch-line that ran close to the wall.

'Now when I say "sprint",' I continued, 'I mean running flat out, as fast as you can possibly go. If you're just going to trot the fourth side, then you're wasting your time.' Several heads nodded as if to reassure me that they would be sprinting flat out. 'Then we trot the three sides again and sprint the fourth. We're going to do this ten times.'

At the mention of 'ten times', several of the players turned to look at each other in consternation. Richie shook his head in disbelief, and the smiles disappeared from the faces of Tom, Jack and Eric.

We started out in two ranks running four abreast, with Niven, Tom, Jack and me in the first. As we went, I realised I would have my work cut out here. Some of them were good sprinters and there would be a lot of competition to beat me. Especially after my defeat of Steve.

But this wasn't going to be just a sprint. It would be the severest test of stamina – and stamina was my long suit.

We jogged along the line behind one goal. Beside me, Tom and Niven were as frisky as colts, holding themselves back with difficulty.

As we turned along the touch-line running in front of the dining hall, strides lengthened a bit.

As we turned into the line behind the other goal, you could feel the tension all around. Deep breathing could be heard as the eight of us filled our lungs with air, ready for the coming sprint. Muscles tensed in anticipation as we gathered ourselves.

Almost leisurely, we turned into the other touch-line, then it was off.

Elbows raised, chin high, legs pumping for all they were worth,

I stared straight ahead as I drove for the corner flag. Niven, incredibly quick across the ground, scooted away from me like a man on a moped. Within half a dozen strides, he was three yards up on me and going away. No one would be able to catch him.

Tom had accelerated quickly, too. He had a more untidy style, but was soon several yards clear of me. I felt Bill and Richie go past and could only stare at their retreating backs as I struggled to keep up.

Niven reached the corner six yards in front of me. Tom was two yards behind him, with Richie and Bill close on his heels. Eric, Jack and Steve all finished more or less level with me.

I jogged to catch up with Niven. Breathing was very heavy now. In a ragged group, we trotted along the lines.

Once again, we drove down the back straight. Again, Niven and Tom ran away from me. They reached the corner three yards in front, with Bill and Richie level with me and the rest a few yards behind.

I caught up with Niven and Tom and jogged with them. All the effort was beginning to take its toll and there was no rush to get to the corner now. They slowed to almost walking pace to ease the pressure on burning lungs and numb, tired legs.

We launched ourselves down the straight for the third time, but there was no acceleration from Niven and Tom. I caught them half-way along the touch-line, and the three of us reached the corner together.

I had to hold myself back to stay with Niven and Tom on the fourth circuit. Their chins had sunk to their chests as their feet dragged across the ground. Hair stuck lankly to wet foreheads. Occasionally they would spit on to the grass. They began to dally, shrinking away from the coming sprint and recognising the inevitable tiredness that would claim them over the next couple of laps.

We ran the straight for the fourth time, but it was little more than a tired gallop for Niven and Tom now. It was my turn to finish three yards clear.

That effectively ended the competition as far as I was concerned. I was into my stride now. My lungs burned, but I was into the rhythm of jogging then sprinting.

I ran on my own, sprinting the fourth side and reaching the corner half the touch-line in front of my closest pursuer, Tom. On the next lap, Niven, Richie and Eric dropped out. The rest dragged round in my wake as I finished what I had set out to do.

I was suffering myself now, but still managed to finish the tenth lap with a sprint. I sat down on the grass to get my breath back and watched the rest struggling to finish.

Tom came in next, immediately collapsing on the grass, breathing deeply. Bill and Steve jogged side by side — there would be no sprint finish for them. Jack doggedly ground on and finished at almost a walking pace.

I felt no sense of triumph at beating them. I was a serious runner and had been training like a professional every day for the past twelve years. In fact, I trained harder than a professional. They at least took a day off occasionally.

It had been an important session, however. Prison was like gladiator school, a warrior society where strength and aggression were all-important. Even at Knightsford, much social interaction was governed by intimidation. It would do my reputation no harm at all to defeat the best of Knightsford's young 'uns in a trial of stamina.

It had also been important because it brought home to the young footballers just how unfit they were. I had made them aware of another dimension of fitness.

I was now rapidly approaching the end of my twelfth year in jail. Barely seven months stood between me and my first parole review. I realised I had better make some preparation to set out a case.

I knew I had no chance of a release date this first time up. Apart from several other factors, I had been in trouble in every jail I had been in. However, there was this period of quiet at Knightsford.

I was looking for this review to give me some indication of how long I would serve. The majority of Knightsford's inmates got a release date or a move to an open prison on their reviews. Very rarely, someone got a straight 'knockback' and would have to stay at Knightsford for another couple of years.

Even the length of the 'knockback' could be revealing. A twelve-month 'knockback' could mean that you had nearly missed getting something this time and would get something the next. The logic was that, if they had intended to make you serve much longer, they would have given you a two-year 'knockback' instead. Needless to say, this was only a rough-and-ready guide. Logic had little place in the running of the lifer system.

I was understandably nervous about the outcome of my review. A two-year 'knockback' would tell me nothing. Three or more years would mean that I still had many more years to serve. Five or more, that they didn't intend to let me out.

I resolved to put forward the best possible case I could. Lifers were assessed on a plethora of criteria. I reasoned that the better the case I presented, the better my chances would be.

Now I had my Ordinary degree on the OU, I was eligible to study for a Master's degree. If I could get accepted by a university on one of their MA courses, not only would this impress the Parole Board, but there might even be a chance – albeit a remote one – of my being let out to study.

I decided to write to three universities asking to be enrolled on their MA course in psychology. It was a subject with an obvious appeal to me. I looked up the names of the relevant professors in a student yearbook and sent an identical letter to each. Several days later, three letters arrived, addressed to me. I had been accepted by all three universities, with the proviso that I be free to take the course. I now had three valuable documents to be copied and put in my parole file.

At least I had done something positive. The criteria governing parole were so vague and intangible that I felt helpless to influence my fate. If only the system had some recognisable logic to it, but it was a victim of its own bureaucracy.

10

As Tom saw Jane almost every weekday, whenever she wanted to see me now she sent a message via him. Not that anything untoward was going on, but this method enabled her to avoid going through official channels and labelling me as one of the education block crowd.

One tea-time, Tom told me that Jane wanted to see me. Evening classes started at 6.00 and I knew she would be busy until the various activities were under way. Therefore I arrived at her office just after 6.30.

She was sitting at her desk, writing intently in a book, a harried look on her face. I guessed that the early rush was just over.

I knocked on the open door and she glanced up. 'Oh, it's you, Norman. Come in.' Smiling she pushed the book away from her and sat back in her chair, indicating for me to sit opposite. She opened a drawer in her desk, took out a letter and handed it to me. She gave me a meaningful look, then returned her attention to her book.

The letter, addressed to the education department, was from a Professor Pat Knox, head of the psychology department at one of the universities that had accepted me, asking to come to Knightsford to interview me.

When I had read through it twice, I put it back on the desk in front of Jane. She immediately replaced it in the drawer.

'Needless to say,' she began, 'you haven't seen that letter. Some of the senior staff are furious that you've been offered places at universities, and there's a battle going on behind the scenes to prevent this interview taking place. But Mr Camber and I have pushed for it. Professor Knox will be coming the day after tomorrow.'

I was experiencing a mixture of emotions. I was pleased that the professor was coming — it could hardly do my cause any harm — and I was grateful to Jane for her help. But I seethed with anger at those senior screws who obviously had it in for me.

'Thanks for your help, Jane,' I said. 'You know, it makes you wonder. I could understand these screws if what I was trying to do was negative or disruptive. But you would think they'd be pleased that someone at Knightsford had been accepted at university.'

Jane shook her head resignedly. 'Yes, I know,' she said, her voice tired. 'So many of them go out of their way to sabotage the work we do in the education block. It's just jealousy really. But it makes me all the more determined to outwit them.' She smiled mischievously. 'And they're not very intelligent, so it's quite easy to do that.'

I laughed. This woman was every bit as rebellious as I was, and not because she was particularly contrary by nature. In many ways, she was an unlikely rebel. However, a natural sense of justice coupled with an indomitable spirit made her a constant thorn in the side of the authorities. I could see why they hated her.

Suddenly, I was aware of someone behind me. I swivelled in my chair. Standing in the doorway was a small, wiry man of about forty. The top of his head was completely bald and his forehead deeply lined. A riot of ginger hair fringed the edges of the bald area, like encroaching countryside around urban concrete. He had a weasel's face, with bright, staring eyes that were constantly on the move. His gaze flickered from me to Jane and on to various objects around the room. You didn't have to be a psychiatrist to realise that he was another patient.

Jane smiled indulgently. 'Hello, Luke,' she said in a bright, cheery voice. She appeared genuinely pleased to see him, but I guessed that this was to spare his feelings.

He stood there grinning foolishly, self-conscious now. Seconds passed, then his attention wandered to a large cupboard standing against the wall. He stared at it fixedly. Suddenly, he walked quickly over to it and knocked sharply on one of its wooden doors. He cocked his head to one side as if waiting for some sort of reply. Then he knocked again and, once more, he cocked his head.

Jane and I watched this little scenario, saying nothing. Eventually Luke lost interest in the cupboard. He faced us, his eyes flitting all around the room again. With a ghost of a smile, he turned and walked out.

I swivelled back to face Jane again. She was laughing silently and shaking her head.

'Friend of yours?' I asked.

Suddenly she wasn't laughing any more. A fierce look scolded me. She wouldn't be party to taking the mickey out of someone who was obviously mentally unbalanced.

'Poor creature,' she said, staring at the doorway through which Luke had just disappeared. 'He thinks there's someone in the cupboard, you know. Every time he's passing and the door is open, he comes in and knocks on the cupboard door. Other times, he comes in and leaves feathers on my desk.'

There was a silence as Jane continued to think about the recently departed Luke. I searched my mind for some symbolic meaning to the knocking on the cupboard and the feathers, but concluded that it was beyond mysticism. Luke was just another Knightsford nutter and another madman that Jane had befriended.

'Norman, I was going to ask you something . . . almost a favour really,' she said, her attention returning to me. She was serious and business-like now.

I didn't know what to expect. I hoped she wasn't going to ask me for something that I would have to refuse.

'There's a friend of mine who lives locally.' She spoke slowly and clearly as if afraid that I might misunderstand her. 'She wants to enrol at the poly for the first year of a psychology course.' She paused, as if to give me time for it to sink in. But she knew I wasn't thick. I wondered what she was leading up to.

'Jean is about your age,' she continued. I smelt the faint odour of a large rat. 'It's a long time since she studied anything.' I felt the suspicion grow in me. 'In view of the fact that you have passed a couple of psychology courses on the OU, I wondered if she might come in one night a week to talk to you?' The suspicion had become reality now and it was a rat indeed.

I sat there, saying nothing, running it over in my mind. First, I considered outright refusal, but I didn't want to seem ungrateful for what Jane had done for me. I wondered what this Jean might be like. Perhaps it wouldn't be too bad to sit with some young student for a couple of hours each week.

Then I remembered that Jane had said that Jean was my age. I was in good shape for thirty-seven and had the outlook of a man ten years younger. However, that didn't mean that Jean would be a Wendy to my Peter Pan. I envisaged an awkward couple of hours where I would have to pretend to be something I wasn't.

That was anathema to me. I hated posers of any ilk. What you saw was exactly what you got, as far as I was concerned. To be anything else would be a denial of my true self. I didn't fancy play-acting with this Jean.

Jane noticed my hesitation. 'Jean's a nice person and she's a friend of mine. She's divorced with four children. She sincerely wants to make a success of this psychology course.'

The added information only confused me more. But the thought of this mother with four children trying to get through college stood out above the rest. What sort of man would refuse to help a mother with four children? Jane had me, and I think she knew it. There was the slightest of twinkles in her eyes as she waited for my decision.

I screwed up my mouth and nodded my head slowly in acknow-ledgement of the *fait accompli*. I would accept now, but there would have to be some ground rules.

'OK, Jane,' I said. 'I'll see Jean for a couple of hours each week, but you must tell her all about me. I don't want her coming in here thinking I'm in for gas meters or something. 'Cause if she asks me, I'll tell her. And then it could be awkward or she might get frightened.'

'I've already told her all about you, Norman,' she replied, smiling broadly, but with no air of triumph.

Her cockiness brought a smile to my face, too. I was rapidly coming to the conclusion that Jane was a very shrewd and intelligent woman.

'What evening would suit you?' she asked.

'Make it Tuesday,' I replied. I had a gym session from the shop on a Tuesday, so it wouldn't matter if I missed the gym session in the evening.

'OK, Norman,' said Jane, 'Tuesday it is.'

I stood up to go.

'By the way,' she called after me, 'don't forget your appointment with Professor Knox the day after tomorrow.'

Later that evening, I talked to Tom about my meeting with Jane. I mentioned the impending visit by the professor and he seemed impressed. Then I told him about the proposed sessions with Jean.

'Four kids, eh, Norm?' he laughed. 'That should keep you busy when you get out.'

'Bollocks,' I replied. 'My name ain't Foxy. Anyway, I'm only doing it as a favour for Jane.'

'Yeah, she's a right cunning bastard, that Jane,' said Tom, laughing harder. The idea definitely tickled him. 'You wait till I tell JB about this,' he said finally.

'By the way,' he added. I looked up, expecting more of the same. 'The Fox has got a new job.'

I was glad he had changed the subject and felt an immediate interest in the new one.

'He's the new canteen orderly,' said Tom, looking quite pleased about it.

I immediately felt pleased about it, too. It was a good job for the Fox, but that wasn't the reason. It was always handy to know someone who worked in the canteen. You could put your 'special orders' in late. You found out what there was on special offer. And, last, but not least, Foxy would get plenty of perks, which should enrich our weekend foodboat.

'Mind you, it's a bit of a double-edged sword for him,' added Tom. 'He's only in the canteen on a Thursday for payday. The rest of the time, he'll be in the Admin with Cyril. And if he throws any of his tantrums in there, that will be the end of him.'

The image of Cyril sprang into my mind. He was a short, bald, dog-end of a man who ran the canteen. He was pleasant enough, but physically repulsive. Only in his fifties, yet looking twenty years older, he weighed no more than nine stone and resembled a recently discharged cancer patient. His skin was an unhealthy, yellowish colour, and his face was permanently wreathed in smoke from an ever-present cigarette. I reflected that he would have his hands full with the Fox.

The following day, Tom brought me another message from Jane. It seemed that there had been further ructions over the professor's impending visit. Maypole had chastised her for being instrumental in arranging it, and by way of recompense, he had ordered her to take a day's leave. She wouldn't be there to meet the professor.

The next morning, I went to work as usual, fully expecting to be called from the shop at any minute. However, the morning passed slowly and dinner-time arrived with no sign of the professor.

As I returned to my wing, Hall was waiting for me on the centre, a sour expression on his fat face.

''Allo, Norm,' he said, attempting a smile that was an abysmal failure. 'You're wanted up the education block right away.'

I hurried up the stairs and into the corridor leading to Camber's office. The door was closed, so I knocked. I heard Camber's voice calling for me to come in.

The professor was wearing a black velvet dress. The *décolletage* revealed an ample bosom, in the midst of which hung a gold pendant. Short, black hair framed a face that was pleasant rather than beautiful. I noticed she wore a minimum of make-up.

'Norman,' said Camber, standing up from behind his desk, 'this is Professor Pat Knox.'

I suddenly realised the 'Pat' must be short for 'Patricia'. But there was nothing short about the professor. As she stood, I could see that she was a good two inches taller than me. She was a well-made woman and I could feel the strength in her as she shook my hand vigorously.

'I'm very pleased to meet you, Norman,' she said, in a manner that implied that the honour was all hers. I was immediately impressed by her friendliness and warmth.

'Norman,' interrupted Camber, 'Professor Knox would like to try a prison dinner. I wonder if you would be so good as to fetch one for her. Then you can go and have yours while she's eating.'

I looked at her, the surprise showing on my face. 'You do realise that it will be on a metal tray?' I said, the doubt clear in my voice.

'That will be all right,' the professor said confidently. I shrugged and went to fetch the dinner.

Within five minutes I was back. I left her with the meal, then went to have my own dinner. I sat with Tom, Bill and Jack and told them what was happening.

Twenty minutes later, I returned to Camber's office. Professor Pat had finished her dinner and was sitting back, drinking a cup of coffee.

'Come in and sit down, Norman,' said Camber. 'No doubt you and the professor have got things to discuss so I'll leave you for half an hour. When I come back, we'll take the professor on a tour of the prison.'

This was another surprise. I wondered how Hall and the rest would take to me showing the professor around the jail. I smiled inwardly, reflecting that I was going to enjoy this.

Camber left me with Professor Knox, closing the door behind

him as he went out. I frantically searched for something intelligent to say, realising that, in spite of the surroundings, this was still an interview for a university.

She was more at ease than I was. 'What's it like here, Norman?' she asked with considerable composure.

I wondered how much I should tell her. After all, she was an academic at a prestigious university. Would she take kindly to a radical critique of one of Her Majesty's penal institutions?

Sensing my dilemma, she leaned forward. 'Look, Norman,' she said, 'I know all the shit they try to tell us about prisons. And I know it's not true. So don't worry about being frank.'

I don't know what surprised me more, her candour or the use of the word 'shit'. But if nothing else, it put me at my ease. It could be that I was in the presence of a kindred spirit here.

'Well, Professor Knox . . .' I began. She put up her hand to stop me.

'Please call me Pat, Norman,' she said. There was to be no standing on ceremony with this woman.

Completely at my ease now, I told her about the set-up at Knightsford. I explained about the false criteria and the hypocrisy. She raised her eyebrows when I talked about the eccentric management style, but she didn't interrupt.

When I had finished, she sat silently for a minute, as if she were weighing up what I had said.

'Well, Norman,' she said, 'I must say that I came here expecting to be surprised, but not as much as I have been.'

I was immediately relieved that she had believed me. Already there was trust between us.

'To be honest,' she continued, 'I'm not particularly interested in prison subcultures or, indeed, management styles, but this has been a revelation. I've learned something here today.'

She paused, as if still thinking about what I had told her.

'Now I'd like to tell you something about the university,' she went on, brightening up at the change of subject. 'We are not without our own eccentric management styles. I must confess that I've had some considerable resistance to your attending our university. Unfortunately, there are reactionary and conservative elements in all our institutions. However, I'm pleased to say that, providing that you are free to attend, there will be a place for you to take your Master's degree.'

I realised that I had reason to be grateful to Pat. She had obviously gone out on a limb for me. The administrators at her university could hardly have taken kindly to the thought of a convicted murderer wandering loose among their students. Although my application was largely an academic exercise as far as I was concerned, I resolved that, should I be allowed to go there, I would do nothing to compromise Pat's position.

Pat talked at length about the university, then we discussed subjects ranging from politics to crime. I wasn't surprised to discover that she shared many of my radical socialist views. She was quite active on the left of the Labour Party.

We were still deep in discussion when Camber came back. He suggested that it was time for Pat's tour of the prison.

We started with the education block, although all there was to see was a succession of empty classrooms. We descended the stairs to look at the gym, then the two specialist classrooms downstairs.

As we came out on to the centre, the last of the 'residents' were making their way to work. There were some curious stares.

Hall was still leaning on the snooker table, surrounded by several other screws. Someone must have nudged him as we came into view, for he turned to look at us.

His face became transformed, a mix of emotions raging across it. His lips actually quivered, but it was his eyes that betrayed him. They burned with an anger that the surrounding flesh could not conceal. He turned away to control himself.

I could imagine his quandary. He hated anything to do with the education department and, if the inoffensive Camber had been on his own, would have found some way to be rude to him. But he wasn't sure about the professor in the velvet dress. He despised her as a woman doing what he would consider to be a man's job. He resented the fact that she had come from a university to visit a prisoner. But he wasn't at all sure about the extent of her power.

We stood on the centre as I pointed out various features to Pat. Either she hadn't noticed the screws by the snooker table or she had decided to ignore them. I tended to think it was the latter, for she looked right through them.

We made our way along B wing and up the stairs to the electrical shop. I was really going to enjoy this.

As Camber entered with Pat, the 'poison dwarf' came running out of his office. Like most minor functionaries, obsequiousness was almost a conditioned reflex with him.

He shook Pat's hand vigorously as Camber introduced her. I got the impression that he had never met a professor before. He kept looking at me out of the corner of his eye. He couldn't quite figure out what I was doing with the party. And, when I started to explain things to Pat and she responded, he looked perplexed at the easy familiarity between us.

As we progressed up the stairs to the telephone shop, we left a very troubled man in our wake. His whole view of the world had just been turned upside down. What were things coming to when convicted murderers promenaded around a prison with professors, and honest, hardworking men like him were introduced just in passing?

If the effect of our visit on the 'poison dwarf' had been traumatic, then our appearance in the telephone shop was positively disruptive.

All four civvies came scurrying out of the office to stand in a semi-circle in front of us, bowing and scraping. It seemed that they, too, had never met a real, live professor before. From the way they were behaving, the distinguished-looking lady in the velvet dress could have been Margaret Thatcher herself – a thought that I'm sure would have tickled Pat.

The effect on the 'galley-slaves' was just as marked. I had never seen the production line come to a halt voluntarily before, but now everyone temporarily lost interest in the telephones. Heads turned as they tried to figure out, first, who the important-looking lady was and, second, what the hell I was doing showing her around the prison.

It was the second question that really bothered them. In the incestuous world of Knightsford, where so many jockeyed for position against each other, this seemed to be a significant coup on my part. My elevation to the role of shop cleaner, on a lower level of pay, hadn't really bothered them that much, although they would have liked to have seen me progress through the ranks first. But this really rankled. Especially as many of them knew of my atrocious prison record.

I had never cared what any of them thought, as long as they kept their opinions to themselves. My attention was wholly on Pat as we progressed down the centre of the shop, with her picking up the odd telephone component.

Leaving the shop, we made a quick tour of the grounds and poked our heads into the kitchen, which was a hive of activity. Then we returned to Camber's office.

As she left, Pat assured me that she had enjoyed herself and said that she hoped I would soon be free to attend university. As she shook my hand, she promised that she would write.

I walked down to my cell and sat drinking a cup of coffee, mulling over recent events. Although it had been the first time I had ever met Professor Knox, I felt we now shared some kind of friendship. For the past twelve years, I had shared comradeship only with men. It was a novel experience for me to have a woman for a friend.

But duty called. They would expect me back in the telephone shop now that the visit was over.

The civvies were in their office when I arrived. I ignored them and walked up the middle of the shop. I was aware of workers' heads turning to look, but I ignored them, too. I went into my office/toilet and closed the door behind me. Let them wonder. They would get no enlightenment from me.

We saw Foxy in the canteen when we spent our wages on Thursday. He loomed behind Cyril like a second shadow, occasionally barking at slow or stupid customers as if he were in charge. Ever the bully, the Fox just couldn't help himself when dealing with those weaker than himself. When he saw Tom and me, though, his attitude changed completely. He smiled and hurried to fetch whatever we asked for.

As we finished off the chicken dinner on Sunday, Foxy suddenly produced a large sponge cake from underneath a cloth.

'Just a little something that Cyril gave me, boys,' he said, grinning like a Cheshire cat. Foxy was never so happy as when he had got away with something. I guessed that he had just taken the cake, rather than been given it by Cyril.

The new job wasn't all cream, though. For the rest of the week, he had to help Cyril in his office in the Admin block. There were lorries to unload, the office to sweep and the Admin toilets to keep clean. Cyril was already beginning to find that the Fox could be a reluctant assistant.

'I've got it sussed out already,' he boasted. 'I can see the gate from where I sit. As soon as I see a lorry coming in, I pick up a broom and start to sweep the office. Then, when it arrives a couple of minutes later, I tell Cyril I'm busy. He has to unload it on his own.'

I reflected on this rather transparent ploy. It wouldn't take Cyril long to get fed up with having to do the heavy work himself. But there was no use telling the Fox. He was sure he knew all the answers. I decided to make the most of the perks while they lasted. I could see the Fox returning to the design shop before long.

The Admin toilets were also problematic for the Fox. At the heart of it was the fact that he resented having to clean toilets after anyone. He moaned to us about the anonymous defecator who regularly shit up the back of the toilet bowl. He pledged to catch the offender and have a word with him.

Then there was the Chief, whose old bowels doubtless weren't what they used to be. He created a considerable stink when he used the toilet. The Fox hated having to clean it after he had been in there.

Tom and I exchanged glances as he told us all this. We could see the seeds of his own destruction as the tale unfolded. But we said nothing. We would only be wasting our breath anyway.

'Here, you know that old Welsh fella, Llewellyn?' asked the Fox suddenly. Tom and I looked blank. 'You know, the one who always stands up in the "crow's nest" every night?'

I dimly recollected a grey-haired old boy who stood on his own, staring down the wings. I nodded.

'Well, he writes really passionate letters to some rich old bird in Cardiff,' declared the Fox, a mixture of mild outrage and self-importance on his face. Clearly, his new job would bring him a degree of secret knowledge.

But how? Had he got it from Llewellyn? Surely Cyril or one of the Admin staff hadn't told him? And how would they know anyway, unless they had read the old man's letters?

A nasty suspicion began to dawn on me. 'How the fuck do you know, Foxy?' I asked aggressively.

A guilty look passed across the Fox's face. He tried to smile, but it wasn't convincing. 'You'd be surprised what I know, Norm,' he said.

'Yeah, how do you know, Danny?' asked Tom, a suspicious look now on his face, too.

Foxy's expression said that he knew he had put his foot in it. He realised we weren't going to let the matter drop. 'I read it in his canteen letter,' he said, decidedly shamefacedly now.

'You what?' said Tom, as what the Fox had said began to sink in.

I knew immediately what had happened. Ordinary issue letters went in the wing letter box. But the extra 'canteen' letters had to have stamps fixed to them in the canteen. The Fox had been going through this mail.

'Here, Foxy,' I piped up. 'I sincerely hope you haven't been reading any of *my* canteen letters.'

'No, Norm, no.' The Fox was panicking now. He realised that he had just confessed to something that was severely out of order, a liberty of the first magnitude. 'I wouldn't read any of your or Tom's mail,' he hastily assured us.

'Well, you better not, Danny, or you and me will severely fall out.' I was angry now. That was the trouble with associating with someone who didn't share your values. You could find yourself in a situation where you were almost conniving at some unacceptable behaviour.

'And that goes for me too, Danny,' said Tom angrily.

'It was an accident really, an accident,' pleaded the Fox. 'The letter fell out of the envelope.'

He could see from our expressions that we weren't having any of that. 'It won't happen again, boys, honest,' he said contritely.

And that was the end of the evening as far as Tom and I were concerned. We helped him clear the dishes away, then left to walk back to our wing together.

'He's a fucking liberty-taker, that Foxy,' said Tom, breaking the silence.

'Well, we've known that all along really, Tom, haven't we?' I answered. 'It's just as well we're only involved in a weekly meal with him.'

'And that won't last much longer if he pulls another stroke like this one,' said Tom.

As Tuesday evening drew near, I began to have second thoughts about my meeting with Jane's student friend. Both Tom and JB had been steadily ribbing me about it over the weekend. Both assured me that Knightsford couldn't stand another tempestuous affair like the Fox's.

After tea on Tuesday, I put on a clean pair of pressed jeans and a new white T-shirt. As I came out of my cell, Tom and Jack were hanging over the railing above me.

'Like the new white T-shirt,' said Tom in a loud, dopey voice.

'Who's a pretty boy then?' added Jack.

'Bollocks' was all I could think of by way of a reply.

'I'll bring you both a cup of coffee at about seven?' shouted Tom in a more sensible voice.

I looked over my shoulder at him. 'Seriously,' he added. 'I'll bring you coffee.'

He sounded like he meant it. 'OK,' I said. 'But don't fuck about, Tom. This could be right embarrassing.' Tom grinned wickedly.

It was difficult to embarrass me in front of men. I was a master of prison uncouth and had long ago learned to give as good as I got. But women were a different matter entirely. I had old-fashioned good manners where they were concerned. I realised that part of the problem was that I wasn't at my ease with them.

I climbed the stairs to the education block and went to Jane's office. She was surrounded by several people, all trying to get information from her. I waved to her over the heads of the crowd and succeeded in attracting her attention.

'Jean's in Classroom 8,' she shouted above the din, and smiled. I didn't like the smile at all. There was a degree of mirth there that troubled me.

But I was committed now. I walked along to Classroom 8, knocked at the door and went in.

Jean was sitting at a desk, looking out of the window. At my knock, she turned, stood up and walked to meet me.

Jean wasn't beautiful by any stretch of the imagination. She wasn't even pretty. But she had a raw-boned, country-pleasant face that wasn't unattractive. She was pale, and her shoulder-length, jet black hair emphasised the pallor. She was about my height, with a slim, well-proportioned build that belied the four children she had borne.

The disaster was the dress. Whether Jane had advised her to dress down for the occasion, I didn't know. But if so, she could hardly have done better. It was a dull chocolate brown, with minimal decoration. It hung, shapeless as a shift. It was a dress your grandmother wouldn't have been seen dead in, and the overall effect was to make her look drab. With her type of looks, she needed a pretty dress.

But what did I care? I wasn't going to marry her. The problem was, I knew that Tom would take the piss.

Conversation was difficult at first. I wondered if I was what she had expected. Years of lifting weights and constantly growling at enemies had given me a tough and brutish manner. I worried that she might feel intimidated by me.

At first, we discussed what she should expect on a first-year psychology course. Then I progressed on to general psychological theory. At times I was sure that I had lost her, but she sat there quietly, taking it all in.

Gradually, bits of our backgrounds crept in. I told of how

learning about psychology had helped me to psychoanalyse myself. I began to suspect that this was one of the reasons she wanted to study the subject herself.

Suddenly, there was a sharp knock on the door. It swung open and there was Tom carrying a tray with two cups on it. He held a long-stemmed rose clamped between his teeth.

Jean immediately burst out laughing. I grinned foolishly, more embarrassed than amused. I dreaded what he would say next.

He placed the tray on the table between us, took the rose from between his teeth and presented it to Jean. 'Norman got this for you earlier,' he said, smiling. 'He must have forgot it.'

Jean covered her flushed face with her hands, laughing into them. 'See you later, Norm,' called Tom as he backed out of the room.

'Who was that?' asked Jean, still laughing.

'Tom, a pal of mine.' I was laughing myself now, partly from relief that he had gone.

The ice had been broken and she began to ask me details of life in Knightsford. Then she told me of how she lived alone with her four children.

She mentioned that she was divorced and that her ex-husband regularly came round to see the children with his new wife. I deduced that they were both professional people and her husband had left her for someone classier, and that this was at the seat of her insecurity. For, as I spoke to her, I became aware that she was a sad and insecure woman.

She put a brave face on it, though. There was no doubt that she was a fighter and determined to raise her four children on her own. I slowly began to admire her as she told me of all the jobs she did around the house in the absence of a man.

The two hours passed quickly. There was another knock at the door and there stood Jane. 'Well, how have you two been getting on?' she asked, smiling.

We both assured her that we had enjoyed ourselves. I shook Jean's hand and said I would see her the following week. I walked back to the wing.

Tom and Jack were both waiting for me. We laughed about the rose and I confessed that it had put us both at our ease. They demanded full details of what had been said, and I told them.

'Well, Norm, that's you spoken for, I suppose,' said Tom.

'You suppose fuck all,' I replied. 'Jean's a nice lady who's trying to bring four kids up on her own. If it helps her out to spend a Tuesday evening talking to me, then so be it.'

'Yeah,' said Tom disbelievingly.

'Tom, you of all people should see the truth in that,' I added.

'Why's that?' he demanded.

'Well, look how I've sorted your life out since I've met you.'

To assorted cries of 'bollocks' and 'fuck off' from Tom and Jack, I went into my cell to change.

Foxy was in top form at the weekend meal. The menu might never change — it was chicken again — but the Fox's tale of his life the previous week always contained many a new twist and turn.

His new job was now a constant source of aggravation to him. Aggravation of his own causing, it must be said.

Cyril had now had quite enough of unloading lorries on his own while the strapping Fox idly pushed a broom around the office. The final straw had come mid-week. Cyril had unloaded a lorry in the drizzling rain with the Fox watching him through the office window.

'I think he saw me grinning at him working in the rain,' confessed the Fox.

The upshot was that Roland, the administrative officer, had stopped Foxy in the corridor.

'Look, Danny,' he said in his most reasonable tone, 'it is part of your job to unload any lorries that come in.'

The Fox's surprise at Roland stopping him was quickly replaced by a surge of sheer rage. 'Has that fucking Cyril grassed me?' he demanded.

Roland blanched several shades lighter. 'That's not the point, Danny,' he insisted. 'The point is that the last orderly did it and you must do it, too.'

'The point is, Roland,' the Fox said, his voice gradually rising through the octaves, 'that someone keeps shitting up the back of the khazi.'

Roland looked aghast. He had heard the Fox raging in the corridor about this very thing, but what did it have to do with him? And what did it have to do with the subject in hand?

'Roland.' The Fox addressed him almost conspiratorially. Roland leaned forward, thinking the Fox was about to impart some secret wisdom. 'If you don't leave off about the lorries, I'm going to put up a fucking big notice saying, "ROLAND SHITS UP THE BACK OF THE KHAZI"!' The last bit was delivered in a roar that reverberated around the corridor.

Whether it was the threat or just the sheer volume of noise, it was too much for Roland. He backed away, looking over his shoulder for an escape route. Suddenly he turned and bolted up the stairs.

The Fox was far from finished, though. Cyril was to be the next object of his wrath. He found him in the corner of the office, head almost buried in the open drawer of a filing cabinet.

'Cyril!' Foxy barked.

Cyril had heard the exchange in the corridor and the Fox's approach, but still he jumped. Slowly he turned to face him, his normal jaundice-yellow fading to a *café au lait* hue.

'Did you grass me to Roland?' the Fox demanded.

'D-Danny . . .' Cyril stammered.

'Never mind about the "Danny". I'm "305 Fox" to you. Did you grass me to Roland?' The Fox was shouting again.

'Danny, I only asked him to tell you what your job was,' pleaded Cyril.

'Huh.' This deep throaty sound unnerved Cyril more than any angry word ever could.

The Fox stood with his hands on his hips, his face white with anger. 'Cyril,' he said through clenched teeth, while Cyril stood petrified, waiting for the Fox to fall on him and tear him limb from limb. 'When you go home tonight, either have a good drink, have a good wank or have a good shit, but whatever you do, make sure you come back in a better mood in the morning.'

With that, the Fox stormed out of the office. He could be heard out in the corridor, clanking and crashing about with a mop and metal bucket.

As luck would have it, the Chief had had his morning bowel movement just before the Fox charged into the toilet with mop and bucket. 'Cor, what a fucking stink!' he roared, tossing the bucket and mop into a corner and storming out. He returned to the office with a broom and with Cyril cowering over some paperwork, proceeded to rap every table, chair and cabinet as he raged around the office in a cleaning frenzy.

As soon as he thought it safe to do so, Cyril slipped out. He spent the next half hour sitting on the toilet, waiting for the Fox to cool off.

As Foxy regaled us with the story, Tom and I sat there, amazement showing on our faces. I just didn't know how the Fox got away with it. If it had been me, it was a sure bet that I would have been on the next bus out. But what the Fox had going for him was that he had never been violent in prison. Perhaps they didn't believe he ever would be.

My next 'tryst' with Jean was more like a visiting-room visit than a psychology seminar. In fact, psychology was hardly mentioned. Instead, we talked about the minutiae of her everyday life in Dartville.

I learned the names of each of her children and the various facets of their characters. We discussed what she hoped to do with her psychology degree, if and when she got it. We even talked about her divorce and her husband's subsequent remarriage.

There was only one nasty moment. It came right out of the blue.

'You know, Norman, my oldest boy came out with something funny the other day,' she said. 'I'd been talking about you and he suddenly asked, "Mum, when Norman comes home, will he come here to be our Daddy?"'

Several thoughts raced around my brain at once. Was this just the ingenuous remark of a young boy who had heard his mother talking about me? Was it a pure concoction by Jean to plant the idea in my mind? Was Tom, who was more knowledgeable in the ways of women than me, to be accurate in his prophecy? And, last and certainly not least, what the hell was I going to say to her?

In the event, I took so long to think about it that I said nothing. There was a long, drawn-out silence, during which neither of us looked at each other.

It is at times like these that the gods sometimes intervene. Suddenly, one of them came through the door in the form of Tom carrying a tray.

The spell was broken as we busied ourselves with the drinks and exchanged banter with Tom. As we sat, sipping our steaming coffee, her son's question was a thing of the past. I certainly wasn't going to mention it and Jean seemed content to let it lie.

Later, talking to Tom, I told him of the remark. He laughed and said that he had told me so. I reflected that he surely had. In future, I would be most circumspect in my dealing with Jean, careful not to give her any encouragement whatsoever in that department. I didn't want her proposing to me right there in the classroom.

11

Jane was growing steadily more worried about Niven, who as day followed day was becoming ever more demanding of her. He had taken to waiting behind after class and protesting his love. Whatever she said, it didn't seem to deter him.

She couldn't report him. It wasn't in her nature and the consequences would be disastrous for him. She had hoped that, when she didn't return his affection, his passion would abate. But her rejections only seemed to encourage him.

He was sitting in class now and every time she looked in his direction, he was staring at her. She had avoided speaking to him, just in case he blurted out something in front of the rest of the class. Tom knew something was wrong, but she couldn't expect him to deal with it for her.

After what seemed like an eternity, the period came to an end. One by one the students left, but Niven remained in his seat. Tom hung around, fiddling with his books and shooting the occasional glance at Niven. Niven ignored him, continuing to stare at Jane.

Eventually, Tom said 'goodbye' to them both and walked out into the corridor. Niven got up and closed the door. Jane looked at him apprehensively.

'Well?' he demanded, walking right up to her.

'What's the matter, Niven?' she asked in her most reasonable tone.

Suddenly, Niven grabbed her by both wrists. Pain lanced up her arms from the tightness of his grip. His eyes blazed with anger.

She wanted to cry out from the pain, but she stifled it, reasoning that she must keep her wits about her. 'What's the matter, Niven?' she repeated more forcefully.

'What's the matter?' echoed Niven. 'You're what's the matter. You've led me on and now I'm in love with you and now you don't want to know.'

'Niven, I've never led you on. Now stop it this minute.' Jane spoke sharply, hoping to shock him out of his mood.

It had the opposite effect. Her passion raised an echo in his.

'No!' he shouted, shaking her by the arms. 'Come down behind the stage with me right now – you owe me that much!' He made as if to pull her towards the door.

Jane desperately searched her mind for something that would stop him. He was still very much a child, a child who had never grown up. Suddenly, her thoughts settled on his parents. They remained in Ireland, but still held considerable sway over him. He came from a strict Catholic family, and his mother still inspired a mixture of fear and reverence in him.

'Think of your mother, Niven. What would she say about this?' Jane cried out.

The effect was instantaneous. Niven's eyes flashed with a surge of pure rage. He released her wrists, but at the same time, he swung his right arm.

A sharp, excruciating pain ran down the side of her face, and a sheet of pure, white light seemed to pass in front of her eyes. A numbing sensation swirled at the base of her skull. She felt herself falling.

Surprisingly, there was little pain as she hit the floor. All sensation seemed to fade away. In the distance, she was aware of the door opening. A voice she recognised as Tom's said, 'Niven, what the fuck have you done? Get out! Go on, get out of it!'

She felt someone take hold of her by the arms. 'Come on, Jane, up you come.' Tom's voice seemed closer now.

She felt his arms around her as she was lifted from the floor. The solid seat of a chair pressed against her buttocks as she was lowered into it.

A wave of dizziness threatened to sweep her fledgling consciousness away. She teetered on the brink of sliding off the chair, but Tom's hands held her firmly by the shoulders.

Slowly, she became aware of his face in front of hers. The rest of the room swam into view, through blurred, water-filled eyes. The dull ache in her jaw was replaced by a painful, burning sensation.

'Can you sit in the chair without falling?' Tom's voice was clearer now. She nodded weakly.

Tom looked around the classroom frantically, then darted towards the back. Pulling a towel from a rail next to the sink, he wet it under the tap and hurried back to her.

The wet towel was cool on her forehead. She allowed her head to fall back and felt trickles of wetness run down her cheeks. She breathed in deeply.

The fresh air seemed to dissipate the fog in her mind, like smoke from a room. As full consciousness returned, the image of an angry Niven filled her mind.

She sat up rigidly in the chair, staring around wildly.

'All right, all right,' said Tom soothingly. 'He's gone now. There's nothing to worry about.'

Jane climbed unsteadily to her feet. Keeping one hand on Tom's arm to balance herself, she walked over to the window.

'Tom, you mustn't say anything about this,' she said in a hoarse, breathless whisper.

'I won't,' he replied, slightly annoyed at her suspicion that he would.

'No.' Jane gripped his arm tightly. 'Don't say anything to anyone. Not even Norman. He would attack Niven, I know it. And then there would be trouble for everyone.'

'I won't say anything, I promise,' insisted Tom.

Jane was herself again now. She wiped her face with the towel and brushed at her clothes. She smiled weakly. 'Thank you, Tom.'

'That's all right, Jane,' said Tom, slightly embarrassed now. 'If you keep something cold on your face, it will keep the swelling down.'

A feeling of panic surged through her. She had forgotten there could be bruising. Luckily, this was her last class of the afternoon. She would duck out of evening classes, saying she felt unwell.

Tom walked with her to her office, along the now deserted corridor. Jane let herself in. She picked up the phone and informed Admin that she wouldn't be in that evening. She collected her things.

'Go on, Tom, you had better go and get your tea,' she said.

'Will you be all right now?'

'I'll be all right,' she assured him, 'and thanks again.'

She locked the office and made her way down the back stairs. The cold air on her face made it feel as if it were swelling already. She wondered what she would tell Robert and the children. Perhaps another fall from her bike would be the best excuse. From the way the dizziness still swam in her head, the lie could easily become fact. She would have to be careful on her way home.

The following morning there was a dark blue bruise under her eye. It wasn't serious, though, and would be gone in a couple of days. As it was Friday, she decided to take the day off. When she returned to Knightsford on Monday, she hoped it would have disappeared.

On Monday, it was overcast and threatening rain as she cycled in. The gates of Knightsford had never looked more ominous. She dismissed the thought from her mind, telling herself that the incident was over. Niven had had a narrow escape. No doubt the experience would have shaken him and so deter him from making any further advances.

She parked her bike and collected her keys from the lodge. The gate-keeper let her into the sterile area and returned to his office. She walked towards the main door of the Admin.

'You dirty slag.' The hoarse, threatening voice seemed to come out of nowhere.

She stared about wildly. The bushes around the sterile area fence shielded most of the jail from her view.

'You fucking whore.' The voice came again, but closer and to her right.

Through the foliage, she saw a short, stocky figure leaning on a rake. The fresh face and gingerish hair could only belong to one person. Niven had been waiting for her in the bushes as he went about his work in the gardens.

But she was safe from him. He couldn't get to her through the fence. She hurried to the Admin door and went inside.

She found she was breathing fast. It had been a shock. She had hoped it was all over, but clearly it wasn't. She wondered if she would be safe in the education block.

Niven appeared for the morning class, but sat, quiet and sullen, at his desk. Tom's face looked strained and angry, and she guessed that he must have said something to Niven. The rest of the class seemed unaware of it, but she felt the tension in the air.

Only Hamid had realised that something was wrong. He looked at her quizzically, his sharp Arab features wrinkled in thought. She didn't want him to find out. She knew he idolised her and could be frighteningly violent when roused. The situation was becoming more difficult by the minute.

Graham caught her eye and smiled intimately. She shot a steely glare in his direction and looked away sharply. She was determined not to encourage any more suitors.

As the class finished, she went to leave, but noticed that Niven was already heading for the door. She dallied by her desk, allowing him time to get away.

She saw nothing of him for the rest of the morning. Work kept her busy and it was only towards late afternoon that she had time to sit alone in the office and collect her thoughts.

Suddenly, a shadow fell across the doorway. Niven entered the office. He stood in front of her desk, glaring at her.

'You fucking whore,' he said throatily. 'You've led me on and you know it.' He pointed a threatening finger at her. 'You won't fucking get away with it.' Then he was gone.

Jane sat there transfixed. She had tried to remain calm when he had come into the office but fear had paralysed her. She fought for control so that, at the least, she could scream if he attacked her again. But he had gone so quickly, that, for a second, it was as if he had never been there. The fear remained, though, and she could feel herself trembling.

She wondered if she could put up with this. The abuse in the sterile area she could handle. She knew he couldn't get at her, even though it was a bit like running a verbal gauntlet. But the education block was sometimes deserted for long periods. There was never an officer in attendance and she often sat alone in the office, marking work. There would be ample opportunity for Niven to attack her if he wanted to.

She still wouldn't report him, though. It would set him back several years and might cost him his sanity. Such a report would also delight the rest of the staff. It would vindicate all they had said about her lack of professionalism. She saw now how other, weaker, members of staff had been forced to join the group for mutual protection. But she refused to become something she abhorred.

As the days passed, Niven regularly ambushed her with abuse, and she began to cringe inwardly as she entered the sterile area in the morning. Whenever she was alone in the office, she awaited his appearance with trepidation. She became nervous and irritable, and began to lose weight. But she was committed now, whatever the outcome. It was a question of who would break first, her or Niven.

I had been blissfully unaware of all the goings-on between Jane and Niven. Tom hadn't said anything and I was rarely in the education block. But finally something happened that made me realise that something was wrong.

Late one afternoon, I took an OU assignment up to the education block for posting. As I entered the corridor between the classrooms, I glimpsed Niven as he disappeared down the far stairs.

The office door was open. I knocked and went in. Jane was sitting in her usual position at her desk.

'Hello, Jane, I've got an assignment for you,' I said, walking over to her.

She looked up. Her face was pasty white and she looked as if she had just seen the proverbial ghost.

'You're very pale, Jane,' I remarked carefully.

'You're very bald, Norman,' she shot back with verve.

I was completely taken aback. I was unaccustomed to anyone being rude to me — I usually managed to intimidate a basic level of civility from most people. And it was right out of character for Jane to be insulting.

I stared at her, trying to figure out what was wrong. I didn't think I had been overly familiar. We weren't intimate friends, but we were certainly beyond mere pleasantries.

She took the assignment from me and maintained a strained distance. She was cold, business-like and unsmiling. I considered the possibility that she was suffering from one of those 'women's problems'.

Later, I mentioned it to Tom. He shrugged, saying that she could be a bit funny at times. He didn't seem very interested, so I let it drop.

The following tea-time, Tom told me that Jane wanted to see us both that evening. I was immediately suspicious. I couldn't figure out why she wanted to see us together and Tom wouldn't be drawn on it.

'Norm, do me a favour,' he pleaded. 'I've given my word that I won't say anything.'

By now, my paranoia was raging. I immediately feared I was under some threat. But Tom assured me otherwise.

'I trust you as a friend, Tom, so I don't expect you to keep things from me that could damage me,' I said.

Tom looked hurt. 'Norm, it's nothing to do with you, I swear. And you should know me better than to think that I wouldn't mark your card if something was up.'

I accepted his assurance, but still waited for the evening meeting with trepidation.

At 7.55, we climbed the stairs to the twos, sauntered round the gallery and wandered into the education block. Other than a few stragglers, the place was deserted.

The office was locked and we found Jane sitting in a classroom on her own. She waved for us to come in and asked Tom to shut the door. My paranoia went into overdrive.

We huddled conspiratorially around a desk, bending our heads closer as she spoke softly. Occasionally, she would look up towards the door.

'Norman, you must promise me that you won't do or say anything about what I am going to tell you,' she whispered.

I was very much caught up in all the secret service stuff now, but I still had my wits about me.

'Jane,' I said, 'if it concerns me, then that's a decision I have to make.'

'No, no, silly,' she said, slapping the back of my hand. I suddenly realised that she was really nervous. 'It's about me.'

'Well, in that case I promise not to say or do anything,' I conceded reluctantly.

She then told me what had been happening between her and Niven. As the tale unfolded, I looked at Tom in amazement. He raised his eyebrows and shrugged. 'Norm, I couldn't say anything to you. Jane made me promise.'

Suddenly, a thought struck me. 'So that's what the matter was the other day when I found you looking so pale,' I said.

Jane nodded. 'Yes, you caught me at a bad time. I'm sorry about the rude remark.' She looked contrite.

'I've been trying to keep it all quiet,' she continued, 'but it's about to come out now anyway. Niven went to his gardens officer today and told him everything. The officer went to see the Governor this afternoon.'

'Well, I don't see that you've got anything to worry about, Jane,' I said. 'It's Niven who assaulted you.'

'But I don't want to say anything about that,' she said stubbornly.

'Jane, he's grassed you. You're a straight person. You're entitled to defend yourself,' I argued.

She shook her head. 'No, I won't do it, Norman.'

I had to admire her. I would have done exactly the same in her position, but then that's the way I had learned to live over many years.

'So what are you going to do if it goes the wrong way?' I pressed her. 'You can bet Maypole will be on Niven's side. You could get the sack.'

'I've got an appointment to see my local union representative first thing in the morning,' she said.

'Do you think that will be enough?' I asked.

'I'm afraid it will have to be, Norman,' she answered.

She stood up, indicating that it was time to go. 'And whatever happens, Norman, don't forget what you promised me.' She looked me straight in the eye.

'And that goes for you too, Tom,' she said, turning to him. Tom nodded his agreement.

We went one way down the corridor while she went the other.

'She's got a lot of nerve for a bird, that Jane,' I said to Tom.

'I did tell you so, didn't I, Norm?'

I had to concede that he had. I didn't like to admit it, but as far as women were concerned, Tom's judgement was proving far superior to mine.

Jane was half an hour late arriving the following morning. The appointment with her union representative had taken longer than she had thought.

She walked through the sterile area and found herself looking around for Niven lurking in the bushes. But there would be no more of that now. That was one positive aspect of the affair being out in the open.

Camber was already well into his morning's work when she entered the office. They exchanged pleasantries, but he asked no questions. She reasoned that he must know something of what was going on, but he was a kind and considerate man. She felt she was lucky to have him as her direct boss.

Her appointment with Maypole was at 11.00. No doubt he would confer with other senior staff first. She might as well get on with her work. She sat down at her desk and started to go through some papers.

The first interruption was from Neil. From time to time, the condition of his joints worsened, and today the first joint of his index finger was swollen and painful and made writing difficult. He had been given paracetamol for it at the hospital, but it still throbbed. Jane excused him from classes for the day.

Hardly had Neil left than Luke came in, clearly upset. He glanced quickly at the cupboard, but there were other things on his mind today. He stood before Jane's desk, shifting from foot to foot and biting his lip.

'Hallo, Luke. What's the matter?' asked Jane sympathetically.

Luke continued to bite his lip and looked on the verge of tears. 'They're going to send me to Parkhurst for observation,' he suddenly blurted out.

'Don't worry, Luke. It's all for the best. They'll just do some tests to work out what treatment you need,' she reassured him, despite feeling a twinge of guilt. He looked far from convinced.

She took her morning class and watched the clock hand creep ever closer to 11.00. At 10.50, she left her students with an essay to write and made her way to the Admin block.

Now she was nervous. She could imagine the pressure that had been brought to bear on Maypole over this, her latest 'indiscretion'. As she passed through each gate and door, the thought crossed her mind that it could be for the last time.

She took a deep breath and knocked on the Governor's door. If these were to be her last hours in Knightsford, then at least she would give a good account of herself. She knew that right didn't count for much in prison; she had learned that very early on. But it did matter as far as her conscience was concerned.

Jane heard a muffled voice shout from within. She opened the door and walked inside. Maypole was sitting behind his desk, telephone in hand.

She hesitated, but he waved for her to sit down. 'Got to go now, call me back later,' he barked into the phone. He replaced the handset and turned to face her.

Jane always had an overwhelming urge to laugh when in Maypole's presence. There was something patently ridiculous in his entire manner. The red, flushed face, bursting out of the neck of the well-pressed striped suit, reminded her of an overstressed executive who feared losing his job. The hair-trigger temper, the insecurity, the personality always on the brink of losing control – in any other half-sane organisation, he would never have risen above lower management level.

But she would never laugh at him. Good manners wouldn't allow it. After all, he was the Governor, and her position demanded she show him some respect. And he had always been well-mannered in his dealings with her.

'Mrs Roman, oh, Mrs Roman.' Maypole shook his head slowly as he almost moaned the words. 'I always feared that, someday, I would have to escort you to the gate and see you off the premises.' He looked straight at her to gauge her reaction.

Jane sat there totally impassive. She wasn't going to make it easy for him. She would let him make the first move, then she would counter-attack.

Already, Maypole felt that the interview was going wrong. He had expected a difficult and emotional time. It would be embarrassing to escort a weeping, distraught woman to the gate, with him having to offer a sympathy he certainly didn't feel.

The pause lengthened. When he saw that there would be no reaction from her, he went on. 'I'm afraid that that time has come, Mrs Roman.' The tone was different now as he tried to add an air of finality to the pronouncement.

'This is a very serious allegation that Niven Brady has made against you. I know he is a volatile and immature young man, but it is quite improper that you have allowed this relationship to develop.'

As Maypole seized the moral high ground with relish, it occurred to Jane that she had always suspected him of being a prude. She could picture him as a rather tubby young boy, forever obsessed with guilt.

But she wouldn't share it with him for she had done nothing to feel guilty about. She felt strangely lightheaded as she became aware of the anger rising within her. She controlled it with difficulty, knowing her time would come very soon now.

Maypole was perplexed. He had warned the woman that he was about to escort her from the jail. He had put the main allegation to her. But still she sat there with no visible sign of emotion on her face. He considered the idea that she might be frozen with shock, but dismissed it as wishful thinking. She had always been a stubborn woman.

With a barely suppressed sigh, he pushed on to the inevitable conclusion. 'I have consulted with other senior members of my staff and they all agree with me that there is no future for you here at Knightsford. We feel that it will be in the best interests of everyone, yourself included, if you resign.' He sat back in his chair and folded his arms across his chest. He had finished.

Jane still sat there. She would let him sweat for a moment. And, her anger having just peaked, she wanted to present a cool and lucid argument.

Maypole fidgeted in his chair. For a situation where he had felt that he held all the cards, it didn't seem much as if he was in control. He opened his mouth to speak.

'Governor Maypole.' Jane cut him off before he uttered a sound. She had spoken so suddenly and unexpectedly that it had made him jump, and he sat there with his mouth still half open.

'Did it ever occur to you to ask me if these allegations are true?' Anger gave a hard edge to her voice. It was a rhetorical question. She didn't wait for a reply.

'I am a married woman. You have met my husband, Robert, a number of times. I am the mother of two children. You have met both of them numerous times. So I find this allegation of having an improper relationship with Niven Brady offensive in the extreme.' Jane paused, confident that Maypole wouldn't interrupt now.

'I take my job very seriously, Governor Maypole. Certainly as seriously as you take yours.' Maypole had been slumping in his seat, but at this mention of his job, he visibly stiffened.

'I take it as a slur on my professionalism,' she continued, 'that you should think that I would pervert the role of teacher in this manner. But far worse than that, it is a slur on me as a woman. How dare you take the unsubstantiated word of someone who, in your own words, is immature and volatile? How dare you take the unsubstantiated word of a prisoner over that of a member of staff? And how dare you hold a meeting with your senior members of staff, and reach a decision, without ever once allowing me the right to speak in my own defence?'

As Jane spoke, Maypole's face became paler and paler. Then the process reversed itself. As she challenged him, he steadily progressed through shades of red until he was now a bright shade of scarlet. Jane reflected that, at this moment, he looked like a large, apoplectic bullfrog.

But she wasn't finished yet. She was about to deliver her final blow. 'Governor Maypole.' She leaned forward to emphasise her words. 'This morning I had an interview with the local representative for the National Union of Teachers. I fully apprised him of the situation. He says that, under union rules, and under the terms of my contract, there are certain procedures that must be adhered to. You have no right to dismiss me without a formal hearing. And, in the first instance, you should submit your complaint to him, in writing.'

At the first mention of 'union', Maypole reacted as if stung. His body convulsed in the chair as he sat bolt upright. He opened his mouth to roar his reply, when he suddenly realised he had nothing to say. The involvement of the union had changed everything. This was now developing into a very messy business indeed and there was no guarantee that he would win.

With this realisation came the change in him. He slumped back in his chair, deflated. Jane reflected that he looked a very small and insignificant bullfrog now.

Suddenly, she noticed tears running down his cheeks. His shoulders began to shake, gently at first, but then more vigorously. Jane realised with horror that he was crying.

The unreality of the situation threatened to overwhelm her. She had always known that Maypole couldn't handle pressure in any form, but she hadn't expected this.

She got up out of her seat and walked around his desk. She put one hand on the heaving shoulders. She felt the deep sobs that racked his body. 'Now, now, Governor. It's all right.' The words seemed trite and inappropriate, but she couldn't think of anything else to say. She looked towards the door, terrified that someone might come in.

Gradually, the sobbing subsided. Slowly, Maypole regained control. He reached into his jacket pocket and pulled out a handkerchief. He wiped his face, then blew his nose loudly.

Jane returned to sit opposite him. She felt terribly embarrassed. It was a situation that she longed to escape from, but she could hardly walk out and leave him now.

'Mrs Roman,' said Maypole, sniffing repeatedly. 'I must give this matter more thought. I want you to return to your classroom and carry on as normal. I want to investigate further.'

A fledgling feeling of triumph surged deep in Jane's bosom, a thrill that threatened to make her cry out. The reprieve had been as sudden as it had been unexpected. It also offered her the ideal opportunity to withdraw.

'I'm sorry for the unpleasantness, Mr Maypole,' she said, getting up from her chair. 'I hope we can settle this matter amicably.'

Maypole wasn't looking at her now. He stared at his desk in front of him, his eyes half closed. He nodded his head slowly in agreement.

Jane turned, opened the door and was through it, all in one smooth movement. As she hurried away down the corridor, she listened for the expected scream or other violent convulsion from the office behind her. But there was nothing, only silence.

She reflected that things would never be the same between her and Maypole now. He had revealed himself to her as being the weak man everyone had suspected. It wasn't in her nature to feel contempt for another human being, but what she was experiencing was certainly tantamount to that. She reflected that she was lucky to be a member of staff. If she was one of his prisoners, she really would have something to worry about.

12

For the first nine-and-a-half years of my sentence, I had been on the 'A' list. While in this top security category, I could only be visited by members of my family and by friends who had been vetted by the police. Needless to say, anyone who had a criminal conviction, or was otherwise deemed to be undesirable, was refused permission to visit.

For the past two years, I had hardly been in a position to take advantage of the more relaxed visiting conditions that went with the lower-security 'B' category, having been shifted about from jail to jail and from chokey to chokey. Now, though, I could think about seeing old friends whom I hadn't seen for years.

Charlie and I went back seventeen years, when we had been young tearaways in the Scrubs together, and later we had renewed our friendship at Parkhurst. Over the years, we exchanged the occasional letter.

Charlie had been with the Krays in the Sixties, running 'long firms'. He had a talent for getting money and a talent for spending it, too: Charlie was a playboy. When he had got out from his last sentence several years ago, he had prospered and now was big in cars and property and lived in a spacious house by a marina. As soon as he had heard I was just down the road from him, he had wanted to visit. I was allowed a visit every three weeks, and as my parents visited only once a month, I had a couple of spare visiting orders. Charlie's visit was set for a Sunday.

The Sunday duly arrived, and as I walked over to the visiting room, I was looking forward to seeing Charlie. It was quite some time since we had been together at Parkhurst.

I was heartily sick of the unspirited cons at Knightsford, who, apart from Tom, were almost universally dull and cowed. Charlie was a kindred spirit. He lived by his wits, had the courage to go after what he wanted from life and had boundless style. He was nearly fifty, yet he still had a young man's life-style.

I sat at my usual corner table and waited. Charlie's large, bulky figure loomed in the doorway. He was much heavier now. Great fleshy jowls made the large, bald head seem almost round. The body-builder's chest was as massive as ever, but his waist and hips had expanded exponentially. You could see the great folds of fat even through his clothes. He was smartly dressed in a casual outfit that was obviously expensive, but the clothes were stretched tight around his enormous bulk.

He held a large cigar between two fingers of his right hand, and seemed to sparkle as he walked, the light reflecting off his gold jewellery. There was a heavy gold chain and pendant around his neck, his cuff links and tie pin were solid gold and on several fingers of each hand were large gold rings.

For a second, I was taken aback. This concession to conspicuous consumption wasn't part of the Charlie that I had known at Parkhurst. There, a man was his word, his personality, his courage and what he stood up in. Window dressing was dismissed as camouflage for posers.

But I was behind the times. Styles had changed. Men wore flamboyant, stylish clothes now, and, for many, personal jewellery was de rigueur. No doubt the man hadn't changed. He was just keeping up with fashion.

As he drew closer, I noticed a young girl following him. She seemed to be with him, yet she was young enough to be his daughter. Long, black hair framed a pretty face that still held the softness of early youth. Her clear, pale skin was highlighted by judiciously applied make-up, cleverly understated. She had on a blue dress that was short but not indecently so. The crochet-knit white cardigan perfectly complemented her long, dark hair. Her breasts moved freely beneath it, and I guessed she wasn't wearing a bra.

As I stood up to greet them, Charlie threw his arms around me and kissed me on both cheeks. His emotional, demonstrative nature betrayed his Jewish origins.

'Norm, this is Helen,' he said, stepping aside to introduce the beautiful child. 'She's a friend of mine,' he added, almost as an afterthought.

I shook hands with Helen and she smiled sweetly, revealing perfect white teeth. 'I'm pleased to meet you, Norm,' she said in a breathless voice.

We all sat down. Charlie and I filled each other in on the details of our respective lives over the past years, but I felt restricted by Helen's presence. My story was one of gloom, despair and violence, and I was ill at ease telling it in front of this young girl. There was also an awkwardness between us, to be expected of strangers.

'Helen, will you go and fetch some tea, please, love?' asked Charlie, handing her some money. 'What do you want, Norm?'

We gave her our order and she went over to the refreshments counter in the corner. Charlie looked over his shoulder, watching her go.

'She's not eighteen yet,' he said to me quietly, grinning.

'You'll get nicked the way you're carrying on,' I said, laughing with him.

'She's got no bra on underneath that jumper, you know,' he added.

'I had noticed, Charlie. I suppose I'll be reading about you in the *News of the World*.'

Charlie roared. It was a deep throaty laugh that carried around the room. A few heads turned. 'She's one of about a dozen young birds I take out occasionally. She's a nice young girl,' he confided.

'You'll be all right if your old woman finds out,' I cautioned.

Charlie was suddenly serious. 'I'm very discreet, Norm. I always take them right off the plot.'

We changed the subject as Helen returned with the refreshments. We carried on as before, with me trying to make small talk to bring her into the conversation.

Helen was intelligent, with a bright, cheery personality. She didn't have the false sophistication that many young girls put on when they're with older men. She was delightful and charming.

She was completely wasted on me, though. There was no place for such as her in my world. I hadn't thought seriously of sex or beauty or love for years now. And to be reminded of it in my situation was like being a hungry child pressing his face against a baker's shop window.

In truth, I would have enjoyed the visit more if Charlie had come on his own. We could have indulged in our old camaraderie and laughed over past times. As it was, Helen significantly cramped my style.

The screw called out that it was time for the visit to end. We looked at each other, surprised that the two hours had passed so quickly. We stood and Charlie hugged me again. Turning to Helen, he said, 'Give Norm a big hug. He hasn't been with a woman for twelve years.'

I felt myself blush. 'Thanks, Charlie,' I replied. 'I feel like a nonce now.' They both laughed.

Helen stepped forward and put her arms around my neck. I put my hands on her waist, not wanting to pull her close. I could be proper almost to the point of prudery with strange women, especially one who was a girlfriend of a close friend.

She pulled herself to me and kissed me lightly on the lips. I felt awkward and slightly embarrassed, but was aware of myriad subliminal reactions. The perfume in her gossamer hair was incredibly sweet and alluring. Beneath her clothes, I could feel the softness of her body against me. Her lips brushed wetly against mine, reincarnating a million erotic dreams that had lain interred for a decade. Her breath was sweet and clean and vital and invited me to drink deeply of it.

An eternity passed in a second. We stepped apart and she smiled. They walked towards the door, half turning to wave goodbye to me. Then they were gone.

That evening, I told Tom about it. He laughed when I

complained that I couldn't talk freely to Charlie because Helen was there.

'You've done too much bird, that's your trouble,' he teased. 'It'll do you good to have a cuddle with a young bird. It might liven you up a bit, too, you old bastard.'

The last part stung. 'Never mind about that,' I said. 'That would be something else that you young 'uns couldn't keep up with me on.'

'Get out of it,' he replied, then changed the subject. However, it stayed in my thoughts for the rest of the evening.

I didn't mention the visit on my next meeting with Jean. After my silence following her last gambit, 'country matters' no longer reared their erotic heads. She seemed content to treat me as a friend with whom she could talk over the events of the previous week. She confided in me and asked my advice. I reflected that her psychology tutor had now become her counsellor.

If some of the world was now beating a path to my door, my main outside contact was still through letters. I wrote to my mother every week and exchanged letters with friends, mostly in other jails. It was a chore rather than a pleasure, though. After 12 years of writing about the same things, the medium had palled on me somewhat. However, I still enjoyed receiving letters, although they were few and far between now.

A letter from Professor Pat confirmed that the university would accept me once I was free. She then went on to talk about her life and her family. She wrote as a friend. I replied in kind.

For many years, the only woman in my life had been my mother. My friendships with Jean and Pat added no romantic dimension whatsoever, though. Increasingly, I looked on others as being exterior to myself. There was no point of contact between us emotionally. But I rejected the notion that I had become hard and callous. It was more a case of becoming desensitised to feeling.

Long months spent in solitary hadn't helped matters. I'd had to survive purely on the warmth of my own company. To assuage the ravages of loneliness, I had convinced myself that I liked to be on my own. Then there had been the shanghais. One moment I would be with close friends; the next, I would be sitting in a strange prison hundreds of miles away. Now, to protect my psyche, I deliberately kept my friendships superficial.

The letter from Helen, the day after Pat's, came as a surprise. I had honestly forgotten all about her, thinking I would never see her again. The next time Charlie visited me, he would probably be accompanied by another of his young birds.

She said that she had enjoyed meeting me and would like to write. She made no mention of Charlie.

For me, though, Charlie was the problem. I was very proper and loyal about things like this. Although I was almost sure he wouldn't mind, I couldn't write to her behind his back.

I wrote to him, telling him about Helen's letter, and he wrote back, giving me his blessing. As far as he was concerned, she was only one of a dozen casual girlfriends.

I was pleased but concerned. I was about to allow romance to enter my lonely world. It was a consummation devoutly to be wished, but there were dangers there. Helen was young love personified. After the ugliness I had been used to, her freshness and beauty had an unreal quality. But what if I grew to love her and wanted to own her?

With two disastrous romances behind me in my youth, love had become synonymous with pain. For me, passion always burned with the fiercest intensity. It was an all-or-nothing affair; there could be no holding back.

Love was an intangible thing that couldn't be controlled. It might grow and change and dissipate. The chemistry that had woven magic between two people could suddenly fail, leaving ashes in the mouth of the one and resentment in the heart of the other.

This time I would control it, though. I would keep my emotional distance so that, if the break came, the wound would be only superficial. And writing was a cool, distant medium. That would aid my cause. It wouldn't be like meeting her in the flesh.

Helen's letters were delightfully irreverent. Her humour was nonsensical and bizarre as only the humour of the young can be. She mocked convention and then mocked the mocking. She was no great writer, but her letters captivated me. I replied in similar vein. Soon we were both lost in our own private world of silliness.

Inevitably, after a couple of weeks she asked if she could visit. I wrote to Charlie to tell him of the latest development, then sent her a visiting order.

Tom had been observing all this with mounting merriment. The fact that I was almost twice Helen's age only added to his mirth.

'Perhaps her father died when she was young and she misses him,' he jibed.

My constant retort was that it was only jealousy since, at the time, he had no girlfriend of his own.

As the day of the visit approached, I grew increasingly nervous. It was hard to rationalise. I, who had stood trial for my life at the Bailey, who had suffered the rigours of solitary, and who, each day, faced the uncertainty of an endless sentence, was frightened of a mere slip of a girl. But it was myself I was frightened of. I was far from content in prison, but I had come to terms with it. I feared a change that would weaken me and make each day seem a lifetime.

I prepared for the visit as if I was going on a date. I pressed my jeans and my tightest white T-shirt. I went to the gym in the morning and pumped up until I felt I would burst. I showered and then spent an age shaving. If I was going to be eighteen again, I would have to work at it.

I sat at the corner table, pleased to be as far away from the screw as I could get. There was no such thing as privacy in the visiting room, but at least I didn't feel so exposed in the corner.

Helen came through the door and I rose to meet her. Should I presume to kiss her or just shake her hand? And if I kissed her, should it be on her lips or her cheek? What was the protocol in a situation like this? I didn't want her to think that, just because she was a casual girlfriend of Charlie's, I felt I could be forward with her.

Helen solved the problem for me, walking right up and kissing me on the lips. I felt her softness against me. Her perfume was a heady aphrodisiac. Her kiss registered on my lips and all over my body at the same time. I felt levels of feeling that had been switched off for years suddenly stir and come alive.

She stepped away and sat down opposite me. Talking to her was surprisingly easy and relaxed. I had worried over what I would speak to her about, but the conversation flowed. As our letters had shown, we had a similar sense of humour, irreverent and silly, and now we were just two people enjoying each other's company. We laughed constantly.

It was a pleasant interlude. The pain and anguish of the past years were almost forgotten now. For two hours, I would escape from my prison in the company of this charming girl. But I knew it would have to end.

As the screw called for time, we both looked up in surprise. Harsh reality had intruded into our make-believe world and now it would tear us apart.

We sat quietly, looking into each other's eyes. We were beyond words now as we savoured these last moments. She reached for my hand across the table and clutched it tightly. Together, we rose and stood beside the table.

There was no thinking about what to do now. Every action seemed to flow naturally into the next. I held her close as she tilted her face up to mine. I kissed her on the lips, lightly, then with passion. We clung to each other.

But I was no Foxy. Public displays of emotion weren't part of my nature and I was aware of the screw looking. As I prised her from me, I felt prison mode begin to take over again.

'Can I come again?' she asked softly.

'Of course you can.'

'I'll write tomorrow.'

'I'll be waiting for it.'

Then she was gone, walking away from me without looking back. She swept through the door and became just a memory.

But it was one that I could examine at my leisure. I lived much in my thoughts now, a trick I had learned in solitary. I would savour this experience, pick it apart and gauge its effect on me.

I was aware that, whatever followed, Helen had brought me

closer to the great body of the human race than I had been in years. Just for that, I would be grateful to her.

Every jail in the country had its local branch of the Prison Officers' Association, and Knightsford was no exception. I had found that committee members were remarkably similar from jail to jail. They were mostly elderly, morose men who, if they ever took any pleasure from life, rarely showed it. They resented prisoners, and this was peculiar because they owed their very livelihoods to them.

Any reforms had to be mediated through their committees, and if they didn't approve, they would not make it easy for reforms to happen. Our local POA branch was usually a model of restraint. In fact, the majority of Knightsford's 'residents' were blissfully unaware of its existence. I knew that the union was there, but for me, it was a question of 'know your enemy'. At the very least, we would certainly be ideological enemies.

The public face of the POA at Knightsford was represented by Mark Collins and Jeff West. Collins was a tall, ill-tempered, bitter man whose permanently red face made him look constantly angry. He also had a facial tic and a permanent half-sneer that revealed one long, yellow fang on the right side of his mouth. With his fat cheeks and his beetle brow, he looked almost canine, like some elderly irate bulldog.

In many ways, Collins and West made for a strange pair. Whereas Collins' evil old soul had been steeped in the acid of hatred for several decades, West was more of the prissy, fussy bigot. His hatred was fuelled by his sense of inadequacy. He knew he cut a ridiculous figure and tried to compensate by being authoritarian. It was patently apparent, however, that he lacked the physical courage to play the role to the full.

The first we knew of any industrial action was when a new notice appeared on the centre notice-board. It had been issued by Maypole and informed us of impending industrial action by the local POA. They were going to exclude all the civvies from the jail, and therefore, there would be no workshops and no work.

In his notice, Maypole emphasised that it was the wish of the screws that we should all be locked up during working hours for the duration of the dispute. He stressed that he had rejected this proposal and had ordered that we be left unlocked. He asked for our co-operation in ensuring that this privilege was not abused.

Needless to say, the notice caused quite a stir. 'Residents' eagerly discussed how the action would affect them. It was generally agreed that, provided it didn't last too long, the break from the workshops would serve as a welcome rest. Long hours of games and lying in bed were envisaged.

But I had experienced similar actions before and had found that, much as workshop labour was a drag, at least it broke up the day and gave it some structure. I knew that the new-found idleness would soon pall on the residents. Before a couple of weeks had passed, they would all be longing for a return to normality.

I couldn't help but reflect for a moment on the nature of the men who had advocated that we be locked up for the duration of the working day. Whatever they might choose to call it, that would be solitary confinement.

Monday dawned and the action began. Men filed down for breakfast, then stood around in groups not knowing what to do with themselves. I promptly returned to bed. Tom hadn't seen fit to get up. In the afternoon, the two of us went to the bath-house for an improvised work-out in a spare room. The evenings were as normal, not being affected by the action.

By day two, Tom and I had our new programme mapped out. Heavy physical exercise in the afternoon and evenings would be followed by a long lie-in the following morning. We were nothing if not survivors.

Maypole wasn't at all pleased with the situation. He fully realised that better governors than he had endured the indignity of having their jails paralysed by the POA, but it still rankled. He could hardly take it out on the staff, though, because this would only exacerbate the situation. And he was notoriously weak with his staff anyway.

He sat in his office and seethed. He itched to do something, but felt helpless. The only section of Knightsford's society he could take his ire out on were the residents, but they were now spending all their time in enforced idleness. There was little he could do to regiment that.

However, he felt that he should be seen to be doing something, and he recalled the military dictum of 'showing the flag'. He left his office to patrol the landings. He just might catch someone doing something they weren't allowed to do. Then he could bawl them out and get rid of some of his frustration.

As he emerged from the Admin on to the centre, he was surprised at how few residents there were about. Admittedly, it was still before 10.00, but the wings looked just as deserted as they usually did when the workshops were operating.

He decided to start on the twos. He would make a complete circuit of the jail, then descend to the ones. He climbed the stairs by the centre and headed down A wing.

He walked slowly from cell to cell, treading softly so as not to make too much noise. Sound carried in these old prisons and inmates were wary and cunning. It wouldn't take them too long to learn that approaching heavy footsteps heralded his imminent arrival.

He crept up to a door and slid its spy-hole cover clear of the Judas hole. The treacherous connotations of this nickname stung him for a moment, bringing a temporary pang of guilt. There was something inherently shameful about creeping up on grown men and spying on them in the privacy of their only living room.

But he was the Governor and this was his jail. He owned everybody and everything in it, and there was no such thing as privacy as far as he was concerned. The residents had surrendered that right the moment they had stepped into prison.

He peered through the opening into the gloom. For a moment, he could see absolutely nothing as his eyes adapted from the strong glare of the landing lights. Then, the daylight streaming through the small window lit a bulky lump obscured beneath bed covers. The form was motionless. Maypole concluded that he must be asleep. But he could hardly censure him for that, even at 10.00 on a weekday morning. There was no work, so sleeping was one of the very few alternatives.

He crept from cell to cell, peering through the spy-holes. Many were in half-darkness, barely revealing sleeping forms. Some were empty. Others were lit like TV screens revealing some mundane domestic scenario. Men sat in chairs reading or writing. Sometimes pairs played games, listened to music or just talked. These were pastimes that defied censure. He crept on.

He rounded the corner and crept along C wing. He moved quicker now, bored with the routine trivia that was meeting his eye.

He came to a cell, swung back the cover and put his eye to the hole. He saw nothing but absolute, inky blackness.

He stepped back, blinked, then looked through again. Still the Stygian darkness glared back at him. He stepped back, puzzled. There was no way this cell could be so unnaturally dark. Someone must have blocked the hole from the inside.

It was a common ploy when clandestine activity was going on. He knew this much from his days as a lowly screw. His heart raced at the thought that he might have caught someone at something. He pushed the door. It refused to yield. Obviously, the same person who had blocked the spy-hole had barricaded the door. This, in itself, was a nicking offence.

It occurred to Maypole that he was being denied access to a cell within his prison. He claimed sovereignty over every square inch of his domain and ceded no rights whatsoever to others. Yet someone was clearly making a determined attempt to annex this cell, albeit temporarily.

Suddenly, he found his voice. A bellow of sheer rage burst from his lips as he threw himself against the door. There was a crash, as his shoulder struck the heavy wood. He gasped in pain as the door still refused to yield.

'This is the Governor! Open this door this minute!' he screamed in rage and pain.

He threw himself against the door again.

This time he heard a scraping sound and felt it budge. Encouraged, he threw himself against it with renewed vigour. It swung open several inches.

By now, feet were running across the ones. The screws had come out of the office and seen Maypole wrestling with the door. Hall launched himself towards the stairs leading to the twos and, breathing heavily, pulled himself up them.

All the noise had roused me from a shallow slumber. I jumped from my bed, hastily threw a towel around me and ran to my door. As I emerged on to the ones, I could see dozens of other 'residents', similarly attired, staring at the door on the twos. I immediately realised it was Bill's cell.

With a final, climactic yell, Maypole threw himself at the half-open door. There was a crash as something fell over and it swung open.

He switched on the light and stepped inside.

Bill and Steve were there, half-naked and blinking in the brightness. Bill's shirt hung open where he had hastily tried to throw it on. Steve had one leg in his trousers. Their faces were frozen with shock and panic.

Maypole gasped. The scene before him spoke for itself. The guilt on their faces removed any vestige of doubt.

It was an outrage. An abomination. Of all the clandestine activities he could have envisaged, this was the worst. They had taken advantage of his good nature in resisting the demands of the screws to lock everyone up. It was a personal affront to himself.

'Get these two men down the block,' he roared. A young screw and a breathless Hall stood outside the door now. They stepped inside.

Their appearance seemed to galvanise Bill and Steve into action. Slowly and deliberately, they pulled on the rest of their clothes, delaying their exit on to the landing as long as possible.

'Hurry up!' barked Maypole, in a considerable state of excitement.

With their heads hanging to their chests, Bill and Steve stepped out on to the landing. Bill's face was stark white and he seemed on the verge of tears. Steve's cheeks burned with colour as he looked wildly about, trying not to meet anyone's gaze.

There was a collective gasp from the assembled 'residents' as they realised the import of what they were seeing. It would be the stuff of gossip for days.

With the two screws following them, Bill and Steve descended the stairs and walked towards the centre. They disappeared round the corner into A wing, heading towards the chokey.

I dressed and climbed the stairs to Tom's cell. He was sitting inside with Jack, and looked up at me as I entered.

'Don't you say nothing, Norm,' he said, a hurt look on his face.

'Oi, Tom,' I replied. 'I ain't said fuck all. Don't put words in my mouth.'

He sat there, staring morosely into space.

'Look, mate,' I said, 'I like Bill and Steve. And I still like them right now. I knew this about them all along, so nothing's changed as far as I'm concerned. I'm not gloating over the fact that I was right. And instead of us arguing about it, we should be talking about what we can do to help them in the chokey.'

This last remark seemed to stir Tom out of his torpor. He adopted a thoughtful expression as he applied his mind to the problem.

'Well, Bill and Steve both smoke, so they'll need some snout,' he said. He slapped his hand on his knee in disgust. 'I've just had a thought: I won't be going out on the Works so I can't get to the chokey windows.'

'Can't we lower it down from above?' I suggested.

'Yeah, of course, we can,' he agreed. 'We'll have to find someone above them who's all right.'

Now he was doing something constructive, Tom's mood seemed to pass. I guessed he was embarrassed that they had been up to nonsense in a cell where he had spent some time himself. I toyed with the idea of making a joke about it, but thought better of it. There would be opportunity enough for that the next time he took the piss out of me.

For the rest of the day, the incident was the most popular topic around the jail. But not with us. A couple of people tried to mention it in passing, but Tom especially was having none of it. The morose look on his face was enough to put most people off.

We ignored the empty place at the table at dinner and tea. Jack seemed particularly bemused. Not only didn't he mention Bill, he sat through both meals in total silence.

The following morning, our thoughts were on what Bill and Steve would get on adjudication. Men on report were always dealt with in their wing PO's office. Normally, for petty, less controversial offences, this was a minor indignity. For Bob and Steve, though, it would mean a highly embarrassing public spectacle.

At just before 11.00 there were an inordinate number of idle loafers hanging around the centre. Some stood against the walls on the ones; others hung over the landing and stared down from the twos. Tom, Jack and I leaned on the railing outside Bill's empty cell to survey the proceedings.

Precisely at 11.00, Bill and Steve appeared from the direction of the chokey, with a screw escorting each of them. They stopped outside Docker's office, heads hanging to their chests.

Bill looked particularly white and drawn. I guessed that he couldn't have slept much the previous night in the face of the coming ordeal on the morrow. He was a sensitive, insecure fella at the best of times, often embarrassed by his Northern gaucherie. This latest incident would do nothing for his confidence.

It was hard to gauge its effect on Steve. He looked white and drawn even on good days, so there was no clue in his face. He, like Bill, hung his head, but I expected him to be the more resilient of the two.

Tom and I forbore shouting out to them in a gesture of support, reasoning that anything that attracted attention would be unwelcome. And as they refused to look anywhere but at the floor, they were unaware of our presence.

Niven had no such scruples. Standing with a group of sycophants in the gallery above the centre, he shouted a boisterous 'Go on, Bill,' as they approached from the chokey.

Bill looked up and smiled weakly, then immediately looked down again. He had cringed at the greeting, like a child expecting a blow.

As they stood below him, outside the office, Niven shouted again. 'Don't worry, Bill. They can't make your wife give evidence against you!' His bray of laughter carried along the wing.

It was a cruel and insensitive remark and typical of Niven. He was never so pleased as when he was making fun of someone weaker.

Suddenly, Maypole appeared through the Admin gate and marched across to Docker's office. His face was flushed, his manner stern, his gaze fixed in front of him. He entered the office and, seconds later, Bill and Steve were ushered in after him. The door closed.

Several minutes passed, then the door swung open again. Bill and Steve emerged, with the two screws in close attendance. In a group, they headed across the centre, back towards the chokey.

'Hey, Bill! Bill!' called out Tom suddenly. Bill's head jerked up at the sound of the familiar voice. 'What did ya get?'

'Seven days,' Bill mouthed back, holding up the appropriate number of fingers. Then he was round the corner on to A wing and out of sight.

In one way, seven days in the chokey would be a welcome relief for them. By the time they emerged in a week's time, the incident would be dead as a topic of gossip.

As the onlookers started to drift away, Docker hurried out of his office and began to write on the large blackboard fixed to the wall outside C wing office. The departing cons stopped, then wandered over to see what the notice was.

The three of us drifted along the twos until we were opposite the office. The notice, written in large, chalk letters, was plain now: 'ALL RESIDENTS ARE REQUIRED TO ASSEMBLE IN THE DINING HALL AT 1400 HOURS TODAY FOR AN ADDRESS BY THE GOVERNOR. THIS IS A DIRECT ORDER. ANYONE NOT ATTENDING WILL BE PLACED ON REPORT'.

It was certainly a curious ultimatum. No one could recall anything like it before. We screwed up our faces in puzzlement, wondering what could be so important that Maypole wanted to address the whole prison about it.

It was the major topic of conversation over dinner. The general opinion was that it was something to do with the industrial action. Others thought it must concern the incident with Bill and Steve, coming so soon after their adjudication.

'With that fucking lunatic Maypole, it could be anything,' I said. Tom and Jack nodded in agreement. 'And whatever it is, you can bet it won't be in our favour.'

Just before 2.00, we sauntered down to the dining hall. We heard the hubbub of voices long before we arrived, and as we entered, we were met by a sea of faces. All of Knightsford's 'residents' must have been there, sitting at tables and facing towards the stage.

There were people we hardly ever saw, Knightsford's eccentric recluses who spent their time in the corner of some workshop or sitting in their cells. All were there, sitting patiently, and not so patiently, for Maypole to appear.

The three of us walked to the back and lounged against the wall, partly obscured by some curtains. With the great dictator holding forth from the stage, we could listen without being seen. It wouldn't do to attract his attention.

At a few minutes past 2.00, Maypole suddenly hurried into the dining hall and climbed on to the stage. The Chief and a bevy of POs and SOs followed in his wake and stood by the side of the stage in a group.

Behind them, Foxy appeared, strolling leisurely into the hall. He ambled to the back, oblivious of the baleful glare that Maypole directed at him.

'Right,' Maypole barked. The hall suddenly fell silent. He thrust his face towards the audience, chin raised aggressively. Already his jowls were the colour of puce. His eyes swept the room.

'As you know,' he began, 'in the face of opposition from many of the staff, I made the concession of allowing you to stay unlocked during working hours for the duration of the industrial action.' He stopped to let this evidence of his good nature sink in. The silence stretched seamlessly as he laboured the pause.

'Unfortunately' – the word lanced through the quiet as he laid maximum emphasis on it – 'two residents have taken advantage of my good intentions. Not only have they let me down; they have let all of you down, too.'

This time he paused to gather his thoughts. He pursed his lips as if trying to decide how to phrase the next bit.

'You are all aware of what happened yesterday.' He seemed ill at ease now, embarrassed even. 'The two men I caught together in a cell . . .' The shade of puce deepened. 'Well, I won't stand for that sort of disgraceful behaviour!' He bellowed this last bit, as if, by his anger, he could distance himself from such activity. He stood tensely, both fists clenched, glaring around the audience.

Suddenly, I felt like laughing. I didn't incline to poofery personally, but it was hardly the stuff for emergency meetings in front of Knightsford's assembled 'residents'. Just because two young men, who had already spent several years without the company of women, had climbed into bed together one morning, it didn't herald the downfall of civilisation as we knew it. It wasn't the prelude to the apocalypse.

But to look at Maypole's face, you would have thought it was. I reflected that any half-qualified psychiatrist would have had a field day with him. That he thought this incident to be so outrageous gave valuable insight into his own personality. And the idea of Maypole as the defender of public morality in Knightsford was too ridiculous for words.

'I want to solemnly warn all of you,' he intoned in his most solemn voice, 'that any repetition of this sort of behaviour will lead to my withdrawing the privilege of free association during working hours as long as this industrial action lasts.'

I stood contemplating this deterrent to mass buggery. I reflected that any particularly mischievous gay couple could condemn us all to indefinite solitary confinement. But Maypole obviously hadn't thought of this. There he stood, a figure of unflinching authority, and clearly pleased with his performance.

There was now a tangible sense of anticlimax. Was this all that he had summoned us to the dining hall for? And what were we to do next? Take a mass oath to read *Playboy* and assiduously masturbate over the centre-fold?

Maypole stalked from the stage. He swept from the hall, the crowd of white-shirts hurrying after him.

It was the sign that the meeting was over. Men climbed to their feet and headed for the door. The three of us pushed ourselves away from the wall and joined the throng.

''Ere, do me a favour,' I said to Tom.

He looked at me questioningly. 'What's that?'

'Don't ever come into my cell with just your underpants on again.'

'Bollocks,' he retorted. 'Don't *you* ever come into mine.'

A week later, Bill and Steve came up from the chokey. That evening, Tom and I went to sit with them in Bill's cell. We asked how they were, but never mentioned the incident. They were clearly embarrassed about it, but that would pass. By the end of the evening, we had them laughing about Foxy. Their transition back into Knightsford society wouldn't be so difficult now.

I had mixed feelings as my next visit with Helen approached. I felt myself being drawn into something over which I could lose control. As survival was my main concern, anything that threatened it was very serious indeed. I had got through years without the sustenance of romance, so why should I risk everything now?

However, I reasoned that, with my new emotional maturity, I should be able to handle the relationship. There was still so much distance between myself and the rest of the human race, that I was able to view even Helen with a degree of detachment.

Over the past years, so many friends had drifted in and out of my life, never to be seen again, that people no longer seemed real to me. I recalled the philosopher who argued that only the self existed and everything else was illusion. It was a state of mind ideally suited to the chokey.

I prepared as before for the visit. When I entered the visiting room, someone was already sitting in my preferred corner seat. So I sat against one wall, my back to the screw, turning in my chair to watch Helen come in.

She hurried towards me, a smile on her face, eyes wide with expectation. Inwardly, I gasped at her child-like beauty. However many times I saw her, I knew she would have the same effect on me. Her youthful innocence was the antithesis of all that was filthy and corrupt in my world. I felt my spirit yield to commune with hers.

We embraced. I kissed her gently, but passion still sent a thrill coursing through me. She sat next to the window, pulling me down into the seat beside her. She clasped my left hand in both of hers, as I put my right arm about her shoulders.

For me, who could go a whole month without so much as touching another human being, such intimate contact was overwhelming. I felt the warmth of her radiate through me, burning fiercely where we touched. Deep inside me, juices ran where before there had only been arid wastes. In the ice palace that was my heart, trickles heralded the thaw.

For a while, we said little, being content just to hold each other. I had watched ten thousand others do this over the past dozen years. Now I knew what I had been missing.

'Norman,' she whispered quietly. I looked intently at her face. 'I want to wait for you.' It was almost like a confession, spoken shyly.

I felt a lump in my throat. There was a vast emptiness in my chest as my heart seemed to expand, and I saw a warm, pink vista open up in front of me.

It would be oh so easy to bask in the warmth of her love, safe from the world and all its rigours. A dozen clichés about the love of a good woman ran through my brain.

But what if it didn't last? What if, after a few years, when I needed her and had come to depend on her, she found someone else? I would be left in a weakened state. Maybe too weak to survive the loneliness again.

The thought was like a deluge of cold water. I figuratively shook myself. I must protect myself.

But maybe there was an alternative. Perhaps I could settle for less and have more.

'Helen,' I said softly, 'It would be very easy for me to say "Yes" to you. You're the nicest thing that has happened to me for many years. But I don't know when I will be free. It could be two years, it could be much longer.' A look of consternation passed across her face. She cuddled closer to me.

'You're still a young girl. It's not right that you should sit at home waiting for me when you should be out enjoying yourself. Let's just be friends, good friends. It will be the best of all possible relationships. We can share our problems and talk them over together. You can go out with who you want. And, if you do meet someone you fall in love with, you'll have my blessing. But if not, when I'm released, we can go out together and take it from there.'

She sat there, dewy-eyed. For long seconds, she said nothing, then, slowly, she nodded. It was the best solution and she had lost nothing. She could still come up and see me, we could still cuddle and be close, but there would be no proprietary, restrictive ownership.

It was a watershed in our relationship. Gone was the heavy pathos of unfulfillable love. We relaxed into an easy-going familiarity. We laughed freely and were comfortable with each other.

At the end of the visit, we clung together and kissed, but there was no desperation in our parting now. We knew we were there for each other and were reassured by the knowledge.

As I walked back to the wing, I was pleased with what I had achieved and proud of my new-found emotional maturity. The child of the institution was growing into the man.

As Christmas approached, there was a subtle change in the atmosphere at Knightsford. It was nothing tangible, nothing you could put your finger on, but nevertheless there was a feeling in the air.

On the one hand, there was anticipation of a golden period when rules would be largely suspended and the boring routine would change. But Christmas in prison was, in many ways, a negation of all that the occasion stood for. It was a family time, to be spent with loved ones and friends. At Knightsford, even the presence of comrades didn't lessen the sense of denial.

And then, just over the horizon, one short day past the 31st of December, lurked a whole new year. Another year identical to the one just gone, during which every one of the 365 days offered only boredom and pain. As a result, Christmas was always a time of tension in prison. As men wondered at the strength that had got them through the year, so they could only be intimidated by the prospect of another one to come. The most highly strung and the mentally ill were always the ones who felt the tension the most. There were inevitably incidents in the pre-Christmas period.

Surprisingly, an unexpected bonus came from the screws. It couldn't have been done out of Christmas spirit and a feeling of goodwill to all men, but they suddenly cancelled the industrial action, perhaps because they realised that they were getting nowhere. Everything returned to normal, or for what passed for normal at Knightsford.

Anyone who had expected the controversy over Jane to slow Niven down a bit would have been rudely disappointed. If it had been a public humiliation, then he wore it like a badge. In an attempt to brazen it out, he was even more boisterous than usual.

The first incident owed more to high spirits than bad temper, however. Just before 9.00 one weekday night, Tom and I were leaning against the rail outside Tom's cell. Below us, Warris shuffled across the ones, his jug of steaming water held out in front of him like a sacrificial offering.

''Ere, Norm, you watch this,' said Tom, nudging me. He pointed surreptitiously along the landing.

My eyes followed the direction he was pointing in. There, lounging against the wall a short distance away from Warris's cell, were Niven and Walt, a pale, thin lad who was Niven's most constant sycophant. I watched Niven raise his eyes as Warris reached the top of the stairs, and he continued to watch his progress out of the corner of his eye.

Warris advanced to the ironing board standing outside his door and commenced the ritual. He stopped, held the jug up to the light and gazed at it, placed it on the ironing board, then went inside to get his cup.

Niven moved quickly. No sooner had Warris disappeared inside the cell than Niven was in his doorway. He grabbed the door-handle and slammed the door, locking Warris inside.

Heaven knows for how many years Warris's ritual had been acted out to its completion. And who could guess what practical or mystical significance it held for him. Tonight, though, it would remain unfinished. A locked door stood between Warris and the jug.

Suddenly, there was a frenzied banging from inside his cell. His 'flag' fell down as he pressed the bell to summon a screw.

Outside on the landing, those in the know were in stitches. Niven had disappeared, together with the jug.

A screw duly appeared up on the twos. He unlocked the door and Warris burst out like a man who hadn't seen daylight for years. He stared around wildly, trying to figure out what had happened.

It was a young screw, one not usually seen on our wing. He seemed both embarrassed by and uninterested in Warris's stammerings. He turned and walked away.

Warris stood there, gazing slowly up and down the landing. If he believed the wind had blown his door shut behind him, that still didn't explain the missing jug. He wandered into the recess in search of it.

I laughed along with Tom, but without enjoyment. I couldn't

help but reflect that, after twenty-seven years inside, a man deserved more than to be tormented by such as Niven. But Warris's mistake was to have allowed himself to become weak. I resolved that such a fate would never befall me.

The pre-Christmas period was a busy time for Bitter Chris. Never had so many bizarre and not-so-bizarre soft toys graced the tables and shelves of his cell. At times it seemed to resemble a set from the *Muppet Show*.

I was looking for two presents. A big, flashy one for the rabbi to auction for charity and a more personal, meaningful one for Helen.

The rabbi's request had come as a surprise. I didn't know we celebrated Christmas. Perhaps he was just a committed democrat when it came to religious holidays. I just hoped he wouldn't ask me for something for Ramadan as well.

I chose a conventional, large white teddy for him. It was just the sort of thing that someone could make a generous, ostentatious gesture for. I could imagine some cigar-chomping Charlie look-a-like, waving a £50 note across the room at it.

Helen's present was far more problematic. I didn't want some sugary-sweet bunny as a clichéd token of our love. It would have to be something that reflected the irreverent humour that we shared.

I saw it straight away, and it was love at first sight. From the gleam in its eye, I knew my feelings were reciprocated.

The crocodile was a good two feet long and a bright, bilious green. Sharp spines ran the length of its back like a line of shark's teeth. Equally sharp white molars ran either side of its jaws, and its gaping maw yawned to reveal a mouth tastefully decorated in red velvet. It would be a pleasure to be eaten by a croc such as this.

Tom laughed when he saw it. He said that it wasn't the sort of thing to give your girlfriend. I reflected that, although he had been right about women before, he knew nothing of the peculiar relationship that Helen and I shared. I wrapped the croc, ready for her next visit.

No season of good will would have seemed quite right in prison without a tragedy. Knightsford might have been spared some of the worst excesses of most long-term regimes, but every so often there occurred an event that brought home to everyone that trying to survive a life sentence was a serious business.

Jane's friend Luke, the one I usually referred to as the 'feather nutter', had duly been sent to Parkhurst for observation. From what I knew, I guessed that this would amount to no more than being locked in a cell for a couple of weeks, followed by an interview with a psychiatrist.

From what little I had seen of Luke, I was sure that he was seriously mentally ill. However, Parkhurst was full of people who were in this condition. The important criterion, as far as the screws were concerned, was whether he was violent.

Obviously, Luke's original offence had involved serious violence, but at the moment, his behaviour lacked an aggressive element. Therefore, the screws were content to let him blither about the landings in his harmless insanity, and at the end of two weeks, they sent him back to Knightsford.

Jane had been sitting in her office daydreaming. As a practising Catholic, the approach of Christmas had particular significance for her, and she had been recalling the shining face of her daughter Linda as she had asked about her present that morning.

Suddenly, she was aware of someone at the door. She started, the feeling of danger rushing to seize her mind, and looked up quickly.

It was only Luke. Since his recent return from Parkhurst, he had been up to see her every day. And far from the period of observation doing him any good, he seemed much worse. He was still obsessed with the mysterious person who lived in her cupboard, but a new demon drove him now.

'What's the matter, Luke?' Jane asked kindly.

'The flood, the flood,' he repeated, a desperate quaver in his voice.

'What do you mean, Luke?' she pressed.

'The flood is coming,' he moaned. 'Everyone at ground level will be drowned. I've asked to be moved upstairs, but they won't let me. I'm going to drown.'

As soon as he left, Jane phoned Dr Gold. She told him what had transpired.

'Mrs Roman,' he said, the exasperation clear in his voice, 'Webster has been for observation at Parkhurst and they have passed him fit.'

Jane tried to put Luke and his problems out of her mind. She resigned herself to having to put up with his regular appearances at the office door. If it helped, then she could do that much for him.

A couple of days passed and she suddenly realised that she hadn't seen him. On the third day, she asked Neil about him. 'Oh, they've sent him back to Parkhurst. I thought you knew,' he told her. 'He kept insisting that he be moved up on to the twos because there is a great flood coming.'

Neil spoke matter of factly. That was what she particularly liked about him. He knew she was concerned and he protected her feelings. If she had asked Tom, he would have undoubtedly made some disparaging remark about Luke.

Several more days passed and Luke slipped from her mind. She was sitting at her desk, hurriedly arranging her notes for the morning lesson she was about to take, when Neil walked into the office. His normally pleasant face was white and doleful. He clutched both hands together as he stood before her, biting his lip. It was obvious that something was wrong.

'What's the matter, Neil?' she asked, fearing the worst.

'Jane, there's some bad news.' His voice was low.

Jane flapped her hands to hurry him along. 'Well, go on then, tell me what it is,' she said impatiently.

'It's Luke,' said Neil. 'He hung himself at Parkhurst yesterday.'

Jane's hand flew to her mouth. The image of the poor creature floated before her. She remembered the knocking on her cupboard and the feathers on her desk. It would happen no more.

She tried to come to terms with the fact that someone she knew, another human being, had taken his own life. As she felt the loss, she also felt a sense of failure, as if she had failed Luke personally.

She tried to reassure herself that she had done all that she could, but it didn't seem enough. She was part of the system, and the system had done for him. It had become patently obvious long ago that she was almost the only member of staff who seemed troubled by conscience. Saying a silent prayer for Luke's memory, she reflected that at least his torment was over now.

13

If Luke's death had an effect on the rest of us, it was not a lasting one. He had had no close friends and if there was an element of 'There but for the grace of God go I' to his suicide, then it wasn't felt by Tom and me. We dismissed him as just another nutter and concentrated on our own survival.

He didn't say as much, but no doubt Niven felt likewise. He wasn't known for his compassion. However, it might have unnerved him a bit.

I missed the weekly yard football, but was told that Niven had been particularly boisterous and selfish. For a change, JB had turned out to play, and a clash was inevitable.

JB had collected a ball and settled on it – he needed time for his sedate game. Niven had come powering in like a train. His shoulder had caught JB in the small of the back and had spun the latter round.

Normally, JB was easy-going enough, and if it had been anyone else, he would have let it go. But Niven's red, angry face had been too much for him. Suddenly, punches were flying.

Bob had run to break it up, and had separated them easily – neither had been keen to continue. If the PTI had reported the matter, it would have been serious for both of them. But in his rough, Marine's way, he had only cautioned them both and said there must be no more.

Perhaps the inconclusive nature of the encounter had served to make Niven worse. That evening, while standing at the pool table, he lashed out with a cue.

Patrick was another young Irish inmate, but several years more mature than Niven. The cue caught him across the forehead, raising a nasty bump. Luckily for Niven, there were no screws about and he had another lucky escape. No one seemed immune to this general groundswell of instability that accompanied the month of December. But then, in a closed society such as Knightsford, nothing ever happened in isolation.

Tom was the next to be affected. As I sat in his cell one evening, he told me that *he* had punched Patrick, knocking him to the floor. It had happened in the small kitchen, while Tom was making some toast.

At first, I was concerned, thinking that perhaps all the training with me was going to his head. I couldn't afford to have Tom going around punching people. It was too close to home.

When he explained, though, I realised that he had had little alternative. Probably smarting from his humiliation at Niven's hands, Patrick had picked on Tom. If it had been me, I would have punched him, too. Luckily, no one had seen it, so little harm had been done.

I suppose it would have been too much to expect for the Fox to remain untouched by all the activity, especially as a fortnight had passed without one of his tantrums. That it was a TV programme that triggered the detonation didn't particularly surprise me. I had learned that Foxy could be provoked by the most mundane things.

We had read in the papers that there was to be a current affairs programme about Wandsworth, which purported to investigate that prison's reputation for violence. Those of us who had been there knew that there would be little difficulty finding the evidence. The screws were particularly brutal at Wandsworth.

We crowded into the downstairs TV room to watch the half-hour documentary. The room was packed. It never ceased to amaze me how prisoners loved to watch programmes about prisoners. All the young 'uns were there, together with some of the older nutters who had been through the system. I noticed a screw standing against the wall, just inside the door.

Tom and I sat together, close to the back. As we squeezed in, I was relieved to see that there were no spare seats near us. I knew the Fox would appear and I didn't particularly want him sitting next to us.

'Let Foxy sit over the other side,' I whispered to Tom. 'He's bound to do something to embarrass us otherwise.' Tom nodded. He had clearly been thinking the same thing.

The programme started with a long shot of Wandsworth's gates. There was a collective moan from the assembled throng, but Tom and I remained silent.

Out of the corner of my eye, I saw Foxy hurry into the room. He looked over to us and saw that there were no seats. He picked up a chair that someone had his feet on and sat against the wall, right next to the screw. Foxy gave no indication that he had noticed him, though.

As the programme progressed, shots were shown of the punishment block and the cells. It brought back old and painful memories for me, and when the interviews with the screws began, I felt a mounting sense of rage. This was indeed the enemy. I hated and despised them. Anyone who had been through the traumatic experience of Wandsworth's punishment block would have felt the same.

One particularly thuggish-looking screw was holding forth about his method of dealing with troublesome prisoners. A couple of sharp, barking comments came from the Fox.

The screw held up his hand and revealed a little finger, twisted at an unusual angle. 'That happened while I was trying to get an inmate into a strip cell,' he explained. 'Now I don't mess about. I put them down right away.'

There was an explosion from the Fox. 'Fucking slag!' he screamed. He jumped up from his chair. 'I can't fucking listen to this!' he roared, both arms flung up in the air above his head. As he made to leave, he grabbed his chair and sent it flying across the room. It smashed against the base of the TV stand with an awesome crash. He stormed from the room.

We were all wound up by the programme, but had managed to retain control. The Fox's tumultuous departure shocked us and increased our anger.

Tom and I buried our faces in our hands. 'What a prick,' I muttered under my breath.

'Thank fuck he didn't sit next to us,' added Tom.

'I would have chinned him,' I replied. 'I wouldn't mind, but the silly bastard's never even been to Wandsworth.'

There was a further, ominous development to come. The screw, who had been near Foxy, suddenly pushed himself upright. Slowly, to attract a minimum of attention, he slipped out the door in the direction Foxy had gone.

'Another nail in the Fox's coffin,' said Niven from somewhere near the front. His assessment wouldn't be too far wrong. I guessed that the screw was on his way to file a report on the incident.

I had never had anything to do with Hamid. I knew that Jane was friendly with him, but if I had shared all her friends, then I would have been in the company of some very strange people indeed.

I had noticed him moving about the jail and had automatically weighed him up for any potential threat. The wickedly hooked nose and restless eyes that flashed with anger made for a visage that was both intimidating and sinister. I thought of the generations of Bedouins who had roamed the deserts of his violent native land.

I had heard that he had a quick temper and that he was in for his second murder. Although he must have been near the end of his tether, I didn't fear him, but I categorised him as someone who it wouldn't be wise to provoke unnecessarily.

Unfortunately, there were others who were not so discerning and one who seemed to delight in putting Hamid down. He was a young fella, who weighed all of fifteen stone. No doubt he looked at Hamid's skinny frame and thought he would have it all his own way.

One Saturday evening, several days after the Fox's latest catharsis, we were sitting in the upstairs TV room watching *Buck Rogers*. As was our habit for this particular programme, Tom, Jack and I were all wrecked.

On the other side of the aisle, towards the front, I saw Hamid stand up, place a cup on his chair and leave the room. A few seconds later, I became aware of a bulky figure moving down the aisle – it was Hamid's heavyweight tormentor. He removed the cup from the Arab's seat, placed it on the floor and sat down.

Now whenever I had a puff, I always found that I became very passive. It wasn't a particularly suitable state of mind for the some-times violent situations I could find myself in in some jails, but at Knightsford, pre-Christmas instability notwithstanding, I didn't have this worry.

However, as I watched the fat bully remove the cup, I went on red alert. I nudged Tom and told him what had happened.

Several minutes passed. Then I saw Hamid returning down the aisle and stopping at the row where his seat had been. He stared around perplexed.

The presence of the big fella and the smirk on his face did the trick. Hamid immediately realised what had happened.

'You're in my seat!' he cried in a high-pitched voice. 'Where's my cup?' he added as an afterthought.

The big fella bent down and picked up the cup from the floor. 'Here it is. Now fuck off,' he said aggressively.

'*Aiee!*' screamed Hamid in a frenzy. He waved his arms in the air and made as if to tear his hair.

The big fella stood up. As he towered over the little man a look of fear passed across Hamid's face. 'You'll see, you'll see!' he shouted as he backed away up the aisle.

'Fuck off,' called the big fella after his retreating figure.

I looked at Tom. Disgust showed on both our faces. Neither of us liked bullies and the big fella was certainly one of those. But it was nothing to do with us. He wouldn't have done it to Tom or me.

We returned to watching the programme. The problems of life in the 25th century seemed much more preferable to the vagaries of living in Knightsford, and soon we were lost in the plot.

The second high-pitched scream made me jump. I looked across the room and saw Hamid standing in the aisle again. But now he was waving what looked like a milk bottle above his head.

Suddenly, he made a lunge into the row. An answering cry of fear rang out as the big fella ducked out of his way, rose from his seat and plunged along the row in the opposite direction. He fell several times before finally reaching the comparative safety of the wall. Several seated viewers now sat between him and Hamid.

'Fucky bastard! Fucky bastard!' Hamid shrieked as he advanced towards him along the row. The seated viewers suddenly lost all interest in the goings-on of the 25th century; the immediate threat in the present occupied all their attention. As they cowered in their seats, they never took their eyes off the bottle that Hamid held in his hand. Whether he hit the big fella or missed, there was the likelihood that they would be showered with glass.

The big fella shrank back against the wall as if he was trying to melt into it, a look of panic on his face. Desperately, he glanced from side to side, searching for a way to escape.

Suddenly, he threw himself across the backs of the chairs in front of him, falling heavily among a flurry of arms and legs in the next row. He rose, only to repeat the action.

Hamid, half-way along the original row, stopped and glared at his tormentor. He realised that he wouldn't be able to catch him now.

He backed out of the row and, still walking backwards, retreated up the aisle. 'Fucky bastard, fucky bastard,' he kept intoning like some Eastern ritual, continuing to wave the bottle above his head. Then he disappeared out the door.

To a disinterested observer, it might have seemed a funny situation. But the suddenness and the immediacy of the violence had robbed the incident of any humour as far as we were concerned. Our gallows humour was a protection against the terrible pathos of our everyday existence. However, we had not yet mastered the art of switching from fear to fun as the situation demanded it.

We returned to watching the antics of Buck Rogers, but now the comicbook violence seemed shallow and unreal. For good, X-rated stuff, I thought, give me present-day prison any time.

*   *   *

Since my first day at Knightsford, I had never cared for the label of 'resident'. It was a euphemism that summarised all that was false and phoney about the place. As I was forcibly detained in a prison, as far as I was concerned I was either a prisoner, an inmate or a convict. The term 'resident' implied a degree of volition with regard to coming and going that I certainly didn't enjoy.

However, one way in which the term did have some relevance was with regard to the length of time an inmate 'resided' at Knightsford. It wasn't unusual for a man to stay there for three years or more. Some had even spent seven or eight years in the place.

As a consequence, there was a very slow turnover. New receptions arrived at the rate of one a week. It was unusual for two to arrive and wholly exceptional for three.

Thursday was reception day. The 'national escort' coach would pull into the sterile area and offload the new arrival, and the first we would see of him would be at dinner-time that day. Because the majority of prisoners who came to Knightsford were weird or nerdy-looking, this often raised a laugh at our table.

Tom would look up and say, ''Ere, have a look at the new one.' There the newcomer would stand, a certified eccentric, blinking bemusedly and staring around the dining hall.

One Thursday, we were eating our dinner as usual when Bill let out a low groan. 'Oh, no, I don't fucking believe it,' he said, staring at the queue.

We all turned to follow his gaze. There, standing self-consciously with a cup in one hand, was a dead ringer for Bernard Manning. He had the same massive head, jet black hair and flabby jowls. His enormous chest and shoulders were more than complemented by a voluminous waist. Thick, horn-rimmed glasses perched on the bridge of a large nose. He must have stood well over six feet tall and weighed all of eighteen stone. With his broad shoulders, he looked like the proverbial brick shit-house.

There was something about the way he cocked his head slightly to one side. Then there was the half-bent arm that held the cup. My 'woodsman's' instinct was aroused.

Suddenly, someone called to him from across the room. As he spun round to see who it was, an amazing transformation came over him.

One enormous arm flew skywards and he wriggled several fat fingers in the fella's direction. A tight-lipped smile split the fat face as he waggled the massive head from side to side in a determined attempt at a simper. In a short-stepping, rumba-like movement, he swung his gigantic *derrière* back and forth. 'Yoo-hoo,' he called across the room in a high-pitched voice.

Any resemblance to Bernard Manning disappeared in a flash. The high-camp manner was more reminiscent of Dame Edna. Knightsford had just acquired its very own screaming queen.

'Who the fuck's *that*?' said Tom, almost hysterical.

Bill had gone quite red and was intent on eating his dinner. 'They call him "Mother",' he muttered.

'Do you know him?' I asked.

The shade of red deepened. 'I was at the Scrubs with him a couple of years ago,' he said. 'He's a right fucking nuisance. He'll come right on to you and embarrass you something terrible.'

'Well, he won't come on to me, I assure you, because I'll hit him right on his fat chin,' I said through a mouthful of food.

'Oh, he won't bother you, Norm. He only goes after the . . .' Bill stopped in mid-sentence and lowered his eyes in embarrassment. 'What I mean to say is that he always chases the young fellas.'

I smiled at Bill's discomfort. 'Are you trying to say that I'm not young any more, Bill?'

Bill looked at me closely to make sure I wasn't serious. He burst into a nervous laugh. 'Oh, you know what I mean.'

We continued to eat our dinner as Mother collected hers and minced across the dining hall, picking her way through the close-set tables like a big ship navigating shallows. On the way, she 'yoo-hooed' to other people she knew and finally sat down at the table of the fella who had called to her in the first place.

I reflected that Mother was as bizarre a fella as I had seen in a long time. However, I didn't expect it would take her long to find a niche here. I guessed that, within a few weeks, she would be just another small part of Knightsford's supremely varied ecology.

With just over a week to go to Christmas, Tom was becoming restless. Usually, he was content to just sit in his cell and drink coffee after we returned from the gym in the evenings, but tonight he had itchy feet.

'Let's go for a walk round, Norm,' he suggested.

I looked at him questioningly. 'Where do you want to go?'

'Oh, I don't know. I just fancy a walk.'

We came out of his cell and descended to the ones. We walked slowly along to the centre and stood by the snooker table. Dougie was in the middle of his umpteenth game of the day. He crept up on the balls, his cue at waist level, pausing every now and then to shout or laugh uproariously. I reflected that Dougie would be a riot at The Crucible.

'Let's see what's happening in the dining hall,' said Tom after a few minutes. I shrugged. Apart from the occasional outside darts match, I wasn't sure that anything else happened in the dining hall other than dining.

As we drew close, I heard the sound of a piano playing. Suddenly, it stopped, then started again. Tom pushed open the swing doors and we walked in.

Over by the stage was a crowd of people. I recognised several well-known faces, and in their midst were four women. They all had sheets of paper in their hands and were intent on discussing something.

'OK, everybody, to your places,' cried a short, stocky woman.

The crowd broke up. Most climbed on to the stage, a couple sitting on chairs just beyond the apron. One of the women, a young, overweight blonde girl, went to sit at the piano. I cringed. I realised that I was in the presence of 'Knightsford's Amateur Dramatic Society' – or 'KADS' for short.

'Cads indeed,' I thought. Perhaps it was just me, but I had a thing about prison amateur dramatics, founded on long years of observing the type of prisoner who was attracted to this sort of activity. To a man, they seemed weak, insecure, unhappy with their own persona and desperately seeking another. Hence the pursuit of acting.

Then there were the posers who just wanted to be around the women. It was pathetic to see them competing with each other in pursuit of something that was quite unobtainable. It might be a savage indictment of the thespian art, but I never knew of any 'chaps' who took an interest in acting.

As the blonde lady began playing the piano, I immediately recognised a few bars from West Side Story. Cliché upon cliché – the play had been done to death in scores of jails over the years.

The Sharks and the Jets shaped up on stage. On the left was Niven, his sycophantic companion Walt, Neil Bowen, Starling and George. Facing them were Graham, Pete, Porter and Alfred E.

Neumann. The latter had on his usual idiotic grin. I assumed he was playing a piece of scenery.

'To the front, to the front, ladies,' trilled the short stocky woman, standing with one foot on the apron. 'In between Niven and Walt, Debbie. And you in between Pete and Graham, Sharon,' she directed.

Debbie and Sharon hurried to obey. They were well-proportioned women in their early twenties. Too many cream cakes and a lifetime spent riding horses had ensured that their bottoms were now extremely large, and they had thighs that the area squat champion would have been proud of.

They squeezed in between the men. Polite smiles were exchanged as space was made. Everybody was on their best social behaviour.

It was hard to discern the role that Derek was playing in all this. He sat on a chair not far from where the short, stocky lady was standing. From time to time, he looked down at the sheet of paper he was holding, then looked up again.

'Paula! Paula!' he suddenly called out. The stocky lady looked over. 'I think there's a mistake here.' She hurried over to him.

Something suddenly struck me. The exaggerated London accent and the 'chaps' mannerisms were gone. Derek was in middle-class mode. I guessed he was some sort of technical adviser. 'Quite right, too,' I thought. 'After all, he's been acting all his life.'

By now, the fellas had seen Tom and me. Some looked embarrassed and a couple waved.

The consultation finished, the stocky Paula hurried back to the edge of the stage. Derek turned in his chair to see who the fellas had been waving to.

''Allo, Norm. 'Allo, Tom boy,' he shouted, the phoney accent back again. It seemed that he could switch modes with amazing dexterity. 'You fancy a bit of acting then?'

Tom just shook his head, but I couldn't resist the opportunity. 'Not me, mate,' I replied. 'I'm quite comfortable with the persona I've got. I don't need another one.'

Derek smiled weakly, not sure of my meaning. It was the word 'persona' that had got him. Paula got my meaning immediately, though. She spun round and shot me a steely glare, before turning to the stage again. She, more than anyone, was aware of the fragile personalities she had under her direction.

It was an appropriate time to leave. I nudged Tom. 'Come on, mate, I've had enough of these wankers,' I muttered.

With a begrudged moratorium on work-outs over the three days of Christmas, time threatened to drag.

By mid-morning, Tom, Jack and I were standing in the gallery overlooking the centre. Several of the other young 'uns soon joined us.

Playful banter passed along this line of 'crows' as we took the piss out of each other and anyone who passed below.

Maypole and the Chief appeared and stood over to the side of the centre near B wing. Other screws came out of their wing offices until a large part of Knightsford's senior management were assembled in that small area.

Inevitably, this collection of brass soon attracted the usual crowd of sycophants and crawlers. They scuttled from their various holes to seize the opportunity to get in a bit of serious Christmas grovelling.

Suddenly, Tom nudged me in the ribs. ''Ere, 'ave a look at who's coming.'

I turned around and looked behind me. Beetling along the ones, heading for the centre, was old Derek, done up to the nines in his best Christmas gear.

He looked quite smart in his well-pressed grey trousers and blue striped shirt. But the *pièce de résistance* was the bright red bow tie with white polka dots.

Apart from the fact that it was outrageously loud, a bow tie wasn't part of official prison dress and so was illegal. It would be a nicking offence at any other time of the year, but today Derek would get away with it.

The amusing thing was that he was obviously wearing it as a conversation piece. He walked up to the nearest screw, wished him a 'Merry Christmas' and virtually thrust the bow tie in his face. Sure enough, the screw remarked on it and they both had a good laugh. Derek then repeated this procedure with Maypole, the Chief and the rest of the screws around the centre. Normally, the assembled young 'uns would have found this unashamed piece of festive grovelling mildly amusing. But recently, tales had been emerging of some particularly vindictive grassing that Derek had been doing behind the scenes, which had got several 'residents' into trouble. Yet he still walked about the jail doing his 'Cheerful Charlie Chester' act as if he meant no one any harm. He was clearly a nasty and treacherous piece of work.

'Look at that wicked old bastard,' said Jack, in a stage whisper that carried right across the centre. Derek spun round and glared up at the line of 'crows'. He cocked his head back and squinted through his spectacles, trying to identify individuals. But it was beyond the power of his old eyesight.

With a muttered curse, he dropped his head and hurried back the way he had come. As he passed below, we heard him say, 'I'll give him ruin my fucking Christmas.' There was a bellow of laughter from us 'crows'. It was like a kick up the backside for Derek. He scooted up the stairs and rushed off in the direction of his cell.

'Well, that's one grass who won't have a Happy Christmas,' said Tom.

At dinner-time we queued for the culinary event of the year. What we got was three dinners in one. It ensured that the waste-bin would be overflowing.

Behind the hot-plate, serving out the stuffing, stood Maypole with a white pinny over his smart, grey business suit. Next to him stood some variety of cleric. It was hard to discern what faith he was, but he was obviously an exhibitionist. A bright red cloak covered him from head to foot. I hazarded a guess that he wasn't a rabbi.

'How d'ya like to do Maypole with a bucket full of shit right now?' muttered Tom as we drew near.

I smiled, savouring the idea. Yes, it would really be something. But I didn't think the humour of it would sustain me over the ensuing years of solitary, so I dismissed it from my mind.

We went to sit at our usual table, but it was slightly out of position. Next to it was another row of tables, and sitting along one side were a dozen old age pensioners of both sexes. The colours of their dresses, suits and jumpers stood out in stark contrast to the dull greys worn by the surrounding 'residents', and on each of their heads was a paper party hat. Sitting opposite them were a dozen of Knightsford's finest arse-lickers. They were to be their company for the duration of the meal.

The hypocrisy was becoming so thick, I almost choked on it. It wasn't that what they were doing wasn't worthwhile. It was just that the 'residents' who were doing it weren't known for their good will to their fellows throughout the rest of the year. In fact, most of them wouldn't have hesitated to do you a bad turn if it helped their own cause.

We hurried to finish the meal. It was good fare, but the presence of the old folk chomping and sucking at their food was off-putting. The final straw came when some poor old girl dropped her teeth into her custard. There was a minor panic as several other old folk helped her fish them out.

Bill gagged on his Christmas pud. 'Fuck that! I'm off,' he said. There was an undignified scramble as we all hurried to join him. We emptied our trays into the slops bin and walked quickly from the hall. So much for Christmas dinner!

The highlight of the afternoon was watching *The Yellow Submarine* completely out of our nuts. We sat there, blithering, as the cartoon Beatles anticked about on the television. There may have been a better way to spend the time, but in the circumstances, we were quite content.

The coming attraction that evening was a drink in Bill's cell. He and Steve had made some 'hooch'. I made the stipulation to Tom that there would be no barricading of the door. 'I don't mind getting nicked for booze,' I said, laughing, 'but fuck having the nonsense on my record.'

At about 7.00pm, Tom, Jack and I went across to Bill's cell.

Richie, Sam and JB were already there. Steve sat in his usual place in the corner. The 'hooch' was in two large plastic buckets in the middle of the cell. We were committed now. There was an unwritten truce at Christmas, but if the screws did come in, it would be on us.

The 'hooch' was typical of most prison brew. It stunk of too much yeast and tasted foul. However, it warmed the back of the throat nicely and caused a delicious shudder as it went down. The alcohol went right to the head.

Within half an hour, we were all thoroughly pissed. The music blared. We talked and laughed loudly, as if we had almost forgotten where we were.

Just after 8.00, Niven appeared with the ever-present Walt. There was a strained atmosphere for a few minutes, but the uninhibiting effect of the 'hooch' soon had its effect. Within ten minutes, they were as drunk as the rest of us.

As 9.15 and the impending bang-up approached, an air of apprehension forced its way through the alcoholic haze. We would have to navigate the open landings back to our cells under the hostile gaze of the screws. Anywhere else, we could have expected a degree of live-and-let-live, but, at Knightsford, the official Christmas spirit was of a very low proof.

We rose to our feet unsteadily and staggered out on to the landing. Three screws stood in a bunch by the office, Hall prominent in their midst. They looked up, grim-faced, as we emerged, disapproval written all over their faces.

There were several small groups of residents scattered about the ones. As they looked up, there was disapproval on their faces, too.

I glared down at them and they dropped their heads. Their disapproval was a symbolic solidarity with the screws. Also, there was a large measure of sour grapes because they never had the initiative or the nerve to secure drink of their own.

We shouted our boozy goodnights to each other and staggered off to our respective cells. I negotiated the stairs with difficulty, clutching tightly at the hand-rail to prevent myself from falling. I meandered towards my doorway and plunged through. In a reflex action, I slammed my door behind me. That was Christmas Day as far as I was concerned.

Dimly, in the distance, I could hear doors slamming as others banged up for the night. I sat on the bed, laughing to myself as I attempted to undress.

Suddenly, I heard a key in the lock. I looked up as the door swung open. Hall's bulk filled the opening.

'OK, Norm,' he said with an attempt at a grin. 'Just checking that you're all right.'

'Just confirming that I'm drunk,' I thought through my stupor.

I stared at him. He backed out, closing the door behind him. 'Goodnight, Merry Christmas,' he called through the narrowing gap.

The stony silence from me was a fitting enough reply.

Christmas was past and a grey, wet and inauspicious January had dawned. Everyone walked around in a cloud of post-Christmas depression. The false jollity had exhausted everyone's capacity to find anything humorous about our situation. Another long, boring year loomed in front of us like the inhospitable, craggy face of some alpine peak.

Tempers were short, appetites jaded and everyday comments liberally laced with vitriol. It was generally agreed that things wouldn't improve until January was out of the way.

Life in the telephone shop ground along, with even the civvies in a bad mood. I reflected that any Christmas spent with them would hardly have been bliss. I felt for their wives.

An unusual event occurred in the second week. I came out of my office/toilet one morning on my way to harass a few ankles with my broom, when I noticed Patel, the hospital screw, standing by the office. He was bending over a table near the checking section. This was where Warris worked.

I walked closer to see what was going on. Warris was sitting in his usual chair, a pained expression on his face. Patel was holding his wrist, taking his pulse. Several of the fellas sitting nearby were nudging each other and grinning.

I walked up to one of them and asked what was happening.

'It's Warris,' the fella replied, sarcasm thick in his voice. 'His parole review is due again so he's having one of his moody heart attacks. He does it every time he comes up for review.' The fella laughed.

I didn't think it was amusing. Warris was a pathetic case, but after twenty-seven years, I felt that a man was entitled to a modicum of respect. I leaned against a wall to watch developments.

Suddenly the other hospital screw arrived. He walked over to Patel, and between them, they helped Warris to his feet and escorted him slowly out of the shop.

That evening, I was leaning on the rail in the gallery with Tom and JB. I mentioned Warris's moody heart attack.

'That's funny,' said Tom. 'I saw old "poison bollocks" down the hospital this morning.'

'I reckon it will be a toss up which one of the old fellas croaks first,' said JB. I smiled a humourless smile, but he had given me an idea.

That night, after bang-up, I sat at my table with a sheet of paper in front of me. I wrote down the names of all the old boys who looked like they might not see out the next couple of years.

Warris, Derek, the German and Brown were obvious choices. The little fat nonce Walker was well overweight and getting on. He could go at any time. Then there was Maypole himself, of course. He had already had two heart attacks.

That gave me a total of six. With a smile on my face, I added JB's name. He was only forty and in the best of health. However, we were always ribbing him about his age.

The following evening, after Tom and I had returned from the gym, it was my turn to want to go for a walk. Staying on the twos, I headed for the gallery, with Tom close behind. We crossed and entered the education block.

I walked past darkened classrooms until I found one that was lit. Inside were the people I was looking for. Sam, Richie, Eddie, Steve *et al* were playing their usual game of Diplomacy.

We walked in and a dozen faces turned to look at us. Even though they had got used to me by now and knew I didn't mean them any harm, there was still apprehension there.

I stood by the table on which they had their game board. Suddenly, with a theatrical flourish, I pulled the piece of paper from my pocket. Several pairs of eyes flinched.

'Gentlemen,' I announced, 'are there any gambling men among you?'

The question hung in the air. Still they stared at me, but suspiciously now. They knew that I had run racing books and card tables in other jails. They suspected a ploy to relieve them of some of their wages.

'Gentlemen,' I repeated, 'I am inviting you to participate in the River Styx Sweepstakes.'

Still they stared, blankly. Beside me, Tom was also looking at me quizzically. I had told him nothing of this.

'On this piece of paper,' I continued, holding it up in front of me, 'I have written the names of seven of our senior residents. Senior, let me add, because of their advanced years.' I paused for effect.

'And here,' I pulled a small, brown paper bag out of my pocket, 'I have a bag containing seven pieces of paper, each with one of the names on it.' I shook the bag in front of them so they could hear the pieces of paper rattling inside.

'The object of the exercise is this. Anyone who wishes to wager a Mars bar can pick one of these names from the bag. They will then have that person in the sweep.' Again I paused to let it all sink in.

'Now. Whichever of these old fellas crosses the River Styx first — that is, snuffs it — then whoever has him in the sweep will win a Mars bar off each of the other six ticket holders.'

There was a stony silence. A sea of wrinkled foreheads confronted me as they mentally digested my proposal. Suddenly, as one, they all burst out laughing. There was a degree of relief in it; they now knew they wouldn't have to search for a polite way to refuse to take part. But there was also whole-hearted amusement at the concept of the River Styx Sweepstakes.

'You're fucking crazy,' laughed Tom next to me.

'Only you could have thought of this, Norm,' called out Eddie.

'I'll have one!' shouted Sam, holding out his hand.

They jumped up from the table and crowded round. I shook the bag in front of them, then handed it to Tom. 'Only the first six can take part!' I shouted over the din. 'I want a ticket for myself.'

I took out a pen and placed the sheet of paper on the table. 'Call out your runner as soon as you get your ticket, please, gentlemen.' I was caught up in the excitement myself now.

Sam plunged his hand into the bag. He pulled out a piece of paper and opened it. 'Cor!' he cried. 'I've got old Arthur Brown!' There were gales of laughter.

'Must have a good chance,' I called out as I wrote Sam's name next to Brown's.

'No way!' shouted Tom. 'He's too wicked to die.'

Eddie was next. He opened the screwed-up paper. 'Fuck me, I've got Alf Walker!' There were more hoots of laughter.

'Trust you to pick a nonce,' called out Steve.

Pete stepped forward for his turn. His eyes widened in surprise and his hand flew to his mouth. For a second he looked scared. 'I've got Maypole,' he said in astonishment.

There was uproar. Hoots and whistles rent the air as someone hammered on the table. 'You'd be a popular winner, Pete!' I shouted.

Suddenly I realised that all the noise could attract a screw. ''Ere, fellas,' I called out. 'For fuck's sake, keep it down a bit. If a screw comes up here to see what's going on and Maypole finds out that I'm taking bets on the likelihood of him dying, I'll end up in Dartmoor!' There was more laughter, but the noise level fell appreciably.

Richie was next and he got JB. 'You ain't got much chance of winning,' I consoled him, 'but think of the fun you can have when you tell him you've got him in the sweep.'

Steve and Eric picked Warris and Derek respectively. There was an enthusiastic cheer for the latter. He, too, would be a popular winner. It was left for me to pick the German.

'It's a fix!' cried Tom. 'You wanted him for yourself all along.'

I folded the paper and put it in my pocket. Tom and I turned to leave. 'Now there's just two things, fellas,' I said, halting in the doorway. 'One. We must keep this between ourselves.' There was a serious look on my face and they all responded similarly. 'Two, no cheating. I don't want anyone bumping his runner off.' I smiled broadly and was out the door.

Over the next couple of weeks, it was a secret joke between us all. When we met, there would be progress reports. Snippets would be passed on. Sightings of any of the runners in the vicinity of the hospital were especially newsworthy. If any of them looked particularly run down, this, too, was discussed eagerly.

Sometimes we would be standing about when one of the

runners passed by. Knowing looks would be exchanged and we would dissolve into laughter. There was nothing particularly wicked or vindictive in it. None of us seriously wished death on any of the runners. It was just a bit of prison 'gallows humour' and helped to take our minds off the pathos that was all around us.

Needless to say, JB wasn't exactly delighted to find himself included. Perhaps it was the way he found out. The very next time Richie met him, his opening gambit was, 'Hey, JB, I've got you in the sweep.' Then he sent him to me to do the explaining.

*   *   *

I had now been at Knightsford for six months – a significant achievement insofar as it was twice as long as I had spent in each of my last six jails. I wasn't about to get complacent, though, for, with the likes of Maypole and the Chief about, anything could happen. However, I had begun to feel more settled than at any time during my sentence.

The six-month period had a further significance in that I was now eligible to apply for a job outside the workshops. These jobs, regularly advertised on the centre notice-board, were usually for orderlies and involved working in close proximity to the screws and making tea for them. I didn't fancy this, but it was all academic anyway as far as I was concerned. Those who got such jobs were mostly 'residents' who had grassed and grovelled their way into them. It was all cut and dried before they ever went in front of the labour board, with the screws speaking up for their particular favourites. I didn't have this kind of help.

The extent of my ambition was to get a job on the 'Works'. Here, civilian tradesmen worked on prison repairs with small teams of inmates. I had heard that there was a vacancy on the 'painters'.

I had never painted for a living before. I had helped redecorate our flat once when I was home, but that had been tiresome and boring. My chosen method had been to paint one small area at a time, like a giant 'painting by numbers'. I realised this wouldn't suffice for commercial painting, but I remembered the old adage: 'If you can piss, you can paint.' I was sure I would get by.

I filled in a 'labour change' form, got my shop supervisor to sign it, then handed it into the office. Two days later, I was called from the telephone shop for an interview.

It was mid-morning when I walked along the ones of A wing in the direction I had seen Tom go every day. I had envied him the freedom of wandering about the jail, doing different jobs in different locations. Much better than sitting about in a workshop, doing the same thing every day. Now, with luck, I could be on the Works myself.

A screw let me out of the end gate of A wing. The Works department was a small, two-storey building, tacked on to the side of the wing, the modern, Fifties-style brickwork in sharp contrast to the eroded stonework of the main building.

I knew the painters' shop was on the ground floor. I walked along a short corridor and knocked on a grimy door. When a voice inside called out, 'Come in,' I pushed it open.

The first thing that struck me was that the room was incredibly cluttered. There were partly used tins of paint stacked against every wall, cans of thinners, varnish and various other fluids perched untidily on shelves, and scores of brushes poking out of glass jars. And over everything, on every wall, the ceiling, the floor, the furniture and the tins, were spots and runs and smudges of paint of every hue and texture.

Sitting, partially obscured among this clutter, were three painters. Their profession was obvious from the spots and runs and smudges that covered their overalls from collars to cuffs. It acted as a camouflage for them, helping them to blend into the paint-smeared background.

Two of them, in blue overalls, were 'residents'. I recognised them from about the prison but had never spoken to either. However, Tom – that fount of knowledge about all things Knightsford – had filled me in. The younger one, a round-faced, anaemic-looking fella in his late twenties, had killed his girlfriend. Whether he had been a bit simple before, or whether the experience had unhinged him, he now had a vacant, docile look. He rarely spoke and, when he did, he did so without animation or feeling. The older one was a Yorkshire fella in his early forties, who had killed his wife after discovering that she was having an affair. He was a dapper, handsome man with a neat, black moustache, but was totally without personality: dour, dull and boring.

The civvy painter was sitting opposite the two resident-painters, on the other side of an old wooden table. Even sitting down I could see that he was short and fat. His overalls ballooned out at the back over an enormous backside and, at the front, over an equally large stomach. He had a florid, pleasant face, with cheeks that were puffed out as if he was permanently out of breath. Clasped tightly between thin, pursed lips was a small, badly stained dog-end. On his head, he wore a white forage-type cap, from the sides of which protruded a riot of curly, gingerish hair. A pair of small, wire-rimmed glasses sat on the bridge of his nose, through which he peered at me owlishly.

All three looked up as I entered. It was obviously tea-break because each had a full cup in front of him. The civvy stopped, cup at chest height, to regard me.

'Mr Butler?' I asked.

'I'm Len,' he replied, with the barest glimmer of a twinkle in his eye. He raised the cup to his lips and drank.

'I've come to see you about a job on the painters,' I continued.

'Have you done much painting?' he asked, almost before I had finished speaking.

I toyed with several answers. I dismissed the notion of lying. The truth would be revealed the moment I picked up a brush. I wondered if he had read any philosophy, considering offering the Cartesian dictum: 'I piss, therefore I paint.' I dismissed this, too, reflecting that he would be provoked either by my intellectual arrogance or the remark's demeaning connotations for his profession. I went for truthful simplicity.

'No, Len, I haven't done much at all.'

A broad smile spread over his ample face. He puffed a few times on the dog-end, but with no success. 'Well, that's good news,' he said. 'Most of those who come over here think they know it all. Then I have a hell of a job telling them how I want it done. I'd rather have someone who knows fuck-all.'

He turned, still smiling, to the two inmate painters. They smiled in return. I recognised it as a private joke between them.

'I'll phone the shop and get you released as soon as possible,' Len said, turning back to me. 'Get your overalls from the stores. I need you right away.' He stood up and held out his hand.

Upright, he looked comically plump. His overalls fitted the large parts of him so tightly that it seemed as if he had been poured into them. He resembled a large, overstuffed toy. With his pleasant, smiling face, he reminded me of a large, amiable teddy bear.

'Thanks, Len,' I said, shaking his hand. I gave a quick wave to the two painters and hurried back to the wing.

Within two days, I was on the painters. Kitted out in my own pair of blue, paint-spotted overalls, I wandered about the prison with Len and the other two, in search of things to paint.

Sometimes ladders were needed, and it was quite a thrill for me to walk close to the wall with a large, extending ladder. A few months earlier, any security department would have balked at the idea. PO Waters would have balked, too, had he seen me mentally measuring the heights of walls and noting the positions of observation boxes. Although I wanted a quiet time, I was still on the look-out for a good escape opportunity.

My second week saw me working in the education block. All the classrooms needed repainting, providing a couple of weeks' work at least. It would give me the opportunity to observe Jane at close quarters.

Necessity being the mother of invention, I soon mastered the art of commercial painting. The secret was to cover up every surface that you weren't working on, then just splash the paint on liberally. This was the reason why Len and the others were covered from head to toe in multi-coloured spots.

The two inmate painters, who were called Gordon and Ed, proved to be poor companions indeed. Try as I might to engage them in conversation, they stubbornly painted away close by, uttering hardly a word. Perhaps it was the ennui that comes from painting areas of unresponding woodwork over many long hours. Maybe they just didn't like me. My considered opinion, though, was that their life sentences had shell-shocked them into a kind of verbal catatonia. It was a common condition in Knightsford.

Len, though, was altogether more lively. At first, he had been a bit reserved, which I put down to the fact that someone must have warned him about me. However, after a few days, he relaxed and we regularly joked together.

He seemed to regard Gordon and Ed with bemused amusement. His jokes and comments went largely unnoticed by them. Often, he would look over at them and shrug. I reflected that he must have been glad to have my company.

There was another side to Len, though, one that I discovered within the first week: he was a totally different man in the afternoons. I was no stranger to bizarre and sudden personality changes, having lived cheek by jowl with assorted schizophrenics over the years. But the source of Len's problem was far from psychological.

Len liked a drink. This was probably no problem in the evenings and at weekends, but when he had a few in the Officers' Club over the dinner-time, he became a definite liability.

This was especially true if you happened to be below where he was working. There would be a muffled cry as a pot of paint plummeted past to smash on the floor, showering paint everywhere. A paintbrush would suddenly fly by, leaving a long, unsightly smudge down a wall. He would regularly overbalance and run down the steps at speed, before tumbling to the floor.

I watched with amusement as he ran through his repertoire. Len would never say a word. Just clean up and start again where he had left off. However, towards the end of the first week, an event happened that brought home to me that, amusing though he could be, he was also dangerous.

We were in a basement alongside the education block. Len was up a ladder, painting a second-floor window. I was standing below, footing the ladder.

As boring as this was, I was keeping my wits about me. Len had returned from lunch with breath that smelled as if he'd been gargling with thinners. I regularly peered up at him, keeping an eye out for flying pots of paint and brushes.

Suddenly, he grunted deeply. He had reached a part of the window that was obscured by the top of the ladder. He heaved it away from the wall to paint behind it.

No doubt this was a trick used by generations of painters. It was potentially quite dangerous but, when performed by a professional, was reasonably straightforward – always assuming, that is, that the professional was sober at the time.

The ladder was already at a steep angle to the wall. We had been constrained by the lack of space in the basement. As Len boosted it away from the wall, it suddenly reached its point of balance. It stayed right where it was, perfectly perpendicular, with Len perched on top. As it moved outwards, I managed to clutch it to my chest. I peered up to see what Len was going to do next. He looked quite comical, right out in the middle of nowhere, hanging on like grim death, but I quickly realised that he wasn't capable of doing anything to help himself. He stood, frozen into inactivity, as the ladder swayed dangerously. I cringed as his brush fell from his hand, bounced off my shoulder and dropped behind me.

I was used to handling heavy weights, but not fourteen stone of inebriated painter twelve feet away at the end of a ladder. I knew that, once he swung beyond a certain point, the strongest man in the world wouldn't be able to hold him. What I did in the next few seconds would be crucial.

If it had been almost any other member of staff, I would have just got out of the way. There was a very real danger that he might fall on me. But Len was a pleasant old boy, and I was sure that we would get someone worse in his place.

I threw myself against the base of the ladder. The weight at the top was daunting, I was seconds away from losing it. I felt sweat break out all over me. The aluminium struts bit into my shoulders as I fought for control.

Then, slowly, the pressure eased. The weight at the top slid out of my control as the ladder fell back against the wall with a resounding crash. There was the scrabble of soles against rungs as Len raced down. I dived to one side as he rushed past me.

He ran over to some nearby steps and sat down heavily, his fat cheeks inflating and deflating rapidly as he gasped for breath. His normally rosy face had gone quite pale. I noticed that the usually ever-present dog-end was missing from the corner of his mouth.

For a split second I almost burst out laughing. The image of Len perched at the end of the ladder stuck in my mind. I imagined the surprise on the faces of the students in the classroom above as Len swung outwards. But fear still lurked in my chest. I didn't need to sit down, but my heart was pounding. It had nearly been a nasty accident.

After about a minute, Len stood up and walked over to the ladder. He glared at it, then pulled the bottom out from the wall another two feet. He picked up the brush from where it had fallen and, with some muttered curses, climbed back. He continued painting from where he had left off.

Back at the foot of the ladder, there was a broad smile on my face. I could see now why Len hadn't wanted an experienced painter. A professional would have been horrified at his after-dinner painting style. In truth, I was horrified myself, but with my own shortcomings, I could hardly complain. Mentally, I amended the Cartesian dictum: 'If you're pissed, you can't paint.'

Although it was obvious to every con in Knightsford that the Chief was something less than the full shilling, his superiors seemed to remain blissfully unaware of it. As his immediate superior, Maypole had to shoulder most of the blame for this. He couldn't have been ignorant of the fact that the Chief, at the very least, was dangerously unstable.

Over the years, one thing that had struck me about the prison system was that it had no means of weeding out unstable and incompetent staff. Governors were a law unto themselves anyway. Quite often, absolute power had corrupted them to the point where they viewed any opposition as a direct challenge to their office. There were apocryphal tales of governors who were absolute monsters. And I had met a couple myself.

As for the uniformed staff, the governors were on dangerous ground here. In the constant war of attrition between management and staff, both sides closed ranks over almost any issue. The POA would automatically rally round an accused officer. A governor couldn't order an officer to undergo a psychiatric examination, so any charge of incompetence or instability would have to be predicated on evidence of actual wrongdoing. This was notoriously difficult to prove, even if the management had the will to do so. As a consequence, every jail had its group of malcontents. And because of their positions of authority, they could wreak havoc out of all proportion to their numbers.

As the most powerful uniformed officer in the jail, a chief was in an almost unassailable position. It was no wonder that Maypole hadn't informed the Home Office about his chief's increasingly bizarre behaviour.

Weeks could pass without ever hearing about an incident involving the Chief. Then, suddenly, he was constantly in the news.

First, we heard that he had again hidden in the bushes on his day off, and nicked two screws for slipping out to dinner early. Then he did the same thing the very next day and nicked two more. Other screws were overheard moaning about the incidents.

We 'residents' thought this was very funny indeed. However, the Chief soon proved that we were not immune from his wrath.

It was dinner-time and Dougie was playing his usual game of snooker. He stalked around the table, suddenly lunging into a shot and sending the balls careering around the table. Reds bounced off cushions and cannoned into each other in a cacophony of clicking concussions. Just when it seemed that they had all come harmlessly to rest, one dropped into a pocket.

'Well, fuck me!' Dougie roared. He threw back his head and brayed a sawing laugh. The sound reverberated around the centre and ran the length of the three wings. You could, quite literally, hear Dougie all over the jail.

Tom and I had been standing on C wing, lounging against a wall about twenty feet from the centre. Opposite and above us on the twos was the Chief's office. As Dougie brayed, we looked towards the snooker table and smiled.

Suddenly the Chief's door flew open, crashing back against the wall inside as he came rushing out. His face was a white mask of fury and his teeth were bared. He was hatless and small tufts of hair stood out at odd angles. There were also red creases down one side of his face, and I remembered that Tom had told me that the Chief often took a quick nap in his office. I guessed that Dougie had just woken him.

He ran along the landing, to the gallery overlooking the centre. 'Taylor!' he screamed.

It was loud and shrill and trailed away raggedly at the end. The scream of an irate madman who had just lost control, it struck a nerve in everyone who heard it and brought them instantly to attention.

Everyone except Dougie, that is. He stared up, smiling his idiot grin and blinking bemusedly through his glasses as he strove to focus on the face above him.

'Taylor!' the Chief screamed again, thrusting his face forward as if to strike Dougie with the power of his voice. It did the trick. The bolt of sound hit Dougie like a physical force, and he recoiled as even his reduced intellect comprehended that someone was very angry with him. But his irreverent humour seemed almost to have a life of its own. Still smiling, he cocked his head back and said, 'Well, fuck me, Chief . . .' but that was as far as he got.

'Shut up!' screamed the Chief, a shower of spittle flying from his gaping mouth. He threw himself against the rail and leaned over, pointing a long arm at Dougie. The smile disappeared from Dougie's face as he took a step backwards. Even he was intimidated by such insane rage.

'Taylor!' roared the Chief. 'If I hear your voice once more this afternoon, I swear I'll put you in the block and have you shipped out!'

All along the wings, men had stopped what they were doing to stare towards the centre. Everyone now froze, lest they attract the attention of the demented Chief.

The Chief, though, was oblivious to them all. He just glared down at Dougie, his eyes burning with hatred. 'Just one more word!' he bellowed, leaving the threat hanging in the air.

Dougie dropped his head under the baleful stare, which seemed to mollify the Chief somewhat. With a grunt, he turned from the rail and stalked back to his office, slamming the door after him.

Below on the ones, Tom and I just looked at each other and shrugged.

'He's fucking nuts, him,' I said, careful to keep my voice down.

Tom laughed. 'Well, I don't have any trouble with him, Norm. I suppose it's just the way you handle him.'

I didn't particularly agree. How do you handle a madman, and a very powerful madman at that?

There was no doubt that Tom enjoyed a special relationship

with the Chief, getting away with things that no one else would have dared to try. However, this was more to do with the Chief's peculiar personality. He just had a soft spot for Tom.

If Tom had been intimidated by the Chief's explosion of rage, he certainly didn't show it. Perhaps it was his irrepressible, mischievous nature. Sometimes, he just couldn't help himself.

It was Friday afternoon, two days after the incident with Dougie. I particularly liked Friday afternoon. We did no painting, just cleaned our brushes and pots and tidied up the shop.

By 3.00, I was finished, and indulging my new-found freedom, I decided to take a stroll around the jail. It was quite a novelty to be able to walk about without having a screw with me.

I walked along the front of the dining hall, past the football pitch and turned to pass C wing. Suddenly I saw Tom bending over a cement mixer in the small, V-shaped builders' yard between C wing and the dining hall. Around him there were several heaps of sand, a dozen or so bags of cement stacked chest high and piles of various types of bricks. Over against one wall, a tangle of scaffolding poles sprawled in disarray. Close by were two wheelbarrows and half-a-dozen shovels. Scattered about the yard were several pieces of plant. Apart from the cement mixer that Tom was working on, there were two dumpers, a compressor and another, smaller mixer.

I called out to him as I approached. As he saw me, a mischievous smile appeared at the corners of his mouth. He turned back to the mixer.

'What you doing, Tom boy?' I asked, stopping next to him.

'I'm just about to annoy the Chief,' came his muffled reply.

I looked around, but could see no evidence of the Chief. 'Well, where is he?' I demanded.

Still smiling, Tom pointed up the side of C wing. I followed the direction of his finger and noticed two over-large windows set in the wall of a cell on the twos. I understood immediately. The Chief's office overlooked the builders' yard.

'He always has a kip on a Friday afternoon at about this time. I'm going to wake the old bastard up,' said Tom. He had finished tinkering with the mixer now and was about to swing the handle.

'Bollocks,' I said, backing away quickly. I hurried to stand close up against C wing wall so that, if he looked out, the Chief wouldn't be able to see me. I didn't share any special relationship with the old madman.

Tom swung the starting handle. At the second turn, it caught and a deep, thudding, thumping sound filled the yard, slowly at first, then faster and faster as the motor picked up speed.

Tom ran over to one of the dumpers. He swung the handle and it, too, started with a deep, coughing, thump-thumping sound. At his second try, the other dumper caught. A throaty whump-whump was added to the growing cacophony.

Scrambling over a heap of sand, Tom pressed the button on the compressor. A sharper staccato barked into the thunderous roar. He headed for the final mixer.

I crouched against the wall, my hands over my ears. The noise was awesome, and in the confined space between the wing and the dining hall, it reverberated back and forth. It was now impossible to distinguish any individual piece of plant. All were roaring at full throttle, contributing to a wall of sound that was almost tangible.

In between watching Tom, I kept glancing up at the Chief's windows. A thin mist was rising from the yard as the wind from the plant stirred up the dust, and tears ran down my face as it tickled my nose and irritated my eyes, mixing with already present tears of laughter. Across the yard, Tom was leaning against the last mixer, laughing fit to bust.

Suddenly, I saw a movement high up the wall of C wing. A white-painted casement window swung abruptly open. The familiar massive tousled head thrust out into the abyss.

'Harris!' the deep voice roared. The rest was lost in the din.

Tom looked up at the Chief. He screwed up his face and put one hand to his ear as if he was trying to make out what he was shouting about. He couldn't keep the smile from his face, though.

As I stared up at the Chief, I could see that he was smiling, too. It was amazing. If anyone else had woken him from his slumber, he would have completely lost control.

He continued to shout, making horizontal chopping movements with his hand, his meaning quite clear.

Slowly, Tom made his way from one piece of plant to the next. First the compressor fell silent, then he went over to the dumpers. One by one, they gave a final, consumptive cough and stopped. The mixer was the last to be turned off.

Tom stood there in the silence and the swirling dust. 'What's the matter, Chief?' he called up, the smile still playing at the corners of his mouth.

'What's the matter, Harris?' the Chief shouted back. 'When you get the toe of my boot up your arse, you'll know what's the matter! Now fuck off with those machines and let me have a bit of peace!' There was a broad smile on his face now. His head disappeared and the window closed.

Tom walked over to me, laughing and holding his sides. 'That livened the old bastard up,' he said.

'You're as fucking mad as he is, you know,' I said between chuckles. Then I held up my hand as if I had just realised something. 'That's it!' I exclaimed. 'That's why you two get on so well together. That's what you've got in common. You're both as mad as each other!'

'As I said, Norm,' replied Tom with a twinkle in his eye, 'it's just the way you handle him.'

I looked at Tom in surprise. He wasn't as completely reckless as he seemed. He often had a profound understanding of human nature. Something about him appealed to the Chief's bizarre sense of humour. That was the secret of the special relationship.

14

Although I was enjoying my new job on the 'painters', something happened that nearly made me want to be back in the telephone shop, if only for a day. Ironically, we might never have heard about it if a 'resident' who came from Dartville hadn't had the local newspaper sent in to him.

When Tom and I heard the rumour, we went in search of the paper. There, buried in the court notices on the back page, was the case. The surname was unfamiliar to us, but the local fella knew it. Colin, one of the faceless civvies from the telephone shop, had been nicked for interfering with another civvy's young son.

It was the scandal of the jail. The screws, to a man, clammed up. They had always looked down on us as a class, because of our criminality. Now, one of their very own had been nicked. And what made it all the more embarrassing was that he stood accused of being a nonce.

Subsequent issues of the local paper were now required reading. For several weeks there were just accounts of the accused being remanded on bail. Already we could discern preferential treatment. Any ordinary citizen would have been remanded in custody.

Eventually, the case came for trial. It was a touchy subject with all the screws. Luckily, they couldn't prevent us from reading the paper, though.

It seemed that Colin had been nonsing Mick's son for quite a while. Colin and Mick socialised when they were off duty, and the offences had occurred when the child had visited Colin's house to play with his young son. From our experience of similar cases, the prediction was that Colin would get a sizeable bit of bird.

The first doubts came when we read that Maypole had been called to give evidence on Colin's behalf – a great surprise considering the Governor's over-reaction to the 'abomination' perpetrated by Bill and Steve. Maypole testified that, because of the nature of his job, Colin had been under great stress. I reflected that he hadn't looked stressed when I had seen him, sitting in the office, drinking tea and joking with his fellow civvies. And the placid and sycophantic lifers he worked with could hardly have put him under pressure. The whole thing began to look like a classic case of a closing of the ranks.

In the circumstances, this surprised me. I could have understood it if the child had belonged to one of the 'residents' or even to a member of the public. But this was the son of another member of staff. It seemed that the authorities would go to almost any lengths to avoid public embarrassment.

Colin was found guilty. It could hardly have been otherwise – he had confessed to the offence. The judge then went into a long dissertation about the pressures on public servants who worked with dangerous criminals. It came as no surprise when he gave Colin a suspended sentence. The only consolation for us was that he wouldn't work in Knightsford again.

Colin's suspended sentence hardly came as a shock to me, confirmed cynic that I was. I had learned long ago that very little was as it should be when it came to the system. While still in my teens, I had been lectured about the law by the judges and the police. I had been made to feel ashamed of my fledgling criminality in the face of men who were such paragons of virtue. But as I grew older, I came to realise that it was all a question of power. The crime was to be poor or of low status. That was what got you nicked.

Spring was in the air. Even the walls and bars of Knightsford couldn't keep it out. I was mostly oblivious to the fine distinctions between the seasons, noticing only the difference between winter and summer. But then, I spent most of my life indoors.

The Fox noticed it, though. We had just finished our meal one Sunday evening when he suddenly announced that he was getting married. I had earlier remarked to Tom that the Fox had seemed quite frisky of late. There had been lots of whistling and loud singing. It was a determined attempt to announce to the world that he was happy – a welcome relief from his usual tense, morose self. And it was just like the Fox to flaunt it.

'What about Caroline's husband? Won't he have something to say about that,' asked Tom, with thinly veiled sarcasm.

If he noticed this, Foxy ignored it. 'She's leaving him,' he said with finality. 'She's found a flat and she'll be moving into it in the next couple of weeks.' He sat back with a smug look on his face.

'Won't it cause a bit of trouble for you?' I asked. 'After all, he is a pal of the Dep's.'

'Fuck him,' replied Foxy. 'It's nothing to do with him. Caroline and I are in love.'

There was no answer to that. The words of a thousand love songs flitted through my head. In nearly all of them, love found a way.

'What about the daughter?' challenged Tom, throwing cold water over the love-struck Fox.

There was an instant reaction. He dropped his eyes and hung his head. A flush came to his cheeks. 'She hasn't made up her mind yet,' he said, embarrassed now. He hesitated, then went on. 'In fact, her daughter's causing more trouble than the old man. The other day she asked Caroline why she was leaving Daddy for a murderer.'

There was an awkward silence. I was surprised that the Fox had told us about it. It was a hell of a thing to have on your conscience, always assuming the Fox had one, that is. However, Tom and I had noticed that, of late, the Fox couldn't help but confess things to us.

It was a remark to end the evening with. I reflected that, if ever a relationship seemed doomed before it started, then it was the romance between Caroline and the Fox.

My own romantic entanglements seemed uncomplicated by comparison. Helen and I had settled into a caring friendship that lacked all the trauma of normal, proprietary relationships between men and women. It had only been a minor thing, the agreement that neither of us owned the other, yet it spared me sleepless nights, wondering what she was up to. Visits with her were a bliss of amusing trivia and tender embraces.

By now, even Jean had accepted that our friendship would remain platonic. There were no more heavy references to remarks by her children and she no longer tried to tie me down to some long-term commitment. This was just as well. I didn't want to lead her on in any way. If she had pressed it, I had resolved to take a radical step. I was going to tell her about Helen (although there was little enough to tell). I was relieved that it never came to that, however.

Professor Knox continued to write friendly and supportive letters, including messages from her husband and children and even enclosing photos of them. And my mother and father still visited every month, both much more relaxed now that I seemed to have settled down.

All in all, I had never felt so at ease. I still bridled at my continuing prison situation, but comparatively speaking, I was more settled than I had ever been. A large part of this was undoubtedly due to the network of caring and supportive relationships that now surrounded me. On the debit side, though, it put increased pressure on me to get out of prison.

Tom was now under pressure himself. His latest parole review had started and he was making the rounds of every conceivable official who might have an opinion about him. Many of these people didn't know him at all and had, in fact, only set eyes on him a couple of times in the past year.

It made a mockery of the whole process. It made you feel helpless, with no influence over events. Your future depended on the good opinion of others, who judged by obscure criteria. Small wonder that so many lifers cracked under the strain.

For one, though, the torment was almost over. There was no general joy at the news and many resented him his good fortune, but old Derek had been given his release date. There would be a period 'working on the hostel' first, then, in nine months, he would be free.

Derek seemed totally oblivious to others' opinions of him now.

He had got what he wanted. When we did see him, which was only in the evenings, he beetled about at his usual frenetic pace, whistling energetically like a budgie on speed.

They had found him a job, working on the restoration of a wrecked ship that had been recovered from the sea. His skills as a wood carver served him well here. There were a few sarcastic remarks about 'a man of his age diving down to the wreck', but the truth was that he had a little office where they brought him salvaged items.

All the to-do about reviews and release dates reminded me that my own review was only a few months away. It awoke thoughts of freedom in me, feelings I had suppressed for over a decade now.

In the background, however, there was a fear. What if they came back and gave me a big 'knockback'? Apart from the implications for my own survival, there was now a whole string of people who wanted me home. I felt increasingly under pressure. Try as I might, I could never put the review completely out of my mind.

Mundane things would bring it back to me. I came in from a run one dinner-time and encountered John Deal. My face was flushed from the exertion.

'Oh, Norm,' he cried, 'do take it easy! You'll have a heart attack the way you're going on.'

The insincerity rang clear in his voice. I could tell he didn't like me, yet I had done nothing at Knightsford to earn this dislike. I suspected that his report wouldn't help me in my review. My only consolation was that, far from *me* having a heart attack, he would go long before I did.

But thinking about it would drive me mad. All I could do was to go through the motions and hope that this period of quiet at Knightsford would count for something. And in the back of my mind, as a last resort, there was always the possibility of escape. However, if I tried and failed, it would be the end for me. They would bury me so deep in the system that I would never get out.

It was at times like these that Jane sincerely felt like giving up. She vacillated between extreme anger and deep depression. It was years since she had cried, but now the tears were only a blink away.

She had just come back from St Jude's Hospice where she had seen Neil, lying in his bed, so pale and so thin. No more than twenty-four hours had passed since he had been informed that he had terminal cancer. Yet it seemed that the very knowing had caused him to deteriorate overnight.

The prognosis was that he had no more than three months to live. It had come right out of the blue, but he had taken it so calmly. It was as if he accepted it as his fate: as due recompense for the life of the wife he had killed.

As in the case of Luke who had hanged himself, Jane searched her heart for blame. Could she have done more? Once again, she felt guilty at being part of such a corrupt and soulless system. Should she vote with her feet and leave, or stay and try to rectify some of the wrong?

She cast her mind back to the morning, less than a week before, when Neil had come to the office. He had stood, too polite to interrupt her writing until she had looked up and noticed him.

'Jane, I won't be in your class today,' he said softly, apologetically. 'My finger has swollen up. It's too painful to write with. I've gone sick with it and they're sending me out for some tests.'

Jane felt a sinking sensation in her stomach. It was very unusual for Gold to send someone out for immediate tests. He must suspect something serious. But she hid her feelings, lest she alarm Neil.

'Can I see it, Neil?' she asked innocently.

Neil held out his right hand and extended the middle finger. It was grotesquely swollen around the second joint and was an angry red.

She reached out her hand and gently grasped his. A thrill of alarm raced through her. The swelling generated a heat that beat against her skin. Gingerly, she released his hand, taking care to avoid his eyes. She couldn't trust herself not to reveal her feelings.

'Well, you've done the right thing going sick, Neil,' she said cheerily, looking steadily at his chin. 'Let me know what they say as soon as you get back.'

'OK,' he replied. 'Sorry about missing your class.' Jane felt a lump in her throat as he turned and walked out.

He hadn't returned. The following day, when he wasn't in her class again, she had toyed with the idea of phoning Gold to ask what had happened to him. But she knew he would tell her nothing. It was Eddie who brought her the news.

At first, she was stunned. Neil was still so young and had already served most of his sentence. It was all so unfair.

The hospital had moved him to the hospice the day before. She had gone along in her dinner hour to see him. In view of the short time left, she felt it best not to delay.

He had been so pleased to see her. His parents had been informed and they would be visiting at the weekend, but he said he felt closer to Jane now. She shuddered at the thought of the coming months, when she would watch him slowly waste away.

He had been a solitary man at Knightsford. He had no close friends. His passing would be mourned by few, but this was no value judgement on the rest. They were all obsessed with their own survival. It occupied all their energies and attention. The death of one of their number would concentrate their minds wonderfully and exhort them to even greater efforts on their own behalf.

That evening, Tom and I made our way up to see Jane. We had heard the news and realised she would be upset. We would offer what words of consolation we could.

Neil's impending death hadn't touched us at all. We felt only for ourselves and our close friends now. The unceasing pathos of our daily lives had served to desensitise us to the suffering of others. I was aware of the process that was progressively hardening my heart, but regarded it as a strength. It would help to ensure that I survived, while others went under.

Jane was on her own when we walked in. She looked up, smiled weakly, then looked down again. I guessed she didn't trust herself to hold her emotions in check. She looked unusually pale and drawn. Increasingly, I felt that Knightsford was no place for someone as sensitive and caring as she was. Yet she had a surprising inner strength. She wouldn't have thanked me for suggesting that she leave.

'Sorry to hear about Neil, Jane,' said Tom softly. I stood at his shoulder in silent agreement.

Jane thrust her chin forward bravely. 'Thank you,' she said, 'thank you both for coming to see me . . . Do you think I could have done more?' This last was said plaintively, almost entreatingly, as if she was begging us to reassure her and so assuage her feeling of guilt.

'There was nothing you could have done, Jane,' said Tom reassuringly. 'We all have trouble getting the treatment we need. That's why it's best to keep yourself fit and healthy.'

'Norman?' She looked at me appealingly.

'There was nothing more you could have done,' I assured her.

Suddenly, as I thought of Neil's predicament, the anger flared in me, too. 'Now you can understand why I am as I am, Jane. I know what they say about me being an animal. The only thing these people understand is a bit of what they rule by: violence and intimidation. I've had to intimidate them into treating me with a basic courtesy and respect. If I had been suffering what Neil suffered, they wouldn't have ignored me because I would have done something to make them take notice.'

Once spoken, I regretted the diatribe. There was an implied criticism of the gentle Neil in it. Yet it was the truth. Neil would die and I would survive, for the present. That was lesson enough.

Jane looked at me with a new understanding in her eyes. She could not condone my violent philosophy, but she recognised its inherent pragmatism. She realised that, with her gentle nature, she would have been unlikely to survive a long prison sentence. With a shudder, she didn't know whether to be sad or pleased at the realisation.

Within a few weeks, Neil's slow decline towards death slipped from our minds. We were aware that Jane went to see him almost daily, but there were other things on our minds. Bad news had struck closer to home.

After several months of waiting for an answer, JB had finally been summoned to the wing office one morning. He emerged ashen-faced. Before he hurried away to his cell, he sought Tom out to tell him that he had been given a two-year knockback.

It was a savage result, just about the worst you could get at Knightsford. He would have to spend another two fruitless years here, before coming up for review again. Then there would be another long period of waiting before he got his answer to that review.

At dinner-time we commiserated with him. Maypole was nowhere to be seen. We had noticed that, when the news was good, the sanctimonious hypocrite congratulated the resident personally as he passed the hot-plate on his way to collect his dinner. Standing at the shoulder on one of the servers, the flushed face would smile broadly and jocularly assure the thankful inmate of his own positive role in the man's success. Yet, when the news was bad, he was always conspicuous by his absence.

Later that evening, Maypole appeared on the centre. JB walked up to him and was immediately joined by a crowd of young 'uns from the nearby pool table.

JB had taken it well. He had accepted the bad news and had come to terms with its implications. He was asking Maypole if he knew of any reason for the knockback.

Maypole prevaricated. He wouldn't commit himself, and made do with generalisations. The crowd stood around him, politely nodding as he spoke, yet said nothing.

I had been watching his performance as Tom and I approached the centre and walked to the fringe of the crowd. Maypole seemed nonplussed by the whole affair. 'Well, Brewer,' he was saying heartily, a broad smile on his face, 'things could be worse. You'll just have to buckle down and work towards your next review.'

It was a masterpiece of understatement. Lifers in JB's situation had been known to kill themselves. Maypole's lack of feeling was almost criminal.

Suddenly, I felt the urge to say something. I strove to prevent it, but before I knew it, it was out. 'Well, Governor,' I said in a falsely cheerful voice that echoed his, 'I must say you're taking it very well.'

There was a stunned silence. The blatant sarcasm had shocked everyone. But the timing, the essence of all humour, was impeccable. Suddenly, the crowd exploded into a communal guffaw of laughter. Men who had been standing with long faces seconds earlier were now laughing fit to burst. Even JB was in hysterics.

Maypole was still smiling, but the eyes that were fixed on mine were as cold as ice. He recognised the humour in the remark, but not my right to make it. His icy glare warned me that I had made my first and only joke at his expense. I quietly cursed my quick wit and loose tongue and resolved not to repeat the mistake.

Humour was the most subversive of mediums. Especially when it was at the expense of a man who was as unsure of himself as

Maypole. I had managed to stay out of his way since I had been at Knightsford. Now, with one remark, I had kindled his enmity. I would do my best to avoid him for a while.

Jeff West was bored. It was 7.15 on a Sunday evening and there were still two hours to go before he was off duty. He strolled slowly along the ones of a deserted A wing, humming softly to himself and thinking of better days.

He hated the regime here at Knightsford. Give him Dartmoor any day. He had spent several blissfully happy years there. A prison officer knew where he stood at Dartmoor.

And prisoners knew their place too. Mostly, it was behind their doors. Even when they were out, at work or on a brief period of association, they had to mind their manners. Officers were to be addressed as 'sir' and all orders were to be obeyed instantly. And woe betide any trouble-makers. It would be a quick trip to the chokey, a good kicking and a night spent in the strip cell. That used to sort them out.

But here at Knightsford, it was the prisoners who seemed to have the run of things. 'Sorry,' he mentally corrected himself. He should have said 'residents' – there were no 'prisoners' in Knightsford.

Many of them were sycophantic enough. However, he still begrudged them their freedoms and privileges. Some of the younger ones, though, desperately needed bringing down a peg. He knew they disliked him, even made fun of him. What was so very frustrating was that there was nothing he could do about it. If only he could catch them at something.

He was nearing the end of the ones now. There wasn't a soul about. No doubt they were all in the TV rooms, or playing snooker, pool or badminton. The place was like a bloody country club for criminals.

The lighting was dim at the far end of the landing. Far away from the activity of the centre, the silence seemed to hum soothingly. He was just about to turn to walk back up the other side when he became aware that he was passing 'Mother's' cell. He stopped.

He particularly detested this one. A disgusting, fat pervert. He couldn't understand how the Governor allowed him to flaunt himself all over the place. The exaggerated feminine movements and breathless manner were travesties of all that was female. It amazed and disgusted him that the man had the nerve to show his face at all.

He was insubordinate with it. West had had reason to caution him about his manner several days ago, and the man had made a joke of it, his shrill, high-pitched voice attracting a crowd. Soon, they were all laughing with him. It was he who had been embarrassed, having to retreat with a red face.

He walked closer to the door. Music was playing softly within.

Carefully, he crept right up close and put his eye to the small hole in the spy-hole cover.

The cell was in darkness. Yet the radio was playing. This was strange.

He pressed his ear to the crack where the door met the jamb. He listened intently. At first there was nothing. The music droned softly, anonymously, in the background. He pressed his ear tighter. Suddenly, there was something else. A deep, rhythmic grunting, overlaid by gasping, heavy breathing.

He stepped back. Could it be the unthinkable? Was the disgusting creature indulging in some filthy perversion? And were there others involved?

West hesitated. What should he do? Should he run to the wing office for help? But by then, it might be over.

He came to a decision and acted all in the same moment. He threw his shoulder against the door and burst into the cell. He groped against the wall in the darkness and switched on the light. His mouth gaped in surprise as his gaze swept the cell. It seemed empty.

But a flicker of movement caught his eye. He spun round. There, in the corner behind the door stood Niven Brady with his trousers around his ankles. Mother knelt before him, his mouth level with Niven's erect penis.

It was hard to tell who was the more surprised.

'Oh fuck!' cried Niven, as he bent to pull his trousers up, his expression a mixture of shock, horror and shame.

Mother's reaction was altogether different. He climbed slowly to his feet, the beginnings of a smirk on his face. There was no shame for him. His social status depended on his ability to outrage and shock. A public liaison with Niven would be the best publicity he'd had in a long while.

West stood there with his mouth open. The early pallor of shock had now given way to the deep red of embarrassment. But he realised that he had to do something.

'OK,' he said unconvincingly. Niven and Mother looked at him. 'OK,' he repeated, unnerved by the smirk he had just noticed on Mother's face. They all stood there, frozen into inactivity.

Suddenly, he seemed to pull himself together. 'OK, you two,' he managed to blurt out, 'come with me.'

'Oh, are you coming?' trilled Mother, raising both his hands to his mouth in mock surprise.

The remark served to galvanise West. Anger and disgust fought for supremacy within him. 'Shut up, you!' he roared, advancing on Mother. 'You just shut your dirty mouth!'

Whatever else he was, Mother was no hero. He disliked violence of any kind. Admittedly, he had killed his lover, but only after long years of torment and abuse. He hung his head, cowed. His manner was that of a little boy now.

Walking behind them, West marched the pair along to the wing office. He ushered them inside and closed the door. Several minutes passed, then the three of them appeared again. He took them back along the ones and they disappeared down the steps of the punishment block.

Within an hour, the news had spread throughout the jail. Just before the 9.15 bang-up, men stood in groups animatedly discussing it, pausing only to break out into bellows of laughter. It was deliciously scandalous. The image of Niven, he of the fiery temper and captain of the football team, in a sexual liaison with the appalling Mother was just too much.

Tom, Jack and I were leaning on the railing outside Tom's cell. Bill and Steve stood talking opposite. 'Well, at least Bill's got some taste,' I muttered quietly.

Tom shot me a hostile look. He glanced across at Bill to see if he had heard. But, of course, he hadn't.

'I suppose you saw this coming, too, Sherlock?' he asked sarcastically.

'Well, as a matter of fact . . .' I said, trailing off into silence. I was already walking away. Tom and Jack looked after me, waiting for the rest. '. . . I thought Mother was having it with you,' I finished.

'Bollocks!' shouted Tom and made as if to run after me, but I was already half-way down the stairs. 'I thought he was having it with *you*!' he shouted after me. But the laughter was all for my remark.

I looked up at the smiling faces of Bill and Steve. 'Revenge is sweet, eh, Bill?' I called up to him. 'Don't forget. When Niven's standing with Mother outside the office tomorrow, waiting to go in, you can shout out about his wife not being able to give evidence against him.'

Bill smiled weakly, more embarrassed than amused. I knew he wouldn't have the nerve to do it.

The following day, in a replay of the Bill and Steve affair, Niven and Mother appeared before the Governor. I would have given anything to have seen his face as the unlikely duo stood before him, but it was all concealed from public view.

They both got seven days in the block and were led away to serve it. Niven looked both relieved and pleased. I guessed he would be glad to escape from all the embarrassment for a week. It would take him a long time to live this down, I reflected, and it would do nothing for his already fragile self-esteem.

Two days had passed since the scandal with Niven and Mother. Jane had been on leave. That evening, Tom told me that he had something to tell her. After our usual gym session, we went up the education block to find her.

She was collecting her papers together as we walked into the office. Her face lit up as she saw us. 'And to what do I owe this pleasure?' she asked brightly.

'It's about what happened in class yesterday, when you were away,' said Tom mysteriously.

Jane looked at him, intrigued now. 'We were sitting there, doing the work you set us,' Tom continued, 'when Hall walked in.' At the mention of his name, a frown appeared on Jane's face. Of them all, he was her sworn enemy.

'He went over to the bookcase and started getting the books out. He opened one book and started to leaf through it. It was a Fay Weldon – you know, the one you got me to read. Well, then he turned to the class and told us we shouldn't read any of those books because they were Marxist. Then he put the books back and walked out.'

Jane's frown dissolved into a smile. 'Fay Weldon would be surprised to hear she's a Marxist. What else did he say?'

'Nothing,' replied Tom.

Jane stood deep in thought for a moment. 'You know,' she said, looking up at the ceiling as if for divine guidance, 'if Hall wasn't so pathetically ignorant, he might make a half-ways worthy adversary. It's always the ignorant who fear knowledge the most, you know.'

She looked directly at Tom. 'Thank you for telling me, Tom. It's very helpful to know what goes on behind my back.'

'I suppose you heard about Niven?' I said, unable to keep the smile from my face. 'It looks like you've got a rival.'

She adopted a pose, her hand on her hip in fake petulance. 'Well, I know when I'm beaten, Norman,' she replied. We all laughed together. She looked quite pleased about the scandal, though. While Niven was chasing after Mother, it would take the pressure off her.

One of the positive aspects of not having a lot of close friends was that most of the bad news I heard concerned people I didn't particularly care for. And while not exactly exulting in their bad fortune, it was nice to see a slag get his comeuppance once in a while.

Alf Walker had had a good run at Knightsford. He had managed to ingratiate himself with the screws to such an extent that he did almost what he liked. In return, he mended their watches and clocks and told them everything he saw.

The true feat, though, was the way he had managed to become Maypole's pet. It was no insignificant concession to be allowed out to paddle on the beach once a week.

Another was that he was allowed to walk around in a filthy state. There were some dirt-birds at Knightsford, but Walker took the prize. He lived in a cell half-way along the ones on A wing. I had regularly seen into it as I passed on my way to the Works in the morning, and its squalor was breathtaking. Steptoe's yard looked pristine by comparison.

It was Saturday morning and there would be no more work until Monday. Walker rarely mixed with the other 'residents'. Even in the

TV rooms he was shunned. Apart from his bizarre personality, there was the sickening smell.

He sat at his table, his door half open, tinkering with a clock a screw had brought in. Suddenly, there was a searing pain in his chest. He clutched at his heart in a reflex as he rose to his feet. He tottered unsteadily for long seconds, then fell, sprawling, to the floor.

He lay there, motionless, gasping for breath. He convulsed, as another bolt of pain galvanised him. With saliva dribbling from his open mouth, he dragged himself to the door. He collapsed unconscious, across the threshold.

He was quickly found. Screws ran from A wing office, a stretcher was fetched and they carried him to the hospital. Mr Patel rang Dr Gold's surgery.

Unfortunately for Walker, Dr Gold was away for the weekend. So another local doctor was contacted. Dr Majul was young, fresh and ferociously committed to the Hippocratic ideal. He never even contemplated the thought that his writ might not run in Knightsford.

Alf Walker lay on a table in the middle of the sick bay. He was barely conscious. His breathing was shallow, and saliva still ran from his open mouth.

Dr Majul circled the bulky figure warily, wrinkling his nose in disgust as the smell from the greasy, stained overalls reached him. He pulled on a pair of protective rubber gloves and gently pushed at the prostrate man's side. With his enormous weight pinning him to the table, Walker hardly budged.

'Cut his clothes off him,' he ordered the hovering Patel.

Surprised, Patel hurried to obey. He produced a large pair of scissors and began cutting up one side of the bib-and-brace overalls. It was hard going to cut through the thick material, but ten minutes saw him finished. He flipped the top layer over on to the floor, so revealing the first surprise.

A blue-striped prison shirt reached down to Walker's hips, but below that he was wearing a suspender belt and and an old, laddered pair of tights.

Dr Majul raised his eyebrows in surprise. Patel stepped back, hesitating. He wasn't sure what to do next.

'Well, go on,' encouraged the doctor. 'Cut it all off.'

Fifteen minutes later, it all lay in an untidy pile on the floor. The last item, on the very top, was an excrement-stained pair of women's knickers. Patel hurried across to the sink to wash his hands.

Dr Majul bent closer to examine the naked figure. Great rolls of grey-white fat hung in folds all over Walker's body. But that wasn't what was attracting the doctor's interest. As he peered through the thick, black hair which virtually covered Walker, he could discern movement.

He stepped back quickly. 'This man is alive with body lice,' he announced loudly. 'How did he get into such a state?' Patel just stood there, hands held out in front of him, shaking his head as if it were all beyond him.

'Call an officer,' Dr Majul ordered. Patel ran to the door and waved one in from outside. 'Take me to this man's cell immediately,' the doctor demanded of the screw.

He followed him out of the hospital and along A wing. When the screw halted outside a cell, Dr Majul walked inside and gasped as the stench hit him.

There was junk everywhere. Piled on the table, the floor and even on the bed were parts of various mechanical devices. Strewn all about the place were soiled articles of clothing.

Picking up a broom which was leaning in a corner, he reversed it and poked underneath the bed with the handle. Suddenly, it snagged on something. He pulled and out came a dusty pile of prison underpants. The once-white material was now an unhealthy shade of grey. The crutch of every one was caked with excrement.

Dr Majul spun on his heel and marched out of the cell. 'Officer,' he said to the screw, 'now listen to me carefully. I want this cell sealed up immediately. I will sign the authorisation, then I want everything taken out and burned and the cell thoroughly fumigated. Do you understand?' The screw stood there, dumbly nodding. Dr Majul headed back towards the hospital, with the screw following behind.

Back in the sickbay, Alf Walker still lay barely conscious. Patel was at the sink, scrubbing his hands with disinfectant as Dr Majul swept in.

'Mr Patel,' he said peremptorily. Patel jumped and spun round from the sink. 'It is my professional opinion that this man is unable to look after himself properly. I will be signing the appropriate papers immediately. I want him removed to a place where they have the facilities to look after him.'

Patel nodded in agreement, his hands clasped before him in as ingratiating a manner as he could manage. There was strong implied criticism of himself here. He had no concern about Walker. He would be pleased if he could avoid censure himself.

'Now I will need to use Dr Gold's office for a short while. I have to make some phone calls,' continued the doctor.

That evening, Tom, Jack and I sat in with Bill and Steve. The talk was all of Alf Walker's recent and sudden departure to, we had heard, Parkhurst. They had a special wing there where mentally disordered patients were kept. The regime was brutal and run on top-security lines. He would have no freedom there.

'Good enough for him, the fucking nonce,' said Bill bitterly. We all nodded in agreement.

'Maypole will have a shock on Monday morning when he comes back and finds his pet nonce gone,' added Tom. We laughed at the thought of Maypole's discomfiture.

'And you can bet your life that poor old Alf won't be doing a lot of paddling at Parkhurst, was my contribution. It got the biggest laugh of the evening.

*   *   *

For a couple of weeks now, Foxy had been building up for an explosion. All the old familiar signs were there: the hunched, taut shoulders with hands tightly clenched, the pugnacious set of the jaw, the cords standing out in his neck. And, last but not least, all the singing and loud whistling had stopped.

At first, Tom and I had thought that he'd had a row with Caroline. We didn't ask, knowing that he would tell us soon enough. We were almost right. It did concern her, but it wasn't a row. It seemed that one of the screws had been going into the shop where she worked and was trying to chat her up.

Foxy pointed out the screw to us. I had noticed him already. He was a young, flash screw who worked on A wing. He looked like just the sort of screw you could easily have a row with, but luckily for us, he never came on C wing.

He definitely fancied himself. With his dark good looks and slim build, he had a reputation for being a bit of a ladies' man in the locality. I couldn't figure out why he was sniffing around Caroline though. She wasn't a bad-looking woman, but she was all of fifteen years older than him. Perhaps he thought that, as she was carrying on with Fox, she would be easy meat.

I was sure he was playing with fire. Of all the subjects that the Fox became dangerously unstable over, Caroline ranked first. I tried to play it down. I couldn't really believe the screw was serious and I didn't want to see the Fox get himself into serious trouble over it.

It was just after 4.00 on a damp and boring Sunday afternoon. Tom and I had just collected our tea, the usual Sunday salad, and dropped it off in our cells to eat later. We were now standing by the pool table at the beginning of A wing, waiting for a game.

I saw Foxy come up C wing from the direction of the visiting room. The neatly pressed greys and the well-starched shirt attested to the fact that he had just come off a visit. But it didn't look as if he had enjoyed himself. He strode along, head down, fists clenched and face screwed up into a scowl.

He stalked right across the centre and on to A wing. We looked at him as he passed, but he totally ignored us, intent on whatever he had in mind.

He marched up to A wing office and looked inside. He obviously didn't find what he was looking for, because he turned away and walked to stand in the middle of the ones. He craned his head backwards as he scanned the length of the twos. Still he didn't find what he was looking for.

He stalked past us again and went to stand by the snooker table. From here, he had a commanding view of the length of all three wings. In between watching the game, he would look up and scan the landings.

The game of pool finished and it was our turn. We racked the balls, chose a cue each and began to play. Within a few moments we were lost in our game.

'Oi, you cunt!' The demented roar cut through the hubbub generated by dozens of men scurrying across the centre in pursuit of their tea. It was loud enough to make me jump. I looked up in time to see the Fox launch himself from the wall against which he had been leaning. He strode quickly across the centre.

The object of his attention didn't seem keen to meet him. In fact, he was hurrying in the other direction as fast as he could without breaking into a run. Looking over his shoulder at the pursuing Fox, the young, flash screw headed for the safety of the A wing office.

He reached it marginally before Foxy and dived inside. If he had thought he was safe, he now had a nasty shock coming. Without hesitation, the Fox plunged in after him.

'I've just about had enough of you, you dirty, fucking bastard!' The scream of a Fox in full cry burst from the office and reverberated around the centre. We had long since lost interest in the pool. Better entertainment was now on offer.

We rested our cues against the wall and stood, listening. There would be several screws in the office. As much as we thought the Fox to be a complete prick, we wouldn't stand idly by if they all jumped on him. It was just the situation we had feared that he would someday create when we were around.

Luckily for us, jumping on the Fox was the last thing the screws had on their minds. Three of them had been sitting in the office, quietly drinking cups of tea. They had been surprised when their comrade had burst into the office, closely pursued by the Fox. They had been shocked when the latter had seized him by the throat and thrust him against the wall. But the blood-curdling scream had been the clincher. Now they huddled together on the other side of the desk, desperately hoping that the Fox wouldn't go completely berserk.

Now, the formerly flash screw wasn't nearly so sure of himself. Eyes bulging from their sockets, he clutched desperately at the hands that gripped his neck. He recoiled as the Fox thrust his face up against his.

'Now for the very last time,' screamed the Fox, 'I'm warning you to keep away from my wife!' It was a line straight out of a B-movie. However, it certainly seemed to impress the young screw. He nodded his head vigorously, desperately seeking to reassure the Fox that he understood.

For long seconds, the Fox glared into the fear-dazed face. Then, with a snort of disgust, he released his grip and stormed out. He marched past us on his way to B wing and his cell. He didn't so much as acknowledge us as he went by.

Tom and I looked at each other, shrugged and smiled. We picked up our cues to continue playing.

'He'll be lucky to survive that one,' I remarked nonchalantly.

'Oh, I don't know,' said Tom. 'It ain't only cats that have nine lives, you know.'

In the event, it turned out that he was right. What saved him was that Caroline had already made a complaint about the screw to the Governor. The Fox could have been nicked for assault, of course. However, it wouldn't have looked very good in front of the magistrates when it came out that the screw had been harassing Foxy's girlfriend. The authorities' overwhelming desire to present a good public image had saved him, but I was sure that the red writing still went down on Foxy's record.

It was a beautiful summer. Long, halcyon days drifted by in a haze of near-tropical heat. Clear blue skies, untrammelled by any vestige of a cloud, over-arched a world that didn't seem to have a care.

Yet none of it seemed to touch Jane. The heat couldn't reach the coldness she felt inside her. The bright colours, the musky odours struck no chord. The cheerful faces of the passers-by stood out in stark contrast to the misery on hers.

For just over three months, she had been making the journey to the hospice each day. It was only a ten-minute walk from the prison, but as Neil grew weaker, it seemed more like a trek. She found herself wishing away each coming meeting, when she would have to gaze on the tortured wreck of her friend's body.

He had died early that morning. His parents had been with him. Jane had looked at the husk-like remains and wondered why God had seen fit to inflict an illness like cancer on humanity. She came away as quickly as she decently could. Now she walked back through the sun-blasted streets towards the place that had undoubtedly contributed to Neil's demise.

The cool of the gate-lodge was refreshing. The darkness of the shade served to conceal a world she had no desire to see at the moment. She would have to carry on, if only for those still living within the walls. But she felt a deep hatred for the very fabric of the place.

Mentally, she steeled herself. Neil's death had been a blow, albeit an expected one, but she would have to come to terms with it. She could expect some of the staff to make disparaging remarks, especially if they thought it would upset her.

The attack came from an unexpected quarter. In the past, she had been no stranger to trouble caused by other members of staff. It was only her naïvety that had caused her to think that they wouldn't pick a day like this.

As she reached her office, she noticed Graham hovering further down the corridor. Mentally, she cringed. She didn't feel up to repelling his romantic advances at a time like this. She walked inside quickly, without looking at him.

She heard a rush of feet behind her. She turned and saw Graham in the doorway. His face was flushed and he was clearly agitated.

'How could you have done it to me, Jane?' he wailed.

Jane looked at him in surprise. 'What in heaven's name are you talking about, Graham?' she demanded.

'My report, Jane. That's what I'm talking about. My report.' He seemed on the verge of tears.

Jane shook her head as if to clear it. This was proving to be a very trying day indeed. Could it be that things were going to get worse?

'Graham,' she said patiently, as if addressing a child, 'will you please explain to me what you're talking about?'

Graham blinked, surprised. He had worked out exactly what he was going to say to her. It had never occurred to him that she would deny it.

'The bad report you wrote about me, Jane. That's what I'm talking about,' he explained.

Now it was Jane's turn to look surprised. 'Graham, I still don't know what you're talking about. I wrote you a good report. Who told you I wrote a bad one?'

Graham looked guarded now. He was an obsequious man at the best of times. He wouldn't have confronted anyone else in the way he had just confronted Jane. He didn't want to get involved in an argument between staff.

'An officer on A wing told me,' he confessed.

'Who was it?' Jane demanded.

Graham shifted from one foot to the other and screwed up his face. 'I don't want to say. I don't want to get into trouble,' he blurted out.

Jane stood, regarding him for a moment. Suddenly, she came to a decision. 'Graham. Wait outside a moment. There's something I want to show you.'

She ushered Graham outside and locked the office door. 'Wait here,' she said, then hurried off along the corridor in the direction of the gallery.

Barely five minutes had passed before she was back. In her hand she held a slim, beige-coloured folder. On its cover it bore the legend 'GRAHAM DARK', followed by a number.

She opened it. 'Graham,' she said, 'I want you to promise me that you won't tell anyone I've shown you this.' He nodded his agreement. 'No, that's not good enough,' she said. 'I want you to promise. I'm only doing this to put your mind at rest.'

'OK, I promise,' said Graham, grudgingly. She handed him the folder.

He stood there, reading intently. He ran his eyes down the page, then started again.

'Well,' said Jane.

Graham looked up. A strange, hunted look flitted across his eyes. His knuckles whitened as he gripped the folder.

Suddenly, he brushed past her, took to his heels and ran along the corridor in the direction of the gallery. 'Graham!' she called after him. He didn't even look back as he rounded the corner and disappeared from sight.

Jane unlocked the door and walked into her office. She could be in trouble now. All records were covered by the Official Secrets Act. They weren't to be shown to prisoners. Her only recourse would be to say that she was reading it when he snatched it from her. That wouldn't be too far from the truth, anyway.

Jane sat at her desk. She wondered if the whole thing had been a set-up. It was common knowledge among the residents that whoever brought her down would be popular with the rest of the staff. But they would be unlucky this time. It would be her word against that of a prisoner. There would be another black mark, but she had long since ceased to worry about her career.

She tried to contemplate the nature of the person who had chosen a day like this to launch an attack on her, but it was beyond her. She contented herself with the thought that she was becoming stronger. What was it that Norman had once said to her? Something about 'That which does not kill you makes you stronger.' Well, they hadn't killed her yet, and, at this rate, she was going to end up a very strong lady indeed.

15

The football season had been over for six weeks, and despite all the arguing and unpleasantness, it was missed. There was a profound vacuum in the social life of Knightsford's young 'uns now. They especially missed the Saturday 'high'.

We had won the league again. Outside, civilian teams claimed that we had an unfair advantage in that we always played at home, and there was a large measure of truth in this. Teams were intimidated by being inside a prison and confused by the peculiar nature of our claustrophobic pitch.

Niven had won the award for being the league's highest scorer, having broken the previous record by a large margin. Most of us took no pleasure in this, though. And Niven certainly regarded it as a personal, rather than a team, achievement.

When I spoke to the other players about the past season, they always complained long and hard about Niven. It was nice to win the league, but winning wasn't everything. Especially when you weren't enjoying the football.

There was, however, little I could do about it personally. Neither Tom nor I had a problem with Niven. He never shouted or screamed at us. The crux of the matter was that most of the rest just wouldn't stand up for themselves.

It was all academic now anyway. The season was over and post-mortems would change nothing. The new season was still weeks away. I was sure that Niven would carry on exactly as he had done in the past.

Suddenly, it all became highly topical. Tom told me that a football meeting had been called. There were two main items on the agenda: the election of a captain for the coming season, and the question of whether screws should be allowed to play in the team.

The captaincy looked like being a foregone conclusion. Tom wasn't interested, I wasn't good enough and none of the rest would have the courage to stand against Niven.

Behind the scenes, when Tom and I met the rest informally about the jail, the general view was that they didn't want Niven as captain again. Eric was suggested as an alternative. He would have been a popular captain. He was an excellent footballer and had a talent for encouraging players without abusing them. However, he was scared of Niven, so there was little chance of him standing against the incumbent.

I had neither the interest nor the inclination to lead a palace revolt. I realised that, even if the others were encouraged to elect Eric, Niven would soon overrule him on the field. As far as I was concerned, he could have the captaincy.

But as for a screw playing in the team, that was a different matter entirely. The Saturday game was an opportunity to escape from all things prison for a while. I had to live side by side with the screws. I didn't particularly want to socialise with them, too.

I wondered how the subject had arisen. Had the PTIs proposed it or was it something most of the players wanted? Tom informed me that it was neither of these. The screw in question was Wade, he of the Welsh origins and hooligan tendency. He had got together with Niven to foist it on the team.

Wade was good enough to get in. He may have been overweight and unfit, but he was better than a good quarter of the players. He was a nasty piece of work, though, and none of us liked him. I guessed he would try to use his uniform to intimidate the rest of us on the pitch.

As much as I wanted a quiet life at Knightsford, I sincerely didn't want to play in the same team as Wade. I was also incensed by the underhand way that Niven was trying to get him in.

I wanted to do something about it, but I would have to be careful. If it became obvious that I was behind a revolt to keep a screw out of the prison team, Maypole would take that as evidence of my subversive and antisocial nature. With my review coming up, it certainly wouldn't do me any good, and there was always the possibility that I could be shanghaied over it.

I talked it over with the others. All were strongly against Wade playing, but they were reluctant to stand up at the meeting and say so. I reassured them that I would start the ball rolling. All they had to do was vote with their consciences.

The meeting was scheduled for a Saturday afternoon. It was to be held in the quiet room, next to the library. Both the PTIs would be there, as well as Wade.

In the days leading up to the meeting, Tom and I met with the others around the prison and continued to exhort them to vote with their consciences. You could see that they were worried, both about upsetting Niven and about voting against a screw.

On the Friday, we heard that Niven was encouraging all his crowd of sycophants to attend the meeting. We were sure that they would vote the way he directed. The unfair part was that none of them ever played. Strictly speaking, any 'resident' could vote, but traditionally, only players attended football meetings.

The meeting was scheduled to start at 1.00. At 12.55, I strolled into the quiet room with Tom, Jack, Bill and Steve. The two PTIs, Ted and Bob, were already there, sitting next to Wade. We nodded to each other, but there was already tension. There were no secrets in Knightsford. Someone had obviously told them about what had been going on behind the scenes.

A score of chairs had been set out around a number of tables pushed together end to end. We went to sit at the far end, on the opposite side to the screws. I mused that it rather reflected the division of opinion among those present.

Suddenly, Niven breezed through the doors, with Walt, Porter, Alfred E. Neumann, Starling and old Derek behind him. A motley crew indeed: sycophants and arse-lickers all. Niven, surprised to see us already there, sat next to Wade. His retinue spread themselves out opposite us.

There was an awkward silence. Niven leaned close to Wade, whispering. His crowd exchanged the odd desultory remark. On our side of the table, we lounged back in our chairs, waiting patiently for the proceedings to begin.

Suddenly, all heads turned as the doors swung open again. Self-consciously, Richie, Eric and Pete walked slowly into the room. With worried looks on their faces, they quickly acknowledged the PTIs, Wade, Niven and his crowd. Grudging acknowledgements were returned, although Niven ignored them all. They drifted around the table, finally to settle on our side.

I made a quick count. The screws and Niven's crowd numbered nine. Even if everyone else present voted against, that made only eight. Clearly, we needed more support.

Everyone looked surprised when Eddie and Sam walked into the room. Neither of them played football and, in fact, had no interest in sport. Both were quite timid by nature, too. I wondered if they had just come along as interested observers.

Before I could think any more about it, the doors swung again, and in sauntered the Fox, followed by JB. They both shouted their greetings to those on our side of the table, while ignoring the rest. There was a moment's confusion as they looked around for a seat. Finally, they settled at the end of the table. It now seemed like everyone was here. I couldn't think of any players who were missing.

Bob must have thought so, too. He rose to his feet. As titular manager of the football team, his was the responsibility to call the meeting to order.

'We've got two things to decide today,' he began, brutally dispensing with any preliminaries. 'The first concerns whether or not officers can play in the team.'

He paused to look the length of the table. Several on our side lowered their gaze, unable to meet his eye. Tom and I stared steadily back at him. I noticed that JB and the Fox were doing likewise.

'Then we've got the business of electing a captain for the

coming season,' he continued. Niven stirred in his seat and smiled at his crew. As one, they smiled back.

I paid it no mind. I was already pleased at the way things were developing. The question of the screw playing would be dealt with first. The major revolt would be over this. If we won it, there was always the chance that Eric would be bold enough to stand against Niven for the captaincy.

'So, firstly, then,' said Bob, 'we'll deal with whether officers should play. Has anyone got anything to say in favour?' He clearly expected that they had, for he immediately sat down.

Niven put his hand in the air. From two seats away, Bob acknowledged him. Niven lowered his hand and, still sitting, began to speak.

'I'm in favour of an officer playing,' he said self-consciously. He stared into the middle distance, avoiding the eyes of any on our side of the table. You could tell that he was embarrassed at speaking up for a screw. 'We're really talking about Taffy here.' He acknowledged Wade sitting at his elbow. Wade nodded his head slightly. 'Taffy's a good player and I think his authority will help to settle us down on the field.' Niven's crew all nodded in unison.

I couldn't help but reflect that what Niven had just said was utter hypocrisy. Apart from any other considerations, the only player who needed someone to settle him down was Niven himself.

He had now run out of things to say in Wade's favour, though. He looked along at his crew, but could find no inspiration there.

'So I'm in favour of an officer playing in the team,' he ended, repeating the statement he had started with.

His abrupt conclusion took Bob by surprise. He leaned forward to stare at Niven, making sure that he had indeed finished. Then he rose slowly to his feet again.

'Well, that's the argument in favour,' he said, nodding at Niven and smiling. 'Now, has anyone got anything to say against?' He remained standing.

I looked around the table. No one made a move. Suddenly, everyone was intent on staring out of the window, at the ceiling or at the table. No one looked at Bob.

With resignation, I put my hand up. I knew I had said that I would speak out, but it would have been nice for someone else to say something too.

Every head turned to look at me. 'Here we go again,' I thought. The memory of a score of past disputes where I had spoken up rose before me like a spectre. I would have to pick my words carefully.

Bob acknowledged me, then sat down. I turned in my chair to face him. A line of blank and unsympathetic faces stared back.

'I'm against an officer playing in the team,' I began. There was no gasp from those present, but I felt a mental intake of breath. It was out in the open now. The unmentionable had been spoken.

'It's not that I've got anything against officers as such.' I looked steadily at Wade and he looked steadily back. 'It's just that every officer has the opportunity to play football on a Saturday if he wants to. There are scores of local teams who they could easily get a game with. Us prisoners, we only have the one team we play for. So if an officer takes up a place, that's one inmate who has to go without a game.' I paused to let it all sink in.

'Now I'm not a particularly good player,' I continued, 'and I'm well aware that I only just get in the team. If Taffy played, it could well be my place he would be taking. I don't think that's right and I'm certainly not going to vote for it. And I wouldn't vote for him taking any other prisoner's place either. That's why I'm against an officer playing in the team.'

There was a stony silence. You could have heard the proverbial pin drop. Wade's face was a picture. You could see that he would have liked to say something. And from the way the muscle in his jaw was twitching, it wouldn't be anything pleasant.

Bob looked along the table to see if anyone else had anything to say. The silence spoke for itself. He rose to his feet.

'OK,' he said, resignedly, 'now we will vote on it. All those in favour of officers playing in the team, raise your right hands.'

Hands rose all along his side of the table. He counted Niven and his crowd, Ted, Wade, then raised his own hand. 'I make it a total of nine in favour,' he announced. I did another quick calculation. There were twenty-one people present.

'And now, will all those against raise their hands,' he said, keeping both of his firmly down by his sides.

Tom and I immediately put our hands in the air. Beside us, Bill, Steve and Jack followed suit. At the end of the table, JB and Foxy raised their hands.

Richie, Pete and Eric had been glancing desperately up and down the table. Reassured, they gingerly put their hands up, staring anywhere but at Niven and the screws. Almost immediately Sam's and Eddie's hands shot into the air.

Crash. I looked up quickly to see that Niven had jumped up, throwing his chair backwards. It ricocheted off the wall and fell noisily to the floor. In the same movement, he turned and stormed out of the room, leaving the doors swinging wildly behind him.

It startled everyone. I wasn't surprised though. It was just the sort of immature behaviour I had expected of Niven.

'Childish little prick,' said JB.

Bob looked decidedly embarrassed now, and beside him, Wade looked uncomfortable. We had just made it crystal clear that he wasn't welcome. There was no further part in the proceedings for him.

Bob cleared his throat. 'The motion is defeated by twelve votes to nine,' he announced. 'Officers will not be playing in the team this season.'

There was no public rejoicing. We all had the presence of mind not to be seen rubbing it in. There would undoubtedly be recriminations of one sort or another. No one wanted to make them worse.

Niven's crew now looked thoroughly deflated. With their leader gone, they were an amorphous group with no common opinions. And their courage had departed with him, too. They sat there, visibly cringing, unable to meet our stares.

The business of the captaincy was a foregone conclusion now. Tom proposed Eric and Richie seconded it. There were no other candidates. We emerged from the meeting thoroughly pleased with the way things had gone.

But there were misgivings already. As we passed along the corridor, I heard Eric say, 'We can't really play without Niven, you know. I think we should leave it open for him to come back in.' It sounded like cold feet to me.

'Fuck him,' said JB from behind. 'Now the little prick has gone, maybe we'll be able to enjoy the football.'

I had spoken to Tom earlier about going for a run. We returned to the wing and changed into our kit. It was a fine, dry afternoon. As we raced around the perimeter of the yard, it provided the ideal opportunity to unwind after the tension of the meeting.

Afterwards, I showered and collected my tea. I was sitting in my cell, eating, when Tom hurried in. 'Have you heard about Richie and Eric?' he asked breathlessly. I shook my head, my mouth full of food. 'Niven caught Richie in the recess and steamed into him. Then he went to Eric's cell and clumped him.'

'Are they hurt?' I asked.

'No,' he replied. 'Richie got a couple of scratches and Eric has a black eye. Niven's taken a right fucking liberty, though.'

I wasn't too concerned. For all his bluster, I never considered Niven to be dangerous. Mostly, it was childish outbursts of sheer, uncontrollable temper. I wasn't worried about a punch-up with him.

'He'll have the hump with you, Norm,' Tom cautioned. 'You were the one who went against him over Wade, so you'd better watch yourself.'

I stopped eating. 'Tom,' I said, 'I've been dying to have a row with that prick. But I knew that, if I went to him, the screws would say I started it. I'd have no chance and they'd ship me out. But if he comes to me, then that's another matter entirely. I really hope he runs in here. I'll make a right fucking mess of him and the screws won't be able to say anything about it, because he attacked me first.'

Tom looked at me with concern. 'As long as you know what you're doing, Norm.'

'I know what I'm doing, Tom, and even if I don't, I can hardly have you sit in here to mind me, can I?' I was smiling now.

Tom smiled in return. 'Well, anyway, Norm,' he said, making

for the door, 'if he does bash you up, you can rest assured I'll do him for you.'

'Bollocks!' I shouted after him. 'You want to make sure he doesn't bash you up first.'

I sat with the door half open until they banged us up for tea. When we unlocked again, I went up to Tom's and told him that I wanted to sit downstairs for a while, just in case Niven decided to make his move. I didn't want anyone to think that I was hiding in Tom's cell.

By 7.30, he hadn't appeared. Deciding that he wasn't going to come now, I went up to sit with Tom and Jack.

A couple of weeks passed and football training started again. I wasn't surprised to see Niven appear for it. He ran around the field with us, with Eric nominally in control. Most of those who had voted against him went out of their way to be pleasant to him, even though he was distant with them. I could discern the emerging pattern. I concluded that, as soon as the season started, Niven would be back in control again.

It was one of those months. Sometimes weeks would pass without anything significant happening. Then there would be a month like this, with several incidents following on top of each other.

It started with Tony the catering assistant. On my regular dinner-time runs around the yard, I had often noticed him going off duty. He would come out the back door of the kitchen, walk past the front of the dining hall and enter the sterile area through a side gate. There was nothing particularly unusual in this. Even my paranoid and suspicious mind wouldn't have dwelt on it too long, but for the two bulging carrier bags he regularly carried.

I often wondered what was in them. If I had been the security PO, I would have wanted to have a look. But it was nothing to do with me. And there were so many other things wrong with Knightsford that a catering assistant stealing rations paled into insignificance.

The security PO, however, was more efficient that I had given him credit for. One dinner-time, PO Waters was waiting for Tony as he arrived in the gate-lodge with his bags. A quick search revealed several joints of meat and a large block of cheese.

For days it was the talk of the jail. Once again, the screws were severely embarrassed that one of their own had been found to share the same criminal tendencies as those that supposedly characterised us prisoners.

But if we had been looking forward to reading about the court case in the newspapers, we would have been disappointed. As usually happened when one of the staff was caught breaking the law, a different kind of justice was applied. Tony was allowed to resign and no charges were formally brought. The only consolation for us was that we wouldn't see him any more and now he would have to work for a living.

No sooner had the furore over Tony died down than the Fox was grabbing the headlines again. It was reliably reported from the visiting room that he had been seen to go down on one knee and propose to Caroline.

I wondered what the visiting-room screws made of it all. Over the months, they had seen the relationship progress from a mild game of footsie under the table to a demure holding of hands. Then it had gone on to passionate, all-in wrestling while seated. And finally, the Fox as traditionalist, down on one knee proposing to his beloved. They could only conclude that things were getting serious. I wondered if anyone had ever been married in a visiting room.

One resident who was wholly oblivious to the goings-on of the Fox – and everything else, for that matter – was the German. He still blithered about the landing like a Teutonic version of Marley's ghost, but he seemed to be getting frailer by the day. He was now the odds-on favourite in the 'River Styx Sweepstakes'. It would be quite an irony if I won my own sweep with the German.

But it wasn't to be. At first, no one noticed he had gone. He had been so much a part of the furniture that we just couldn't put our finger on what was missing. It was JB who finally noticed. He asked in the office and was told that the German had been moved. It smacked of the usual cover-up. They didn't want him dying in a show-piece jail like Knightsford.

His going had revived interest in the sweep, though, and once again it was the topic of conversation among the young 'uns. But with all the four remaining runners looking hale and hearty, it didn't look as if it would be resolved in the near future.

I was eating my dinner with Jack and Bill when Bill asked where Tom was. I hadn't seen him, which was unusual. We normally came down to dinner together.

Suddenly, I saw him hurrying into the dining hall. He waved then shook his head as if something was troubling him. He collected his dinner and sat down opposite me.

'Fuck me, what a morning!' he exclaimed.

'What's the matter?' I asked. Bill and Jack both looked at him enquiringly.

An impish grin appeared on his face. 'Old "poison bollocks" is dead,' he announced.

There was a stunned silence as we all stopped eating. I stared into his face to see if he was joking. The grin was still there, but somehow he seemed serious.

'It was me who found him,' Tom continued. 'I've been down the hospital all morning filling out forms.'

'Where did you find him?' asked Bill.

The grin broadened into a cackling laugh. 'On the khazi in our recess.'

Again we looked at him carefully to see if he was winding us up. 'Honestly?' asked Bill.

'Yeah, honestly,' assured Tom. 'It frit the life out of me. I went in there for a crap, opened the door and there he was – sitting on the khazi stone dead.'

As one, the three of us hooted with laughter. Heads turned from nearby tables to look. Guiltily, we stopped. It was hardly decent to laugh at someone's death, but it wasn't Brown's demise we were laughing at. It was the manner of his going. To die sitting on the khazi with your strides around your ankles lacked a certain dignity. It was just the sort of thing that could make a laughing stock of an otherwise distinguished life.

In Brown's case, this consideration didn't arise, however. Other than the fact that he was one of the few ever to be twice found guilty of murder, there was little distinguished about his life. And as he would have been going to die in prison anyway, perhaps this was a fitting end.

Humour had now given way to pathos. Each of us stared into our dinners, lost in morbid thoughts. It was time for a bit more laughter.

'Tom, did you help them move the body?' I asked innocently.

'Yeah. It was really awkward getting it out of there.'

'Tom, before you pulled his trousers up . . .?' I paused, letting the half-question hang in the air. Tom looked at me, suspicious of what was to come. '. . . did you wipe his arse for him?'

Bill and Jack laughed with me. 'Bollocks,' said Tom, 'that's what the medical screws are paid for. And come to think of it, they just pulled his strides up and put him on the stretcher.'

We now had a winner for the 'River Styx Sweepstakes'. Later, we jokingly congratulated Sam, but no Mars bars changed hands. I cautioned everyone to keep talk about the sweep among ourselves. With my review so close now, if Maypole heard I was taking bets on the demise of his 'residents' it could have had serious implications for my release.

It had been an eventful month. It wasn't over yet, however. A momentous event was still to come. No one was surprised that it involved the Fox.

Tom and I, just returned from dinner, sat in his cell, leafing through the newspapers and drinking coffee. It was a mirror image of a thousand other boring dinner-times.

Suddenly the Fox hurried into the cell. We looked up, startled. He stood there, hands clenched, jaw set, pale. You didn't have to be a drama student to recognise that Foxy was trying to tell us that he had been the recipient of bad news.

'I've been sacked,' he announced peremptorily.

That certainly qualified as bad news. There would be no more freebies from the canteen for our foodboat.

'It's that fucking Cyril.' As the Fox became more animated, Tom and I involuntarily recoiled. We could expect an incandescent display of emotional pyrotechnics.

'He must have made another complaint,' he went on. 'The Dep just called me up. I've been sacked for not doing my work.'

I didn't say as much, but I reflected that he'd had a good run. He hadn't been doing his work for several months now, so he certainly had it coming. I wondered what had taken them so long.

'I've been told that I'm in the electrical shop in the morning, but they can *go fuck themselves*!' The Fox screamed this last bit, raising both fists head high.

'Do you think that's wise, Danny?' I asked matter-of-factly.

'I don't give a fuck,' he replied aggressively.

'If you're dealing with the Dep, he'll probably dig in his heels over this one to get even with you over what's happened with Caroline and her husband,' I suggested.

'Fuck him,' barked the Fox.

I shrugged. Tom raised his eyebrows as if to say that I was wasting my time. No doubt I was, but, prick that he was, I didn't want the Fox to self-destruct unnecessarily.

'You should always leave yourself a way out, Danny. If they refuse to back down, you could end up being shanghaied,' I added.

'I don't care any more,' he said petulantly. 'I've had enough of this place anyway.'

I knew he didn't mean it. A shanghai could set him back years. And anywhere else he went wouldn't be as easy as Knightsford. But his mind seemed made up.

The following morning Foxy refused to go into the electrical shop. Inevitably, he was nicked for refusing labour, and within the hour he appeared before the Dep.

We later heard that he still refused to go into the shop. They took him straight from the wing office to the chokey, and that afternoon loaded him and all his kit into a van. They shanghaied the Fox to Winson Green.

It was the end of an era, and it had all happened so quickly. Foxy had survived so many crises that he – and everyone else for that matter – had thought he was fire-proof. But, in jail, everyone is expendable.

Tom and I wouldn't miss the Fox; he hadn't been a friend. It had been one of those strange prison relationships in which we had tolerated rather than liked him. In the free world, we would have told him to piss off right from the start. But, as far as we were concerned, in Knightsford Foxy had been like an elephant. Whatever your feelings about him, you couldn't ignore him. He would be missed, but only because of the empty space he left behind.

Now it was my turn to go through the trauma of the interviews for my parole review. The chaplain sent for me, then the doctor. I sat through an interview with Hall and then another one with Docker. Camber called me up to the education block half an hour before Deal had a session with me in his office. My outside probation officer, whom I had seen only once during the past 12 years, came up to interview me in the visiting room. Finally I was summoned into the presence of the Dep.

It was astounding that so many people should have an opinion about me, especially as they had seen so little of me over the past year. But it was a ludicrous system. It was all a method of control. Everyone who had the right to compile a parole report about you exercised power over you. The message was that, if you did exactly as you were told, you had a good chance of getting a positive parole report.

I wondered what relevance this had to living in the outside world. There were drink, drugs and sexual elements to most lifers' offences. Of course, the rapists settled down in prison – there were no women to rape. And no wonder the child molesters made obedient tea-boys for the screws – prison was a world without children. The screws certainly never brought their kids in to play with them.

It was all very frustrating. If I had kow-towed to every petty official in all the jails I had been in, my spirit would have been broken by now. I would have become just as dull and as institutionalised as many of Knightsford's residents. And would that better fit me for life outside?

But for keeping my spirit strong, I had been categorised as a rebel and my independence had been interpreted as wilfulness. Instead of praising me for being articulate, they condemned me for being manipulative.

It isn't only beauty that is in the eye of the beholder. I was confronted by a hall of reflecting mirrors. Each official had his own particular slant. Whatever type of behaviour I might set out to display, the individual might well interpret it to the contrary. So to try to act a part would drive me mad with frustration. I would just have to be myself and damn the consequences.

There was an opportunity for me to add my own contribution, though. I was given a single sheet of foolscap to write my representation on. I reflected that it was woefully inadequate to summarise the developments of a dozen years.

However, I described the way I felt I had changed and matured. I detailed the exams I had passed and the universities that had offered me a place to take a Master's degree. Finally, I mentioned the situation of my elderly parents. There was still a family home for me to return to, but it wouldn't be there indefinitely.

All that was left now was for me to see my Local Review Committee representative. He (or she) would put my case to the LRC. They would make a recommendation, which would then go to the main Parole Board in London. This Board would then sit and make a recommendation to the Home Secretary, and he would either accept or reject this.

My LRC rep turned out to be an elderly gentleman who still retained his former military rank. He explained that he could only advise the Board and had no power himself. He didn't seem too enthusiastic about my chances. However, I had already dismissed any hope of getting a release date. I would be more than pleased to get a move to an open prison.

With that last interview over, I was now officially 'waiting'. Parole answers were taking an average of nine months or more to come through. It was a state something like pregnancy. Except that, after a nine-month wait, there was no guarantee that you would have anything to show for it. But at least I could live in hope for a while.

As Jane made her way out of the education block towards the Admin, she wondered what Maypole wanted with her. It was very unusual for him to summon her like this. On past occasions, it had been to tell her off. Communications were normally in the form of terse notes.

She suspected that it wouldn't be good news. She had heard that there were changes afoot. Camber, her immediate superior, was definitely going, and his replacement had already been chosen. Another rumour had it that Maypole himself would shortly be moving on to a new jail.

She felt her heart start to pound as she neared his office. She reflected that any replacement could only be an improvement. Surely, there weren't worse governors than Maypole?

His voice summoned her inside. 'Good morning, Mrs Roman,' he said, smiling a sickly sweet smile. He waved her to a chair in front of his desk.

'Mrs Roman,' he began, 'when we originally employed you as assistant education officer at Knightsford, there might have been a misunderstanding that you were working for the prison department. In fact, you were working for the local education authority. You were, and always have been, an employee of theirs.' Maypole paused, allowing the information to sink in.

Jane looked puzzled. She didn't recall this being mentioned at the time, or subsequently for that matter. And what was its relevance anyway?

'It just so happens,' continued Maypole, cutting into Jane's train of thought, 'that a vacancy has occurred at a local school. We, on the other hand, have no further need of your services. Therefore it has been proposed that you be transferred to work at the school.'

Maypole leaned forward, placing both elbows on the desk. He looked directly at her. 'I've spoken with the headmaster there and he has agreed to employ you as a teacher in media studies. He will be writing to you in due course.'

Jane was stunned. A more obvious ploy she couldn't imagine. This was the latest in a long line of measures that Maypole had used to try to get rid of her.

'But I don't want to go to work at the school, Mr Maypole,' she said, trying to keep her tone reasonable and not show the anxiety she felt.

'Mrs Roman,' said Maypole, in a voice that was all cold logic and reason, 'it's not a question of what you want. It's a question of what's best for the prison and what's best for the school. As an employee of the local education authority, you will have to go where you are needed most. We no longer have a need for an assistant education officer at Knightsford. There is a vacancy at the school. You have been chosen to fill it. It's as simple as that.' He sat back in his chair, a look of satisfaction on his face.

Jane stood up from her chair. Maypole's quiet confidence had unnerved her. She wondered if he had finally found a way to get rid of her. But she wouldn't go without a fight.

'Mr Maypole.' She couldn't keep the quaver out of her voice as she spoke. 'I'm sure that what you're doing is unlawful. I refuse to accept it. You can rest assured that I will be seeing my local union representative in the morning.'

Similar threats in the past had unnerved Maypole. This time he just sat there, smiling. 'Mrs Roman, that is your prerogative,' he said confidently. 'This time it will do you no good. I assure you that you will be going to work at the school.'

Back in her office, Jane immediately phoned the local union office and made an appointment for the following morning. Her meeting with Maypole was still on her mind as she went through her post. Absent-mindedly she opened one letter and noticed the heading with surprise: it was from Dartville Comprehensive. She was being summoned for an interview later in the week for a post of teacher there.

Maypole certainly hadn't wasted any time. The whole thing looked more and more like a set-up now. She was pleased that she had managed to secure an interview with her union rep for the morning.

The interview with the union went well. They, too, were of the opinion that what Maypole was trying to do was unlawful, and promised Jane the full support of the union to fight it.

The interview with the headmaster of Dartville Comprehensive was a disaster, although it had started off pleasantly enough. Jane had explained that she just didn't want to work at the school and was happy where she was.

The head had obviously been primed by Maypole. He insisted that she didn't have a choice in the matter and would work where she was needed most. The argument became heated. Eventually, Jane had refused point blank to work at the school.

'In that case,' said the headmaster solemnly, 'I will have no choice but to terminate your employment with the local education authority.'

'But my union representative says that you can't do that. That it's unlawful,' she insisted desperately.

'Oh, I assure you that I can do it and that it is lawful,' affirmed the headmaster.

And there the argument had rested. On her return to Knightsford the following day, Maypole had suspended her prior to her dismissal for refusing to take up the post at the school. Now she sat at home, awaiting the outcome of the battle between the union and the Home Office over her legal entitlement to work at the prison.

With both Jane and Foxy gone, the old place just didn't seem the same. And further ominous changes seemed to be afoot. Mr Camber duly went and his replacement arrived. John Leventhal was a weedy, academic-looking man in his late forties. He lacked Camber's warmth and if he found anything amusing about life, it certainly didn't show in his demeanour.

I wasn't too concerned. My dealings with the education department were minimal now. I received my OU units from them and handed in my assignments to them, and that was the extent of my involvement.

The second major change was that iron gates were installed at either end of the education block, which served to bring it more under the control of the screws: you now needed one of them to let you in. Nothing could have emphasised more clearly Maypole's commitment to changing the educational regime now that Jane had gone.

For Tom though, it was suddenly all academic. I was standing in the painters' shop one morning, about two weeks after Jane had gone, when he suddenly burst in in a state of great excitement.

'I've got it, Norm, I've got it!' he shouted ecstatically, throwing his arms around me and hugging me.

I knew immediately what he meant. 'When is it?' I demanded, prising him off me.

'I go out in twelve months' time,' he explained excitedly. 'I'm going to Sudbury for six months, then there will be six months on the hostel. Then I'm out.'

I was genuinely pleased for him. For many years now I had learned to live vicariously, getting pleasure from the good news received by my friends. It didn't make up for all the bad news in my own life, but it served to prevent me from becoming too bitter and heightening my sense of martyrdom.

But in the pleasure was also a deep sense of loss. Tom had become a close and loyal friend, and life in Knightsford would be that much more empty without him. It had happened to me many times before: good friends had gone, leaving me behind.

There would, however, be a couple of weeks before he was off to the open prison. During that time, we walked around like a doomed couple. He was pleased to be going, but he curtailed his exuberance out of respect for me, and others, who had to stay. Nothing was worse than a lifer who paraded his good fortune in front of others who still only lived in hope.

Eventually, the day came. I walked with Tom to the stairs leading to the reception. He put down his kit and we shook hands. It was a 'man' friendship, but there was still deep emotion there.

'Norm, you keep your chin up. Your answer won't be long coming now.' He threw his arms about my shoulders and hugged me.

'Take care, Tom,' I said as he stepped back. 'Remember that you ain't out yet. Don't get into any trouble at Sudbury.' He nodded reassuringly.

Suddenly, the irony was too much. Here were we, two big, hairy cons, clinging to each other in a maudlin parting like a couple of silly schoolgirls.

'Well, Tom, I suppose it's just as well you're going before me. You wouldn't have been able to handle it if I had gone first,' I said provocatively.

'Bollocks!' he retorted, stung. 'I'm worried that you won't survive without me to look after you, baldy.' He threw a playful punch.

I laughed and backed away. 'Take care, Tom,' I said seriously.

'Take care yourself, Norm. I'll be in touch.'

I turned and walked away without looking back. I knew that when I came in from work at dinner-time, he would be gone.

Now the place really did seem empty. I hung around with Jack occasionally, but my close mate had gone. I knew I would recover; I always had in the past. It was a bit like observing a decent period of mourning. I resigned myself to the desperately lonely path I was destined to walk throughout my sentence.

One consolation was that Jane had come back. There had been a couple of articles in the local press and even a few mentions on the local radio. It wasn't a *cause célèbre*, but there was a lot of sympathy for her.

It wasn't sympathy that had swayed the Home Office, however. The union had finally managed to convince them that they would be the losers in any court case. It had taken them two whole months to do so, but that wasn't long when gauged against the torpor that usually imbued all negotiations with the Home Office.

It was a significant slap in the face for Maypole. Under normal circumstances we could have expected a reign of terror, as he took out on us what he had been unable to take out on Jane, but he was surprisingly subdued. We soon found out the reason. He was to leave for a new jail within the month.

It really was the end of an era. But for those subject to the rule of the tyrant, the main concern was who would take over from him. Maypole was a weak, selfish and uncaring man, but he was by no means unique within the system. And there were those who had an added streak of gratuitous cruelty.

We were reassured somewhat to learn that the new governor was a woman. Some argued that, by the very fact of a woman's more caring nature, we would be far better off. I urged caution. I had never encountered a woman governor, but I was sure that the type of woman the Home Office would choose to run a prison wouldn't be typical of the species. After all, Margaret Thatcher had been chosen to run the country, and whatever her other qualities, no one could ever have accused her of being caring.

But, suddenly, the nature of our new governor became academic for me, too. My answer had come through. I had only been waiting for four months, a very short time indeed for a parole answer. I immediately suspected that it couldn't be good news. It would hardly have had time to go all the way up to the Home Secretary, for him to approve a positive result.

I had been working with my painting party at the side of one of the wings when the Works orderly hurried up and told me that I was wanted back on the wing immediately. Surely, it was too soon for my answer, but I couldn't think what else it might be.

I strolled back to the wing, refusing to be rushed. I had seen scores of others brought to the verge of nervous collapse by a summons of this nature. It was all entertainment for the screws. I was determined they would get no mileage out of me.

At C wing office, I was surprised to be directed to the PO's office on A wing. This was even more confusing. A wing staff had nothing to do with me.

I knocked on PO Mann's door and, at his summons, went in. Mann, a short, greying man in his mid-fifties, had a hearty, phoney air about him that I had never liked. His special interest was charity projects. The irony was that there was little charitable in his nature.

He was writing as I entered, but stopped immediately. He smiled and motioned for me to sit down. He reached over into a wire basket and took out a sheet of paper. He placed it on the desk in front of him.

'Parker,' he began, leaning forward with his elbows on the table and steepling his hands in front of him. He looked pensive, worried even. 'As you well know, Mr Docker is your wing PO. It should be his job to give you the result of your parole answer, because that is what I've called you here for.'

In spite of myself, I felt a sinking sensation in my stomach. So much would depend on the words he would say in the next few moments. It was impossible to remain cool and detached from the proceedings. The answer could, quite literally, mean life or death for me.

'Unfortunately, Mr Docker has gone sick today.' He peered over his fingers at me. The wistful look spoke in silent condemnation of the man who had left him to do his dirty work. I resigned myself to the worst, while at the same time resolving to show no sign of disappointment.

PO Mann looked down at the piece of paper as if to remind himself of its contents. 'Your parole answer isn't very good, I'm afraid,' he warned. I barely took note of his words. My mind was whirling with a dozen different thoughts. What would I do if it was a really big knockback? How would I tell my family and friends? And what if it drained me of the strength to carry on?

Mann's hesitation was sheer torture for me. I felt like screaming at him to get it over with. I had been in his office for several long minutes now and still he had told me nothing concrete.

He picked up the paper from the desk and held it in front of him. He looked up at me, then down at the paper, as if to say that these were the words of the Parole Board and not his. He cleared his throat.

'Will you please inform the above-mentioned prisoner that the Secretary of State has considered his parole application and is unable to recommend his release on licence at the present time.' Mann paused and looked up. I stared back at him, unmoved. This was no surprise at all. I had never thought I would get a release date. It was the next part that was crucial to me.

'However,' Mann continued, 'it is proposed that the prisoner be moved to Category C conditions at Coldingley and reviewed again in twelve months' time.' He continued to stare at the paper as if searching for something more. But he had lost me. I was transported by the news.

For the average Knightsford lifer, anything more than a twelve-month release date was viewed as an unmitigated disaster. Many looked on a twelve-month knockback and a move to open conditions as a poor consolation prize. I, though, ever the realist, was more than pleased with my move to Cat C conditions. And a wait of only twelve months before my next review was even better news.

At Coldingley I would have much more freedom. Further, there was a tradition that lifers only spent a couple of years there before moving on to an open prison. I was sure it heralded light at the end of the tunnel.

The twelve-month knockback told me nothing in itself, but logic dictated that they could hardly intend to keep me for many more years. Otherwise they would have given me a two-, or even three-year knockback. I reasoned that they wouldn't want to waste their time with unnecessary reviews.

'Thanks very much, guv,' I said, smiling broadly. 'Can I have a copy of that answer, please?'

Mann looked at me in amazement. Perhaps he had been

expecting a flood of tears. Or even for me to jump across the desk and attack him. But I was satisfied with what I had heard.

He said he would have the answer photocopied and give me a copy. He examined my face carefully to see if I was putting on the good mood. As I walked out of his office, I could imagine him shaking his head in amazement.

For the rest of the day, and part of the next, a constant stream of people came up to me to offer their commiserations. They, too, were surprised when I expressed my satisfaction at the result. Little did they realise what a career pessimist I had become over the years. I had been given a significant step forward. The authorities could only take it away from me if I gave them some excuse, and I resolved not to do that.

At the back of my mind lurked another, unspoken, option. Escape was never far from my thoughts as a last resort. Cat C conditions were, by definition, notoriously lax on security. I had been a determined escaper in Category A conditions. If push ever came to shove, I rather fancied my chances of having it away from Coldingley.

It would be a couple of weeks before I went, but I made preparations for my departure immediately. I wrote to my mother with the news. She was coming up at the weekend, so I saved the explanations until I saw her.

I wrote to Helen and knew she would be disappointed. I had never played the optimist with her, but without being specific, had warned her against hoping for too much. I enclosed a VO for her to visit as soon as she could. I wrote several more letters to my circle of friends and, in these, detailed what I thought were the implications of the answer I had received.

Now I didn't mind Knightsford at all. I knew it was only a matter of days before I would be away. All the things I detested about the place wouldn't have to be tolerated for much longer. I didn't care if they put security gates and bars all over the jail now. It had no relevance for me.

I was leaving no close friends behind either. I admired and respected Jane, but unlike so many others, I hadn't allowed myself to become emotionally involved with her. I would miss her as a trusted and valued comrade, but I knew she wouldn't lack for affection. Anyway, I had hardened my heart to such an extent that virtually nothing could touch me now.

It was several days before I saw her. I had spoken to her briefly when she had first returned. There had been no crowing over her victory. She had seemed more concerned that Tom had gone without her being able to wish him goodbye. Now I chose a time when I knew she would be alone in her office, even though I still wasn't completely at ease with her.

'Congratulations,' she said as I walked in. 'Are you pleased?' Jane knew my thinking on my parole chances and my limited expectations.

I smiled and nodded. 'Well, I'm not disappointed. The move to

Cat C is a positive step, and twelve months isn't long to wait for my next review.'

She nodded in agreement. 'It's just as well you're so realistic about these things. I'm sure you'll get a good result next time.'

There was an awkward silence. Previously, I had almost always been with Tom when I had spoken to her, and I continued to be aware that, however sympathetic to the prisoners' cause, she was a prison official. I knew this was unworthy of me and she deserved better, but it came from years of conditioning.

Then there was the fact that I really didn't know how to handle women. I had it all worked out with men. At any stage of a conversation, I could always resort to intimidation or violence. But with Jane these methods weren't available to me. Sometimes her penetrating wit was disconcerting. Not to put too fine a point on it, she regularly took the piss out of me, albeit mildly. Her femininity emasculated me, though. I either had to reply in kind or walk away. It was a whole new experience for me.

I always also felt that, with her gentle nature, she was horrified by my capacity for violence. We were so many worlds apart. She could identify with me on an intellectual level, but that was the extent of it. The two people I had killed stood between us like monoliths.

'How are you settling back in?' I asked, to break the silence.

'It's just like I've never been away,' she replied pertly. I smiled with her, impressed by her spirit.

'And how are you going to survive with both me and Tom gone?' I asked sarcastically.

Jane raised her eyebrows in mock surprise. 'Probably the same as I did before you both arrived,' she replied. It was a good answer and certainly put me in my place.

'How's Tom? Have you heard from him?' she asked quickly, her concern taking the sting out of her previous remark.

'Yeah, he phoned my mum,' I replied. 'He's settling in well.'

Again there was an awkward silence. I searched for something meaningful to say. Something that would get over to this woman that I respected her strength and was grateful for her help. But I didn't want to sound presumptuous. I wasn't at all sure what sort of bond we shared, if we shared one at all.

She was looking at me, slightly amused now, but taking pains to hide it. She was well aware of my discomfiture. I never could come to terms with the fact that, in all our meetings, it was she who was invariably in control. Strangely, I didn't resent it now.

'Jane, I want to thank you for all the help you've given me whilst I've been here.' It was an effort. I rarely conceded to anyone that I needed help.

She smiled sweetly. 'And I want to thank you for all the help you've given me.'

It wasn't the greatest of partings. Bogart would certainly have made more of it. But then he wouldn't have been playing opposite a spirited and liberated woman like Jane.

'Take care,' I said as I turned to leave.

'You take care, too.'

My parting from Jean was a lot easier. It had always been a one-dimensional relationship, acted out across a table in a classroom. With my going, that was all that would be missing from our lives.

She asked where Coldingley was. I explained and saw her face drop as she realised she wouldn't be able to afford to visit. I promised to write and would do so. But I knew it would inevitably tail off. Our friendship was for Knightsford only.

The visit with my mother and father was entirely more traumatic. She couldn't understand why the probation officer had come round to the flat to examine the home I would be returning to if I wasn't going to be released. I explained that I was satisfied to achieve limited goals, and that a move to Cat C conditions was a significant step forward. By the end of the visit, she had accepted that we had cause to be pleased, if not ecstatic.

Saying goodbye to Helen was a tender parting. I hadn't realised just how much she had been hoping that I would be coming home. She clung to me, visibly upset. I stroked her hair and assured her that I would have a good chance next time. But to talk in terms of years to one so young could only depress her further.

'And Coldingley is so far away,' she moaned plaintively. 'It's easy for me to get to Knightsford.'

I cursed the fates that looked so unfavourably on me. If only I had been like so many others at Knightsford and had been given a move to open conditions. But I wasn't like them, and I always dealt with the reality of the situation.

It occurred to me that I was taking my parole knockback a good deal better than my family and friends. I reflected that it was just as well that they weren't the ones who had to do the time.

There were tears as Helen left. I assured her that it was only *au revoir* and not goodbye. She didn't look convinced. I felt a fledgling fear that Coldingley might be the rock on which our relationship would founder.

I was relieved when my farewells to outside friends were over. There was only the rabbi to deal with now. As we sat in the visiting room early one Saturday morning, I thanked him for his support. He took it that I meant the spiritual support he had given me. I didn't contradict him, even though I had meant his commitment to visit me every second Saturday throughout my stay at Knightsford.

As the day of my departure drew near, I cut all my ties with Knightsford. I hadn't enjoyed my stay, but it had been a period in which I had been able to regroup and regather my strength. It was an experience I would rather have missed, but there were worse places I could have been.

On my last evening, I had a surprise visitor. I had spent the evening saying goodbye to JB, Jack, Bill, Steve and the rest of the young 'uns. They had all expressed regret at my departure and had given me a card they had all signed. I reflected that I had assumed the status of a rallying point for them. Thankfully, it hadn't become too obvious to the screws.

During my comings and goings on that final day, I had noticed Niven hanging about on the ones. I was always hypersensitive to any possible threat and had been watching him out of the corner of my eye. I hoped he wasn't plotting up on me on my last evening. A row could well delay, or even cancel, my departure.

Suddenly, as I approached my cell, he walked quickly over to me. I turned to face him.

'Can I have a word with you, please, Norm?' he asked softly.

I looked into his face and saw deep emotion there. It could be a row, but I didn't think so. After so long in prison, I could read situations pretty accurately now. And if he did want a row, I could hardly walk away from it.

I went into my cell and waved for him to follow me. I sat on my bed, because standing up would have been too threatening. It was good psychology. He would see that I wasn't particularly worried about him.

He pushed the door to and sat in the chair opposite me. I saw him bite his lip.

'Norm, there's something I wanted to say to you before you went,' he said.

He stopped, fighting for control and seemingly close to tears. He tried to speak, but nothing came out. His teeth closed over his lower lip as his face worked furiously.

'I couldn't help it with Jane,' he suddenly blurted out. And then the tears came. They coursed down his cheeks and his shoulders shook.

I wanted to tell him to let it all come out. That to fight it would only make it worse. Clearly, he was terribly embarrassed to be crying. But there was still that barrier between us. Any acknowledgement of this supposed weakness might only humiliate him more. I sat there, saying nothing.

All at once, I saw him in a new light. He was so desperately immature. He'd had to compete with men in an unequal contest. Emotionally, he was still a child.

I reflected on how I would have felt had I come to a foreign country at fifteen and been nicked for murder. I tried to remember how I had been at that tender age. Small wonder that, growing up in our prison system, he had become so unstable and unsure of himself.

'I was terribly in love with her, Norm,' he mumbled between sobs. 'And I don't care what anyone says, she did lead me on,' he added defiantly.

I forgave him this last bit. I was sure that, with his restricted knowledge of women, he couldn't make this judgement. He had probably mistaken kindness for something altogether more serious. I reflected that the experience could only have matured him.

'It's not all your fault, Niven,' I said gently. 'You came into prison when you were so very young. The good thing is that you're over the worst of it now. You will have other hurts in this life. There will be other relationships that fail. You will be able to handle them all the better for this.'

As I spoke, I couldn't help but think of my own experiences. I was a fine one to give advice. Both my serious romances had ended in disaster. Yet, perhaps this was what qualified me to speak on the subject. If it was true that you learned by your mistakes, then I should be a very wise man indeed by now.

I handed him a towel to wipe his face with, then put a hand on his shoulder and helped him to his feet.

'Niven, I'm going tomorrow, but I wish you well. I've seen this fucking system break down too many good people. You've got to make sure it doesn't break you. You're a strong fella and you're through the worst of it now. You've got to survive not only for yourself, but for your mum and dad back in Ireland.' I put out my hand and he shook it.

'Thanks, Norm. I hope everything goes all right for you at Coldingley.'

I was pleased that it had ended like this. Prison threw us together like rats in a sack. Small wonder that we regularly turned on each other and bit.

As I drifted off to sleep that night, I thought of the friends and enemies I would be leaving behind in the morning. I suddenly realised that I hadn't said goodbye to a single screw. There was nothing to thank them for; none of them had shown me any kindness. They must have known it, too, for none of them had come near me since my answer.

I would have liked to have had one last look at Maypole. Not to speak to him, but to exult in the knowledge that, shortly, I would no longer be subject to his power. However, in the transition period of changing governors, he had rarely been seen of late. I hoped I would never see him again.

The following morning I collected my last breakfast. I saw the monstrous Hall on the centre, but ignored him. I was free of his poisonous personality. He would have to live with it for ever.

I had put most of my kit in the reception the previous day. I now collected my remaining few things together and left my cell. As I slammed the door on nearly eighteen months of my life, I felt an overwhelming sense of relief.

I walked to reception without looking back. The good memories I had with me in my head; the bad ones I didn't want to be reminded of.

Within twenty minutes, I was sitting in a taxi, handcuffed to an A wing screw. As we drove out of the gate, I suppressed a shudder. I silently prayed that I would never see the 'Goldfish Bowl' again.

16

For Jane, change was all around her. Her remark to Norman that it was as if she had never been away, had been a patent lie. The new gates either end of the education block had been an ominous portent of the way things were changing.

Her first meeting with her new boss, John Leventhal, set the tone for their future relationship. There was no easy, informal camaraderie as there had been between her and the avuncular Camber. Leventhal was serious, austere and lacked warmth, and he soon made it very clear that the men were inmates first and students a poor second. The uniformed staff would have no difficulty with him when it came to 'co-operation'.

'There have been some changes around here, Mrs Roman, and there will be some more,' had been his opening remark, once he had quickly dispensed with the pleasantries. 'Mr Maypole has briefed me on what he feels were the shortcomings of the way things used to be. Miss Lacy has assured me that her thinking is completely in line with his.'

Jane could imagine what Maypole had said about her. That might explain Leventhal's aloof manner with her, but she suspected that he was like that with everyone. The remark about Miss Lacy agreeing with his view concerned her, though. She had yet to speak to the new governor, although she had seen her from a distance and she had looked friendly. But appearances were deceptive. If her view agreed with Maypole's, then Jane could expect little sympathy from her.

As if he had read her thoughts, Leventhal suddenly said, 'Miss Lacy has intimated to me that she will be speaking with you within a couple of days. I will leave it to her to fill you in on the details. However, I feel that, as your immediate superior, I should warn you of the changes to come.'

Now Jane was seriously concerned. What exactly was it that he was warning her about? More gates wouldn't affect her. It was only a question of unlocking them to pass through. What new assault on her position lay in store for her?

She already had less space to work in. Leventhal had pushed her desk further into the corner. She was pleased there wasn't an outer office – she was sure that Leventhal would have relegated her to that.

Increasingly, Jane wondered if she still wanted to carry on. So many people she had been close to had gone. She would miss Tom, and Norman's presence had been reassuring. There were still many who depended on her, though – Hamid immediately sprang to mind. He had been so relieved when she returned, and she feared for him if she ever had to leave.

But the skies were darkening. She was now totally isolated among the staff. She had entertained great hopes for a new and better regime under Miss Lacy. She would have to see how things developed, but it wasn't looking good.

The following morning the summons from Miss Lacy came. As she walked towards what had once been Maypole's office, she ran through the few details she knew about the new governor.

Miss Lacy was a slim woman in her mid-forties. She had never married and lived alone. Jane wondered if she had sufficient experience of men to deal with an all-male institution. However, she had come through the system, so there could be little that would be new to her. She didn't seem to be Thatcherite woman, but Jane would soon find out for sure.

'Ah, so pleased to meet you, Mrs Roman. Do sit down.' Miss Lacy welcomed her with a warmth that Maypole had never felt necessary. Whatever she had been told about Miss Lacy, she wasn't letting it show in her demeanour.

'Now, as you know, I am completely new here,' she began. 'I'm very much finding my feet. I am taking advice from all sorts of people and weighing it up. I want you to know that I am my own woman and that I will listen to reasonable argument. However, I do accept that the education block in the recent past has left a lot to be desired.'

Sitting opposite, Jane felt her stomach sink. This was obviously a strong implied criticism of herself. If she had expected support from this fellow woman, it looked as if she was going to be disappointed.

'Now I have discussed the matter with Head Office …' Miss Lacy paused and looked meaningfully at Jane to make sure the import of this registered with her. It wasn't purely a domestic matter now, but a situation where she would have the Home Office looking over her shoulder. 'They have made certain recommendations. A new post of deputy education officer is to be created here. A well-qualified young lady called Maureen Burgess will be joining the staff within the next few days. I'm sure she will enjoy your full co-operation.' She spoke this last without any hint of threat, but Jane felt it all the same.

'Unfortunately, there will now be no need for an assistant education officer at Knightsford,' she continued. Jane managed to suppress a gasp, biting her lower lip instead. Just when she had thought that the Home Office had backed down, it looked as if they were going to try to get rid of her again. But, in this, she was being premature.

'I value your services here, Mrs Roman. It seems that you have considerable rapport with some of the prisoners. This is no bad thing,' said Miss Lacy, in a manner suggesting that maybe it was. 'You will continue here as a teacher on exactly the same pay as before.' She smiled as she made this concession. However, it made way for a frown as she went on. 'Unfortunately, as an ordinary teacher, you will enjoy none of the privileges you had before. You will have no keys, you will no longer sit on any of the inmate assessment boards and you won't have access to any of the prisoners' files. Last but not least, and this is most important, Mrs Roman, you will only communicate with uniformed staff and governor grades through your immediate line manager of the day. That will be, of course, Mr Leventhal when he is here, and Miss Burgess when he is sick. Is this all perfectly clear to you?'

Jane reflected that it was all crystal clear. Her victory over Maypole and the Home Office had been a pyrrhic one indeed. They intended to strip her of all her status. Obviously, they were hoping that she would now resign.

Suddenly, she felt very angry. It was like a white heat that grew and grew in her. Well, they weren't going to get rid of her as easily as that. To walk out now would be to betray the local union branch, which had fought long and hard for her. And then there were the prisoners who depended on her. No, she would continue until they physically threw her out.

She wondered how many of the new changes were Miss Lacy's responsibility. She had mentioned the intervention of the Home Office, but that could have been a smokescreen. She had obviously been well briefed by Maypole. The future would soon reveal just how much of her own woman she would be.

Over the next few weeks, Jane discreetly asked her students about the new governor – but only the ones she trusted, which tended to be the more rebellious ones. Feelings were mixed, though. Some were all praise for Miss Lacy. Already she had initiated reforms that had benefited the residents. There were ominous rumblings among the screws about her being too liberal, which, in Jane's eyes, was no small praise.

On the other hand, there were those who said she was two-faced. That, while pretending to be sympathetic, she was a ruthless career woman who would do the Home Office's bidding no matter what. Certainly, Jane's conditions of work hadn't eased since their initial meeting.

The new deputy education officer duly arrived: Maureen Burgess, a rather plain woman in her forties. Outwardly, she was friendly to Jane, but she made it very clear that she would interpret Miss Lacy's instructions to the letter.

It was all very frustrating. Jane now had to watch her job being done less efficiently. Miss Burgess went through the motions, but whenever there was a conflict of interest between the prison and a student, the student inevitably came second. The human face of education at Knightsford had taken on a significantly different expression.

Jane's personal circumstances were a source of irritation, too. Now she had no keys, she had to rely on officers to let her through gates and, needless to say, they often kept her waiting. It was especially inconvenient with regard to the staff toilet, which, for security reasons, was always kept locked. This hadn't mattered at all while Jane had a key, but now she even had to ask an officer or one of her superiors to unlock it, and sometimes they were slow to do so.

She could put up with these petty indignities, though. The loss of status also meant nothing to her. She didn't do the job for the kudos it brought her. However, the new restrictions meant that she was spending less time in the prison than before.

There were other teachers who just came in to teach specialist classes. When their class was over, they left the prison. Jane now found that she was required to do the same. Even when she had a later class, she had to leave the jail and return.

She had no office now. Miss Burgess had been given her old desk. No doubt it wouldn't have mattered if she sat in one of the classrooms until her next lesson, but Leventhal had been adamant. His instructions were that, when she wasn't teaching, she was to leave the premises.

In practice, this meant that she spent a lot of time sitting in the little cemetery just outside the prison walls. It was quite pleasant when the weather was fine. She would sit on one of the benches, with her papers and sandwiches spread out around her, and do her marking while she ate her lunch.

When it was cold or raining, she retreated to the small Catholic church just up the road. It was quiet and private there, but the lighting was poor and she had to squint to mark the papers. It was all a trial, but she was determined they wouldn't beat her.

Her classes were still a delight, though. Hamid was like a child with her, his natural reserve melting in her presence. It was very obvious that he had come to depend on her completely.

Dougie, in his own way, had come to rely on her, too. He even moderated his rough uncouthness when in class, no mean feat for someone with as uncontrolled a personality as his. He, too, was childlike in the way he sought her approval. She reflected that, long ago, her role had transcended that of a teacher. To many of the residents she was more like a surrogate mother now.

Gradually, she got used to her new routine. Her job was not as personally rewarding now, but she still felt that she was doing something worthwhile. She believed that, if they had thought she would tire of the restrictions and resign, they must be having second thoughts now. This served to comfort her whenever she felt that things were getting on top of her.

But they hadn't finished with her yet. At first, she didn't recognise the new threat. Tim Fry had seemed just like any other resident/student when they had sent him to her, although her suspicions had been aroused somewhat by the unusual request that she teach him poetry for an hour every Tuesday morning. But she'd had other requests for personal tuition, albeit usually in basic skills. She just put it down to him having some influence with one of the wing staff.

His appearance hadn't rung any alarm bells either. His rough, flabby face was unremarkable except for his left eyebrow, which was split in two by an old scar. His wavy brown hair had been well greased – his only concession to style. He wore untidy, crumpled prison greys.

Jane waited for him in the classroom, sitting at the teacher's table, facing rows of empty seats. As an ordinary teacher, she had no access to the office now. In any case, neither Leventhal nor Miss Burgess were on duty on Tuesday mornings. The office was locked and she didn't have a key.

A screw had let her into the education block fifteen minutes earlier. There were no other staff on duty up there, so she was effectively locked in on her own. It didn't bother her, though. She had been on her own in similar situations hundreds of times. She felt under no threat. Many of her students had been with her for years.

Suddenly, there was a knock on the door. She looked up.

'Good morning, Mrs Roman. I'm Tim Fry,' the man at the door reminded her, putting out his hand.

Jane was taken aback. His manner, although formal, had an air of familiarity to it. He grasped her hand limply, then gave it a little squeeze. As she withdrew it, his fingers briefly clung to hers.

She suddenly realised that she hadn't replied to his greeting. He was standing there, head cocked to one side, looking at her enigmatically.

'Oh, good morning,' she said, feeling the colour rise in her cheeks. There was something strange here that she couldn't quite put her finger on. Tom and Norman had always warned her of the importance of having a sixth sense. Theirs was well developed from years spent in prison, but hers was virtually non-existent.

She shrugged. Perhaps she was just being silly. What with all the intrigue that had characterised her life in Knightsford of late, maybe she was becoming paranoid.

'Well, Tim, take a seat,' she said, waving to a row of desks at the front of the class.

He smiled brightly, positively beamed, at the use of his first name. He went to the first row of desks, took a chair and brought it up close to her table. He sat down opposite her.

Deep in her consciousness, a warning bell rang. She became aware of the tangible sense of unease that she had felt since he had first entered the room. But she had denied it and so stifled it. She began to understand the nature of the sixth sense. You had to suspend rationality and give rein to your inner feelings.

'What poetry do you like?' she asked in as business-like a fashion as she was able.

But it was as if she had uttered an endearment. He smiled and leaned closer across the table. 'Love poems, Jane,' he said in a breathless, husky voice.

Now she felt real alarm, but strove to hide it. She was locked in the education block, completely on her own. She was in the presence of a man who was undoubtedly disturbed. There were, however, students in other classrooms doing private study, and as a last resort she could go to them for help. But, for the moment, she would have to deal with this Tim Fry as best she could.

'In that case, I suggest we start in the seventeenth century,' she said, ignoring the implications of his manner. She tried to keep a hard edge to her voice. She didn't want to seem to encourage him in any way. She pushed a small, blue-covered book across the table towards him, then quickly withdrew her hand.

'We'll begin with Andrew Marvell's "To his coy mistress". Page one hundred and fifty-nine.' She stared down at the page.

A sharp knock at the door made her jump. She looked up quickly to see if Fry had noticed. She saw a grimace of displeasure pass over his face. He turned to look at the door and she turned with him.

It flew open and in stalked Eddie. 'Jane, I've got an OU assignment here. Could you take it, please?' he said loudly.

She was grateful for the interruption and put her hand out to accept it. But she was puzzled. OU assignments were usually handed in to the office. And Eddie was normally a shy, reserved young man, not the type to burst into her class when she was teaching and virtually demand her attention.

'And how are you and the family, Jane?' he asked conversationally.

Surprise nearly robbed her of her poise. Eddie never asked her personal questions about her home life. And certainly not when she was in the middle of teaching. What in heaven's name was going on?

'Oh, we're all OK,' was all she managed to reply.

'Well, I won't keep you, Jane, but I know that Steve and Sam both want to speak to you in a while.' Eddie smiled, looking directly at her. She realised that he hadn't so much as acknowledged Tim Fry sitting just across from her.

As the door closed behind Eddie, she immediately felt vulnerable again. But he had said that Steve and Sam wanted to see her. She savoured that knowledge and it gave her comfort. There was help at hand if she needed it.

She turned back to Fry. There was a peeved look on his face. He had been irked by the interruption. Mentally she prepared a story if he should complain. As the only teacher on duty, she was liable to be sought out by all the students in the education block.

'Oh, where were we?' From Jane's tone, it was as if she had forgotten all about the love poems. 'Ah, yes, Andrew Marvell,' she said. 'I'll read it through first, then you try.' Before he could say anything, she started reading.

At the end of the first verse, she looked up. She immediately regretted it. Fry was still staring at her intently, the enigmatic smile back on his face.

She was just starting the last verse when a knock came at the door again. There was a sharp intake of breath from Fry. The door opened and there was Sam. His large, bulky form had never looked so welcome.

'Hello, Jane,' he chirped. He bowled into the room and came up close to the table. He had some papers in his hand. 'Could you just have a quick look at the first paragraph there and tell me if I've used the gerund correctly?' he asked, placing a sheet in front of her.

Jane was beginning to understand. 'Certainly, Sam,' she replied. 'Excuse me, Tim,' she said, looking across the table. 'This won't take a minute.'

In fact, it took five. She read and reread the paragraph and almost smiled when she realised there was no use of the gerund at all. She longed to ask Sam what was going on, but would have to wait until later. She was grateful that it was Fry's poetry hour that was being wasted.

She picked up a pencil and wrote 'THANK YOU' in small letters between one of the lines. She handed the paper back to Sam.

'Thanks, Jane,' he said. 'Sorry to interrupt your class.' He walked out without having once acknowledged Fry's presence.

For a moment she was tempted to start the poem from the beginning again, but that would have been too obvious. Reading slowly and deliberately, she finished the last verse. Reluctantly, she raised her eyes to look at Fry. He was still staring directly at her. He hadn't followed one line in the book.

'Well, it's your turn now, Tim. Take your time and see if you can understand Marvell's meaning. Then we'll discuss it.' She hoped that, by then, Steve would have been in. That would leave very little time to discuss anything.

The book still lay on the table in front of Fry. 'You read that wonderfully, Jane,' he said, in the same breathless husky manner he had used earlier.

Jane was lost for words. 'Thank you,' she managed to mumble, embarrassment raising spots of colour on both cheeks again.

The silence hung between them like a tactile thing. The awareness that it was of his creating and that she was sharing it with him unsettled her. It was as if he had physically touched her.

Inexplicably, the image of Norman suddenly filled her mind. She wondered what had made her think of him, and then she knew. Norman would have known exactly what to do in this situation. He would have leaned across the table and punched Fry smartly in the face.

The thought almost brought a smile to her face. The corners of her mouth twitched as she fought it, but Fry registered its fleeting presence. He wrinkled his brow as the cloud of anger passed behind his eyes. He regained control quickly, though, and forced a smile.

'Do you believe in love, Jane?' he suddenly asked.

Any thought of smiling was immediately forgotten. It wasn't just the question, it was the manner of asking. Fry seemed to have an inexhaustible talent for becoming passionate with absolutely no encouragement. Her mind raced over how to answer him.

Then it came to her. 'Yes, I believe in love,' she replied. 'As a Catholic, I believe in love within marriage. I love my husband and my two children. Does that answer your question?'

Again the cloud passed behind his eyes. He maintained the smile, but it was a fiction. He took a deep breath and opened his mouth to speak.

A sharp knock cut him short. Steve walked briskly into the room.

'Sorry to interrupt, Jane,' he said, 'but I have a note here for Mr Leventhal. I'm on a visit this afternoon so I wondered if you could give it to him for me.'

'Of course, I will, Steve,' said Jane, reaching out for the letter he held in his hand. 'How's the writing coming along?'

It was a cue for an interruption that would run and run. Steve had recently started writing articles for the prison magazine. He talked for all of five minutes without pause. When he left, he, too, walked straight to the door without acknowledging Fry.

As the door closed behind him, Jane resigned herself to the fact that there would be no more interruptions. Desperately, she searched her mind for ways to sidetrack Fry from embarrassing subjects. But as the subject under discussion was love poems, it was inevitable that he would wax romantic.

The door suddenly opened again. Jane turned, thinking it was Steve returning to add something to his previous instructions. Her mouth opened in surprise as she saw Hamid's swarthy face. He wasn't on a class this morning. She wondered how he had managed to get in the education block.

'Jane, you are all right?' As he asked the question, he glared at Fry. The latter dropped his head and, for the first time, picked up the poetry book and pretended to read.

Jane couldn't help but smile. Someone had obviously told Hamid that something was up. In his totally unsophisticated way, he couldn't be anything but frank. The question was to reassure Jane; the glare was to deter Fry.

'Yes, I'm quite all right, thank you,' she said. 'Now you just run along and I'll see you in class tomorrow.'

The sinister face with the wickedly hooked nose suddenly broke into the sweetest smile. The transformation was amazing. It was as if everything good and wholesome had flowed out of him in that second. It was the smile of a child.

Then he turned to Fry and his face changed again. Cold, cruel hatred charged his stare, and Fry was transfixed like a rabbit in the headlights. He cowered, unable to meet the other's eyes even for a moment. Then Hamid was gone.

All the effrontery had disappeared from Fry now, and he read the poem in a much subdued fashion until the time was up. Sulkily, he thanked Jane for the lesson and hurried from the class.

Hardly had he gone than Eddie, Sam and Steve walked in. They were all smiling broadly.

'And what was that all about?' Jane asked.

They were suddenly serious. 'Jane, he's a very dangerous man with women,' said Eddie sombrely. She looked at him with interest. 'He killed his girlfriend, her husband and her mother. He waited for them to come home one by one. He tried to kill himself in Brixton. He stood in a bowl of water, connected an electric flex to the light socket, then wound it around his hands. Unfortunately, it only burned his hands.'

Jane flinched at this seeming callousness. The usually placid Eddie was being uncharacteristically brutal.

'He's got an ego the size of a house. He fancies he's a ladies' man, and every jail he's in, he pesters the female staff. He's been involved in several incidents with them and been shipped out. In other jails, they won't let him near the women.'

Jane's eyes widened in surprise. 'You mean that it was official policy to keep him away from women staff?' she asked.

'Yes,' said Eddie, nodding vigorously.

'Therefore, it must be on his record,' said Jane, thinking aloud.

'Exactly,' said Eddie with emphasis. 'The screws have set you up here. They know what he's like. They knew you'd be on your own with him. They were hoping that something would happen.'

A chill passed right through her. They really did hate her. Her feeling for them had been one of mild contempt, and outwitting them had been something of a game. It frightened her now to realise that they would go to any lengths to get her.

'Thank you for coming in like you did,' she said to the three of them.

'That's OK,' said Sam. 'We'll do the same next week, too.'

'Hopefully, he won't come back next week after what's happened today,' said Jane wistfully. She dismissed the idea of making a complaint. She wasn't allowed to see prisoners' records now, so the staff would only deny that Fry was a menace to women.

In the event, she was wrong. The following Tuesday, Fry turned up for the class again. He was subdued this time, though. There were a couple of *double entendres* and some mild innuendo, but nothing like the previous week.

Eddie, Steve, Sam and Hamid all interrupted the class again, and this time they were joined by Richie and Pete. It seemed that hardly five minutes passed without someone calling in.

The next week, Fry failed to turn up for the class. There was no explanation and she didn't go looking for one. She assumed he had tired of all the interruptions. She mused that even Andrew Marvell would have found it difficult to wax romantic with his coy mistress if he'd had to suffer all those interruptions. And Tim Fry was obviously no Marvell.

How strange that a place of the dead should be so restful. The rows of stones stood in silent testimony to the frailty of the human condition. A frightening reminder that one could be snatched from this life at any time.

But no doubt, at nightfall, this cemetery would assume an ominous aspect. Shadows would lengthen, then the darkness would close in. Little else about the place would change, but all those nightmare things that swam in the unconscious would find form in a fertile imagination.

Jane suppressed a shudder. It was too nice a day to think of such dark things. The sun shone brightly overhead and the heat warmed the ground until the haze seemed to shimmer, melting the harsh lines of solid objects.

The bench backed on to the prison wall. In front of her, a riot of fecund greenery shielded the road from view. She felt protected here. Hidden from prying eyes, she could relax and, when she could stir herself, do some marking.

The papers were spread on the bench next to her. A partly eaten sandwich lay in the lunch-box on her lap. The flask at her feet had long since been drained of coffee. Her appetite had been sated. She lolled back, eyes half-closed, dozing in the soporific heat.

''Ave ya got a smoke, miss?' The low, husky voice seemed to come out of nowhere. Jane opened her eyes. Off to one side stood a young man. As she focused more carefully, she noticed that he was a thoroughly dishevelled young man.

He was short and painfully thin. The stubble that covered his chin was fluffy and sparse. He could have been no older than twenty, yet his eyes spoke of harsh experiences beyond his years. His black, greasy hair cascaded about his ears, adding the final scruffy touch to a head that was far from noble.

He was wearing a shapeless grey jumper over stained and faded jeans. All down one side there was an ingrained mud stain. He certainly slept in his clothes. Jane wondered if he ever slept in this cemetery.

These details she took in in an instant. Her mind was racing. She had become so accustomed to danger of late that she immediately weighed up a situation by reflex now. She was aware that she was alone in a deserted graveyard with a dishevelled and wild-looking young man. It had all the ingredients of danger.

''Ave ya got a smoke, miss?' The question came again, but more insistent this time.

Trying to hide her fledgling alarm, Jane sat upright on the bench. She tilted her head slightly to catch sight of her bag, which she had propped alongside the bench. She tried to calculate how she could sweep all her papers into it and run if the situation demanded it.

But the young man was well schooled in the ways of deceit. His gaze followed hers, finally resting on the bag.

'I'm sorry, but I don't smoke,' said Jane, starting to gather the papers together. She looked skywards, play-acting as if she feared rain or a squall. It was a patently obvious ploy and the young man's gaze never left her bag.

''Ave ya got any spare cash then?' he said in a tone that was little short of demanding.

Jane picked up her bag. She crammed a handful of papers into it. 'I'm sorry. I haven't brought any out with me,' she replied.

Suddenly, his silence spoke more eloquently than his words. Jane looked up quickly. His eyes glinted brightly now. They darted between her and the surrounding greenery. He was clenching and unclenching his hands. Clearly, he was on the verge of attacking her.

He stepped closer, more confident now. Her fear had served to encourage him. 'No smokes, no cash, I'll just have to have you then, won't I?' His voice was low and threatening.

Jane launched herself off the bench. She made to run, but he was on her immediately. They struggled briefly, then fell headlong into the long grass. She felt a sharp pain as prickly gorse cut into her face.

She tried to scream, but the wind had been knocked out of her. She emitted a thin wail, part-way between a gasp and a squeal. She heard him gasp in return, then utter a low, cackling laugh.

She tried to rise, but only made it to her knees. She felt his hand between her legs. For the first time, she was grateful that the prison insisted that she always wear trousers to work.

She felt his other hand claw at her breast. He was panting heavily now and obviously aroused. Almost in a dream-like state, she observed and experienced the attack.

She became strangely calm. She wondered if this was what a rabbit felt like as it froze before a fox. She reflected that this was the traditional response of the female to the male: to be passive in the face of violence.

The thought stirred her. A flicker of anger kindled deep in her psyche. Her mind screamed 'No!' at the realisation of what the ultimate consummation would be. There had to be an alternative. She must resist.

But despite his small stature, he was remarkably strong. She had never been into fitness and had all the weakness of the sedentary worker. She recalled Tom and Norman and their work-outs in the gym. She bitterly regretted that it hadn't inspired her to do the same.

The thought of Tom brought back something he had once said to her. The conversation had been about violence. Jane's position was that it was never justified. Tom had laughed and said that she would soon change her mind if she were ever attacked.

Her reply had centred on the fact that she wasn't capable, either mentally or physically.

'The fear will give you the mental motivation,' he had insisted, 'and what you lack in strength must be made up for in cunning.'

She had looked at him quizzically. He had shaken his head impatiently at her silent question.

'Pretend you like it, Jane,' he had said, with a false smile on his face. He had paused, causing her further puzzlement. Was that it? But he had only been pausing for effect. 'Then knee him right in the nuts,' he had added gruffly.

She had smiled at the time and immediately dismissed it, but it all came back to her now.

'OK, OK,' she heard herself cry, 'but don't hurt me.' She stopped struggling.

She felt his grip on her breast relax a trifle. 'Turn over then,' came his gruff demand.

'Not on the ground,' she insisted. 'The marks will show on my clothes and then I'll have to report it.' She was amazed at how coldly logical she was now that she was working to a plan. 'Let's do it on the bench,' she suggested.

Still gripping her breast, he helped her roughly to her feet. He turned her around and pulled her to him. Immediately, his hand sought her crotch again.

She backed awkwardly towards the bench. He shuffled with her. His face was close to hers. She saw his stained and broken teeth. His fetid breath nearly caused her to retch, but she couldn't afford to lose control even for a second. Carefully, secretly, Jane positioned her feet. She realised that she would only have one good shot. Slowly, she drew a deep breath.

When it came, his scream of pain surprised her. It was so primal and so close. As she drove her knee deep into his groin, she felt his whole body suddenly stiffen, then relax. A blast of hot breath basted her face.

In reflex, he scratched at her eyes. She felt his nails rake across her cheek and his fingers enter her open mouth. She bit down on them with a savagery that shocked her. He howled in agony and tore his fingers from her. She was aware of the warm, salty taste of his blood in her mouth.

She spun away from him and ran. Headlong, with no thought of where she was heading, she plunged through the undergrowth. A trailing creeper briefly caught her ankle and she stumbled, but fear kept her upright.

She emerged into a narrow clearing. Beyond, she saw the railings and the road. She knew where she was now. She headed for the gate and safety.

Behind her, there was no sound of pursuit. But still her pace didn't slacken. She threw herself through the opening and was immediately reassured by the proximity of the passing traffic and an approaching group of schoolboys.

'Help, I've been attacked!' she cried as she ran up to them. They looked surprised, then frightened. Their eyes fixed on her exposed breasts, the group flowed around and past her like water around a rock.

She looked around wildly. Still no sign of her attacker. Quickly doing her blouse up, she hurried up the road in the direction of a phone box.

The phone was a good 200 yards from the cemetery entrance. She glanced back as she reached it and was reassured by the empty street. She stepped inside and hurriedly dialled for the police.

There were more people passing now, so she stepped outside. She hid behind the phone box, peering back down the street. Still there was no sign of her dishevelled attacker.

The rest was a nightmare, almost worse than the attack itself. The police arrived — all men. She explained what had happened and they insisted on her escorting them back to the scene. She was reassured by their presence, but the site of the attack renewed the trauma.

By now, a crowd had gathered. Embarrassment replaced her fear. She scanned the faces, dreading that she might see any prison staff. This would give them a good laugh. She had survived in the midst of murderers and rapists, but had been nearly raped in the shadow of the prison walls.

She hid what had happened from the children, but that evening, Robert and she had agonised for hours over her lucky escape. He shared her passive nature, but was highly incensed at the risk she had been exposed to. In a fit of pique, he had written an angry letter to the Prime Minister. If his wife hadn't been excluded from the prison in a vindictive and petty campaign, he argued, it would never have happened.

After that, events just seemed to follow on from each other. She wasn't hurt, just bruised and badly scratched. She decided to take a fortnight off work.

The following day, the police came round again, this time with a woman officer. She took full details of the attack before leaving.

Later, the phone started ringing. The local press wanted to know her version of events. They remembered her from the union dispute, and the police had already hinted at her exclusion from the prison outside teaching times. They sensed a story.

The reply from Mrs Thatcher gave them one. Suddenly, the national media was interested, too. A television crew appeared on her doorstep and refused to leave until she gave them an interview. She told of the campaign to force her out of Knightsford. Once again, she was the centre of very public embarrassment for the prison.

The scratches on her face were taking longer to heal than she had expected, so she took another week off sick. When she returned, she was summoned to Miss Lacy's office.

The Governor was all apologies.

'Mrs Roman, how can I ever express how sorry I am about your being attacked in the very shadow of Knightsford. I hope you have recovered from your ordeal now.' Jane assured her that she had.

'I do feel partially responsible,' the Governor continued. 'We can't have you sitting about in cemeteries while you wait for your next class.

'When it is fine, it is quite nice round by the bowling green. There's all that flowering shrubbery alongside B wing and some wooden benches. And when it's raining, I'm sure you would be comfortable in the waiting room in the gate-lodge.'

'I'm sure I would,' replied Jane, trying to keep the sarcasm out of her voice.

She reflected that there was nothing like a bit of bad publicity to concentrate the minds of the prison authorities. She hoped that she wouldn't have to suffer another serious assault before they made their next concession to her. However, she conceded that it was possibly the only way that she was ever going to get anything out of them.

'I know it is the will of Allah,' said Hamid passionately, 'but it is so hard to understand.'

Jane had never seen him so agitated. She had noticed him waiting outside the classroom for her to finish teaching, and he had rushed in before the last students had left. Whatever it was, his problem was urgent.

None the less it had taken her the best part of ten minutes to get it all out of him. There had been much wailing and prophesying that this was the end. And when she finally knew the problem, she really had to agree that it just might be, even if she would never tell him so to his face.

Of late, Jane had been reading a great deal about the Home Secretary's new plan for lifers, part of a radical 'law and order' initiative, timed for the Tory conference in October. It involved categorising lifers according to the nature of their offences and fixing a tariff accordingly.

It was a blatant piece of politicking, though, with no foundation in rationality. It retroactively sentenced lifers to increased time in prison in response to a perceived public concern about the rise in violent crime.

Hamid had been called to the PO's office that afternoon. He had previously been informed that his next review would be held the following year. He had already done ten years on this life sentence, but then he had served a life sentence before. To his horror, the PO had told him that, under the new policy, his next review had been put back until he had served a further ten years.

It was a cruel and savage thing to do. Where there had been hope, now there was just hopelessness. Hamid expressed doubts that he would survive.

At his next class, Jane had sat down with him to draft a letter to a prominent firm of solicitors that specialised in the grey area of life-sentence prisoners' legal rights. They had been active in several recent cases in the High Court. It was an outside chance, but at least it would give Hamid something to hope for. When he left Jane, he was in better spirits than he had been for days.

But it couldn't last. Jane was so kind and caring, and when he was with her, there was hope and he could find the strength to carry on. He marvelled that he had come to rely so much on a woman. In his country, women were little more than servants.

How he hated Knightsford now. He had only ever barely tolerated the place. He could have held out for another year. But ten years was an eternity. He knew his strength would run out long before then.

Increasingly, he found it hard to sit in his cell. He spent long hours in the TV room, but his English wasn't good enough for him to understand all the programmes. Also, the promiscuous sexuality shown on some of them was an affront to his Muslim beliefs. England was such a strange country. So advanced in material things, yet so decadent in moral values.

He wandered along the twos of A wing. Some evenings he walked many miles along the landings. It was something to do and it made him tired so that he could sleep at night.

As he neared the centre, a large figure came around the corner. Hamid had been ambling along, staring at the ground. He was only aware of the man as a large shape looming up.

He gasped as the man's elbow caught him in the ribs, and he cried out in pain as he was brushed aside and thrown against the railings.

'Fucking wog,' he heard the man say as he swept past. Hamid clung to the railing with one hand and spun round. He saw the back of his giant tormentor receding up the landing. He recalled his previous trouble with him in the TV room. 'Fucky bustard!' he screamed at him. The big fella turned quickly and, smiling, held up one finger to Hamid before carrying on.

It was a gesture that was universally understood, and for Hamid, it was the last straw. He hurried back to his cell, muttering darkly.

He grabbed an empty sauce bottle and quickly wrapped it in a towel. He hit it smartly against the wall. The small shards of broken glass he shook into his bin; the fiercely jagged neck he clutched tightly in his hand.

Hurrying back out on to the landing, he was just in time to see the big fella heading back towards the centre. He broke into a trot as he sought to catch him up.

Perhaps the big fella heard his approaching footsteps; maybe it was just a sixth sense. As he turned his head, his eyes widened in fear. He saw Hamid running towards him, the jagged neck of glass glinting in his hand. With the Arab in hot pursuit, he ran around the gallery, lines of startled 'crows' watching in disbelief.

It was immediately apparent that Hamid was never going to catch the big fella, who was younger and fitter and motivated by fear. In his frustration, Hamid kept calling out, 'Fucky bustard! Fucky bustard! I keel you!'

If it hadn't been so serious, it would have been funny. But no one wanted to get slashed with a broken bottle, brandished by an unbalanced double-lifer. The 'crows' scattered, leaving the arena to the two protagonists.

The disturbance had attracted the screws, and the gallery soon filled with dark blue uniforms. They positioned themselves between the two men.

Hamid was quickly persuaded to hand over the broken bottle-neck. It was this object that persuaded the screws he was the aggressor. They immediately led him away to the punishment block.

The following day, he appeared before the Governor. It was known that the big fella was a bully, but Hamid's possession of the bottle-neck was a serious offence. He was sentenced to fourteen days' solitary.

The 'chokey' was cool and silent. As usual, Hamid was the only occupant. They rarely had more than one inmate on punishment at any one time at Knightsford. He lay on the floor, flat on his back, and stretched out his arms and legs until he lay in the shape of an 'X', each limb reaching out for a corner of the cell. Strangely, he felt comfortable like this. It was as if he could plug into power points by stretching in this way. He mentally reached out to the universe and felt cosmic energy flowing along his limbs.

But it was a passing fancy. Soon his shoulders grew stiff and the cold concrete floor chilled his spine. He rolled over on to his side, then crawled to the rough, wooden bed-board.

A deep sigh escaped his lips. Life was so empty. There was no pleasure left. Each painful moment was followed by another, equally painful moment. And on the horizon, there was only more pain.

He thought of the time, about a year before, when he had lain in a similar cell in Parkhurst hospital, when he had been sent for 'observation'. It had been the lowest point of his life. Only the letters from Jane and little Linda had kept him going. He had them to thank for his survival.

He returned to the present and his eyes focused on his books which lay in the corner. Jane and Bernie from the polytechnic had spent hours working with him on his English, but despite their efforts, he had made little improvement.

Suddenly, he came to a decision. He crawled over to the pile and took out a small exercise book. He selected a pencil and tested its point. He returned to the bed-board and, slowly, laboriously, began to write.

Jane was worried. She was sure that this was the day that Hamid was due to finish his punishment, but she hadn't seen him. She had been expecting him all day, to let her know that he was all right and tell her his latest worries. But she had just finished her last class for the day and there was still no sign of him.

She contemplated asking Leventhal about him, but immediately dismissed the idea. He would have said that it was nothing to do with her. Maureen Burgess would have just raised her eyebrows and shaken her head, not wanting to get involved. Jane resolved to ask one of her trusted students if they had heard anything.

Suddenly, there was a knock at the open door. She looked up quickly and saw Hamid standing on the threshold. He hung his head, as if in shame. She had never seen him look so dispirited. He was a picture of misery.

'Well, come in then, Hamid,' she said gently. He shuffled forward. She noticed that he had a pile of books under his arm. They were a mixture of English textbooks and the notebooks he had written in.

Still he was hesitant. He seemed dazed. She wondered if it was an effect of the solitary. She had heard that sensory deprivation caused people to become disorientated.

'How are you?' she asked softly.

He raised his head, but found it difficult to meet her eye. He lowered his eyes again. Suddenly, a tremor shook him. He looked up quickly. 'Please take my books,' he said. 'I won't be needing them any more.'

Jane was so surprised that she just stood there. Putting the pile of books on the table next to her, Hamid raised his head and opened his mouth as if to speak, but nothing came. His eyes brimmed with tears.

Abruptly he turned and quickly walked away. Without looking back, he swept through the doorway and was gone. Jane looked after him in astonishment.

She searched her mind for anything she might have done to upset him, but she knew that she hadn't. There was no way she could have kept in close touch with him while he was in the punishment block. As it was, she had sent him several cards, from both herself and Linda. She concluded that it must be just the lingering effects of his recent bad news about his next review.

She went through his books absentmindedly as she gathered them up. There would be no sense in handing in the exercise books. She would put them aside in case he ever wanted them back. The textbooks could always be reissued to him.

As she stacked the exercise books on one side, two small envelopes suddenly fell from between them. She picked them up casually, thinking that they were just letters he had forgotten to send. She froze when she saw 'JANE' written on one and 'LINDA' on the other.

With a rising sense of panic, she quickly tore open the one addressed to herself. Written in Hamid's normal, barely legible script, it was a rambling letter, with many crossings-out. He thanked her for all she had done for him. He said he would always be grateful for her kindness. But it was the last part that sent a chill racing down her spine: 'I wish you goodbye, Jane. I go to Allah now.'

Feverishly, she tore open Linda's letter. It concluded with the identical line. Leaving the books lying on the table, she rushed out of the classroom.

Leventhal was on the telephone as she hurried into the office. He looked up, wrinkling his nose in disapproval at her hasty entrance. She waved to attract his attention and pointed at the letter she held in her hand. He waved back dismissively and looked away.

With growing impatience, Jane waited for him to finish his call. She tried to calm herself, knowing that Hamid's safety might depend on her ability to convince Leventhal that he meant to harm himself. After what seemed like an age, Leventhal replaced the phone in its cradle and turned to regard her disdainfully.

She guessed that he was about to reproach her, but she got in first.

'Mr Leventhal, it's Hamid. I think he's going to kill himself.'

Leventhal had opened his mouth to speak, when Jane had cut him off. Now it gaped wider. Concern showed clearly in his eyes. Suddenly, though, his expression changed. It was as if he had reminded himself to whom he was speaking. Caution replaced concern.

'What on earth are you talking about, Mrs Roman?' he demanded.

'Hamid has just handed in his books. I found this note amongst them. He talks about "going to Allah". I'm sure he intends to kill himself,' she said in a rush.

Leventhal put out his hand for the letter. He started to read, but immediately wrinkled his brow.

'You can read this?' he asked.

'Not all of it,' replied Jane impatiently, 'but I can make sense of most of it.'

Leventhal returned to the letter. He read it to the end, then read it again. He laid it on the desk in front of him. 'And what do you want me to do about it, Mrs Roman?' he asked softly.

Jane was annoyed by his seeming calm. Or was it a lack of concern? 'There is a Home Office circular regarding the reporting of potential suicides, Mr Leventhal. I would like you to act according to that.' Her tone was cold, logical and incisive now. In the face of Leventhal's dithering, she would have to take control.

He looked puzzled. 'I don't think I've seen this circular,' he said.

Suddenly, Jane's control snapped. For all she knew, Hamid could be killing himself right now while Leventhal sat here wondering about correct procedures. She leaned forward and placed both hands on his desk so that her face was level with his. 'Just phone his wing PO, Mr Leventhal, and inform him of the contents of that letter,' she said angrily.

Leventhal recoiled as if he had been slapped. Her aggression had taken all the bluster out of him, though. Averting his eyes, he reached for the directory containing the extension numbers.

'Three five two, Mr Leventhal,' Jane said, trying to keep the sarcasm from her voice.

Petulantly, Leventhal dropped the directory. He reached for the phone. This was a strange situation, one he had never experienced before. But he resented the way that Jane had taken control.

Jane listened as he told Hamid's PO the details of the letter. She felt reassured when he promised to send it across to him. She would have liked to have gone to the PO herself, but had been expressly forbidden to communicate with uniformed staff. And, anyway, she had no keys to get out of the education block. She would have to be satisfied with what had been done.

Jane returned to the classroom and locked Hamid's exercise books in her cupboard. She put Linda's letter in her handbag, but she had no intention of giving it to her daughter. She didn't want to distress her, and with luck, the message would have no relevance now.

Nevertheless she was uneasy as she left the prison. She asked herself if there was anything more she could have done. Reluctantly, she had to accept that there wasn't. In her position of an ordinary teacher, she could only pass on the message. She would have to hope that they had acted on it quickly enough. But as she cycled home, she couldn't put the thought of Hamid out of her mind.

It was still with her as she cycled towards the prison the following morning. She would be relieved only when she had spoken to someone who could confirm that Hamid was all right. She hurried through the sterile area and skipped up the steps leading to the Admin. She stopped in surprise when she saw Hall in the doorway.

He had obviously been waiting for her. He stepped forward with the ghost of a smirk on his face. He drew himself up, his enormous bulk dwarfing hers.

'Mrs Roman,' he began in a bored tone, 'I've been charged with the responsibility of writing a report on Hamid Anwar. It will be necessary for me to talk to you sometime today because you are . . .' He paused momentarily, his voice trailing off. 'Correction, you *were* his teacher.'

Jane's hand flew up to her mouth. This could only mean that Hamid had killed himself.

'Yes,' Hall continued, nodding in confirmation of her reaction. 'He killed himself last night.'

Shock temporarily robbed her of all reason. She stood there, just shaking her head. A lump came to her throat and she felt her eyes fill with tears. She had failed him. In his hour of need, she had failed him – and the system had claimed another victim.

Hall stood there impassively, his lack of concern as bad as if he had sneered. Suddenly she was angry. 'But what about the suicide note I handed in?' she demanded.

Puzzlement appeared in Hall's face.

'Suicide note?' he asked querulously. 'I don't know anything about any suicide note.'

'I handed one in to Mr Leventhal yesterday afternoon,' Jane insisted. 'And I was there when he phoned the wing PO about it.'

Hall shook his head. 'No, I haven't heard anything about it,' he said stolidly.

Jane realised that she was wasting her time with Hall. She moved forward, forcing him to step aside. She hurried into the Admin block.

It was too early for Leventhal to be in his office, so she climbed the stairs in search of Deputy Governor Bone. In the past, his aristocratic good manners had always ensured her of a sympathetic hearing.

Knocking on the door to his office, she was relieved to hear his voice. She hurried in. She explained the events of the previous afternoon. He confessed his ignorance of them and said he would investigate. As she left, a deep sense of helplessness settled on her.

She was waiting outside Leventhal's office when he came in. At first, he looked peeved at her presence, but when she informed him of Hamid's suicide, his expression turned to concern. She could see him considering whether his role in the matter was open to criticism.

She stood by as he phoned Bone. She listened intently to his replies. 'But I saw the suicide note myself. I took it over to PO Jones on A wing. I don't see how it could have disappeared,' she heard him say.

Jane leaned over and tapped him on the arm. He looked up to see her waving Linda's letter in front of him. 'This is another suicide note. Hamid wrote it to my daughter,' she said, handing it to him.

'Just a minute, Mr Bone,' he said. He scanned the letter quickly. 'Mrs Roman has just handed me another copy of the suicide note. Yes, it is amazing,' he said in answer to Bone's unheard comment. 'I'll bring it over to you immediately.'

For the rest of the morning, Jane could only go through the motions. All her students had heard the news and, if they hadn't particularly cared for Hamid, they sympathised with her grief. At the end of the morning, she took Hamid's books from her cupboard. Turning the pages, she found his unfinished attempts at earlier notes. It made for disturbing reading. She put them in her bag for safekeeping.

Suddenly, she just had to get out of the place. She was overwhelmed with horror at an institution that could regularly consume its residents with so few repercussions. She began to understand how the rest must feel. It must be like warfare. They were too concerned with their own survival to dwell long on the fall of a comrade.

In the ensuing days, all urgency seemed to go out of the investigation. Whenever she saw Bone, all he would tell her was that investigations were in progress, and Leventhal was very tight-lipped about the whole affair. He had obviously been briefed by someone. Her only source of information was her students.

What she heard was disturbing. They spoke of no special precautions being taken to watch Hamid. According to the guidelines of the Home Office circular, he should have been checked in his cell every quarter of an hour throughout the night. Her sources swore that this hadn't happened. It seemed that they had just ignored the note.

It was by chance that she heard of the inquest. She phoned the coroner to ask why she had not been asked to attend. He informed her that it was the first he had heard of her and that he had no knowledge of any suicide note.

Fearing a cover-up, Jane phoned a solicitor, who advised her to contact Inquest, an organisation that helps the families and friends of those who have died in custody. When Jane contacted them, they promised to attend the inquest.

Jane arrived at the coroner's court early, wanting to be available for any last-minute questions from the Inquest team. She was surprised to find that they had sent a barrister to act on Hamid's behalf. He promised Jane that he had some awkward questions for the authorities.

But by now, though, they had closed ranks. It was admitted that a suicide note had been received prior to Hamid's death. Bone swore that proper precuations had then been taken, that a twenty-four-hour watch had been placed on Hamid, with him being checked every fifteen minutes. A record was produced purporting to show where Hamid had been during every hour of the day he died. To Jane's good knowledge, it was grossly inaccurate.

Jane watched the proceedings with growing disgust. That government officials should lie under oath was totally repugnant to her. These were the very people who were charged with the custody and rehabilitation of criminals. Small wonder the inmates had so little respect for them.

When she was called, Jane's evidence contradicted the official version in almost every aspect. She told of Hamid's depressed state since receiving the bad news about his parole review. She described finding the suicide notes and her taking one of them to Leventhal. She related how she had been told by Bone that there was no trace of it. She handed in as evidence the half-finished copies of the note in Hamid's exercise book.

That it had been suicide wasn't in doubt. What was in question was whether Hamid's death had been due to lack of care. This was very hard to prove, especially as the authorities controlled all the official records.

Jane was disappointed when the jury brought in a straight suicide verdict, but she wasn't surprised. It was a watershed in her relationship with the prison. It came at a time when she had thought that there was nothing more they could do to shock and disgust her.

In the following days, she felt weak and tired. Reluctantly, she took time off work. She had wanted to go in, just in case they thought that her nerve had gone after confronting them in court. If they had hated her before, they would regard this as the ultimate treachery.

She consoled Linda, who had grown very attached to Hamid. Over the years, they had regularly met at concerts and carol services.

The child couldn't understand why anyone would want to kill himself.

Jane had heated conversations with Robert. For so long now, she had stood alone against the prison authorities, but it was a losing battle. Her family was being affected, and it was no longer just a question of what she wanted to do.

She resolved to resign. No longer could she work side by side with people whose values she so despised. Merely to be present added legitimacy to their position. It could only lead to her compromising her own principles, simply to have a quiet life. It would be better to leave.

She returned to Knightsford to collect her personal things and clear out her cupboard. She had expected to be quickly escorted in and out, but was surprised when they left her alone in the education block.

More than anything, she had returned to say goodbye to her students. As word went round, they crowded into her classroom. For the first time in his life, Dougie was speechless. He hovered around her, too upset to speak. Eddie and Sam thanked her for everything she had done. Richie, Steve, Pete and JB shook her hand and hugged her. Even Graham appeared and apologised for what he had done.

When it was time to leave, she had gone to the office to hand in her cupboard keys. Leventhal was at his desk as usual, but she was surprised to see Bone standing at his shoulder. 'Come in and close the door a minute, Mrs Roman,' said the Deputy Governor.

Warily, she closed the door behind her. Surely they didn't have any more nasty surprises in store.

Bone waved her to a chair. 'Thank you, but I prefer to stand,' she countered. He smiled and nodded, accepting that, even now, she intended to concede nothing.

'Why did you want to cause the Prison Department embarrassment in public, Mrs Roman?' he asked. 'Surely you understand that employees owe a certain duty to the Department and that, when they betray that duty, they can't expect to receive any co-operation or respect from their colleagues?'

Jane simply stood there, looking at him. She felt calm and in control of the situation. Beneath his outer charm, Bone was just as big a hypocrite as his colleagues. The Oxford education had done nothing to instil in him morals or principles.

It was unusual for her to feel morally superior to anyone, but she couldn't help but despise these people. They murdered with the stroke of a pen, then sought to justify their actions by calls for loyalty.

'Mr Bone, if you expect me to salve your conscience over what has happened, then you are going to be sadly disappointed,' she began. 'Because of your incompetence and lack of concern, a man has died. That is between you and your maker.' She paused, watching a rush of blood inflame his face.

'And as for my duty to the Department and my colleagues,' she continued, 'that was overtaken long ago by my duty to my fellow citizens, to the law of the land and to God. How can you expect the inmates to reform their criminal ways when they see people like you engage in behaviour that is similar to theirs? No, Mr Bone, you will not shame me. I can walk out of here with a clear conscience. The question you need to ask yourself is whether you can do the same.'

Bone's face was scarlet now, as contending emotions fought for control. For a second, Jane thought he was going to burst into tears. Seated beside him, Leventhal cringed and stared at his blotter.

Without waiting for Bone's reply, Jane turned smartly on her heel and walked out of the office, closing the door behind her. She didn't want to hear any remark he might shout after her.

Her students were still waiting in the corridor, and she called a cheery goodbye. 'I'll be in touch,' she promised.

An officer was waiting by the gate. He let her through and they descended to the centre together. As she passed the covered snooker table, she suddenly stopped. It was as if unheard voices were calling to her.

She looked along A wing to where the cells of Hamid and Neil had been. She stared the length of B wing and picked out those of Foxy and Luke. She glanced at the railing outside Tom's cell, where she had so often seen him leaning with Norman.

The old place was peopled with ghosts now. It was time to leave. She had done all she was able, so she couldn't be condemned for leaving too soon, even by her own fierce standards. She had made some wonderful friends, among men who had committed the worst of crimes. She had sought the human being and invariably found him. These were memories she would carry with her for ever.

The officer had stopped beside her. He was young and Jane couldn't recall ever having seen him before. He stood there silently, respecting her wish for this last wordless farewell.

'Well, come on then. I must be going,' she said to him brightly.

Without ever once looking back, she walked through the Admin and out to the gate. She had seen enough of Knightsford to last a lifetime. She was leaving with her memories and that was souvenir enough.

As she passed through the gates, the shade of Knightsford fell from her shoulders. She felt the spirits of her dead friends leave with her.